D1118829

'Those who were originally called radicals and afterwards reformers, are called Chartists', declared Thomas Duncombe before parliament in 1842, a comment which can be adapted for a later period and as a description of this collection of papers: 'those who were originally called Chartists were afterwards called Liberal and Labour activists'. In other words, the central argument of this book is that there was a substantial continuity in popular radicalism throughout the nineteenth and into the twentieth century.

The papers stress both the popular elements in Gladstonian Liberalism and the radical liberal elements in the early Labour party. The first part of the book focuses on the continuity of popular attitudes across the commonly assumed mid-century divide, with studies of significant personalities and movements, as well as a local case study. The second part examines the strong links between Gladstonian Liberalism and the working classes, looking in particular at labour law, taxation and the Irish crisis. The final part assesses the impact of radical traditions on early Labour politics, in parliament, the unions, and local government. The same attitudes towards liberty, the rule of law, and local democracy are highlighted throughout, and new questions are therefore posed about the major transitions in the popular politics of the period.

Contributors: EUGENIO F. BIAGINI, KENNETH D. BROWN, GRAHAM D. GOODLAD, JON LAWRENCE, ROHAN McWILLIAM, ALASTAIR J. REID, JOHN SHEPHERD, JONATHAN SPAIN, DUNCAN TANNER, MILES TAYLOR, PAT THANE

Currents of Radicalism

Currents of Radicalism

Popular radicalism, organised labour and party politics in Britain, 1850–1914

Edited by

Eugenio F. Biagini

Research Fellow, Churchill College, Cambridge

and

Alastair J. Reid

Fellow and Lecturer in History, Girton College, Cambridge

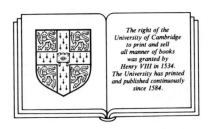

The right of the
University of Cambridge
to print and sell
all manner of books
was granted by
Henry VIII in 1534.
The University has printed
and published continuously
since 1584.

Cambridge University Press

Cambridge
New York   Port Chester
Melbourne   Sydney

Published by the Press Syndicate of the University of Cambridge
The Pitt Building, Trumpington Street, Cambridge CB2 1RP
40 West 20th Street, New York, NY 10011, USA
10 Stamford Road, Oakleigh, Melbourne 3166, Australia

First published 1991

Printed in Great Britain at the University Press, Cambridge

British Library cataloguing in publication data
Currents of radicalism: popular radicalism, organised
    labour and party politics in Britain, 1850–1914.
    1. Great Britain. Radicalism, history
    I. Biagini, Eugenio F.   II. Reid, Alastair J.
    320.530941

Library of Congress cataloguing in publication data
Currents of radicalism: popular radicalism, organised labour and
    party politics in Britain, 1850–1914 / edited by Eugenio F. Biagini
    and Alastair J. Reid.
      p. cm.
    Includes index.
    ISBN 0 521 39455 4
    1. Political parties – Great Britain – History. 2. Radicalism –
Great Britain – History.   3. Great Britain – Politics and
government – 1837–1901.   4. Great Britain – Politics and
government – 1901–1910.   I. Biagini, Eugenio F.   II. Reid, Alastair J.
DN 1120.C87   1991 90-40489   CIP
324.241′009 – dc20

ISBN 0 521 39455 4 hardback

US

Contents

Notes on contributors

Eugenio F. Biagini is a Research Fellow at Churchill College, Cambridge. He is the author of a forthcoming book on popular Liberalism in the age of Gladstone.

Kenneth D. Brown is Professor of Economic and Social History at Queen's University, Belfast. His publications include *The English Labour Movement, 1700–1951* (London, 1982) and *A Social History of the Nonconformist Ministry in England and Wales, 1800–1930* (London, 1988).

Graham D. Goodlad was a research student at Magdalene College, Cambridge, and is now a schoolmaster at Notre Dame Senior School, Cobham.

Jon Lawrence was a research student at King's College, Cambridge, and is now a Research Associate in the Faculty of History, University of Cambridge.

Rohan McWilliam is a Lecturer in History at the University of Kent, Canterbury. He is the author of a forthcoming book on the Tichborne cause and mid-Victorian popular radicalism.

Alastair J. Reid is a Fellow and Lecturer in History at Girton College, Cambridge. He is the author of a forthcoming book on social classes and social relations in late-nineteenth-century Britain.

John Shepherd is Principal Lecturer (Staff Development and Research) at Anglia Higher Education College, Cambridge. He is currently preparing a book on George Lansbury.

Jonathan Spain was a research student at King's College, Cambridge, and is now a research assistant for a firm of solicitors in Lincoln's Inn.

Duncan Tanner was a Research Fellow at St. Catharine's College, Cambridge, and is now a Lecturer in History at the University of Wales, Bangor. He is the author of *Political Change and the Labour Party, 1900–1918* (Cambridge, 1990).

Miles Taylor is a Research Fellow at Girton College, Cambridge. He is the author of a forthcoming book on radical politics in mid nineteenth-century Britain.

Pat Thane is Reader in Social History at the University of London. Her publications include *The Foundations of the Welfare State* (London, 1982) and, as editor, *The Origins of British Social Policy* (London, 1978).

Preface

First of all we would like to thank the other authors of the contributions in this collection, whose continued support and enthusiasm has been a major factor in making our role in organising it so enjoyable and rewarding. We are particularly grateful to Dr Miles Taylor for all his help during the editing stage.

The conference at Churchill College, Cambridge in the spring of 1989, at which the papers were originally presented, would not have taken place without the generous financial support of the Nuffield Foundation, of Churchill College itself, and of King's College, Cambridge. And it would not have been so successful without the participation of the following scholars, who acted as chairs and discussants, or otherwise provided valuable support: Professor Derek Beales, Dr John Breuilly, Professor Kenneth Brown, Dr Peter Clarke, Dr John Davis, Dr John Dunbabin, Dr José Harris, Dr Colin Matthew, Dr Henry Pelling, and Dr Gareth Stedman Jones. We are particularly grateful to Dr Peter Clarke for all his support during the process of publication, and to Professor Kenneth Brown for agreeing to write a paper at short notice, after discussion at the conference had revealed an important theme which needed more detailed attention.

Even this did not fill all the gaps though, and we are very aware of the inadequate coverage in this volume of such important issues as co-operation, land reform, and the position of women. What we have produced therefore cannot claim to be fully comprehensive, but we hope that it will provide a stimulating perspective on some of the central problems in the field.

1   Currents of radicalism, 1850–1914

Eugenio F. Biagini and Alastair J. Reid

I

'Those who were originally called radicals and afterwards reformers, are called Chartists'[1] declared Thomas Duncombe before parliament in 1842, a description which if adapted for a later period would provide an apt quotation to set the theme for this collection of essays: 'those who were originally called Chartists, were afterwards called Liberal and Labour activists'.[2] For our central thesis is that there was a substantial continuity in popular radicalism throughout the nineteenth and into the twentieth century, and as a result the essays stress both the popular elements in Gladstonian Liberalism and the radical liberal elements in the early Labour party.

The continuity between Chartism and Liberalism has not gone unrecognised in the previous literature on the subject of radicalism itself, but the insight has had only a limited impact on more general approaches to the study of the popular politics of the period.[3] Perhaps this can be explained, at least in part, by the fact that many of the major contributions to the history of mid-nineteenth-century British radicalism have come from American scholars. For while their own national background has made them more appreciative of the intellectual content of liberalism

We would like to thank the other contributors to this collection for their helpful comments on earlier drafts of this introduction, but would also stress that it reflects only our own views and is not intended as a collective statement.

[1] G. Stedman Jones, 'Rethinking Chartism', in *Languages of Class. Studies in English Working Class History, 1832–1982* (Cambridge, 1983), pp. 90–178, quotation from p. 90.
[2] For links between old Chartists and Liberal and Labour politics, see E. P. Thompson, 'Homage to Tom Maguire', in A. Briggs and J. Saville (eds.), *Essays in Labour History*, vol. 1 (London, 1960), pp. 276–316, especially pp. 281–2, 288; B. Harrison and P. Hollis, 'Chartism, Liberalism and the life of Robert Lowery', *English Historical Review*, 82 (1967), pp. 503–35; P. F. Clarke, *Lancashire and the New Liberalism* (Cambridge, 1971), pp. 33–4.
[3] The political activists involved were themselves often very conscious of their debts to previous generations, as will emerge in several of the chapters in this book; see also J. Clayton, *Leaders of the People. Studies in Democratic History* (London, 1910); A. Barratt Brown (ed.), *Great Democrats* (London, 1934).

and of the importance of democratic traditions,[4] it has also tended to exclude them from full participation in the debates taking place between British historians.

Thus Frances Gillespie's important study of the influence of organised labour on the politics of parliamentary reform between 1850 and 1867, which anticipated many of the general themes of this collection and which was published as long ago as 1927, has been largely neglected.[5] Similarly, the more ambitious, if ultimately rather antiquarian, collection of material which Simon Maccoby started in the early 1930s is rarely referred to, even though it argued for a continuity in radicalism from the 1760s into the early twentieth century, taking in Gladstonian and Edwardian Liberalism in its sweep, and only dying out during and after the First World War.[6] More recently, and especially since the late 1960s, there has been a growing interest in the life histories of radical working men, which in Britain has produced a number of useful sets of reprints and an invaluable guide to working-class autobiographies, both published and unpublished.[7] However, it is striking that once again most of the new full-length biographical studies of mid-Victorian radicals have been carried out by American scholars and it may be this, as well as the necessarily narrow focus on individual lives, which has reduced their impact on wider discussions, despite the strong emphasis in most of them on the personal continuities from early nineteenth-century radicalism, through Chartism, and into the Liberal party.[8]

As a result of this unfortunately rather self-contained nature of the history of mid-nineteenth-century radicalism, the predominant interpretations of popular politics in Britain, as well as of labour and social history

---

[4] Important work by American scholars along these lines in other periods includes W. Haller, *The Rise of Puritanism* (New York, 1938), and *Liberty and Reformation in the Puritan Revolution* (New York, 1955); R. R. Palmer, *The Age of the Democratic Revolution. A Political History of Europe and America, 1760–1800*, 2 vols. (Princeton, 1959 and 1964).

[5] F. E. Gillespie, *Labor and Politics in England, 1850–1867* (Duke University Press, 1927).

[6] S. Maccoby, *English Radicalism*, 6 vols. (London, 1935–61); S. Maccoby (ed.), *The English Radical Tradition, 1763–1914* (London, 1952).

[7] The main reprints were by Europa, and MacGibbon and Kee; J. Burnett, D. Vincent and D. Mayall, *The Autobiography of the Working Class, 1790–1945*, 3 vols. (Brighton, 1984–9).

[8] F. M. Leventhal, *Respectable Radical. George Howell and Victorian Working Class Politics* (London, 1971); L. Grugel, *George Jacob Holyoake. A Study in the Evolution of a Victorian Radical* (Philadelphia, 1976); J. O. Baylen and N. J. Gossman (eds.), *Biographical Dictionary of Modern British Radicals. 1770–1914*, 4 vols. (Hassocks, 1979–88); and one by an Australian, F. B. Smith, *Radical Artisan. William James Linton, 1812–97* (Manchester, 1973).

more generally, still tend to emphasise major discontinuities.[9] For example, despite the recent trend towards the more general acceptance of Chartism as a development of eighteenth-century radicalism rather than as a forerunner of socialism,[10] there is still a widespread tendency to see it as the last outburst of revolutionary working-class politics before the rise of 'mid-Victorian reformism' and the triumph of 'middle-class values' allegedly embodied in political and economic liberalism.[11] Some historians go so far as to see this as part of 'a broadly successful vaccination programme undertaken by capital ... against labour's associated potential',[12] and this tendency is generally combined with the notion of a period of political quiescence from 1850 to the 1880s, during which the working classes accepted a 'non-political ideology' of improvement and self-help, and voted for the '"non political" Liberal party'.[13] As epitomised by Royden Harrison's well-known title *Before the Socialists* (London, 1965), only the subsequent developments in popular politics are seen as fully appropriate for a modern working class.

At the root of this widespread approach is the Marxist assumption that the fundamental feature of capitalist society is class struggle, that all politics which is not a direct expression of the interests of one class is a direct expression of the interests of another, and that the only appropriate politics for a mature working class is state socialism of a more or less revolutionary type.[14] This frame of mind has been surprisingly dominant in the study of popular politics in this period, whether explicitly phrased in

[9] For recent examples of the emphasis on discontinuity see N. Kirk, *The Growth of Working Class Reformism in Mid-Victorian England* (London, 1985); G. Claeys, 'Mazzini, Kossuth, and British radicalism, 1848–1854', *Journal of British Studies*, 28 (1989), pp. 225–61.

[10] Stedman Jones, 'Rethinking Chartism'.

[11] J. Belchem, '1848: Feargus O'Connor and the collapse of the mass platform', in J. Epstein and D. Thompson (eds.), *The Chartist Experience. Studies in Working-Class Radicalism and Culture 1830–60* (London, 1982), pp. 269–310, especially pp. 303–4; D. Thompson, *The Chartists* (London, 1984), pp. 332–9; J. Saville, *1848. The British State and the Chartist Movement* (Cambridge, 1987), pp. 8–15, 226.

[12] S. Yeo, editor's introduction to *New Views on Co-operation* (London, 1988), p. 5.

[13] Thompson, *Chartists*, p. 334. It is significant that in Kirk, *Working Class Reformism*, there is no sustained discussion of working-class radicalism. The chapter on popular politics focuses on popular Toryism, and the implication is that connections with Gladstonian Liberalism were confined to trade union leaders.

[14] For a recent example see, K. D. Wald, 'Advance by retreat? The formation of British Labour's electoral strategy', *Journal of British Studies*, 27 (1988), pp. 283–314, especially pp. 288–91. By dividing the history of the period between P. Adelman, *Victorian Radicalism. The Middle Class Experience, 1830–1914* (London, 1984) and D. G. Wright, *Popular Radicalism. The Working Class Experience 1780–1880* (London, 1988), the relevant Longman texts give a distorted picture of the period, and lead to the latter volume being dominated by assessments of the presence or absence of revolutionary and socialist politics. However, the assumption that radical liberalism was a predominantly middle-class affair has a long pedigree, see for example, J. W. Derry, *The Radical Tradition. Tom Paine to Lloyd George* (London, 1967), pp. 403–6.

terms of Lenin's distinction between 'trade union consciousness' and an allegedly higher 'socialist or revolutionary consciousness',[15] or derived more indirectly from traditions in the social and political sciences since the Second World War.[16] As a result, most British historians have found working-class liberalism somewhat embarrassing, and have tried to explain it away as an unfortunate interlude between the 'early socialism' of the Chartists and the 'revival of socialism' in the late nineteenth century. In particular, there has been a strong tendency to relate it to deviations from the expected development of the industrial working class supposedly unique to Britain, above all through the embourgeoisement of the 'labour aristocracy'.[17] This particular theory has, however, come under growing criticism from historians who have studied the material conditions of the groups in question more closely, and have found it difficult to justify the claim that there was a distinct 'artisan elite', in terms of wages, skills, or separate lifestyles.[18] Other historians have advanced the alternative claim that the early-nineteenth-century radical alliance of popular classes collapsed in 1848 when its 'most proletarian' section became more militant.[19] But this too has been challenged, in this case by an emphasis on the impact of the events of 1848 themselves in renewing and reinvigorating the co-operation between radicals of all social backgrounds.[20] In our view this in fact remained a leading characteristic both of Gladstonian Liberalism and of the Labour party itself, and it is for this reason that we frequently refer to 'popular' or 'plebeian', rather than to either 'artisan' or 'working-class', radicalism.[21]

Our approach to the subject has been particularly influenced by the

---

[15] E. J. Hobsbawm, 'Notes on class consciousness', in *Worlds of Labour* (London, 1984), pp. 15–32, especially p. 27.

[16] J. R. Vincent, *Pollbooks. How Victorians Voted* (Cambridge, 1967); M. Barker, *Gladstone and Radicalism. The Reconstruction of the Liberal Party in England* (Hassocks, 1975).

[17] E. J. Hobsbawm, 'The labour aristocracy in nineteenth-century Britain', in *Labouring Men* (London, 1964), pp. 272–315, and 'The aristocracy of labour reconsidered', in *Worlds of Labour* (London, 1984), pp. 227–51.

[18] H. Pelling, 'The concept of the labour aristocracy', in *Popular Politics and Society in Late Victorian Britain* (London, 1968), pp. 37–61; H. F. Moorhouse, 'The Marxist theory of the labour aristocracy', *Social History*, 3 (1978), pp. 61–82; A. J. Reid, 'Class and organization', *Historical Journal*, 30 (1987), pp. 225–38, especially pp. 232–5.

[19] G. Crossick and H. G. Haupt, 'Shopkeepers, master artisans and the historian: the petite bourgeoisie in comparative focus', in their *Shopkeepers and Master Artisans in Nineteenth Century Europe* (London, 1984), pp. 3–31, especially p. 15.

[20] R. Quinault, '1848 and parliamentary reform', *Historical Journal*, 31 (1988), pp. 831–51.

[21] K. Tiller, 'Late Chartism: Halifax 1847–58', in Epstein and Thompson, *Chartist Experience*, pp. 311–44, especially pp. 338–40; S. A. Weaver, *John Fielden and the Politics of Popular Radicalism 1832–1847* (Oxford, 1987), pp. 272–3; B. Lancaster, *Radicalism, Co-operation and Socialism. Leicester Working Class Politics 1860–1906* (Leicester, 1987), p. 182; T. C. Smout, *A Century of the Scottish People 1830–1950* (Glasgow, 1986), pp. 234–40; Reid, 'Class and organization', especially pp. 235–8.

work of Gareth Stedman Jones and Peter Clarke, who have stressed in turn the importance of reconstructing the nature of the thinking involved in popular political movements, and the vitality of the liberal intellectual and political tradition.[22] Our 'rethinking of post-Chartist radicalism' therefore begins from the assumption that popular politics needs to be assessed in the first instance within its own political context, rather than in terms of what it 'ought' to have been, defined for example in terms of its consistency with external norms of revolutionary rhetoric or with teleological models of historical development. What ordinary people thought, and the way in which they expressed it, matters and ought to be taken seriously by historians; what the politically active among them demanded cannot be assessed in abstraction from their own needs, desires, and capacities.[23]

Once we place mid and late-Victorian working-class Liberal and Labour activists back into their own political context in this way, enough continuity in popular radicalism can be demonstrated to make the search for social explanations of major changes unnecessary. Indeed, the labour movement activists of the second half of the nineteenth century were remarkably successful in achieving most of the political reforms which had been pursued in vain by previous generations of plebeian radicals, and eventually also in obtaining a number of social and economic reforms which were of greater practical significance to the industrial working classes than anything asked for by the Chartists. We therefore maintain that popular radicalism not only survived after 1848, but remained a major political force, with a substantial impact both on the Gladstonian Liberal party and on the Labour party in its formative years. As Gillespie put it, 'from the special point of view of the political history of the working classes ... the divisions between its various phases in the nineteenth century were not so sharp as it is sometimes believed. Its development was uneven, it is true, but its transitions were made without any great degree of abruptness.'[24]

Thus the central demands of progressive popular politics remained largely those of radical liberalism well into the twentieth century: for open government and the rule of law, for freedom from intervention both at home and abroad, and for individual liberty and community-centred democracy. Some of these themes were voiced in popular slogans like

---

[22] Stedman Jones, 'Rethinking Chartism'; Clarke, *Lancashire*, and *Liberals and Social Democrats* (Cambridge, 1978).

[23] For examples of the application of this approach to the history of Marxism itself, see S. McIntyre, *A Proletarian Science, Marxism in Britain, 1917–1933* (Cambridge, 1980); F. Andreucci, 'The diffusion of Marxism in Italy during the late nineteenth century', in R. Samuel and G. Stedman Jones (eds.), *Culture, Ideology and Politics* (London, 1983), pp. 214–27.

[24] Gillespie, *Labor and Politics*, pp. 291–2.

'anti-corruption' and 'fair play', usually directed against familiar 'parasites' like the landed aristocracy, financiers, and the established Church. And some of them were embodied in a vision of the ideal citizen–patriot who would be independent of both government pressure and excessive party loyalty, and who would therefore be able to decide on political and social issues in a conscientious and public-spirited way. Within this broad tendency there were differences over how far government ought to be *by* the people, but demands for the extension of the franchise were one of the most outstanding continuities in the main stream, and radicalism in general was democratic in its commitment to government *for* the people and with their consent, and to the prevention of tyranny through the constitutional separation of powers. The re-combination of these elements in different currents could also involve varying degrees of influence by strands of rationalism (Utilitarianism, Marxism) and idealism (Romanticism, Ethical Socialism), and thus lead to contrasting programs of social and economic reform. However, in general radicalism was characterised by a broad emphasis on pragmatism, in its acceptance both of constitutional methods and of the already existing aspirations of the people. The resilience of these attitudes through a range of different political contexts can be understood in terms of their very deep historical roots, which can be traced back through the eighteenth-century 'country' opposition, and the seventeenth-century 'Puritan Revolution', to the impact of Renaissance humanism, above all in the form of the Calvinist project for the Reformation of the Church.[25]

II

In reexamining the period between the 1850s and the 1880s in these terms, we distance ourselves not only from the materialist approaches mentioned above, but also from those interpretations which tend to disparage popular politics as something essentially irrational. Drawing on Shannon's reevaluation of the political importance of religion, John Vincent and David Hamer have alleged that coherent thought and rational argument had little relevance in mid and late-Victorian constituency politics, since local peculiarities, religious animosities, 'fads', and Gladstone's charismatic power were what really mattered. Moreover, in this view the Gladstone that working men admired and followed bore little resemblance to the real statesman, being instead a product of their

---

[25] Stedman Jones, 'Rethinking Chartism', especially pp. 102–4; J. G. A. Pocock, *The Machiavellian Moment. Florentine Political Thought and the Atlantic Republican Tradition* (Princeton, 1975); W. J. Bouwsma, *John Calvin. A Sixteenth Century Portrait* (Oxford, 1988).

collective imagination: in short, Liberalism had a purely psychological and symbolic meaning for its working-class supporters.[26]

Valuable as Vincent's and Hamer's contributions are, the explanations they suggest create more problems than they solve. In the first place, it is not clear why such irrational political behaviour should have prevailed in a period of increasing levels of information and political discussion, based on the growth of a mass-circulation newspaper press and on the proliferation of political associations and debating societies.[27] Moreover, it is difficult to see how Vincent's devaluation of the actual Liberal reforms fits with the impressive record of Gladstone's achievements, some of which (like free trade finance) were later to be incorporated into the programme of the Labour party itself. Similarly, Vincent's low opinion of Liberal intellectuals is rather at odds with the pervasive influence, not only in Britain itself but also throughout the world, of such thinkers as Macaulay, Grote, and Mill. Finally, Hamer's view of 'faddism' as a collection of disparate societies seeking incompatible ends has been undermined by Brian Harrison's demonstration that many 'faddists' were members of more than one association of moral reform, had a complex and articulated vision of how society should be improved, and made a major contribution to the development of later forms of socially oriented Liberalism.[28]

These objections to the prevalent irrational approach to popular Liberalism are of equal force in relation to a recent tendency to interpret the popular politics of the period more generally in terms, not of 'reasoning, opinion or understanding, but perhaps of discipline exacted or, more often, identification with a community',[29] in fact of semi-feudal loyalty if not even of tribal allegiance.[30] As Derek Beales has shown, such an approach is also vulnerable to two further objections: firstly, that it cannot account for the existence of significant minorities of irrepressible

[26] R. Shannon, *Gladstone and the Bulgarian Agitation, 1876* (London, 1963); J. R. Vincent, *The Formation of the British Liberal Party* (Harmondsworth 1972; 1st edn 1966) p. 265; D. A. Hamer, *Liberal Politics in the Age of Gladstone and Rosebery* (Oxford, 1972), pp. xi, 42, 57–78, also *The Politics of Electoral Pressure* (Hassocks, 1977), and 'Gladstone, the making of a myth', *Victorian Studies*, 22 (1978), pp. 29–50. The allegedly irrational character of popular politics is stressed even more in M. Cowling, *1867. Disraeli, Gladstone and Revolution* (Cambridge, 1967); A. Jones, *The Politics of Reform* (Cambridge, 1972).

[27] H. J. Hanham, *Elections and Party Management* (Hassocks, 1978; 1st edn 1959), pp. 104–105.

[28] B. Harrison, 'State intervention and moral reform in nineteenth-century England', in P. Hollis (ed.), *Pressure From Without in Early Victorian England* (London, 1974), pp. 289–322, especially pp. 290, 319, and Harrison, *Drink and the Victorians* (London, 1971), pp. 19, 27.

[29] D. E. D. Beales in a critical review of D. C. Moore in 'Victorian politics observed', *Historical Journal*, 31 (1978), pp. 697–707, quotation from p. 702.

[30] D. C. Moore, *The Politics of Deference* (Hassocks, 1976); P. Joyce, *Work, Society and Politics* (Hassocks, 1980).

dissidents in the very heart of the constituencies which allegedly provide the strongest evidence for the 'politics of deference';[31] and secondly, that the undoubted growth of democratic practices in other major types of constituency is completely left out of its overall view of Victorian popular politics.[32] These criticisms are further strengthened when we consider that the best studies of popular radicalism in the second half of the nineteenth century demonstrate that self-conscious working men often asserted their social and political autonomy. In fact 'independence' was the most widespread and typical of articulated working-class values, and to some extent characterised the actual experience of labouring people from Lanarkshire to Kent.[33] Indeed, Edward Royle has shown the extent to which the plebeian radicals could go on the basis of a consistent loyalty to this value and, while the secularists and republicans that he has studied were small in number, the radicalising influence of working-class Nonconformity had similar effects on a much wider scale.[34]

Even movements focusing on erratic personalities like David Urquhart or the 'Tichborne claimant' were in fact quite 'rational' in their motivations, and only look eccentric because their methods were becoming anachronistic. For theirs was still the style and the spirit of the radicalism of the days of the Duke of York affair and the Queen Caroline agitation, when the immoral conduct of certain members of the ruling elite provided a focus for out-of-door agitations.[35] However, then, as later, the occasional enthusiasm for an aristocratic figure or for an increase in royal power was not necessarily the manifestation of an underlying popular 'deference' but rather, as Rohan McWilliam and Miles Taylor show in their contributions to this collection, could be a confirmation of popular commitment to such Whig and radical principles as 'fair play' through a strict adherence to the rule of law, and the prevention of tyranny through the constitutional separation of powers. It was therefore radical notions of justice and democracy which were seen at work in the Tichborne and

---

[31] Beales 'Victorian politics', pp. 702–4; K. McClelland, review of Joyce in *History Workshop*, 11 (1981), pp. 169–73, especially p. 173.

[32] T. J. Nossiter, *Influence, Opinion, and Political Idioms in Reformed England* (Brighton, 1975), pp. 144–61; D. Fraser, *Urban Politics in Victorian England* (London, 1976), pp. 178–233.

[33] T. Tholfsen, *Working Class Radicalism in Mid-Victorian Britain* (London, 1978), pp. 108–9, 243ff; G. Crossick, *An Artisan Elite in Victorian Society* (London, 1978), pp. 134–8; A. Campbell, *The Lanarkshire Miners* (Edinburgh, 1979), pp. 2, 26–48, 272–3.

[34] E. Royle, *Victorian Infidels. The Origins of the British Secularist Movement, 1791–1866* (Manchester, 1974), and *Radicals, Secularists and Republicans. Popular Freethought in Britain, 1866–1915* (Manchester, 1980); R. Moore, *Pit-Men, Preachers and Politics* (Cambridge, 1971); N. Scotland, *Methodism and the Revolt of the Field* (Gloucester, 1981); A. Howkins, *Poor Labouring Men* (London, 1985). See also the contributions of Kenneth Brown and Alastair Reid in this collection.

[35] I. Prothero, *Artisans and Politics in Early Nineteenth Century London* (London, 1979), pp. 132–55.

Urquhart agitations, involving a sense of equity which was more than Whig, more nearly 'whiggamore', and which was closely linked with the ethic of Old Dissent. This also emerges from Kenneth Brown's contribution on the Nonconformist support for the reform of the labour laws, but as he points out, in the 'age of urban democracy' and the mass press this emphasis on the rule of law could be a double-edged sword applied to criticisms of, as well as support for, the labour movement. This was one of the most important lessons learned by the 'New Model' unionists, who realised that their success depended on their ability to use and modify the law, rather than to challenge or subvert it. A similar conclusion was reached on the political front by what we might refer to as the 'new model' radicals, and this led to the replacement of the Tichborne style of campaign with one which was more completely committed to ordinary parliamentary procedure and to the articulation of its demands in the moral rhetoric of Gladstonian Liberalism. Such assumptions, indeed, had become so closely identified with political opposition that by the end of the century, as Jon Lawrence's contribution on local politics in Wolverhampton shows, even strong reactions against particular party organisations only led to shifts of the popular vote between the various parliamentary options: voting Conservative and voting Liberal could, in different contexts, both be seen as assertions of popular independence.

Victorian popular politics, then, may well have been characterised by arguments about community and status more than by arguments about class. However, especially after the democratisation of the system of local government, the form of local allegiance which prevailed was not that of D. C. Moore's instinctive and subservient 'deference groups', but rather that of Peter Clarke's 'interest communities', based on a conscious commitment to, and a positive evaluation of, relationships of mutual dependence and trust which covered a wide range of human needs.[36] Popular radicals and intellectual liberals alike stressed that individual liberty had a meaning only within the collective identity provided by local self-governing units, and in this way Victorian liberalism was also clearly quite different from the dogmatic individualism which has been championed by the 'New Right' in the 1980s, frequently under the banner of 'Victorian values'.[37]

---

[36] P. F. Clarke, 'Electoral sociology of modern Britain', *History*, 57 (1972), pp. 31–55 especially pp. 37–41; for a contrasting approach see S. and E. Yeo, 'On the uses of community', in Yeo, *Co-operation*, pp. 229–58; and for an example of the impact of changes in local government see J. Davis, *Reforming London* (Oxford, 1988), pp. 115–28.

[37] Harrison, *Drink and the Victorians*, p. 32; J. Davis, 'Radical clubs and London politics, 1870–1890', in D. Feldman and G. Stedman Jones (eds.), *Metropolis: London. Histories and Representations since 1800* (London 1989), pp. 103–28; J. S. Mill, *Autobiography* in his *Collected Works*, vol. 1 (London, 1981), p. 151, and 'On civilization' in his *Collected Works*, vol. 18 (London, 1977), p. 132.

The full implications of this line of interpretation for the formation and growth of the Liberal party as a mass movement have yet to be brought into focus. But it can be suggested that, far from being irrational in its motivations and aims, support for the Liberal party resulted from the fact that its reform programme offered convincing solutions to many of the problems which were perceived as the central questions of the time. More generally, working-class Liberalism was not the fruit of the ideological success of 'bourgeois ideology' during the mid-Victorian decades, but rather of the institutionalisation of older and genuinely plebeian traditions.[38] In fact most of the ingredients of Gladstonian Liberalism were already present in earlier popular movements: anti-state attitudes, free trade, anti-clericalism, and franchise reform had been energetically promoted by plebeian radicals since the days of Thomas Paine.[39] Even in foreign policy a precursor of the Gladstonian non-interventionism of the 1870s can be found in the new trends in popular radicalism stimulated by the Urquhartite movement from the 1850s, as Miles Taylor shows in his contribution to this collection. Similarly, as John Shepherd shows, Irish Home Rule itself had been debated for years by the Lib.–Labs. before its adoption as the official policy of the Liberal party in 1886 and as a result, as Graham Goodlad establishes in his contribution, when the crisis came it was Gladstone who remained consistently more popular than even an avowed social reformer like Joseph Chamberlain.[40] This suggests that the charisma of popular liberal leaders did not depend on mere rhetorical powers and popular gullibility but, as Colin Matthew has argued for Gladstone and Derek Beales has argued in his study of Garibaldi, depended rather on moral empathy, ideological affinity, and established reputations based on actual achievements.[41]

Thus if a change took place in the second half of the nineteenth century it was not so much in the attitudes of the lower classes as in those of the ruling classes: symbolised in the career of Joseph Arch, who was representative of a group which by the 1880s was accepted as the leadership of the 'respectable' working classes, when only a few generations previously they

---

[38] E. F. Biagini, 'British trade unions and popular political economy, 1860–1880', *Historical Journal*, 30 (1987), pp. 811–40.

[39] E. P. Thompson, *The Making of the English Working Class* (Harmondsworth 1981; 1st edn 1963), pp. 88–9, 104–5.

[40] See also chapter 11 by Pat Thane in this collection for the centrality of Home Rule in later popular radicalism.

[41] H. C. G. Matthew, editor's 'Introduction' to *Gladstone Diaries*, vol. 9 (Oxford, 1986), pp. liii–lxix, and 'Rhetoric and politics in Great Britain, 1860–1950', in P. J. Waller (ed.), *Politics and Social Change* (Oxford, 1987), pp. 34–58; D. E. D. Beales, 'Garibaldi in England: the politics of Italian enthusiasm', in J. Davis and P. Ginsborg (eds.), *Essays in Honour of Denis Mack Smith* (Cambridge, 1990), pp. 184–216.

would have been dealt with in the fashion reserved for the 'Tolpuddle martyrs'. However, the suddenness of this change should not be exaggerated, for historians of a wide range of views now generally agree that since the eighteenth century the British legal system had been developing firmly in the direction of equal rights for all citizens, and was thus able to play an increasingly important role in mediating conflicts between (and within) social groups.[42] As a result, the traditions of British popular radicalism had in fact from their very inception been predominantly legalistic and constitutional, and remained so even in the heyday of Chartism. In the second half of the nineteenth century this process of social mediation was maintained by such crucial steps as the removal of one-sided labour laws, analysed by Jonathan Spain in his contribution to this volume. Moreover, this period also saw the opening up of the political system to previously excluded groups,[43] and an increasing responsiveness of governments to popular pressure, above all over fiscal reforms and free trade, as is shown in Eugenio Biagini's contribution.[44]

It was, of course, the Liberal party under Gladstone which was most closely associated with all of these reforms, and it is therefore time to reopen the questions not only of the relationship between the Liberal party and the people after the 1860s, but also of the attitude of 'Old Liberalism' to public intervention and social reform. We would not only argue that the Liberals continued to develop policies which were favourable to the working classes throughout the 1870s and 1880s, but also challenge the view, originating in the debates within the next generation over 'New Liberal' and Keynesian proposals, that Gladstone himself was dogmatically committed to a 'minimalist' state.[45] In fact it is clear that Gladstone could be remarkably interventionist,[46] and that he presided over a Liberal party which was responsible for a long series of impressively 'constructionist' or even 'collectivist' measures, ranging from the 1870

---

[42] E. P. Thompson, *Whigs and Hunters* (Harmondsworth, 1975), pp. 258–69; J. Brewer and J. Styles (eds.), *An Ungovernable People. The English and their Law in the Seventeenth and Eighteenth Centuries* (London, 1980); C. Harvie, 'Revolutions and the rule of law', in K. O. Morgan (ed.), *The Oxford Illustrated History of Britain* (Oxford, 1984), pp. 421–60.

[43] C. Harvie, 'Gladstonianism, the provinces and popular political culture, 1860–1906', in R. Bellamy (ed.), *Victorian Liberalism* (London, 1990), pp. 152–74.

[44] See also H. C. G. Matthew, 'Disraeli, Gladstone and the politics of mid-Victorian budgets', *Historical Journal*, 22 (1979), pp. 615–43 especially p. 616; R. McKibbin, 'Why was there no Marxism in Great Britain?', *English Historical Review*, 99 (1984), pp. 297–331, especially pp. 322–4; Stedman Jones, 'Rethinking Chartism', especially pp. 177–8.

[45] See, for example, F. W. Hirst, *Gladstone as a Financier and an Economist* (London, 1931).

[46] H. C. G. Matthew, *Gladstone 1809–1874* (Oxford, 1986), pp. 118–19, and his introduction to *Gladstone Diaries*, vol. 10 (Oxford, 1990), pp. xxxvi–xxxix, clii–cliii; also the interesting review by P. Smith, 'Liberalism as authority and discipline', *Historical Journal*, 32 (1989), pp. 723–37, especially pp. 726–9; and for a later period, Barker, *Gladstone and Radicalism*, pp. 197–8, 254–6.

Education Act, to Irish and Scottish land reform, and the extension of the powers of local government. Further moves in this direction would not have been easy, given the widespread hostility among popular radical activists and labour leaders themselves to state 'interference' in matters which they felt ought to be left to the self-organisation of working people.[47] This hostility was, however, less marked at the local level where, as Pat Thane's chapter demonstrates, radical programmes for political and social democracy merged into 'municipal socialism'. As this was inspired and strengthened by the decentralising emphasis of Old Dissent, it is therefore also now time that this tradition was more fully recognised as a major influence among both Liberal and Labour activists, and as a central component of the cultural and intellectual inheritance of the British left.[48]

III

Interpretations of the way in which this inheritance generated a distinct Labour party in the early twentieth century fall broadly into three main approaches. Committed socialists like E. P. Thompson have seen the emergence of the Labour party as the direct consequence of the formation of new socialist groups and 'New Unions' in the 1880s. They maintain that the foundation of the new party in 1900 was mainly the result of a major advance in working-class politics, which in turn was closely related to the latest developments in the organisation of industry. This led to an intensification of economic conflict, and to a growing sense of a separate working-class community which culminated in an increasingly sharp break with the 'bourgeois' Liberal party and with 'middle-class' Noncon-formity.[49] The historians of this school manage to recreate the sense of energy and enthusiasm felt by many of the local labour activists at the time, and also emphasise the creativity shown by working people in establishing new political organisations. Moreover, the most sophisticated among them recognise the presence of the same qualities within estab-

---

[47] See the discussion of Robert Knight's views in Alastair Reid, chapter 10 in this collection.

[48] K. O. Morgan, 'The New Liberalism and the challenge of labour: the Welsh experience, 1885–1929', in K. D. Brown (ed.), *Essays in Anti-Labour History. Responses to the Rise of Labour in Britain* (London, 1974), pp. 159–82; A. Cyr, *Liberal Party Politics in Britain* (London, 1977), pp. 253–9; W. W. Knox, 'Religion and the Scottish labour movement, 1900–1939', *Journal of Contemporary History*, 23 (1988), pp. 609–30.

[49] Thompson, 'Tom Maguire'; F. Reid, 'Keir Hardie's conversion to socialism', in A. Briggs and J. Saville (eds.), *Essays in Labour History*, vol. 2 (London, 1971), pp. 17–46; S. Yeo, 'A new life: the religion of socialism in Britain, 1883–1896', *History Workshop*, 4 (1977), pp. 5–56; A. Howkins, 'Edwardian Liberalism and industrial unrest: a class view of the decline of Liberalism', *History Workshop*, 4 (1977), pp. 143–61.

lished political parties and, consequently, the variations in local Liberal responses to the emergence of the new labour groups.[50]

However, the central assumption of these historians, that the 'New Unions' were fundamentally different from the 'Old' is no longer tenable, for it is now well known that the bodies which survived the initial outburst of enthusiasm were those which converged the most with established forms of organisation, and that the causes of industrial conflict after 1880 were not as new as was once widely assumed.[51] As a result, these writers cannot account for the support which the unions gave to the Labour party after 1900 and, perhaps in overreaction to other interpretations, they do not seem to be very concerned with the danger that they will end up by equating the Labour party with the much smaller Independent Labour party (ILP). A second area of weakness derives from the fact that, while the local research on the ILP stimulated by this school has of necessity recognised the importance of older radical traditions in shaping the political outlook of early labour activists, it has also tended to see radicalism as increasingly out of touch with economic and social developments in the late nineteenth century, and therefore as a significant barrier to the creation of a truly modern socialist party. In this way these historians, instead of paying 'homage' to the early labour activists, end up by portraying them as ultimately unable to think their way out of outdated, and essentially sentimental and unreflective, political habits.[52]

Though this approach is therefore seriously flawed, it is striking how early and how strongly it established itself in the Labour party's own self-image, and how, even after decades of historical criticism, it still remains as an emotional backdrop which has to be revised, or indeed disposed of, in order to develop more sophisticated interpretations.[53]

The second main approach is that of historians like Eric Hobsbawm who are influenced by more orthodox forms of Marxism, and are therefore interested less in the idea of the Labour party as a channel for

[50] D. Howell, *British Workers and the Independent Labour Party, 1888–1906* (Manchester, 1983), pp. 129–282. For further discussion of this point see Pat Thane, ch. 11, in this collection.

[51] E. J. Hobsbawm, 'The "New Unionism" reconsidered', in W. J. Mommsen and H. G. Husung (eds.), *The Development of Trade Unionism in Great Britain and Germany, 1880–1914* (London, 1985), pp. 13–31; S. Pollard, 'The New Unionism in Britain: its economic background', in *ibid.*, pp. 32–52; A. J. Reid, 'The division of labour and politics in Britain, 1880–1920', in *ibid.*, pp. 150–65; J. Zeitlin, 'Industrial structure, employer strategy and the diffusion of job control in Britain, 1880–1920', in *ibid.*, pp. 325–37.

[52] Howell, *British Workers*, pp. 343–97; D. Clark, *Colne Valley: Radicalism to Socialism* (London, 1981).

[53] See, for example, H. Tracey, *The Book of the Labour Party, vol. 1* (London, 1925); A. Wright, editor's introduction to *British Socialism. Socialist Thought from the 1880s to 1960s* (London, 1983), pp. 1–33.

the socialist activism of a minority, and more in its relationship to the position of the working class as a whole within the latest stage in the development of capitalism. Thus, while they stress similar developments in industry and culture to the first school, they are both more deterministic in their analysis of the ways in which these produced a new sense of class unity and separateness, and more pessimistic about the degree to which this new working-class consciousness was contained within the political status quo.[54] These historians attempt to locate changes in labour politics more rigorously within the context of the wider developments taking place in late nineteenth and early twentieth-century Britain and, as a result of their insistence that the position and attitudes of the majority of working people must be properly accounted for, they have stimulated an increasing body of theoretically informed research on the social background of popular politics in the period.[55]

However, as an overall interpretation this approach has simultaneously become vulnerable to the findings of the new research it has itself stimulated, for this is now highlighting both considerably more continuity and considerably more diversity in all areas of working-class life within a mature industrial society than Marxist theory had predicted.[56] Thus, for example, it now seems that previous emphases on mechanisation and the erosion of the position of skilled workers have been exaggerated, and that in the workplace and in the labour market there remained a wide diversity and a significant degree of sectionalism: the phrase 'working classes' would still seem to be the more accurate description.[57] Similarly, in the area of cultural life, recent accounts have stressed both the persistence of older forms of recreation and association and the variety of personal preferences, rather than the emergence of an increasingly homogeneous

---

[54] E. J. Hobsbawm, 'Custom, wages, and workload in nineteenth-century industry', in Briggs and Saville, *Essays*, vol. 1, pp. 113–39 (reprinted in *Labouring Men* [London, 1964], pp. 344–70); J. Saville, 'The ideology of labourism', in R. Benewick, R. N. Berki, B. Parekh (eds.), *Knowledge and Belief in Politics* (London 1973), pp. 213–26; G. Stedman Jones, 'Working-class culture and working-class politics in London, 1870–1900: notes on the remaking of a working class', *Journal of Social History*, 7 (1974), pp. 460–509 (reprinted in Stedman Jones, *Languages of Class* [Cambridge, 1983], pp. 179–238); E. J. Hobsbawm, 'The making of the working class, 1870–1914', in *Worlds of Labour* (London, 1984), pp. 194–213.

[55] McKibbin, 'Why was there no Marxism'.

[56] For two general surveys which synthesise this recent research, see F. M. L. Thompson, *The Rise of Respectable Society. A Social History of Victorian Britain, 1830–1900* (London, 1988); J. Benson, *The Working Class in Britain, 1850–1939* (London, 1989).

[57] C. More, *Skill and the English Working Class, 1870–1914* (London, 1980); R. Harrison and J. Zeitlin (eds.), *Divisions of Labour. Skilled Workers and Technological Change in Nineteenth Century England* (Brighton, 1985); J. Benson, 'Work', in J. Benson (ed.), *The Working Class in England, 1875–1914* (London, 1985), pp. 63–88; Reid, 'Division of labour'.

working-class culture with unambiguous political consequences.[58] This growing body of research therefore leads us to the conclusion, firstly, that any interpretation based on a clear-cut succession of stages in the development of nation-wide classes will be misleading, and secondly, that, in so far as we are prepared to accept that political behaviour is influenced to some degree by economic and social conditions, there will be strong grounds to expect significant continuities in popular radicalism into the late nineteenth and twentieth centuries.

Though the second approach is therefore also seriously flawed, it is striking how much of the political history of the period has until recently been based on its propositions about social change. Thus in the important debates over the Liberals' ability to adopt new social policies, over the speed with which Labour constructed an effective national organisation, and over the implications of the franchise extension of 1918, the background assumption has generally been that the two parties were competing to gain support from an electorate increasingly dominated by an unambiguous sense of class.[59] These debates have been invaluable in demonstrating that, whatever underlying economic and social changes are assumed, reductionist explanations of political events will always be inadequate, and that the form eventually taken by popular politics will depend on the relative success of appeals from rival parties and programmes.[60] However, the new emphases in the social history of the period outlined above would not only support those historians who argue that the continued appeal of the 'Old Liberalism' to working-class voters should not be underestimated,[61] but would also strongly suggest that more attention ought to be paid to the political content of Labour's appeal in particular places and periods, rather than assuming that, once

---

[58] See, for example, R. McKibbin, 'Work and hobbies in Britain, 1880–1950', in J. Winter (ed.), *The Working Class in Modern Britain* (Cambridge, 1983), pp. 127–46; P. Johnson, 'Credit and thrift and the British working class, 1870–1939', in *ibid.* pp. 147–70; A. J. Reid, 'Intelligent artisans and aristocrats of labour: the essays of Thomas Wright', in *ibid.*, pp. 171–86.

[59] H. Pelling, 'Labour and the downfall of Liberalism', in Pelling, *Popular Politics and Society in Late Victorian Britain* (London, 1968), pp. 101–20; P. F. Clarke, *Lancashire and the New Liberalism* (Cambridge, 1971); R. McKibbin, *The Evolution of the Labour Party, 1910–1924* (Oxford, 1974); H. C. G. Matthew, R. I. McKibbin and J. A. Kay, 'The franchise factor in the rise of the Labour party', *English Historical Review*, 91 (1976), pp. 723–52. D. Tanner, 'The parliamentary electoral system, the "Fourth" Reform Act and the rise of Labour in England and Wales', *Bulletin of the Institute of Historical Research*, 56 (1983), pp. 205–19 raises a number of questions about this assumption.

[60] See especially Clarke, *Lancashire*.

[61] H. Pelling, 'The working class and the origins of the welfare state', in *Popular Politics and Society*, pp. 1–18; Morgan, 'New Liberalism'; M. Pugh, *The Making of Modern British Politics, 1867–1939* (London, 1982), pp. 150–2. For further discussion of this point see chapter 9 by John Shepherd in this collection.

the organisational structures and electoral opportunities were in place, the Labour party would be the most natural channel for the expression of working-class consciousness.[62]

The third main approach has been subscribed to mainly by scholars initially connected with the right wing of the Labour party like Henry Pelling, who, while seeing the socialist groups and social change as significant background influences, highlight the important contribution of the established trade unions to the actual formation of the Labour party, largely as a result of the threatening developments in labour law which culminated in the Taff Vale case.[63] Instead of arguing for a new departure in socialist activism or a new phase in the development of working-class consciousness, these historians see the Labour party largely as the latest manifestation of a long-standing trade union involvement in politics: its existence as a separate organisation being due more to local Liberal resistance to the selection of working-class candidates and national Liberal reluctance to institute the payment of MPs, than to any major difference in political aims or values.[64] This interpretation has the advantage of allowing for a considerable degree of continuity in popular experiences and attitudes, at the same time as making a close analysis of the actual political events involved, both in the foundation, and in the early development of the new party. Moreover, the historians of this school who emphasise the impact of the First World War on trade union growth, changing popular attitudes, and the relative coherence of party leaderships, are able to offer the most plausible accounts of how it was that the Labour party eventually began to emerge as a serious electoral rival to the Liberals after 1918.[65]

However, though we therefore find this interpretation the most convinc-

[62] M. Savage, *The Dynamics of Working-Class Politics. The Labour Movement in Preston, 1880–1940* (Cambridge, 1987); D. M. Tanner, *Political Change and the Labour Party, 1900–1918* (Cambridge, 1990). For further discussion of this point see chapter 4 by Jon Lawrence in this collection.

[63] H. Pelling, *The Origins of the Labour Party, 1880–1900* (London, 1954); H. A. Clegg, A. Fox and A. F. Thompson, *A History of British Trade Unions since 1889*, vol. 1 (Oxford, 1964); J. Lovell, 'Trade unions and the development of independent labour politics, 1889–1906', in B. Pimlott and C. Cook (eds.), *Trade Unions in British Politics* (London, 1982), pp. 38–57.

[64] Pelling, *Origins*, pp. 222–7; McKibbin, *Evolution*, pp. 236–47; K. D. Brown, 'The Edwardian Labour party', in K. D. Brown (ed.), *The First Labour Party, 1906–1914* (London, 1985), pp. 1–16.

[65] J. M. Winter, *Socialism and the Challenge of War. Ideas and Politics in Britain, 1912–18* (London, 1974); Pugh, *Modern British Politics*, pp. 161–220; C. Wrigley, 'Trade unions and politics in the First World War', in Pimlott and Cook (eds.), *Trade Unions*, pp. 79–97; K. D. Brown, *The English Labour Movement, 1700–1951* (Dublin, 1982), pp. 212–40; A. J. Reid, 'Dilution, trade unionism and the state in Britain during the First World War', in S. Tolliday and J. Zeitlin (eds.), *Shop Floor Bargaining and the State. Historical and Comparative Perspectives* (Cambridge, 1985), pp. 46–74.

ing of the various approaches, it is not without its own shortcomings. In particular, it frequently echoes the second school in presenting the early Labour party as essentially 'a-political', because of its role as a trade union pressure group and its focus 'merely' on increased representation of the working classes (this is no doubt due, at least in part, to the long-standing influence of the Webbs, who could be just as condescending as more recent Marxist historians towards trade union leaders and Labour MPs). As a result this third approach generally under-states the degree to which Labour's political pragmatism and convergence with Liberalism were based on conscious intellectual and political choices, rather than on unexamined habits and loyalties. Moreover, when the importance of the radical inheritance is recognised, it is frequently treated in ways which echo the first school, implying that radical liberalism was something of a barrier to the development of a fully appropriate modern politics, because of the elements of individualism and self-improvement which were involved, and because of the apparently incoherent range of ideas which were consequently embraced within the Labour party.[66]

In effect, then, the third approach to the history of the Labour party, while the most convincing on the sequence of political events, has generally lacked a distinctive account of the political content of the new party's appeal. The essays in the final part of this collection can therefore be seen as a contribution towards remedying this shortcoming, by placing alongside the first school's 'religion of socialism' and the second school's 'ideology of labourism', a strong emphasis on the 'continuity of radicalism'.

In the first place, as John Shepherd and Alastair Reid establish in their contributions, this involves a clearer recognition that the older generation of trade union leaders and Lib.–Lab. MPs were just as deeply rooted in radical Nonconformist traditions as the younger generation of ILP activists. Whatever evaluation one makes of these traditions, this recognition casts new light on the process by which the Labour party developed as a reasonably coherent organisation. For as Duncan Tanner shows in his chapter, old liberals and new socialists of a moderate hue were able to communicate with each other and to establish a common commitment to a programme of social democratic reforms because they already shared a set of common intellectual reference points, and even their more militant critics were still speaking in the language of radicalism.

In the second place, it is our view that the various currents of radicalism were in fact more intellectually coherent and remained more politically appropriate to the problems faced by trade unionists and Labour

---

[66] D. Martin, 'Ideology and composition', in Brown (ed.), *First Labour Party*, pp. 17–37.

politicians than has generally been recognised.[67] As living political traditions they were handed on and developed largely through direct communications addressed to specific problems: speeches, sermons, organisational reports, and spontaneous discussions. Despite, or perhaps indeed because of, this relatively informal transmission, they proved themselves to be both rigorous and capable of adaptation to the new circumstances of the late nineteenth and early twentieth centuries. As Pat Thane and Duncan Tanner demonstrate in their contributions, the seriousness of the analyses produced by such autodidact radicals as Ramsay MacDonald has all too often been undervalued in favour of supposedly 'more theoretical' continental traditions, even though MacDonald was able to develop a wide-ranging approach to early-twentieth-century progressive politics, covering economic and social developments, the problems of state power and individual citizenship, and the questions of short-term political tactics.[68]

Finally, it is very important to place the development of the early Labour party alongside the previous history of the Liberal party as it had evolved within an expanding democracy, and this we have attempted to do in the structure of this volume as a whole. For, as Jon Lawrence's contribution shows, labour activists still retained a strong sense of loyalty not only to radical traditions but also to the Liberal party itself, even as they were establishing their own independent organisations. This can only be fully understood if we appreciate how much organised labour had been able to gain from its alliance with Gladstonian Liberalism, even after the end of the triumphant reforms of the 1860s. For not only had the 'final settlement' of the central questions of financial policy and labour law been achieved by the Liberals, this was also long remembered by activists within the labour movement.

If from this point of view the Labour party begins to look like the major party of twentieth-century radical liberalism, it is not as a result of some decline from the ideals of its founders, or of some deficit in their political thought, but rather of an understandable commitment to a political tradition which has proved its effectiveness in both theory and practice over a long period of time.[69] For while it is often suggested that radicalism is in its very nature an 'Old Analysis', unable to address the central problems of a genuinely modern society, we would argue that the

---

[67] For a similar argument in relation to middle-class intellectuals see Clarke, *Liberals and Social Democrats*.

[68] For important exceptions, see the illuminating discussions in R. Barker, 'Socialism and progressivism in the political thought of Ramsay MacDonald', in A. J. A. Morris (ed.), *Edwardian Radicalism 1900–1914* (London, 1974), pp. 114–30; K. O. Morgan, *Keir Hardie. Radical and Socialist* (London, 1975), pp. 201–17.

[69] Pugh, *Modern British Politics, passim*; J. Smith, 'Labour tradition in Glasgow and Liverpool', *History Workshop*, 17 (1984), pp. 32–56.

essays in this collection demonstrate that this was certainly not the case up to 1914. Moreover, a reconsideration of debates within the Labour party thereafter is likely to show that radical traditions retained considerably more relevance and appeal than has previously been recognised: even in the context of the growth of the welfare state and the nationalisation of major industries, many prominent figures remained outspoken in their concern for individual liberty and local democracy.

Once this perspective is adopted, one of the central controversies over the party's history begins to seem to be in need of rephrasing: the question is no longer so much why the Labour party emerged, as why significant groups of middle-class liberals have been unable to co-operate with it at key moments in its history.[70] We suspect that part at least of the explanation for this is to be found in the confusions arising from the Labour leaders' continual labelling of their policies as 'socialist'. Given the predominantly radical liberal nature of much of their substantive outlook, the question of why they have done this must also be considered, especially since it has given genuine state socialists convenient opportunities to attack them for betraying the party's true cause, which in turn has given the political centre and right convenient opportunities to accuse the party as a whole of intending to betray the nation. Moreover, given the strength of libertarian attitudes within the population at large, such accusations have reaped major electoral rewards, even when the subsequent actions of Conservative governments have failed to fulfil the promises of their borrowed radical rhetoric.[71] Thus, if as well as asking questions about the past we may conclude on a more prescriptive note, it seems to us that the Labour party's ability to play a leading role in broad progressive movements in the future will be strengthened if it becomes more restrained in its tendency to legitimise its policies primarily in relation to 'socialism', and if it develops more self-consciousness of, and more pride in, its relation to currents of radicalism.

---

[70] P. Clarke, 'The social democratic theory of the class struggle', in Winter (ed.), *Working Class*, pp. 3–18; G. Stedman Jones, 'Why is the Labour Party in a mess?', in *Languages of Class*, pp. 239–56.

[71] For a lucid analysis of the relationship of modern socialists and 'New Right' conservatives to the liberal tradition see R. Eccleshall, editor's introduction to *British Liberalism. Liberal Thought from the 1640s to the 1980s* (London, 1986), pp. 1–66, especially pp. 55–62.

Part I

Continuities in popular radicalism

2 The old radicalism and the new: David Urquhart and the politics of opposition, 1832–1867

Miles Taylor

I

Few enigmas have survived intact from as much study as David Urquhart (1805–77). Despite being the subject of a biography, a doctoral thesis and several monographs, it is still the eccentric side of Urquhart's character and the irrational and obsessive nature of his following which continue to constitute his chief historical significance. Studies of Urquhart himself have tended to concentrate on his Russophobia, his lifelong preoccupation with the 'secret' diplomacy of Lord Palmerston and his messianic aspirations towards leading an enlightened working class.[1] Accounts of the movement which Urquhart inspired – the 'working-men's' foreign affairs committees of the 1850s – have faithfully reproduced this particular focus, emphasising, *inter alia*, their proliferation during the Crimean war, their doctrinal belief in Palmerston's diplomatic duplicity and their complete subservience to Urquhart's Tory demagoguery.[2] In a few of these studies there has been some attempt to offer a more structural explanation for the Urquhart movement – as a response to the *anomie* of a

I am grateful to the Master and Fellows of Balliol College, Oxford for allowing me to use and cite material from the Urquhart bequest.

[1] Gertrude Robinson, *David Urquhart. Some Chapters in the Life of a Victorian Knight-Errant of Justice and Liberty* (Oxford 1920); John Howes Gleason, *The Genesis of Russophobia in Great Britain. A Study of the Interaction of Policy and Opinion*, Harvard Historical Studies, 57 (1950), ch. 7; A. J. P. Taylor, *The Trouble Makers. Dissent over Foreign Policy, 1792–1939* (London, 1957), esp. pp. 46–50, 58–60; Margaret H. Jenks, 'The activities and influence of David Urquhart, 1833–56, with special reference to the affairs of the Near East', unpublished Ph.D. thesis, University of London (1964); cf. William H. Maehl Jr's entry on Urquhart in Joseph Baylen and Norbert J. Gossman (eds.), *Biographical Dictionary of Modern Radicals*, vol. 2, *1830–70* (Hassocks, 1981), pp. 506–12.

[2] Asa Briggs, 'David Urquhart and the West Riding foreign affairs committees', *Bradford Antiquary*, 39 (1958), pp. 197–207; Olive Anderson, *A Liberal State at War. English Politics and Economics during the Crimean War* (London, 1967), pp. 139–52; John Salt, 'Local manifestations of the Urquhartite movement', *International Review of Social History*, 13 (1968), pp. 350–65; Richard Shannon, 'David Urquhart and the foreign affairs committees', in Patricia Hollis (ed.), *Pressure from Without in early Victorian England* (London, 1974), pp. 239–61.

'complex industrialising society' (Salt); as a form of natural religion (Shannon); and, most persuasively, as an integral part of a backward-looking radicalism peculiar to the 1850s (Anderson). However, the overall effect has been one of isolation. Historical fashions come and go, yet Urquhart and the 'working-men's' foreign affairs committees remain a phenomenon set apart from and almost immune to the historiography of mid nineteenth-century England.

One of the main sources of this puzzle has been Urquhart himself. Both in his lifetime and posthumously through his papers he left a deceptively simple trail of evidence which leads to the plausible conclusion that Russophobia was indeed his one fixed idea and the foreign affairs committees little more than his unwitting dupes. However, it is clear that the remote and self-referential nature of the movement was a product of the distance which Urquhart sought to place between himself and the clandestine and corrupt political system he abhorred. In stressing the single-minded and didactic character of the Urquhart movement, historians have thus laid emphasis precisely where Urquhart would have wished, but not necessarily where it is due. The purpose of this chapter is to relocate Urquhart and the foreign affairs committees within the mainstream of the political culture from which they emerged.

II

There are good empirical grounds for treating Urquhart's account of the foreign affairs committees with some scepticism. In the first place, it is by no means clear that it was the Crimean war which provided the impetus for the formation of the majority of the committees. Three pieces of external evidence suggest that 1857–8 rather than 1854–5 was the key period so far as the establishment of the majority of the committees was concerned. Firstly, most of the committees' correspondence contained in the Urquhart papers does not commence until the spring of 1857. Secondly, from the reports of the proceedings of the committees contained in the *Free Press* which began publication in London in October 1855 it is clear that the bulk of the committees in the West Riding and in the Manchester area were formed between February and October 1857. A third source of external evidence is provided in the Reports of the House of Commons Select Committee on Public Petitions. Petitioning the Queen was something to which Urquhart and the committees attached great significance, but there is little indication of a great wave of committee petitions until the Government of India Bill was being debated in parliament in February, 1858, during which time over twenty different committee petitions were presented in the space of six days.[3] This same campaign on behalf of the East India Company during the winter of 1857–8 also appears to have been the only time during the 1850s when Palmerston was particularly concerned by the activities of the committees. In the middle of October 1857, he suggested to the Foreign Secretary, Lord Clarendon, that a prosecution against Urquhart for sedition might be worth while.[4]

In comparison with this upsurge in committee formation and activity during 1857–8, the fortunes of the Urquhart movement in the Crimean war years are less impressive. It is difficult to provide an accurate figure for the number of committees formed during the war but it is doubtful whether the total ever reached more than twenty. Well-publicised committees were formed in Newcastle in November 1854 and in Sheffield and Birmingham in the summer of 1855. A three-day delegate conference was held at Birmingham during July 1855, reassembling a month later, with fourteen towns represented altogether. There just is not the evidence to substantiate the picture of what Salt called a 'frenzied' working-class foreign affairs movement emerging during the Crimean war under Urquhart's auspices. Indeed, before he had heard of the formation of the Newcastle committee in November 1854, Urquhart confessed that he had been on the verge of quitting the country.[5]

If the majority of the foreign affairs committees were established in 1857–8 rather than during the Crimean war this would seem to suggest that Urquhart's Russophobia was not, as is usually maintained, the main reason why he attracted such widespread support. This raises a second main problem regarding Urquhart's version of events in the 1850s. Who made up his following? His own view was that he had saved the 'democracy' from itself – meaning, in other words, that he had wrested the working class away from Chartism and set them on a course of instruction and revelation whereby, as he expressed it, '[s]tatesmen have been formed out of Revolution'.[6] Some historians have accepted this claim and depicted Urquhart as a key precursor of Disraelian strains of working-

---

[3] By comparison, the signing of the Treaty of Paris inspired three petitions of complaint from foreign affairs committees in June and July, 1856 – the same number who petitioned in February, 1857, after the bombardment of Canton; overall, thirty different foreign affairs committees petitioned between mid-February and mid-June, 1858: *Appendices to the Reports of the Select Committee of the House of Commons on Public Petitions*, Sessions 1856, 1857 (1), 1858.

[4] Palmerston to Clarendon, 15 Oct. 1857, Bodleian Library, Oxford, Clarendon deposit, MS Clar. dep. c. 69, fols. 580–4.

[5] *Morning Advertiser*, 26 December 1854, p. 4.

[6] 'An Account of the formation of the committees', (8 Apr. 1862), Balliol College, Oxford, Urquhart bequest, 1/G/24 (Misc. letters).

class patriotism.[7] However, few of his closest and most consistent supporters can be considered as working class, no matter how loose the definition. Three of his staunchest colleagues – Charles Attwood, George Crawshay and Isaac Ironside – had inherited the manufacturing and mercantile wealth of their fathers; another loyal Urquhartite, Stewart Rolland, was a newspaper proprietor.

Urquhart's support was politically as well as socially heterogeneous. Although his supporters were often characterised as a retinue of misfits, there were several points at which Urquhart's analysis converged with that of mid nineteenth-century radicalism, as Olive Anderson has shown in her study of domestic politics during the Crimean war. She dwells in detail upon Urquhart's 'zeal for the ancient constitution' which was his antidote to all the ministerial and parliamentary abuse of power unleashed since the Whig settlement of 1688. She argues that this was a particularly compelling critique in 1855, given the collapse of the coalition government, but which in its purest form was profoundly undemocratic and thus ultimately unacceptable to most radicals, for it advocated the restoration of royal prerogative and a limited suffrage. Thus, Urquhartism, in Anderson's account, was part of the backward end of the 'Janus-face' of mid nineteenth-century radicalism and, as such, was soon eclipsed by its modern, liberal reforming countenance.[8] However, Urquhart was considerably more appealing than this. What Anderson's account overlooks is the extent to which Urquhart was adopted by radicals, not for his 'ancient' constitutionalism, but, rather, for his free trade liberalism and advocacy of non-intervention in foreign policy. In other words, there was a much greater congruence than Anderson allows, between Urquhart's views and some of the modern tenets of mid nineteenth-century liberalism.

There are thus several areas where the empirical evidence does not seem to fit Urquhart's own depiction of what the foreign affairs committees were – a picture, it has been argued, whose authenticity has been accepted too readily by historians keen to demarcate a distinctly plebeian or working-class movement. Urquhart's version of events probably says more about his aspirations than the actual nature or timing of his influence. At the same time, Urquhart's account of his political progress has proved an attractive one to historians wanting to emphasise the discontinuities between early-nineteenth-century radicalism and Gladstonian liberalism. Not only does he seem to have diverted working men

[7] Victor Kiernan, 'Working class and nation in nineteenth-century Britain', in Maurice Cornforth (ed.), *Rebels and their Causes: Essays in Honour of A. L. Morton* (London, 1979). 123–39; Hugh Cunningham, 'The language of patriotism, 1750–1914', *History Workshop Journal*, 12 (1981), pp. 8–33.

[8] Anderson, *Liberal State at War*, and 'The political uses of history in mid-nineteenth-century England', *Past and Present*, 36 (1967), pp. 87–105.

away from Chartism but also he appears to have temporarily checked the radical impulse towards reform as well. Indeed, if Urquhart had not existed, those historians who believe in the watershed significance of 1848 might have had to invent him. Perhaps they have anyway. The rest of this chapter attempts to fill some of the gaps in Urquhart's version of events and suggest a reconsideration of his place within mid nineteenth-century radical politics.

III

Urquhart is usually characterised as a natural Tory whose radicalism was at most an exigency created by the Crimean war. In fact, if his political career is studied at any length, it emerges that he was, by inclination, a Whiggish radical whose Toryism arose out of necessity rather than conviction. Urquhart belonged to a particular generation of aspirant politicians whose entry into public life in the 1820s brought with it a distinct lesson in partisanship. With his background, Urquhart could not reasonably expect many doors into the Tory establishment of the day to open before him and thus it was from the more liberal fringe of the Whigs that he sought patronage as a young man. Whilst at Oxford, Urquhart was introduced into Jeremy Bentham's circle of friends and admirers. Urquhart certainly used his acquaintance with Bentham as a character reference, carrying a letter of introduction from the old man on his Greek travels, as well as urging both Bentham and John Bowring to help him find a consular appointment.[9] Urquhart also seems to have been genuinely disposed towards the intellectual content of Benthamite radicalism during the 1820s. At Oxford he was intimate with some of the members of the utilitarian debating society set up in London by John Stuart Mill and J. A. Roebuck and he himself was part of a similar society in Oxford.[10] This engagement with the Benthamites was perhaps one of the inspirations behind Urquhart's decision to go and fight on the side of the Greeks in the war of independence against Turkey.[11] Whilst there he became more interested in the commercial resources of Turkey and their potential use to Britain and it was his knowledge of Turkish affairs which

---

[9] Bentham to John Bowring, 12 July 1825, Urquhart bequest, 1/A/6.
[10] R. Doane to Urquhart, 8 Jan. 1824, Urquhart bequest: 1/A/15. On the utilitarian debating society, see Francis E. Hyde, 'Utility and radicalism, 1825–1837. A note on the Mill-Roebuck friendship', *Economic History Review*, 16 (1946), pp. 38–44; W. E. S. Thomas, *The Philosophic Radicals: Nine Studies in Theory and Practice, 1817–41* (Oxford, 1979), pp. 156–7.
[11] For Urquhart's service in the war, see D. Dakin, *British and American Philhellenes during the War of Greek Independence, 1821–33* (Salonika, 1955), p. 204.

led to his diplomatic appointments. In the second of these, in 1833, he was instructed to enquire into trade conditions in Turkey and the Near East.[12]

On his return, Urquhart attempted to impress upon both Whig and Tory administrations the importance of developing commercial links with Turkey at the expense of England's relationship with Russia. At this stage, Urquhart had no complaint with the Whig government – it was the Duke of Wellington (and not Lord Palmerston) who, in 1834, vetoed Urquhart's upgrading to a consular position in Constantinople[13] – but his campaign in 1834 coincided with widespread radical frustration with the Whig record in government. During 1834–5, as William Thomas has shown in his study of the philosophic radicals, a number of publishing initiatives developed through which radicals attempted to establish an independent opposition. Some of the most important of these were Roebuck's *Pamphlets for the People*, J. S. Mill and William Molesworth's *London Review*, and the *British and Foreign Review* which had the active participation of Lord Brougham.[14] In this latter Whig–radical journal, Urquhart's criticism of Anglo-Russian relations found its most congenial home.[15]

In other words, Urquhart's success in the second half of 1835 and early 1836 was not simply an index of a latent Russophobia in the British reading public, as J. H. Gleason's influential study of 1950 suggested. Rather, his attacks on a Whig cabinet departing from the true course of diplomatic retrenchment and non-intervention in Europe was precisely in line with radical criticism of the way in which the Whigs had allowed the reform spirit of 1832 to evaporate completely. By way of contrast, by the time of Urquhart's involvement in the abortive attempt to send the ship, the *Vixen*, to break down Russian commercial barriers in Circassia at the end of 1836 – according to both his own mythology and later accounts his most infamous act – radical opposition within the Whig party had died down and Urquhart's escapade received little coverage in the press.[16]

At the end of the 1830s and during the early 1840s, having sacrificed his diplomatic career over the *Vixen* affair, Urquhart moved to a more overt

---

[12] *The Taylor Papers, Being a Record of . . . the Life of Lieut.-Gen. Sir Herbert Taylor, etc* arranged by Ernest Taylor (London, 1913), pp. 294–300; Charles Webster, 'Urquhart, Ponsonby, and Palmerston', *English Historical Review*, 62 (1947), pp. 327–51; Jenks, 'The activities and influence of David Urquhart', p. 9.

[13] G. H. Bolsover, 'David Urquhart and the eastern question, 1833–37: a study in publicity and diplomacy', *Journal of Modern History*, 8 (1936), pp. 444–67; Vernon John Puryear, *International Economics and Diplomacy in the Near East. A Study of British Commercial Policy, 1834–1853* (London, 1935), pp. 24–6.

[14] Thomas, *Philosophic Radicals*, chs. 5–7; H. B. de Groot, 'Lord Brougham and the founding of the *British and Foreign Review*', *Victorian Periodicals Newsletter* (1970).

[15] See, in particular, his 'The quadruple treaty', *British & Foreign Review*, 1 (June, 1835), pp. 217–37, esp. 218–24.

[16] Gleason, *Genesis of Russophobia*, pp. 195–6.

attack on Whig foreign policy since the beginning of the decade. He now began to court a manufacturing and mercantile audience – in Glasgow, Hull, Newcastle and Sheffield (where he unsuccessfully contested the seat in the 1841 election) – emphasising how British preeminence should be sought through commerce and commercial men and not through state-craft and diplomats.[17] This same concern lay behind Urquhart's involvement with cross-party opposition to the Afghan war in 1842–3.[18]

Urquhart's election to parliament in 1847 as Tory MP for Stafford seems, on the face of it, to be unequivocal evidence of his party creed. In fact, his electoral campaign combined an extravagant commitment to free trade with a fashionable attack on Peel's Bank Charter Act of 1844, an attack which intensified as the contest developed. With such views it is not surprising that the Tory *Morning Herald* called him a 'radical'.[19] As an anti-Peel free-trader he was certainly something of an atypical Tory and, indeed, only adopted the label at the onset of the new parliament.[20] Once elected, Urquhart immediately associated himself with the independent Irish MPs and declared privately that he was for the repeal of the Union (in addition to every other statute on the book).[21] He spent much of the August following the election in Dublin, discussing with Charles Gavan Duffy how the case for repeal might be presented as a European question and how the Irish independents' parliamentary fortunes might be allied with those of the protectionists.[22] Given Urquhart's election pledges on free trade, this was curious advice and only makes sense if it is seen not as an attempt to join the tail of Bentinck and Disraeli's party outright, but rather, as a commitment to work with them in opposition when the occasion arose. During 1847–9, the radicals Bright and Cobden, for

[17] Urquhart, *Foreign Policy and Commerce: Speeches Delivered at a Meeting of the Chamber of Commerce of Newcastle-upon-Tyne, etc ... 15th and 20th November, 1838* (Newcastle, 1839), p. 20; cf. 'To the electors of the borough of Sheffield' [9 June 1841] in *Sheffield Mercury*, 12 June 1841, pp. 2–3.

[18] Urquhart, *An Appeal Against Faction, In Respect to the Concurrence of the Present and Late Administrations, to Pervert the House of Commons from Performing its Highest Duties* (1843). This pamphlet was the product of Urquhart's participation in an offshoot of the Colonial Society which met during 1842, lobbying Disraeli, amongst others, over the Afghan war. 'Proceedings of the sectional committee for the East Indies, Ceylon, China and the Mediterranean', Urquhart bequest, 1/J/6; cf. Urquhart to Disraeli, nd [1842], Cambridge University Library, Hughenden papers (microfilm), B/XXI/U/6.

[19] Alex Sinclair to Urquhart, 10 Aug. 1847 [copy], Urquhart bequest, 1/J/6; 'To the worthy and independent burgesses & electors of the Borough of Stafford' (24 June 1847), Urquhart bequest, 5; cf. Urquhart, *The Parliamentary Usurpations of 1819 and 1844, In respect to Money Considered: In a Letter to the Burgesses and Electors of Stafford* (1847).

[20] During the election he made no party professions and took as his colours the Circassian flag, *Staffordshire Advertiser*, 10 July 1847, p. 5.

[21] Urquhart to Sinclair, 17 Aug. 1847 [copy], Urquhart bequest, 1/J/6.

[22] Duffy to Meagher, 18 Aug. [1847], Urquhart to Sinclair, 18 Aug. [1847], Urquhart bequest, 1/J/6.

example, showed much the same sort of pragmatic understanding with protectionists such as Henry Drummond, particularly on questions of taxation and army estimates. Associating the question of Irish repeal with the European situation was, for Urquhart, also a means of mustering new support for a traditional attack on Whig interventionism in Europe.

Nominally a Tory in the 1847 Parliament, Urquhart in fact stood on common ground with many radicals. Like Cobden in his 'National Budget' of 1849, Urquhart attributed many of the present discontents to the fateful year of 1835, since which time national expenditure in the form of army and navy estimates had increased alarmingly.[23] His attitude towards parliamentary reform, rather than stemming from an innate diehard Toryism, in fact reflected a scepticism common to a variety of radicals. Instead of ensuring control over the executive by introducing independent members into the House of Commons, the 1832 Reform Act, in Urquhart's opinion, had fuelled party differences and muted a principled opposition. He reserved special venom for Joseph Hume, who, although the advocate of further parliamentary reform, was a living example of how reform had 'corrupted this House, and changed its Members' – in Hume's case, from a 'staunch economist' to a vehement Whig supporter.[24] Although the attack on Hume was somewhat zealous it was not unusual, for Hume's quiescence in the 1846–7 session had disappointed many of the new radical MPs returned in the 1847 election. On the whole, these MPs, like Urquhart, were highly critical of the laxity and malleability displayed by the older radical section of the Liberal party and, although few went as far as Urquhart did in his rejection of further parliamentary reform, many put financial reform ahead of political reform precisely because they felt that the 1832 Reform Act had done little to preserve the independence of individual MPs.[25] Using a tried and tested analogy, Urquhart likened this encroachment of executive power and the abnegation of opposition to ancient Rome, where the expansion of military commitments overseas had eroded the freedom of the polity at home.[26] Once again, this allusion was staple radical fare in the late 1840s and shows how the classical connection between imperialism and corrup-

[23] For Urquhart's views on the merits of an 'old' Tory opposition to Whig expenditure, see *Hansard*, cv (10 May 1849), col. 220.

[24] Urquhart, *Some Incidents of the Session Reprinted for my Constituents* (London, 1848), pp. 13–14, 17.

[25] For Hume in 1847, see: Ronald K. Huch and Paul R. Ziegler, *Joseph Hume: The People's MP*, Memoirs of the American Philosophical Society, vol. 163 (Philadelphia, PA, 1986), p. 136; on the radical position in parliament generally in the late 1840s, see my unpublished Cambridge Ph.D. thesis, 'Radicalism and patriotism, 1848–59', chs. 1 and 2.

[26] Urquhart, *Wealth and Want: Or Taxation. As Influencing Private Riches and Public Liberty. Being the Substance of Lectures on Pauperism. Delivered at Portsmouth, Southampton, etc in February and March, 1845* (1845), pp. 103–4.

tion, derived from early-eighteenth-century Tory reactions to the aftermath of the Whig revolution of 1688, served as a model for the radical critique of the Whig party after 1832.[27]

After two parliamentary sessions, Urquhart seems to have lost interest in the House of Commons. As well as ill health, shortage of funds may have taxed his enthusiasm. Towards the end of 1848 he dashed off a volume based on his travels in Spain and Morocco earlier in the decade and then left England for a two-year stint in the Near and Middle East, spending much of the time in the Lebanon before visiting Lajos Kossuth, the Hungarian leader in exile in Turkey.[28] Whatever the immediate reasons behind Urquhart's departure, it is significant that the waning of his interest coincided with the beginning of the demise of the independent opposition in the House of Commons. After 1850, the frequency with which Peelites, protectionists and radicals joined with each other in motions against Whig financial policy abated and MPs like Roebuck came in from the cold to give uncritical support to Russell and Palmerston.

Two main themes emerge from this consideration of Urquhart's political career up to the onset of the Crimean war. Firstly, his hostility to political power stemmed from his distrust of the Whig party's record in office after 1832. Secondly, his criticisms of Whig foreign policy were centred around a commitment to free trade rather than a wild Russophobia. In many ways these two attitudes were natural to someone who expected from the Whigs the fulfilment of the promises and principles of Canningite liberalism. It was thus not surprising that it should be Lord Palmerston who provoked Urquhart's deepest resentment, for Palmerston was not only the main connecting thread between the Canningites and the Whigs, but he was also, as Whig foreign minister, perceived to be breaking with the liberal European foreign policy pursued by Canning.[29] Whilst imbued with the spirit of the 1820s, however, Urquhart was also a product of the reformed state of the 1830s, owing his diplomatic posting to the institutional rejuvenation instigated by the Whigs. Dependent on the Whigs for his vocation, yet suspicious of their chicanery after 1832, Urquhart, like J. A. Roebuck or A. H. Layard (a later example), displayed a lifelong propensity to bite the hand that fed him. Thus, it was Urquhart's own ambiguous relationship with the Whigs, more than

[27] For Urquhart's fondness for Swift and Bolingbroke, see M. C. Bishop, *Memoir of Mrs Urquhart* (London, 1897), pp. 79, 132.

[28] Contract with Richard Bentley (9 Sept. 1848), BL, Bentley papers, Add. MS 44,615, fol. 125; cf. Jenks, p. 274–5; for Urquhart's visit to Kossuth, see Denes A. Janossy, *Great Britain and Kossuth*, Archivuum Europae Centro-Orientalis, vol. 3 (Budapest, 1937), pp. 110–13.

[29] Roger Bullen, 'Party politics and foreign policy: Whigs, Tories and Iberian affairs, 1830–6', *Bulletin of the Institute of Historical Research*, 51 (1978), pp. 37–59.

anything else, which lay behind his characteristic sensitivity to the distinction between private motives and public profession – between self-interest and patriotism. Moreover, it was his belief that the Whigs and, in particular, Palmerston, were not adhering to a policy of peace and retrenchment which took Urquhart to the manufacturing districts, not in search of working-class men, but in the pursuit of those very same commercial classes that the Whigs had enfranchised in 1832.

IV

Urquhart's position during the prelude to the Crimean war in 1853–4 was more or less in line with his Whig-radicalism of the 1830s and 1840s and had little to do with Russophobia *per se*. For him, what lay at the root of the 'Eastern question' was the Whig propensity for interventionism abroad and faction at home. Unlike many radicals who found it difficult at first to decide whether Russian barbarism or Turkish corruption was the greater evil in the Near East, Urquhart was convinced of the cause of the Russo-Turkish dispute from the start. The danger lay not in the East – neither in Russian aggression nor Turkish supineness – but in Europe, where Whiggish England and imperial France were predisposed to intervention – to 'becoming mutually involved in false courses in *third* countries'.[30] Russia, Urquhart argued, lacked the necessary resources to attack Turkey – indeed, since 1828 her military power had diminished greatly whilst Turkish defences had been strengthened.[31] What Russia coveted in Turkey was not her territory, but her commercial trade with England, in particular, the export of grain from the Danubian principalities. By imposing a tariff on grain exports in the Anglo-Turkish treaty of 1838, England had already given the Anglo-Russian grain trade an unfair advantage. Now, firstly through diplomatic negotiation and latterly, as a *fait accompli*, through occupation of Moldavia and Wallachia (the Danubian principalities excluded from the 1838 treaty), Russia hoped to gain a monopoly of the grain trade.[32] English support for Turkey was thus a complete fallacy and Urquhart supplemented his most widely read writings of 1853 with a plea for non-intervention. By her diplomatic interference in the Turkish tariff England had already fuelled Russian ambition and to now impel Turkey into a European war would load her

---

[30] Urquhart, *Progress of Russia in the West, North and South: By Opening the Sources of Opinion and Appropriating Channels of Wealth and Power* (London, 1853), p.lviii.

[31] *Ibid.*, pp. vii–ix; (2nd edn), p. xlvi; Urquhart, *The War of Ignorance and Collusion; Its Progress and Results: A Prognostication and a Testimony* (London, 1854), pp. 25–6; *The Occupation of the Crimea. An Appeal from Today to Tomorrow* (1854), pp. 28–31; *Recent Events in the East. Being Letters, Articles, Essays, etc* (1854), pp. 15–16, 26–8, 212, 216–17.

[32] Urquhart, *Progress*, pp. 294–5; *Recent Events*, pp. 70–4.

domestic economy with debt, precipitate her decline and deliver her commerce over to Russia.[33]

Urquhart's free trade liberalism had changed little since the early 1830s. The Whigs, in his eyes, had opted once again for diplomacy instead of commerce. Urquhart's position in 1853 was thus closer to Cobden than has been suggested.[34] Cobden also argued that Russia was not equipped to attack Turkey and that without English commerce Russia would have remained in a backward condition. Where Urquhart and Cobden parted ways was over the relative merits of Turkish civilisation – Cobden doubted that a corrupt Muslim empire was worth Europe spilling blood over; Urquhart was certain of the liberal credentials of the Turkish polity and believed that, if left alone to fight Russia, she might save Europe.[35] Urquhart and Cobden's arguments not only started out from the same point of disagreement with Whig policy, they were also directed at much the same audience. As in 1838–41, Urquhart sought to pitch his criticisms to a manufacturing and mercantile audience and two of his Stafford contacts, William Peplow and S. Langley, spent some time in October and November 1853 trying to set up a public meeting in the symbolic home of free trade – Manchester.[36] The meeting did not come off until the following April and, by then, Urquhart had been adopted by radicals, not as he would have liked, as the unraveller of English secret diplomacy, but as the champion of Turkish liberalism.

Much to Cobden and Urquhart's annoyance, it was Whiggery and not free trade which dictated the terms in which the 'Eastern question' was discussed in 1853–4. Radicals, in particular, attempted to link the 'Eastern question' to the wider issue of European nationalism. From the late summer of 1853 onwards, radical energies were concentrated in demonstrating on the one hand, that Russia, though backward, was capable of westward expansion and encroachment and, on the other, that Turkey was not in a state of decline, but was going through a process of civil and religious reform. Urquhart, whose travel writings on Turkey and the Near East were well known, was a natural authority to turn to for evidence of Turkish progress and this, along with his hostility towards *The Times*, was one of the main reasons why he secured a regular place in the columns of the *Morning Advertiser*, then in the midst of a circulation drive against *The*

---

[33] Urquhart, *War of Ignorance*, Appendix, p. 43; *Recent Events*, pp. 284–6, 307–10.

[34] Taylor, *Trouble Makers*, ch. 2.

[35] For Cobden's position in 1853–4, see John W. Derry, *The Radical Tradition: Tom Paine to Lloyd George* (1967), pp. 209–15; and Taylor, 'Radicalism and patriotism', ch. 4.

[36] Langley to Urquhart, 25 Oct. [1853]; Peplow to Urquhart, 10 Nov. 1853, Urquhart bequest.

Times.[37] His knowledge of Turkey was also cited approvingly by the *Leader*,[38] another paper which, like the *Morning Advertiser*, was pressing for English intervention in the Crimea. It was from this unlikely source of predominantly pro-Italian and pro-Polish nationalism that Urquhart derived his main support during 1853 and 1854. Although run by close colleagues of Urquhart, the 'Association for the Protection of Turkey and Other Countries from Partition' had many members of the 'Society of Friends of Italy' on its committee and in attendance at its meetings.[39] For pro-interventionist radicals, Urquhart's Turcophilia was considerably more significant than his Russophobia.

In addition to his pro-Turkish views, Urquhart inspired support from a range of radicals during the winter of 1853–4 by his attack on the 'secret diplomacy' of the Aberdeen cabinet. Not only was this, he argued, giving Russia the upper hand in the Danubian delta, but also at home it meant that ministers were encroaching upon the independence of the House of Commons by not allowing MPs to debate the negotiations over the Porte.[40] Finsbury radicals such as Charles Dobson Collet and Washington Wilks joined in with Urquhart, declaring 'rend open the Foreign Office',[41] John Bright presented petitions on their behalf in the House of Commons,[42] and, in their papers, George Jacob Holyoake and William James Linton endorsed Urquhart's unmasking of executive influence.[43] Some of these radicals wanted English intervention in the east, some did not. What they all desired was that the facts of the 'Eastern question' should be presented to the House of Commons and the issues involved in the dispute be properly debated. Urquhart's personification of 'secret diplomacy' in Palmerston was, in some respects, incidental to this wider radical concern for the sovereignty of parliament. Indeed, some of those radicals who agreed with Urquhart's criticisms of 'secret diplomacy', such as George Crawshay of Newcastle and Isaac Ironside of Sheffield, looked upon the main target of Urquhart's animus – Palmerston – as the one 'statesman' who might conduct an 'upright' and more accountable foreign policy.[44] Once the war began, demands for ministerial accountability and

---

[37] Jenks, 'The activities and influence of David Urquhart', pp. 292–6; for the *Morning Advertiser*'s rivalry with *The Times*, see James Grant, *The Newspaper Press*, 3 vols. (London, 1871–3), vol. 2, p. 59.

[38] *Leader*, 15 Oct. 1853, pp. 996–7.

[39] *Association for the Protection of Turkey and other Countries from Partition – Proceedings* (1854).

[40] *Morning Advertiser*, 12 Aug. 1853, p. 3.

[41] *Ibid.*, 31 Mar. 1854, p. 6.

[42] *Hansard*, cxxxi (13 Mar. 1854), cols. 673–4.

[43] *English Republic* (1854), pp. 196–8; *Reasoner*, 30 Apr. 1854, pp. 289–91.

[44] *Leader*, 24 Dec. 1853, p. 1235; *Sheffield Free Press*, 24 Dec. 1853, p. 5, 31 Dec. 1853, p. 5.

expressions of opposition to the war became incompatible, as both Urquhart and John Bright were to find to their cost.

Given his account of the origins of the 'Eastern question' and his opposition to English intervention, Urquhart's chances of remaining in alliance with the supporters of European nationalism were never very great. Once war was declared, the separation between the two partners became imminent. Urquhart's advocacy on behalf of Turkey was no longer as immediately relevant as it had been in the previous autumn and his criticism of the cabinet provoked little response. As the *Daily News* noted when Urquhart tried to contest Lord John Russell's City of London seat in the middle of June 1854, '[t]his may be modern conservatism, but it is wondrously like old-fashioned destructiveness'.[45] Radical opposition to the coalition's war policy increasingly took the form of the call for the restoration of an independent Poland and the opening up of the war against Russia on her East European and Baltic fronts. Urquhart, whose grand plan was limited to a Turkish legion, was an unhelpful guide. On the same day that Urquhart was contesting the City of London, Lajos Kossuth was telling a Nottingham audience that the solution to the war lay in Hungary and Poland and not in the Crimea.[46] Over the next six months Kossuth's presence completely overshadowed Urquhart's, with the Hungarian being warmly received at many of the venues in the Midlands and in London where Urquhart had spoken the previous autumn. By the end of the year the 'Society of Friends of Italy' had metamorphosed into the 'Anglo-Polish Committee' and in the new year of 1855 Kossuth began the first of two stints as leader-writer for metropolitan weeklies – the *Atlas* and *The Sunday Times*.

With his own star falling and Kossuth's in the ascendant, it is not surprising that Urquhart was somewhat disillusioned towards the end of 1854.[47] What organised opposition existed during the first nine months of the war showed little sign of his influence. There is no direct evidence, as Anderson suggests,[48] to connect Urquhart with the committees formed in Sheffield and Newcastle in August and September for 'asserting the right of people to interfere directly in foreign affairs'. Isaac Ironside, the editor of the *Sheffield Free Press*, was the inspiration behind the Sheffield committee and, although during the summer he had supported Urquhart's call for the establishment of a Turkish army, as a member of the 'Society of Friends of Italy' his sympathies were broadly in line with the liberal

---

[45] *Daily News*, 14 June 1854, p. 3.

[46] *Authentic Report of Kossuth's Speeches on the War in the East, and the Alliance with Austria, at Sheffield, June 5, and at Nottingham, June 12, 1854* (1854), pp. 18–20.

[47] Cf. n.12.

[48] Anderson, *Liberal State at War*, pp. 147–8.

nationalism of Kossuth. The following April, for example, he was still calling for the restoration of Poland, Hungary and Italy.[49] Not until the summer of 1855 did he state that he had been won over by Urquhart's arguments. George Crawshay, another member of the 'Society of Friends of Italy', established the Newcastle committee in August with Charles Attwood, who knew Urquhart from the late 1830s. Their invitation brought Urquhart to Newcastle on 23 October and just over three weeks later the 'Newcastle-upon-Tyne Foreign Affairs Committee' was organised for the first time, with Attwood as president and Joseph Cowen Jr as secretary. This latter committee was the one whose formation Urquhart attributed to his influence,[50] but this was something of a delusion on Urquhart's part. Almost immediately the committee reiterated the programme of the 'Society of Friends of Italy' and called for the restoration of Poland. At the end of the month the committee organised a meeting to commemorate the anniversary of the Polish revolution of 1830 and it also published a pamphlet advocating an attack on Russia's eastern front.[51] This was Kossuth's strategy and not Urquhart's. Crawshay did his best to impress upon Urquhart that the committee was moving in Attwood's direction,[52] but in the ensuing months Cowen and George Julian Harney (another committee member) snubbed Crawshay's involvement in the committee, declared themselves for parliamentary reform and set an explictly republican agenda to accompany their monitoring of the war.[53] Eventually, in March 1855, Crawshay and some other Newcastle radicals set up a rival 'Committee for watching the war' which was set more in the Urquhart mould.[54]

In 1854, therefore, Urquhart gained little support on his own terms. It was not until the series of resignations from the coalition cabinet in February 1855 that Urquhart's constitutionalist critique became wholly

[49] *Sheffield Free Press*, 19 Aug. 1854, p. 5, 30 Sept. 1854, pp. 2–3, 21 Oct. 1854, p. 8, 28 Apr. 1855, p. 3.

[50] Newcastle-upon-Tyne Foreign Affairs Committe minute book, 14 Dec. 1854, Tyne & Wear Archives Dept., Newcastle-upon-Tyne, Cowen collection. The committee's reservations about Urquhart were made quite clear in the *Northern Tribune* (1854), pp. 389–92.

[51] General L. Mieroslawski, *Poland, Russia, and the Western Powers. A Memorial, Historical and Political, Addressed to the British and French Nations* (Newcastle-upon-Tyne, 1854). For Mieroslawski and the Anglo-Polish movement at the beginning of 1855, see Peter Brock, 'Joseph Cowen and the Polish exiles', *Slavonic and East European Review*, 32 (1953), pp. 52–69; Marian Zychowski, *Ludwik Mieroslawski, 1814–1878* (Warsaw, 1963), p. 697; M. J. E. Copson-Niecko, 'Pro-Polish agitation in Great Britain, 1832–1867', unpublished Ph.D. thesis, University of London (1968), pp. 146–50.

[52] Crawshay to Mrs Urquhart, 1 Dec. 1854, Urquhart bequest, 1/J/3.

[53] Newcastle-upon-Tyne Foreign Affairs Committee minute book, 30 Nov. 1854, 7 Feb. 1855, 26 Feb. 1855; *Republican Record* (Jan. 1855), pp. 1–3; cf. *Northern Tribune* (1855), pp. 105–6.

[54] See this committee's *Constitutional Remedies: evidence of Mr. Urquhart before the [Newcastle] committee* (Newcastle-upon-Tyne, 1855).

credible. With the departure of Russell, quickly followed by the Peelites, circumstances were ripe for an acceptance of the traditional vocabulary of opposition which was Urquhart's hallmark. At one and the same time, a succession of ministers had put their own private reputations before their public duties and yet there was no parliamentary opposition to call them to account.[55] The quality of both the executive and the legislature became the subject of sustained discussion in the radical press. As the one minister whose personal position was strengthened by the events of February, Palmerston's motives, in particular, were the subject of speculation.[56] So too were the credentials of all the MPs who professed independence but who allowed themselves to be compromised by party patronage and the lure of office. Securing the political independence of the House of Commons was prized by many radicals above further reform of the franchise. In this, their views were similar to those of Urquhart.[57] Initially, radicals such as Ironside, Cowen and George Dawson (in Birmingham), looked to Austen Henry Layard to spearhead an opposition to Palmerston's ministry, but with the slow progress in the early part of the summer of the Administrative Reform Association, to which Layard attached himself, more immediate remedies were sought.[58]

At the beginning of July, Urquhart was invited to speak in Sheffield and Birmingham. By now, perhaps wary of radical overtures, he was careful to define his position and that of other opponents of the ministry. In Sheffield on 4 July he called into question J. A. Roebuck's course in pressing for a vote of censure of Palmerston's conduct.[59] The following day, he went with Ironside to Birmingham to address the first of three meetings at Bingley Hall. Urquhart told his audiences there that 'in proportion as the corruption of the Executive power increased, so in proportion did their power of self-government for the removal of evils diminish and decay'. He recommended impeachment but, noting the weakness of the Commons, also pointed out that there was no tribunal or court where the 'treason' of ministers could be investigated properly. Thus, he declared, there was a need for local committees to make such investigations on their own accounts. The series of Birmingham meetings

[55] For Urquhart's views on the weakness of the opposition, see his *The Home Face of the Four Points* (London, 1855), pp. 17–18.

[56] E.g. [T. C. Grattan], 'Lord Palmerston as premier', *Westminster Review*, ns, 7 (Apr., 1855), pp. 398–424.

[57] *Sheffield Free Press*, 10 Mar. 1855, p. 5, 24 Mar. 1855, p. 5; cf. [F. W. Newman], 'Administrative example of the United States', *Westminster Review*, ns, 7 (Apr. 1855), pp. 492–516.

[58] For the slow progress of the Administrative Reform Association, see Olive Anderson 'The Administrative Reform Association, 1855–1857', in Hollis, *Pressure from Without*, pp. 262–88.

[59] *Sheffield Free Press*, 7 July 1855, p. 3.

concluded with the drawing-up of a petition calling for the impeachment of ministers and it was also agreed to form a local committee to discuss Urquhart's claims regarding English collusion in the Russian encroachment in the Danube.[60] Two weeks later, a conference assembled in Birmingham, organised by two local radicals, George Dawson and J. A. Langford, both old members of the 'Society of Friends of Italy', at which the various reports of different committees on Urquhart's claims were presented. To make quite sure he was not misunderstood in such company, Urquhart made it clear that he thought Mazzini was a Russian spy and European republicanism a means of furthering Russian influence. Such a clarification of Urquhart's position certainly cleared the air and, as Langford feared it would, depleted the conference of most of its pro-republican participants.[61] When the conference reassembled the following month half the delegates who attended in July were missing, including most of those from Birmingham. The so-called 'Address of the Men of Birmingham', which was published by this reduced gathering and which has often been deemed an authentic example of Urquhart's influence, contained hardly a word with which Dawson, Langford or any of the other Birmingham radicals would have agreed and was probably put together by Steward Rolland from Urquhart's notes.[62]

The year which ended in September 1855 can thus hardly be considered as the most 'successful' of Urquhart's life, as Anderson claims.[63] Rather than organising a faithful band of converts up and down the country, Urquhart and 'Urquhartism' had been rejected in Newcastle and Birmingham and misunderstood elsewhere. Even where he had secured a hold, Urquhart remained cautious. In Sheffield, Ironside's protestations of faith did not impress Urquhart and he despatched a reliable local Stafford newspaper reporter to the town to act as sub-editor on the *Sheffield Free Press* and keep Ironside on the right track.[64] Nor had Urquhart made any inroads on radical support for continental nationalism. The Newcastle committee ended the year as it had begun, calling for the restoration of

---

[60] *Birmingham Daily Press*, 6 July 1855, p. 3, 7 July 1855, p. 3; *Morning Advertiser*, 9 July 1855; *Empire*, 14 July 1855, pp. 516–17.

[61] *Birmingham Daily Press*, 23 July 1855 (Supplement); Langford to Urquhart, 4 Aug. 1855, Urquhart bequest, 1/J/3.

[62] *Birmingham Daily Press*, 14 Aug. 1855, p. 3; *Address of the Men of Birmingham to the People of England, Adopted at a Meeting of the Conference, Held at Birmingham, Monday, August 13, 1855, etc* (Birmingham, 1855); Langford penned his own version of events: *Kossuth, Mazzini, Urquhart and the Conferences: with a letter from George Dawson, M. A.* (London, 1855); Kossuth distanced himself from the conference as well: *Atlas*, 8 Sept. 1855, pp. 576–7.

[63] Anderson, *Liberal State at War*, p. 147.

[64] 'Statement of the facts of Mr Cyples connection with Mr Urquhart, and the Sheffield Free Press' (24 Jan. 1857), Urquhart bequest, 1/G/18.

Poland and, in addition, protesting against the expulsion of Victor Hugo and other French republicans from Jersey.[65] The only part of Urquhart's arsenal of argument which retained any degree of persuasion at the end of 1855 was his claim that the Crimean war had originated in Russian attempts to snuff out the Turkish grain trade. As bread prices rose towards the end of the year Collet, Rolland and Richard Hart attempted, with some success, to convince the Finsbury and Paddington 'People's Provision Leagues' of the connection between bread shortages and English diplomacy.[66] 'Urquhartism' thus ended the war as it had begun, preaching the cause of free-trade liberalism.

V

Urquhart's most successful year was 1857–8 and not 1854–5. Between February 1857 and March 1858 foreign affairs committees proliferated, particularly in the Manchester area and in the West Riding of Yorkshire. In this year too, Urquhart's well-worn theme of overseas intervention, imperialism and corruption for once made perfect sense in the light of the English bombardment of the Chinese port of Canton and in the aftermath of the Indian mutiny. Whereas the Crimean war had been dominated by a Whiggish debate over the destiny of European nation states – a debate in which the superiority and security of English institutions was taken for granted – Palmerston's entanglements in Asia awakened dormant fears that overseas conquest would destroy constitutional liberties at home. Here was Urquhart's vindication. Since the Afghan war of 1842 he had been warning that the source of the decline of the English polity lay in military conquest in the Indian sub-continent. In 1857–8, however, this was no longer the prophecy of an isolated radical. The perception that Palmerston was a 'second Chatham', endangering the freedoms of England, united a range of disparate groups and proved to be one of the strongest forces which bonded together the component elements of a 'liberal' party before 1859.[67]

When news of the English attack on Canton reached London in January, Urquhart's response followed its usual course. The *Free Press* denounced the bombing as a blow aimed by Palmerston at the sovereignty

---

[65] Kenneth Ward Hooker, *The Fortunes of Victor Hugo in England*, Columbia University Studies in English and Comparative Literature, no. 134 (New York, 1938), pp. 112–32; Monica Partridge, 'Alexander Herzen and the younger Joseph Cowen, M.P. Some unpublished material', *Slavonic and East European Review*, 41 (1962), pp. 50–63.

[66] *Empire*, 10 Nov. 1855, p. 786; *Free Press*, 10 Nov. 1855, p. 3, 24 Nov. 1855, p. 3; Thomas Johnson to Urquhart, 5 Feb. [18]56, Urquhart bequest, 1/G/24.

[67] For a fuller discussion, see Taylor, 'Radicalism and patriotism', ch. 5.

of parliament and likened England to Rome in the age of Nero.[68] As in 1853, Urquhart looked to Manchester for a response and on this occasion was able to arrange a public meeting immediately. Urquhart and Rolland addressed a gathering at the city's Corn Exchange on 2 February and the first meeting of the aptly named 'Manchester Free Trade and Foreign Affairs Association' was held four days later and an address was issued. Most of the address was vintage Urquhart – the benefits of free trade had been denied because of an interfering foreign policy through which, by imposing tariffs on Poland and Turkey, English ministers served the interests of Russia. However, the address concluded with the observation that there was some common ground between the association and the Anti-Corn Law League, the local Chamber of Commerce and, in particular, the Peace Society.[69] This open-ended declaration denoted a very different approach to political organisation to that of Urquhart. Over the next nine months the Manchester committee, run by John Buxton and Frederick Carr, demonstrated both a degree of independence from Urquhart and a willingness to cooperate with other radical groups. One of its first acts was to petition parliament on the Canton bombing through one of the local MPs, Thomas Milner Gibson, not necessarily Urquhart's first choice.[70] During March, April and May, together with the Bradford committee, Buxton and Carr visited towns on both sides of the Pennines, organising new foreign affairs committees and, on occasion, crossing the paths of Peace Society lecturers without any of the acrimony which had characterised such confrontations in 1855.[71] In Manchester, the committee seems not to have become involved in the borough election in March, but in Bradford the local committee came out in active support of Thomas Perronet Thompson, who stood successfully as an anti-Palmerstonian liberal.[72] Following his election, Thompson began a regular correspondence with the *Bradford Advertiser*, in which he took up many of the issues raised by the local committee.[73]

Despite showing themselves to be increasingly independent of Urqu-

[68] *Free Press*, 28 Jan. 1857, pp. 196–7.
[69] *Free Press*, 11 Feb. 1857, pp. 209–10, 214–15.
[70] The committee published the petition as *Illegality of our Proceedings in China*, a copy of which is in the T. P. Thompson papers, Brotherton Library, University of Leeds, MS 277/5/23; cf. Urquhart to Buxton (8 Mar. 1857), reprinted in the *Free Press*, 18 Mar. 1857, pp. 249–50.
[71] *Free Press*, 25 Mar. 1857, pp. 257–8, 13 May 1857, pp. 326–8; *Herald of Peace*, 1 Apr. 1857, p. 192. In its *Report no. 2: 'What Constitutes Lawful War?'* published in May, the Bradford committee cited extracts from Peace Society material.
[72] T. P. Thompson to Richard Cobden, 9 May 1857, Archives Dept., Brynmor Jones Library, University of Hull, T. P. Thompson papers, DTH/4/14.
[73] This correspondence was later published as *Audi Alteram Partem. Letters of a Representative to His Constituents*, 3 vols. (London, 1858–61).

hart's organisational strategy, the foreign affairs committees formed during 1857 agreed with the broad thrust of Urquhart's analysis of events. They accepted that Palmerston had subverted the functions of the Privy Council and that his diplomatic representatives in the Indian sub-continent knew no lawful restraints on their exercise of power. Much of the committees' activity during 1857, besides the organisation of new committees, involved exposing and detailing examples of the inconsistencies of public officials overseas. The Bradford and Bristol committees took up the case of the dethroned King of Oude, the annexation of whose principality, they argued, had been an act of diplomatic collusion.[74] Other committees reopened the investigation into the policies pursued by Sir Alexander Burnes (since deceased), the British envoy to Kabul on the eve of the Afghan war in 1842.[75] All of this was perfectly in accordance with Urquhart's expressed conviction that, in extinguishing party, Palmerston had helped to make the nation and its policy overseas 'dependent on the dispositions of individual men' in much the same way as Louis Napoleon had done in imperial France. In England, in Urquhart's opinion, imperialism had now succeeded faction and political collapse was imminent.[76] The committees' campaign against the Government of India Bill the following year, which saw the peak of their activities, encapsulated, in a single issue, the main themes of Urquhart's critique of the Whigs since 1832. Instead of leaving India to be developed, like Turkey, through the agency of free trade in the form of the East India Company, ministers were planning to control India from Westminster by transferring power to a Board of Control. From being a medium of commerce India would become a tool of partisanship and corrupt the parliamentary system.[77]

As in the 1830s and in 1855 radicals could go some way with Urquhart's diagnosis, but not accept his remedies. It was difficult to sustain enthusiasm for an institution like the East India Company. Moreover, Crawshay, who led the campaign, was known to be a stockholder in the company and this lent an air of vested interest to the attack on the government. However, perhaps the greatest check to Urquhart's wider appeal in 1857–8 lay in the very conventionality of his views. Across a

[74] *Free Press*, 20 May 1857, p. 335; C. Bartholomew to Urquhart, 11 May 1857, Urquhart bequest, 1/G/4.
[75] The Newcastle committee's report was later published in London as *Falsification of Diplomatic Documents: the Affghan Papers. Report and Petition of the Newcastle Foreign Affairs Association* (1860).
[76] *Free Press*, 18 Mar. 1857, pp. 249–50, 5 Aug. 1857, pp. 417–21; cf. Urquhart, *The Rebellion of India* (1857).
[77] See George Crawshay's arguments in *The Immediate Cause of the Indian Mutiny, as set forth in the Official Correspondence* (Newcastle, 1857) and *The Catastrophe of the East India Company* (London, 1858).

broad spectrum of the opposition many of the same connections were being observed between Palmerston's foreign policy and the subservience of the House of Commons, as those emphasised by Urquhart. Gladstone, Bright, Cobden – even Ernest Jones – did not require conversion to Urquhartism for their analysis of the effects of Palmerston on parliamentary politics.

The reemergence of liberal radicalism in 1858–9 thus spelled the demise of the Urquhart movement. In mid-April 1858 the *Free Press* switched from weekly to monthly publication – most of its issues, from then on, devoted to special numbers, reprinting large parts of the *Portfolio* and others of Urquhart's writings, as well as monitoring Crawshay's prolonged campaign on behalf of the East India Company. During 1859 some of the committees battled on against the reform movement, whilst others reported that their numbers were being depleted by the '[m]ania' of reform.[78] With the return of Lord Palmerston to office in June 1859, Urquhart mustered forces once more and warned of the perils of English intervention in Italy – perils which seemed to be realised by most radicals anyway.[79] The Lancashire cotton famine of 1862 revived Urquhart's interest in exposing to a Manchester audience the connections between diplomacy and food shortages, but, by then, committee organisation in Manchester was at a low ebb.[80]

VI

By the end of the 1850s there were too many points of confluence between Urquhart's views and those of many other radicals for him to retain the kind of distinctive appeal he had acquired in earlier years. To attribute all the present discontents to the policy of intervention abroad which the Whigs had pursued since 1688 was something of a commonplace by 1859. Of course, Urquhart was fairly unique in believing that Russia was the

---

[78] 'Report of the Proceedings of the Foreign Affairs Committee during August, 1859', pp. 14–15, Urquhart bequest, 1/G/24; 'Report of a district meeting' (27 June [1858]), Urquhart bequest, 1/G/14.

[79] *Mr Urquhart on the Italian War . . .; English Aid to Garibaldi, on his Invasion of the Sicilies. Is it Lawful and Just? Correspondence between the Manchester Foreign Affairs Association and Mark Philips, Esq., etc.* (Manchester, 1860); for attitudes in general towards Italy in 1859–60, see Derek Beales, *England and Italy, 1859–60* (London, 1961) and M. P. Urban, *British Opinion and Policy on the Unification of Italy, 1856–61* (New York, 1938).

[80] Buxton to Mrs Urquhart, 18 Jan. 1862, Foden to Urquhart, 29 June 1862, Urquhart bequest, 1/G/14; Rolland to Mrs Urquhart, 19 Feb. 1862, Urquhart bequest, 1/G/24. Urquhart and several of the committees did temporarily revive the campaign for Circassian independence in 1863/4, by climbing upon the back of the pro-Polish agitation of that year. See John F. Kutolowski, 'English radicals and the Polish insurrection of 1863–4', *Polish Review* (1967), pp. 3–26.

main beneficiary of this policy and that the remedy lay in restoring the royal prerogative. But, as this chapter has tried to make clear, neither of these two more colourful aspects of his analysis were ever the main reason for his support. Throughout his political career, Urquhart's appeal was always greatest when the differences between Whigs and radicals were most intense – in the parliamentary party in 1835, amongst manufacturing audiences disillusioned with the Whig position on the Corn Laws at the end of the 1830s and in the opposition to Palmerston in 1855 and 1857. Once this breach between Whigs and radicals had been healed, Urquhart's arguments were largely irrelevant and quite naturally soon took on shades of eccentricity.

During the 1860s, the only campaign in which Urquhartites figured significantly was that of the Jamaica Committee, which sought to bring Governor Eyre to trial for his actions before and during the Morant Bay uprising in Jamaica in 1865. Collet was on the committee, Urquhart gave moral support and the Bradford foreign affairs committee met and petitioned over the issue.[81] The Governor Eyre case was a fitting swansong for the Urquhart movement, for it involved the question of to what extent men vested with political power could be held accountable and subject to popular restraint. For those of Urquhart's generation, this was in many ways the key problem posed by the 1832 Reform Act. On the one hand, it had introduced a popular element into parliament, but, on the other, it had consolidated party government and weakened principled opposition. In this limited sense, Urquhart was not a democrat, for he believed that the 'patriotism' of individual MPs, rather than the existence of an extended electorate, would protect the constitution from the forms of executive influence unleashed in 1832. By the mid-1850s Urquhart had come round to the view that the reformed Commons no longer constituted an effective countervailing power. He turned to the royal prerogative as an alternative constitutional check; other radicals and liberals began to look to an extended franchise. Urquhart then, did not make the transition to mid-Victorian democracy. However, the concerns for independence and accountability which he expressed became central to radical liberalism after 1867, for example, dominating discussions about the fitness of the working man to vote and featuring in reactions to the development of the party caucus, as Jon Lawrence shows elsewhere in this volume. In this way, the ideals of old radicalism did not die away, but became relocated as the polity was extended.

[81] J. S. Mill to Urquhart, 16 Sept. 1866, Urqhart bequest, 1/G/24; J. S. Mill to Thompson, 10 Oct. 1866, University of Hull, T. P. Thompson papers, DTH/3/26.

3 Radicalism and popular culture: the Tichborne case and the politics of 'fair play', 1867–1886

Rohan McWilliam

I

For mid-Victorian radicals, the Tichborne cause was the farcical sequel to the heroic and democratic politics of the 1830s and 1840s. Whereas previous radicals and workers were concerned with such movements as Chartism and Owenism, many in the new generation were devoted to the less egalitarian task of restoring the property of a long lost aristocrat. We do not know how one contemporary radical, Karl Marx, felt but it is unlikely he approved.

Similarly, historians have tended to reflect the desperation of George Potter and Charles Bradlaugh who complained that so much working-class energy was devoted to such a worthless cause.[1] Tichborne has barely rated a mention in historical accounts of this period although, as David Kynaston has pointed out, the 1870s are an 'under-researched decade'.[2] There have been several books on the case but they have scarcely affected the prevailing historiography.[3] On the face of it, this is understandable; in many respects, the Tichborne cause *was* absurd. And yet the relative silence among historians ignores the fact that Tichborne was one of the largest (if not *the* largest) popular movements between the end of Chartism and the development of socialism and independent Labour politics in the 1880s and 1890s. Between 1872 and 1886 some 250

I am grateful to Dr Hugh Cunningham and Kelly Boyd for their comments on this chapter.

[1] *Bee Hive*, 27 Feb. 1875, p. 11, 9 Oct. 1875, p. 3; C. Bradlaugh, *Letter to E. V. Kenealy* (London, 1875).

[2] D. Kynaston, *King Labour: The British Working Class, 1850–1914* (London, 1978), p. 46. Kynaston does in fact refer to Tichborne in this book (pp. 59–60).

[3] The best books on the Tichborne case are undoubtedly D. Woodruff, *The Tichborne Claimant: A Victorian mystery* (London, 1957) and M. Roe, *Kenealy and the Tichborne Cause: A study in mid-Victorian populism* (Melbourne, 1974). This chapter is drawn from McWilliam, 'The Tichborne claimant and the people: investigations into popular culture, 1867–1886', Ph.D., University of Sussex (1990), in which I examine the popular movement itself. Among other historical accounts that deal with Tichborne, J. Saville makes some good observations in 'The background to the revival of socialism in England', *Bulletin of the Society for the Study of Labour History*, 11 (Autumn 1965), pp. 13–19.

Tichborne associations were formed all over the country. In 1875, 283,314 people signed petitions in support of the Claimant. For Thomas Wright, he was 'the best-beloved or most-grieved-over personage in the country'.[4] To ignore the cause is simply an example of the 'enormous condescension of posterity'.[5]

The cause was a curious pastiche of previous radicalisms, borrowing freely from the political language of the past – in particular, from the ideology of radical constitutionalism and the myth of the freeborn Englishman. Tichbornism provides evidence for the survival of such radicalism beyond Chartism. It was libertarian and atavistic in the way so many such movements were and maintained traditional forms of protest that resembled the early modern spirit of carnival, with its emphasis on inversion and the world turned upside down. Its language also overlapped, as it did in several radical causes of the nineteenth century, with melodrama and popular fiction.[6] This gave it a relevance to popular culture that other agitations lacked. The cause was a form of popular theatre, gently subversive and evocative of an alternative morality, a sense of what a 'just' society would be like. This was not expressed in precise demands for social transformation but was dramatised in a key phrase: the need for 'fair play'.

II

The case itself was one of the most extraordinary *causes célèbres* of the Victorian period.[7] Sir Roger Tichborne was a discontented aristocrat, heir to the estates of an old Catholic family who belonged to the Hampshire gentry. Frustrated when his family opposed his marriage to his cousin, Katherine Doughty, he decided to tour South America. He was last seen alive in 1854 on the *Bella* which sailed from Rio de Janiero bound for Kingston, Jamaica. The ship was never seen again and everyone on board was assumed to have drowned. However, Sir Roger's mother, the Dowager Lady Tichborne, refused to believe that her son had died and ten years later placed advertisements for him in the press. In 1865, a poor

4   T. Wright, *Our New Masters* (London, 1873), p. 330.
5   E. P. Thompson, *The Making of the English Working Class* (London, 1963, 1968) p. 13.
6   On melodrama and politics, see G. Kitson Clark, 'The romantic element, 1830–1850', in J. H. Plumb (ed.), *Studies in Social History* (London, 1955); T. Laqueur, 'The Queen Caroline affair: politics as art in the reign of Geroge IV', *Journal of Modern History*, 54 (September 1982), pp. 417–66; I. McCalman, *Radical Underworld: Prophets, Revolutionaries and Pornographers in London, 1795–1840* (Cambridge, 1988), ch. 10; J. Walkowitz, 'Science and the seance: transgressions of gender and genre in late Victorian London', *Representations*, 22 (Spring 1988), pp. 3–29.
7   The following is a heavily simplified account of a complex case. For further details, see Woodruff, *The Tichborne Claimant*.

butcher named Tomas Castro from Wagga Wagga in Australia came forward as Sir Roger. He claimed that the *Bella* was overturned at sea but he and several members of the crew had escaped in a lifeboat which was then picked up by a ship bound for Melbourne. The Claimant looked nothing like Sir Roger who, when last seen, was decidedly svelte. In contrast, the Claimant was sixteen stone (a weight that almost doubled over the next two years to twenty-eight stone). Nevertheless, this extraordinary figure travelled to Paris, where the Dowager then lived, and in January 1867, she recognised him as her son. It was a rags-to-riches tale come true.

However, most of the Tichborne family refused to acknowledge the new Sir Roger, believing him to be an imposter. For the Claimant, this did not matter as long as he was supported by the Dowager's testimony, but in 1868 she died. The Tichborne family then resolved to bring the matter to court.

Evidence from Chile (where Sir Roger had travelled) and Australia began to connect the Claimant with a man called Arthur Orton, a native of Wapping. The Claimant never denied that Orton was a friend of his but several witnesses claimed that the two were one and the same. In his defence, many former associates of Sir Roger came forward confirming that the Claimant was the long-lost heir. These included many army officers who had known Sir Roger during his brief military career and Andrew Bogle, an old retainer of the Tichborne family. After many legal wranglings, the case began as a civil action in May 1871 and became one of the longest law suits in history, lasting until March 1872. The Claimant was rigorously cross-examined and found wholly ignorant of Sir Roger's past; in particular, he could not speak French (which Roger had been brought up speaking), or read Latin (which he was taught at Stonyhurst). The most explosive moment of the trial came after his assertion that he had seduced Katherine Doughty in 1854 and, on his departure for South America, feared she was pregnant. For his opponents, the Claimant was therefore not just an imposter, but a cad who had insulted the reputation of a respectable married woman (she was now Lady Radcliffe). The trial was suddenly brought to an end after ten months when Lord Bellew, a friend of the undoubted Sir Roger, revealed that he had once tattooed the young aristocrat. As evidence, this was suspicious. Why had such crucial evidence not been introduced earlier? Some speculated that the story had actually been invented to halt the proceedings – which it did. The Claimant did not have any tattooes and the judge, Sir William Bovill, directed that he was guilty of perjury and should be tried in a criminal action.

The Claimant was bankrupt and could not pay for his own defence. In contrast, the crown engaged six of the finest lawyers of the day to prosecute him. To the popular mind, it was clear that he could not get a fair trial and that the government and the legal profession were closing ranks to crush him. The Claimant became a popular martyr and hero.

Local supporters around the country began to establish defence funds. He was supported in parliament by two Liberal MPs: George Whalley (an ultra-Protestant who helped turn the case into an anti-Catholic agitation) and Guildford Onslow, who had known Sir Roger in earlier days and believed the Claimant was genuine. Most of the established press dismissed him (with the exceptions of *Reynolds's Newspaper* and the *Morning Advertiser*) and so two Tichborne newspapers were established: *The Tichborne Gazette* and *The Tichborne News and Anti-Oppression Journal*. The Claimant began a 'stump' agitation and spoke at venues all over the country, supported by Onslow, Whalley and many who had known Sir Roger. The agitation only came to an end when the court rigidly applied the *sub judice* rule, and Onslow and Whalley were fined for contempt (even though their hostile remarks on the conduct of the case were made outside the courtroom). A further contempt case resulted in the imprisonment of G. B. Skipworth, a republican lawyer, for denouncing the judiciary at a public meeting. The cause was also expressed through petitions and popular cultural forms such as Staffordshire pottery, ballads and broadsides. It was an extraordinary spectacle.

The criminal trial began in April 1873 in the form of a trial at bar before the Lord Chief Justice, Alexander Cockburn. The Claimant was defended by Edward Vaughan Kenealy, a bizarre eccentric. An Irish lawyer and littérateur, he devoted much of his life to producing immense and incomprehensible works of theology. He believed he was the twelfth messenger of God – part of a line that included Adam, Jesus Christ and Genghis Khan. The trial again took almost a year. Kenealy's defence proved disastrous. He harangued the judiciary, asserting it was part of a conspiracy against his client. As a result, when the trial ended, the Claimant was not only found guilty and sentenced to fourteen years imprisonment but Kenealy was disbarred by the legal profession. The cause had found its second martyr.

Undaunted by the loss of his career, Kenealy took over the Tichborne movement. He founded a weekly newspaper devoted to the cause, the *Englishman*, and followed it with an annotated edition of the trial account which appeared in weekly instalments and took five years to complete. He launched a second stump agitation and appeared all over the country supporting the Claimant and complaining of his own plight. To centralise the movement, he established the Magna Charta Association, which attempted to turn Tichbornism into a wider political cause. Its proposals included the abolition of income tax, triennial parliaments, the exclusion of lawyers from parliament, the restoration of the crown to the queen and votes for women. In February 1875, Kenealy stood at the by-election in Stoke-upon-Trent and was elected as a people's candidate. It was the high point of the agitation. He obtained a majority of almost 2,000 over the favoured Liberal candidate, Alfred Walton.

Thereafter, although support remained strong at least until 1877, the movement declined. At Westminster, Kenealy's attempt to obtain a royal commission into the Tichborne case failed and his parliamentary career was negligible. The Magna Charta Association began to split badly. Kenealy lost his seat in the election of 1880 and died soon after. Clearly the Tichborne moment had passed. When the Claimant emerged from prison in 1884 he failed to revive the agitation and took to appearing in circuses, still claiming he was Sir Roger Tichborne. This tactic, lacking in decorum, only served to distance him from many of his supporters and in any case was not a great financial success. He died penniless in Marylebone in April 1898.

Despite its dismal conclusion, it would be wrong to simply write off the cause as a failure. Parliament received a stream of petitions on behalf of the Claimant up until the early 1880s. The Magna Charta Association established itself as a prominent radical club and in 1881 assisted in the establishment of Hyndman's Democratic Federation, which, in 1884, became the first organisation to assist in the revival of socialism. According to Andreas Scheu, Hyndman actually modelled his agitation on Kenealy's.[8] The *Englishman*, although by no means entirely devoted to Tichborne, remained in publication until 1886 – the year that marked the end of the movement to all intents and purposes. Although the Tichborne cause failed to achieve its aims (the Claimant remained in prison for ten years), its longevity was striking – especially for a supposedly absurd movement concerned with the rights of a dispossessed aristocrat. This should have been on the periphery of popular consciousness, yet, as late as 1884, a decade after the end of the trial, a parliamentary candidate canvassing in the West Country was astonished by the number of questions addressed to him on the case.[9] Why did this ridiculous lost cause still create so much interest after ten years?

---

[8] E. P. Thompson, review of C. Tsuzuki's *H. M. Hyndman and British Socialism*, in *Bulletin of the Society for the Study of Labour History*, 3 (Autumn 1961), p. 68. The association between the Magna Chartists and the Democratic Federation lasted less than a year. However, the *Englishman* came to interest itself in the doctrines of socialism as it developed during the 1880s. See McWilliam, 'The Tichborne claimant', ch. 9.

[9] The unknown candidate was a friend of J. B. Atlay. See his *Famous Trials of the Century* (London, 1899), p. 391.

III

To properly evaluate the cause, it is necessary to understand its dimensions, although, as often happens with studies of this kind, it is difficult to find reliable statistics. The established press frequently refused to report the movement and much of our information comes from self-acknowledged Tichbornites, whose estimate of their own strength was no doubt subject to some hyperbole.

When it emerged in 1872, the movement was national. There were Tichborne societies from Southampton to Dundee, although there was little activity in Ireland. It was mainly urban but there were exceptions. Many tenants on the Tichborne estates continued to support the Claimant and his original stump campaign began at Alresford, near Tichborne House. As for its class composition, the movement was genuinely popular, in that it was trans-class. Whilst many middle-class authorities tried to imply that it was based exclusively on the working class, it is clear that this was not so. When Kenealy toured Britain, he usually held two meetings in a town – one aimed at the middle class and another at the working class with reduced prices.

Within the working class, it is more difficult to generalise about support. Walter Bagehot, writing in the *Economist* about a Tichborne demonstration in Hyde Park in 1875 noted that it was made up of 'the better order of working people'.[10] Other contemporary observations confirm the impression that it was supported by skilled workers. For example, the Claimant was known to be warmly supported by glovers in Yeovil.[11] East End artisans turned out in large numbers when the Claimant spoke in Millwall in July 1872.[12] It was probably the more affluent sectors of the working class who voted for Kenealy at the Stoke-upon-Trent by-election in 1875. Subscription lists for the Tichborne Defence Fund showed a wide range of proletarian professions that tended to cluster around the skilled working class: joiners, metal founders, chair makers, cabinet makers, tailors, saddlers, vellum binders, hatters, shoe makers, railway workers, plasterers, servants, soldiers and cab drivers.[13] However, the subscription lists are an imperfect source. First of all, many recorded their subscription anonymously or used a soubriquet (see below, pp. 55–6). Secondly, it is not surprising that subscription lists should reflect support from skilled

[10] N. A. St John-Stevas, (ed.), *The Collected Works of Walter Bagehot* (London, 1974), vol. 5, p. 241.
[11] *Western Gazette and Flying Post*, 12 Apr. 1872, p. 7; *Hampshire Chronicle*, 20 Apr. 1872, p. 3.
[12] *Tichborne News*, 13 July 1872, pp. 1, 3; *Morning Advertiser*, 8 July 1872, pp. 3, 4; *Hampshire Chronicle*, 13 July 1872, p. 3.
[13] The subscription lists are in *The Tichborne Gazette*, 28 May 1872, p. 1; 18 June 1872, p. 1; 2 July 1872, p. 1.

workers as they would have been the workers who had the money to subscribe. The lack of evidence about casual labourers does not mean that they were not involved or did not entertain opinions on the matter. In any case, casual labour by its very nature is difficult to organise in any political movement.

Another test of interest in the cause is the readership of the *Englishman* (no figures exist for the other Tichborne papers). In a court case that George Potter of the *Bee Hive* brought against the paper for libel, one of the printer's employees claimed that its average circulation was 70,000 copies a week 'though it went up when they had a portrait'.[14] This was in September 1875 when, if anything, the cause was on the decline. To take the sales of a comparable Chartist paper, the *Northern Star* sold 36,000 copies at its peak in 1839.[15] However, the *Northern Star* was a more expensive paper than the *Englishman*, which sold for 2d – cheap enough to be bought by the working class. Furthermore, not only was the literate population larger in 1875 but the *Englishman* was part of a new market of popular newspapers sold at the weekend which did not exist in the same way in the 1830s.[16] On the other hand, the figures do constitute an argument for taking the *Englishman* and indeed the Tichborne cause seriously. The sales figure, of course, reflects only the number of copies sold and tells us little of the actual reach of the paper.

The high figure is also remarkable given that the newspaper was very difficult to obtain. W. H. Smith's, the booksellers, refused to take it on the excuse that it did not receive papers published on a Saturday, an impediment that galvanised local Tichbornites. H. Masters of Aldershot, finding that his local railway station would not stock the paper, wrote in offering to 'work up the sale in this town'. The problems in distribution may explain why the *Englishman* was often distributed through appointed agents, rather than news agents. For example, the *Englishman* stockist in Lincoln was T. Dowd, a coal merchant.[17]

The organisation of the cause emerged in a relatively spontaneous way. The Tichborne leadership always claimed that the cause was the true expression of the feeling of the people and no effort had been made by outsiders to encourage support.[18] After the civil action in 1872, local

---

[14] *The Times*, 25 Sept. 1875, p. 8. I am assuming that as the printer's statement was made under oath in court, it is true.

[15] J. Epstein, *The Lion of Freedom: Feargus O'Connor and the Chartist Movement* (London, 1982), p. 86.

[16] V. S. Berridge, 'Popular journalism and working-class attitudes, 1854–1888: a study of *Reynolds's Newspaper, Lloyd's Weekly Newspaper* and the *Weekly Times*', unpublished D.Phil. thesis, University of London (1976), ch. 1.

[17] *Englishman*, 23 May 1874, p. 110; 2 May 1874, p. 61; 29 Aug. 1874, p. 332; 26 Dec. 1874, p. 603.

[18] *Englishman*, 20 Feb. 1875, p. 725.

Tichborne societies began to appear. The cause was usually organised around a network of pubs and temperance halls – this was not as contradictory as it might seem as both simply provided venues for meetings. However, the drink connection was extremely important. The cause was supported by the *Morning Advertiser*, owned by the Incorporated Society of Licensed Victuallers. Many publicans took the lead in publicising the movement. For example, J. T. Peacock of the Green Dragon, Doctor's Commons, collected three pounds in two days from the pockets of working men.[19] Money was also collected in the workplace. Thus, in Leeds, the employees of J. and C. Boyle, brickmakers, began a weekly subscription on behalf of the Claimant.[20]

Between the two trials, the main purpose of the local groups was to encourage the defence fund. In itself, this was an old form of radical culture. The defence funds for Joseph Rayner Stephens and Peter M'Douall had been major Chartist activities and there had also been defence funds for Governor Eyre in the 1860s. The groups were also involved with petitioning parliament and arranging visits from the Claimant and his leading supporters.

Between the two trials, the activities of local organisations were fairly spontaneous. Most do not appear even to have had names. When the criminal trial finished, many took up the cause of Kenealy. A testimonial fund was created which became an important focus of activity. There remained a great deal of spontaneity in the movement as is shown by the diversity of names in 1874: the 'Tichborne Release Association' in Shadwell, the 'Tichborne and Kenealy Association' of Leicester and the Leeds 'Tichborne Liberation Society'.[21] By March 1875 there were eleven committees in the East End of London, eight of them located in pubs and three at private addresses.[22]

All over the country, societies devoted themselves to publicising Tichborne matters. For example, the Birmingham and District Tichborne Release Association produced facsimiles of a letter by the undoubted Roger and a letter by the Claimant to show that they had similar handwriting.[23] The groups also organised visits by people connected with the case (especially Kenealy) and, most of all, supported the petitioning campaign.

---

[19] *Morning Advertiser*, 8 Apr. 1872, p. 1.
[20] *Tichborne News*, 3 Aug. 1872, p. 1.
[21] *Englishman*, 21 Nov. 1874, p. 522; 19 Dec. 1874, pp. 581, 587.
[22] *Englishman*, 13 Mar. 1875, p. 779.
[23] Birmingham and District Tichborne Release Association, *Fac-Simile of an Acknowledged Letter from Roger Tichborne ... with a letter of the 'Claimant', Sir R. C. D. Tichborne* (Birmingham, 1876).

There had been only a small number of petitions between the trials, but during the second trial the number began to increase. In 1873, 24,029 people signed petitions. The number rose to 47,087 in 1874 and peaked a year later at 283,314. Even as the cause went into decline, the figures remained high. There were 97,593 signatures in 1876, and 25,882 in 1877; 1878 was a bad year with only 488 signatures, but the number crept up again in 1879 with 14,971. There was little significant petitioning thereafter, but Hampshire in 1882 did manage to raise 4,984 signatures, testifying to the strong local feeling engendered by the cause.[24]

It is true that the same people probably signed the petitions from one year to the next and therefore the figures do not necessarily suggest new supporters adopting the cause after 1875. If anything, however, the numbers probably underestimate the levels of national support. Some areas of known Tichborne activity did not send petitions. Others returned petitions after a public meeting with only one signature (that of the chairman) on the form. The unknowable feature about the petitions is how many people signed 'for a lark'. However, it is clear that at its height (roughly 1872–7), the Tichborne cause was one of the largest radical movements of the mid-Victorian years.

IV

For many, the Tichborne cause meant the monster demonstrations that were held all over England in support of the cause and serve as an index of commitment. The 'mass platform' has been the subject of much historical interest recently, notably in the important work of James Epstein and John Belchem.[25] Their attention has been focused on the first half of the nineteenth century and assumes that this distinctive form of activism which had grown up in the mid eighteenth century ended on Kennington Common. For Belchem, the Chartism of 1848 was 'the last great mass platform agitation'.[26]

However, in many ways the stump agitations of the Tichborne movement are comparable to those of Henry Hunt and Feargus O'Connor.

---

[24] Report of the Select Committee of the House of Commons on Public Petitions, 1872–82. These figures collapse together all the figures for Tichborne petitions as most of them demanded the same thing: release of the Claimant or a select committee of inquiry into the trial.

[25] Epstein, *The Lion of Freedom*; J. Belchem, *'Orator' Hunt: Henry Hunt and English Working-Class Radicalism* (Oxford, 1985); J. Belchem, '1848, Feargus O'Connor and the collapse of the mass platform', in J. Epstein and D. Thompson (eds.), *The Chartist Experience: Studies in Working-Class Radicalism and Culture* (London, 1982), pp. 269–310.

[26] Belchem, '1848, Feargus O'Connor and the collapse of the mass platform', p. 269.

Platform politics remained integral to popular political life, as is shown by the examples of Charles Bradlaugh, John De Morgan or the Gladstone of the Midlothian campaigns ('The People's William'). Further, Tichbornites employed the language of radical constitutionalism that had serviced popular orators from the time that the platform was born. Its gentlemen demagogues (such as Kenealy or Onslow) were part of a tradition that can be traced from Burdett, Cochrane and 'Orator' Hunt to Hyndman and beyond. Admittedly, there were fewer meetings in the open air and more in town halls and places of amusement, but this only reflected the more urbanised world of the 1870s. Indoor meetings were also essential so that money could be charged for the defence fund.

The Claimant began the first stump campaign on 14 May 1872, at Alresford, near the Tichborne estates in Hampshire. Subsequent meetings rejoiced in a carnivalesque atmosphere. There was usually a demonstration at the station at which the Claimant arrived, followed by huge meetings in the local town hall. When the Claimant arrived at Bristol, the *Western Telegraph* compared the excitement generated at the station with that inspired by Garibaldi.[27] In all, the Claimant addressed at least sixty meetings around the country between May 1872 and March 1873.

A month after the close of the criminal trial, 2,000 working men demonstrated in Leicester to protest at the way Kenealy had been treated. His manliness was celebrated and some favourite lines of the Leicester Chartists were recited:

> The lion of freedom had come from his den
> We will rally around him again and again

The speeches reflected an alienation from the contemporary terms of jurisprudence. Mr Godfrey, a 'trades-unionist', said 'no well-conducted trades' union would have been guilty of such an act as the Benchers of Gray's Inn had adopted in reverence [sic] to Dr Kenealy'. One resolution complained that 'the verdict had not been in accordance with the majority of the witnesses because the verdict had been declared in favour of the minority'.

G. B. Skipworth advised that republicanism was the answer. Whilst this may have chimed with the sensibilities of the locals, it was not typical of the cause which, if anything, tended to court popular royalism.[28] Kenealy maintained Tichborne links with Leicester, where the cause was supported

---

[27] Quoted in E. V. Kenealy (ed.), *The Trial at Bar of Sir Roger C. D. Tichborne*, 9 vols., (London, 1875–80), Introductory volume, p. 110.

[28] *Englishman*, 18 Apr. 1874, p. 18. The cause became more avowedly republican after the death of Kenealy. See McWilliam, 'The Tichborne claimant', ch. 9.

by the *Leicester Evening News*, and began his own stump campaign there in September 1874. He was greeted at the station in the afternoon by about 2,000 people. In the evening, he addressed a packed meeting in the Leicester Temperance Hall. The hall was decked out with banners showing Biblical mottoes that had a bearing on the case: 'For we wrestle not with flesh and blood, but against principalities and powers, against the rulers of darkness in this world, against spiritual wickedness in high places', 'That it may please Thee to bring into the way of truth, all such as have erred or are deceived', 'My kinfolk have failed, and my familiar friends have forgotten me'. The cause was sometimes interpreted at a local level in religious terms – as a contest over truth. Therefore, it is appropriate that the vicar of Aylestone supported one of the resolutions at the meeting. Kenealy gave a speech recounting important incidents in the trial and expressed sympathy for the Claimant. The following evening a second meeting took place in the Temperance Hall aimed at a more popular audience with reduced prices.[29] He proceeded to address meetings all over the country in 1874–5, including Leeds, Peterborough, Loughborough, Grantham and Bradford.

Tichborne meetings were a regular occurrence especially in London where a demonstration was held (usually in Hyde Park or Trafalgar Square) on Easter Monday, up to the mid-1880s. These ranged from the spectacular to the amateur. It is the former quality that illustrates an important objection to their use as evidence. Was it not the spectacle that drew crowds rather than concern for the Claimant and Kenealy? The events certainly functioned as a day out for the participants. The point was noted by Walter Bagehot in his account of the 1875 Hyde Park demonstration:

No doubt a large proportion of the spectators ... were moved by mere curiosity, but that was also notoriously the case in the reform demonstrations ... it was clear that a greater number of the gathering on Monday was acted upon by a strong conviction and emotional excitement than was the case with those who took part in any of the reform demonstrations.[30]

The exact proportion of committed support at these meetings is unknowable. It is true that some meetings were broken up by hooligans,[31] but no observer failed to be impressed by the strong number of concerned followers present.[32]

[29] *Ibid.*, 10 Oct. 1874, pp. 418–23.
[30] St John-Stevas (ed.), *The Collected Works of Walter Bagehot*, vol. 5, pp. 241–2.
[31] E.g., *The Times*, 19 May 1875, p. 7; 24 Jan. 1877, p. 9; 25 Jan. 1877, p. 7; 27 Jan. 1877, p. 6.
[32] E.g., see C. Davies, *Mystic London: Or, phases of occult life in the metropolis* (London, 1875), ch. 12.

V

The ideology of Tichbornism was a kaleidoscope of popular concerns.[33] One way to get at this culture is through the subscription lists for the cause between the trials. Many chose not to give donations under their own names but instead adopted soubriquets which reveal a great deal about their reasons for involvement. Some simply believed in the Claimant on the basis of the case he presented. Hence one subscriber described him or herself as 'one who has faith in a mother's recognition'. Others were suspicious of the way Lord Bellew's tattoo evidence had brought the trial to an end. This spawned a range of pseudonyms:

Anti-tattoo Humbug.
C. M., no faith in his L's [Lordship's] Tattooing.
Seven workmen who do not believe the tattoo marks.
Did Lord Bellew dream of the tattoo marks?
Tattoo marks too late to be true [meaning that the evidence should have
    been introduced earlier, being crucial to the case].
From three who think the L. C. J. [Lord Chief Justice] and A. G.
    [Attorney-General] ought to be tattooed . . .

Some responded to the cause in the name of republicanism: 'Oliver Cromwell', 'E. K., who sees this pressure of might against right will help on republicanism . . .'. The religion of the Tichbornes and the Jesuit education of Sir Roger stimulated hostility: 'An enemy to the Jesuits and their permissive system of lying', 'R. M. B. who believes the tattooing to be a got-up Popish plot', 'one convinced that Jesuit influences have been exercised against the Claimant'.

But the majority of pseudonyms concerned themselves with the alleged misuse of justice suggesting that this was the central issue. Sir William Bovill, the Judge, and John Duke Coleridge, the Attorney-General, who appeared for the Tichborne family and who demolished the Claimant in a lengthy cross-examination, were both subject to abuse:

Judge Jeffreys and his jury coming to life again.
One who despises the Attorney-General's language.
Liberals who protest against C. [Coleridge] being A. G. any longer.
One who would like to see the A. G. get the cat.

[33] The term 'popular' is problematic, not respecting differences of class, gender or region. This chapter is about only one strand within popular culture. However, the Claimant was supported by men and women of all classes, drawn from the whole country. Hence the term 'popular', though imprecise, is arguably merited. See S. Hall, 'Notes on deconstructing the "popular"', in R. Samuel (ed.), *People's History and Socialist Theory* (London, 1981), pp. 227–40.

Many reflected the feeling that the Claimant did not get a fair trial:

One who regrets the trial so ending as to prevent a full and rightful reply for the Claimant.

D. P. and C.'s work people who protest at effigy burning . . .

H. Tate, Godalming, who has suffered from false swearing, and therefore feels for Sir Roger.

Some names showed a cynical bloody-mindedness: 'One who thinks the Claimant too fat to be an imposter . . .'. Others veered towards the licentious: 'A peep through the Barn Door' (the barn at Tichborne where Sir Roger was alleged to have seduced Katherine Doughty). Finally, there was a clear sense of class distinctions, particularly over the tattoo evidence: 'One who thinks no more of a peer than a peasant's word.'[34] Many working-class people who had known Sir Roger testified to the Claimant's identity and it was felt that their evidence was as sincere as that of Lord Bellew.

Of all these different reasons for support, the critique of the law was the most central because it highlighted an alternative morality. The Claimant was believed not to have had a fair trial. The tattoo evidence was highly suspect as was a series of correspondence produced between the Claimant and Mrs Pittendreigh, whose husband worked as a clerk for the solicitors of the Tichborne family. Mrs Pittendreigh offered to steal documents from their office in return for financial help. At least two of the Claimant's replies used by Coleridge in court as evidence against him were found to be obvious forgeries that had been written by Mrs Pittendreigh. The fact that the prosecution employed them at all suggested a network of corruption. For Tichbornites, the conclusion was clear: there was a conspiracy backed by the Tichborne family, the legal profession and even the government against the Claimant, pitting their wealth against his penury. There was therefore one law for the rich and one for the poor.

This sense of moral outrage must be seen in the context of a popular culture contemptuous of the law as a corrupt force in society and one in which the poor could not find redress. Lawyers were condemned as simply out to make money, regardless of morality. In a ballad entitled *A Sketch of Roguery*, one verse runs as follows:

> The lawyers do it brown
>   When ever they go to law,
> And if you have ought to do with them.
>   Your money they will draw.

34 *Tichborne Gazette*, 28 May 1872, p. 1; 18 June 1872, p. 1; 2 July 1872, p. 1.

They will take you to the county court,
There the matter to decide.
They will rob you of every screw
And humbug you beside.[35]

In broadsheets following the world upside down pattern, it is possible to find instances where the client defends the lawyer and the peasant tries the judge. Lawyers were despised for their readiness to prosecute as well as defend, reflecting a longing for integrity in public behaviour. In a ballad of 1866–7, Disraeli and the Tories were put on trial but were undefended 'as no one could be found willing to take their cause in hand on account of their previous bad character'.[36] Such sentiments can be found elsewhere within Victorian culture, most notably in the work of Charles Dickens and particularly *Bleak House* (1852).

In opposition to the corruption of the law, Tichbornites counterposed a distinctive language and set of symbols, based on radical patriotism. When the Claimant launched his appeal to the public between the two trials, he wrote to the press as follows:

Cruelly persecuted as I am, there is but one course that I could see, and that is, to adopt the suggestion so many have made to me, *viz*, to 'appeal to the British Public' for funds for my defence, and in doing so appeal to every British soul who is inspired by a love of justice and fair play, and who is willing to defend the 'weak against the strong'.[37]

This appeal, printed in most national newspapers, set the terms for the Tichborne cause. It dramatised the Claimant's predicament: one mere individual against the state with its full panoply of legal power.

The most important phrase that the Claimant used was 'fair play'. This was taken up all across the movement. For instance, the sub-title of *The Tichborne News and Anti-Oppression Journal* was a 'weekly newspaper advocating fair play for every man', and the phrase cropped up constantly in popular broadside literature:

Whoever the Claimant is
Through the country they say,
From first to last,
He has not had fair play.

[35] British Library Ref. no. 11661 dd. 20, p. 7.
[36] D. Kunzle, 'World turned upside down: The iconography of a European broadsheet type', in B. A. Babcock (ed.), *The Reversible World: Symbolic Inversion in Art and Society* (Ithaca, 1978), p. 51; *The Life, Trial and Probable Sentence of the Derbyites, Dizzyites and Adullamites*, British Library Ref. no. 12230 i. 42, p. 17.
[37] *Daily Telegraph*, 27 Mar. 1872, p. 3. On radical patriotism, see H. Cunningham 'The language of patriotism, 1750–1914', *History Workshop Journal*, 12 (Autumn 1981), pp. 8–33.

> F stands for Fair Play,
> right throughout the nation,
> And every man should have it too,
>   No Matter what his station.
>
> Keep up your blooming pecker, you're
>   Sure to win the day,
> If judge and jury see it out and let
>   Him have fair play.[38]

One ballad was actually entitled *'Fair play' for Tichborne and Kenealy.*[39] The term was used on banners at meetings and most strikingly of all was adopted as a pseudonym by subscribers to the cause: 'Fair Play', 'Fair Play is a Jewel', 'Lovers of Fair Play, at Messers Simpsons, Pimlico'.[40]

The phrase exemplified the movement. It was a criticism of oppression couched in a sporting metaphor comprehensible to all. It was a demand for straight dealing in social behaviour. The term helps us to understand how 'politics' was constructed by the working class – the feeling that a corrupt world can be restored by purity amongst the rulers.[41]

The term was certainly not peculiar to Tichbornism. Instead it was a conventional term within the radical vocabulary. In 1831, when an orator denounced the established church before a crowd in Huddersfield, there were shouts of 'fair play for the people'.[42] In the East Anglian song 'Pity Poor Labourers' the complaint is that

> Fair Play is a stranger these many years past,
> And pity's bound up in an old oaken cask.
> But the time's fast approaching, it's very near come
> When we'll all have the farmers
>   Under our thumb.[43]

[38] *Conviction of the Claimant*, Leeds Record Office, Radcliffe papers, I 659 Box E; *The Tichborne ABC*, Bodleian Library Collection, Ref. no. 2803 d.3; *The Great Tichborne Trial* Broadside Scrap Book: Birmingham Central Library, Ref. no. F A082 2 LL, p. 5. I argue in my thesis (ch. 10) that ballads are close representations of popular culture even in the 1870s.

[39] Copy in possession of Dr D. Thompson.

[40] See note 34.

[41] See also M. Taylor, ch. 2, in this collection for a similar emphasis in the Urquhartite campaigns of the previous decades.

[42] R. D. Storch, 'Please to remember the fifth of November: conflict, solidarity and public order in southern England, 1815–1900', in R. D. Storch (ed.), *Popular Culture and Custom in Nineteenth Century England* (London, 1982), p. 79.

[43] British Library Ref. no. 1876 d. 41, vol. II, p. 1330. The song can also be found with slightly different words in A. Howkins, 'The voice of the people: the social meaning and context of country songs', *Oral History*, 3 (Spring 1975), p. 68.

During the Queen Caroline agitation of 1820–1 (a similar movement, in some respects, to Tichborne) William Benbow published a broadsheet urging: 'Englishmen! You who love Fair Play and Open Trial, now open your eyes and read! Green Bags, SEALED UP, were sent to the Parliament about the Queen.'[44] The green bag in which the evidence for the prosecution was delivered to parliament was a much used metaphor for the secret and conspiratorial behaviour of the government. These criticisms of 'behind closed doors' politics as opposed to 'open' political behaviour and 'fair play' were a constant thread in the radical tradition. A comic ballad attacking food adulteration was entitled *New Intended Act of Parliament, agreed to by Sir John Fairplay, and seconded by Mr Steady, for the Public Good*.[45] These terms, 'fair play' and 'steady', both express a belief in a coming social harmony if only purity of behaviour can be restored to public life.

That the term 'fair play' was in constant use should not surprise us. It was employed as an ideal for how the law should operate and harked back to an eighteenth-century view of the law as intimately linked to virtue and manners.[46] This system of ideas in effect rejected the basis of the 1873 Judicature Acts – a codified, regularised approach to the world, where jurisprudence exists as a science in itself separated from morality. Instead, it demanded that the law should equal justice: the essence of the popular critique of the law. It insisted that the law have social as well as purely civic responsibilities. It was an argument in favour not only of common law, but of natural law itself.

Another feature of Tichbornism was its use of symbolic inversion.[47] The Lord Chief Justice caused offence through his closing remarks to the jury during the criminal trial. 'I am sure that the verdict you will pronounce will be received on all hands, except by fanatics and fools, as the judgment of twelve men who have brought to the consideration of this great cause the utmost and the most vigilant attention . . .'[48] Tichbornites disliked their views being dismissed as those of 'fanatics and fools' and the phrase became a central motif throughout the movement. The *Englishman*

---

[44] *Bill of Pains and Penalties* (London: William Benbow, 1820) in Public Record Office, Home Office papers 40/14, f.49.

[45] M. Vicinus, *The Industrial Muse: A Study of Nineteenth Century British Working-Class Literature* (London, 1974), p. 30.

[46] J. G. A. Pocock, *Virtue, Commerce and History* (Cambridge, 1985), p. 49. Natural and civil law both retained the concept of 'manners' and 'chivalry' as part of their science of society even though the terms were not part of the 'operational vocabulary of jurisprudence'.

[47] The literature on this subject is now immense, but see Babcock, *The Reversible World*; M. Bakhtin, *Rabelais and his World* (Bloomington, 1984); Y.-M. Bercé, *Fête et révolte des mentalités populaires du XVIe au XVIIIe siècle* (Paris, 1976); P. Burke, *Popular Culture in Early Modern Europe* (London, 1978).

[48] Kenealy (ed.), *The Trial at Bar of Sir Roger C. D. Tichborne*, vol. 8, p. 630.

claimed that the crowds awaiting a visit by Kenealy exhibited 'as little of the FOOL and FANATIC as our sober middle-class and trained operatives ever do'.[49] In time, the phrase was inverted, becoming a defiant gesture of pride. Thus the movement took on a carnivalesque dimension in which the world appeared to be turned upside down. Onslow, surveying a crowd assembled in the Victoria Hall in Leeds wished that the Lord Chief Justice could have been present to judge of the 'fools and fanatics' who filled the hall. At the same meeting, Kenealy developed the theme:

Mr Chairman, Ladies, and Gentlemen – I dare not call you female fanatics and Yorkshire fools, though I have high authority for asserting that anybody who doubts the Lord Chief Justice of England and his asseveration is both a fanatic and a fool. I can only say that if that be true, there are more fanatics and fools in England than I expected to find there; and I should not be at all surprised if, after a very short time, the fanatics and fools were found to be in a tremendous majority of Englishmen, and the wise men in a miserable minority. (Cheers)[50]

Moreover, the term was taken up by members of the movement and carried on banners. One Tichbornite wrote to Kenealy asking that he visit Liverpool: 'there will be a hearty welcome from the many thousands of "fools and fanatics" . . .'.[51]

By employing the language of *mundus inversus* and of fair play, the Tichborne movement employed an alternative morality, based on an emotional hostility to the intrusion of the state. It appealed because it dramatised popular feelings about power relationships in society (in particular, the individual's powerlessness before the law).

Kenealy attempted to develop Tichbornism into a more coherent political philosophy in the form of the Magna Charta Association. Much of its programme admittedly reveals more about his personal preoccupations than contemporary politics, but it was cast in the language of traditional radicalism.

The title itself was important because Magna Charta had been an important emblem in radical movements, and was part of the language of popular constitutionalism. Sir Francis Burdett was depicted holding it triumphantly in early nineteenth-century iconography. In 1809, on discovering that he was to be arrested for breach of parliamentary privilege, he imprisoned himself in his house and was apprehended in the process of reading Magna Charta to his son.[52] John Wilkes' Society for the Supporters of the Bill of Rights played on this language as did the

[49] *Englishman*, 24 Oct. 1874, p. 451.
[50] *Englishman*, 31 Oct. 1874, p. 467.
[51] *Englishman*, 5 Dec. 1874, p. 555.
[52] A. Pallister, *Magna Carta: The Heritage of Liberty* (Oxford, 1971), pp. 67–71.

'People's Charter'.[53] The language drew its inspiration from the myth of the freeborn Englishman: a viewpoint that venerated the independence of the working man – it tended to be constructed in masculine terms – and resented any interference from outside, whether from the state (taxation, the Poor Law), the legal profession ('One law for the rich and one for the poor') or from conspirators (scheming Jesuits in the case of Tichborne). For historians, this radicalism has gone under several names: 'the Old Analysis' or 'populism'.[54] It was not strictly a 'class' vocabulary but was dependent on the ambiguous term 'the People' (usually defined in relation to their corrupt leaders).

In drawing up the new Magna Charta, Kenealy invoked the names of Hampden, Milton and Fairfax, suggesting a link with an older form of commonwealth radicalism, but also part of the Victorian interest in the English Revolution.[55] The first aim of the Magna Charta Association was to 'bring back Magna Charta and the Bill of Rights'. The second was 'to establish a free and honest press' (a complaint against the treatment of the cause in virtually every major newspaper) and the third was to send 250 'people's representatives' to parliament. These were to come from the 'middle and the operative class' and were intended to overcome 'class legislation'. The charter also had echoes of Chartism in its support for payment of MPs, opposition to bribery and accountability through triennial parliaments (although of course the People's Charter sought annual parliaments). Whilst it never explicitly celebrated it, the *Englishman* occasionally looked to Chartism for inspiration. On one occasion, it asked for information about O'Connorville with a view to developing its own land policy.[56] In contrast to Chartism, the programme did not seek universal manhood suffrage, although it contained a vague commitment to support votes for women.

The Magna Charta Association also planned 'to abolish the Income Tax Act' and 'to secure a free breakfast table'. The latter was a reference

[53] See C. Robbins, *The Eighteenth Century Commonwealthman: studies in the transmission, development and circumstance of English liberal thought from the restoration of Charles II until the war with the thirteen colonies* (Cambridge, Mass., 1959); J. Belchem, 'Republicanism, popular constitutionalism and the radical platform in early nineteenth-century England', *Social History*, 6 (January 1981), pp. 1–32.

[54] P. Hollis, *The Pauper Press: A Study in Working-Class Radicalism of the 1830s* (Oxford, 1976), ch. 8; W. D. Rubinstein, *Elites and the Wealthy in Modern Britain: Essays in Social and Economic History* (Brighton, 1987), ch. 11; for the freeborn Englishman, see Thompson, *Making*, ch. 4.

[55] This account is based on *Englishman*, 12 Dec. 1874, pp. 560–4. On Victorian interest in the English Revolution, see T. W. Mason, 'Nineteenth-century Cromwell', *Past and Present*, 40 (1968), pp. 187–91.

[56] *Englishman*, 16 Oct. 1875, p. 496. The other old radical figure venerated by the movement was Junius, whose name was used as a soubriquet by one columnist in the *Englishman*, e.g. 8 Jan. 1876, pp. 622–63.

to John Bright's move to abolish the duty on tea, coffee and sugar.[57] Concern with income tax was part of the radical tradition and Kenealy turned it into an argument about surveillance by the state:

The Income Tax has made every individual Englishman an absolute slave ... Much better would it be for all of us, as the Eastern Despotisms, that the government came down when its necessities required it, and demanded a certain sum than that it should insult us every year, by prying into our means; that it should degrade us, with all our books and accounts, before our neighbours, the Income Tax assessors.

This located the cause within the anti-statist tradition in popular politics.[58]

These proposals were coupled with such apparently conservative objectives as 'To support the House of Lords' and 'To restore the crown to the Queen'. However, these were intended in the spirit of radical constitutionalism as the two were considered to be checks on despotic ministers in government. Hence the programme constituted an argument in favour of the separation of powers. The restoration of the crown to the queen also echoed the radicalism of Queen Caroline's supporters.

Although there were problems in its organisation, the Magna Charta Association programme was taken up and actively discussed by local associations. Amongst its adherents, Jack Williams (later of the SDF) considered it to be comparable to socialism. He admired its denunciation of the 'cheap and nasty Manchester school' and claimed 'there was more interest displayed in purely social questions than by any other political body' at that time.[59] This was perhaps because the programme was a colourful and dramatic statement of popular political themes.

Nevertheless, the Magna Charta Association had much in common with other radical pressure groups. It opposed compulsory vaccination and the Contagious Diseases Acts. Support for monarchy did not prevent republicans from associating themselves with it. Although Kenealy was a maverick, his movement was in many ways a typical product of mid-Victorian radical culture.

VI

It is difficult to establish exactly who voted for Kenealy at the Stoke by-election in Feburary 1875. However, it was a Liberal seat and it seems

---

[57] See *The Times*, 6 Nov. 1868, p. 5. Kenealy also wanted to secure a 'Free Meat Dinner Table', but did not define what this meant.

[58] H. Pelling, *Popular Politics in Late Victorian Britain* (London, 1968), ch. 1; P. Thane, 'The working class and state "welfare" in Britain, 1880–1914', *Historical Journal*, 27 (1984), pp. 877–900. See also the contributions by E. Biagini and A. Reid in this collection.

[59] *How I Became a Socialist* (London, 1894), pp. 37–8.

likely that he was supported principally by the workers enfranchised in 1867 and who were expected to support the advanced Liberal Alfred Walton.[60] In many respects this was understandable. The libertarianism of the Tichborne movements had some affinities with popular liberalism.[61] Two Liberal MPs, Onslow and Whalley, were prominent in the movement and in 1862 Kenealy had contemplated standing for Stoke as a Liberal.[62] There are records of known Liberals attending and sometimes supporting Tichborne meetings.[63] However, the affinities are not exact. Kenealy was a former friend of Disraeli and the *Englishman* on one occasion argued that the Tories were better friends of the working man than the Liberals.[64] In parliament, Kenealy tended to support Disraeli – especially over the Eastern Question – as did many Magna Chartists.[65]

Tichbornism should not be examined in conventional political terms but rather should be seen as a symbol of distrust of the political process.[66] At the Stoke by-election, Kenealy claimed to belong to 'no party . . . but to England'.[67] In many ways two-party politics were the antithesis of the 'fair play' tradition; supporting or opposing a government for reasons of party lacked the requisite integrity. Kenealy's position signalled a retreat from parliamentary politics towards an older form of radical patriotism. This was appropriate for a man whose newspaper was called the *Englishman*.

The Tichborne case may have been a farcical re-enactment of previous radical scenarios but this does not mean that its supporters' desire for 'fair play' was unimportant and should not be recovered. It is tempting to dismiss the movement as either absurd or something that was in effect highly conservative. At best it might appear to be an example of what Gareth Stedman Jones calls 'the culture of consolation', a resignation to the fact that capitalism could not be beaten.[68] However, the symbols of the Tichborne movement and the energy of its supporters reveal a deep

---

[60] P. Anderton, 'The Liberal party of Stoke-upon-Trent and parliamentary elections, 1862–1880: a case study in Liberal–Labour relations' unpublished MA thesis, University of Keele (1974).

[61] See J. Vincent's definition of popular liberalism in his *The Formation of the Liberal Party, 1847–1868* (Hassocks, 1976), pp. xxvii–xxviii.

[62] Anderton, 'Liberal Party', pp. 22–3.

[63] G. Crossick, *An Artisan Elite in Victorian Society: Kentish London, 1840–1880* (London, 1978), pp. 232–3.

[64] *Englishman*, 5 Jan. 1878, p. 219.

[65] H. Cunningham, 'British public opinion and the Eastern Question', unpublished D.Phil thesis, University of Sussex (1969), pp. 128–30.

[66] V. Hart, *Distrust and Democracy: Political Distrust in Britain and America* (Cambridge, 1978). See also J. Lawrence, ch. 4, in this collection.

[67] Leeds Record Office: election poster in Radcliffe papers I 659, Box E.

[68] G. Stedman Jones, *Languages of Class: studies in English working-class history, 1832–1982* (Cambridge, 1983), p. 237.

disquiet in the popular culture of the 1870s – the end of a time normally perceived as the high point of Victorian capitalist confidence. The Tichborne movement enables us to grasp a yearning for an alternative morality: a desire for integrity and justice. For many, this was what politics was all about.

4   Popular politics and the limitations of party: Wolverhampton, 1867–1900

Jon Lawrence

I

This chapter adopts the case study approach to develop a detailed analysis of English popular politics in the thirty or so years between the passing of the Second Reform Act and the emergence of the Independent Labour Party in the 1890s. If the work has an underlying theme it is that, in endeavouring to recreate something of the texture and vitality of popular politics, we must focus special attention on the complex, and often deeply ambiguous, relationship between political activists – be they Liberal, Conservative or Labour – and the people they sought to represent. To many this must appear glaringly obvious: is this not everyone's common-sense understanding of the stuff of politics? And yet this basic insight has informed only a small fraction of the post war historiography of British working-class politics. The dominant approach has been to treat major political movements such as Chartism, socialism, or for that matter working-class Conservatism, as little more than the natural (i.e. causally determined) outgrowths of prior social and economic realities. Rarely has there been any attempt to understand the complex web of aspirations and identities which sustained popular political movements; in effect political history has been depoliticised. In recent years this approach has been challenged by a growing body of historical writing which has sought to reassert the importance of the specifically political dimension in popular movements whilst rejecting both the elitist assumptions of the 'high politics' school on the one hand, and the countervailing tendency to focus exclusively on the internal dynamics of political organisations on the other.[1]

Thanks to Gareth Stedman Jones, Alastair Reid, Miles Taylor, Pat Thane and all those who participated in the Churchill conference.

[1] For instance, see G. Stedman Jones, *Languages of Class: Studies in English Working Class History, 1832–1982* (Cambridge, 1983), Introduction and ch. 3; D. Feldman and G. Stedman Jones, *Metropolis: London, Histories and Representations since 1800* (London, 1989), or, from a different perspective, A. Reid, 'Class and organization', *Historical Journal*, 30, 1 (1987), pp. 225–38 and B. Harrison, *Peaceable Kingdom: Stability and Change in Modern Britain* (Oxford, 1982), especially the introduction.

This chapter is intended as a contribution to this wider reassessment of popular politics in modern Britain.

In many respects Wolverhampton is an ideal town upon which to base a case study of Victorian popular politics. Unlike many nineteenth-century manufacturing towns it possessed a diversified economic structure with strengths in both iron and coal production (thanks to the proximity of the mineral-rich Black Country), and high-value finished goods trades. In particular, Wolverhampton was famous for its light-metal trades such as lock making, tinplate working, brass moulding, and, from the late nineteenth century, the manufacture of bicycles and engine components. Other strengths included paint and chemical production, electrical goods, boots and shoes, beer and railway rolling stock.[2] Consequently, although certain local trades might possess strong and distinctive political traditions (occupational cultures), no industry was ever able to dominate the political culture of Wolverhampton as a whole.[3]

More importantly, however, Wolverhampton demands attention because it witnessed a major transformation of political allegiance during the late Victorian period. After decades of almost unchallenged Liberal dominance the town's political culture changed rapidly during the 1880s and 1890s as the Liberal party found itself squeezed between the genteel Conservatism of the new suburbs and the increasingly strong populist Toryism of central working-class districts. As such, Wolverhampton stands alongside Birmingham, Manchester, Sheffield and Nottingham as one of those important urban, manufacturing communities whose lurch towards Conservatism in the late nineteenth century effectively killed the 'Liberal Dream' of an inexorable march towards an enlightened, progressive polity.[4] For this reason alone it justifies the detailed attention of the historian.

---

[2] See G. C. Allen, *The Industrial Development of Birmingham and the Black Country, 1860–1927* (London, 1929) and W. H. Jones, *The Story of the Japan, Tinplate Working and Iron Braziers Trades, Bicycle and Galvanising Trades and Enamelware Manufacture in Wolverhampton and District* (London, 1900).

[3] This is in marked contrast to places such as Northampton or County Durham, where preponderent occupational groups, shoemakers and miners respectively, were able to impose their strong organisational and political identities on the wider community.

[4] John Vincent highlights 'the rise of a popular Tory party in the great towns between 1859 and 1885', in *The Formation of the British Liberal Party, 1857–1868* (2nd edn, Hassocks, 1976) p. xxxvii. An analysis of party performance in the ten provincial parliamentary boroughs with the largest electorates in 1874 confirms that this trend continued into the 1890s. At the General Elections of 1868 and 1874 the Liberals won an average of eighteen of the twenty-four seats in these large boroughs; at the General Elections of 1885 and 1895 they averaged just seventeen and a half out of forty-seven. Even allowing for the distorting impact of the new single member constituencies this represented a serious decline for urban Liberalism.

II

Wolverhampton Liberalism won its political spurs during the reform agitations of 1831–2 and consolidated itself during the subsequent campaign for the repeal of the Corn Laws. Major election-day disturbances in 1832, 1835 and 1837 all confirmed the popularity of Wolverhampton's Liberal leaders,[5] and yet there was never any attempt to broaden Liberal organisation to embrace the plebeian Radicals[6] who had led these popular demonstrations. On the contrary, the Wolverhampton Liberal party remained confined to a small group of wealthy manufacturers, merchants and professionals, who organised local politics through an informal, yet impenetrable, oligarchy known as the Liberal Committee.

It was not until after the Second Reform Act of 1867 that Wolverhampton Liberalism began to assume a more democratic character. In 1871, Henry Walker, a veteran of the 1832 reform agitations, announced that the town's Liberal leaders had decided to establish a new organisation, the Liberal Association, based on open and fully democratic ward parties.[7] Significantly, neither this reorganisation, nor the subsequent adoption of the Birmingham 'Caucus' model in 1878,[8] proved capable of establishing the Liberal party on a genuinely popular basis. But if the mass-based Liberal Association failed to materialise in Wolverhampton this was less because the working class was profoundly anti-Liberal, than because it was violently anti-party. For decades 'party' had been synonymous with corruption, intimidation and intrigue. Once the prerogative of Staffordshire's Whig and Tory worthies, political influence had, by the mid nineteenth century, largely transferred to a new urban elite comprised of manufacturers, factors and their professional friends. Hence, when the powerful local iron master 'Baron Sam' Griffiths ran as an independent Liberal at the Wolverhampton by-election of 1861, he did so specifically pledged 'to smash this great oligarchy [the Liberal Committee] which has bound the borough and beaten down and trampled on [its] rights for the last five and twenty years'.[9]

---

[5] *The Wolverhampton Chronicle*, 5 and 12 Dec. 1832, 3 June 1835 and Jones *Story of the Japan Trades*, pp. 16–20. For a more extensive treatment of many of the themes discussed in this chapter see J. Lawrence, 'Party politics and the people: continuity and change in the political history of Wolverhampton, 1815–1914', Ph.D. thesis, Cambridge (1989).

[6] Throughout this chapter upper-case 'Radical' is used to denote an identification with the advanced wing of the Liberal Party or Liberalism as a political movement. It is not, however, assumed that Radicals were in other respects necessarily a homogeneous political grouping.

[7] *The Wolverhampton Chronicle*, 10 May 1871.

[8] *The Midland Examiner and Wolverhampton Times*, 9 Feb. 1878.

[9] *The Wolverhampton Chronicle*, 3 July 1861.

Significantly the 1861 by-election also demonstrated that Liberal leaders could no longer rely on the public's violent hatred of Toryism to bolster their own popularity. When Griffiths addressed a crowd of between 15,000 and 20,000 supporters after his defeat by the 'official' Liberal candidate T. M. Weguelin, he was able to draw an enormous cheer by praising the defeated Tory, Alexander Staveley-Hill of nearby Dunstall Hall. Clearly the Tories were becoming politically less obnoxious as their local power and influence declined.

One might also contrast the rather poor turn-out at the 1868 hustings, about 1,500 Liberals failed to fill the Agricultural Hall, with the nomination day gatherings seen in the 1830s. Local press reports estimate that over 10,000 attended the 1832 hustings in St James's Square, a figure equivalent to over 40 per cent of the town's population at that time.[10] It would be wrong, however, to push this argument too far; there can be no doubt that throughout the mid-Victorian period Liberalism remained immensely popular among the plebeian classes of Wolverhampton. Even prominent ex-Chartists like Joseph Linney, who had been imprisoned for his part in the great strike movement of 1842, had become closely identified with Liberalism by the mid-1860s;[11] although for him, as for most plebeian Radicals, Liberalism meant, not loyalty to an organisation, but loyalty to a set of political principles and to the individuals thought to embody those principles: which in Wolverhampton meant William Ewart Gladstone, the Liberal Chancellor, and Charles Pelham Villiers, the local MP who had pioneered free trade and the repeal of the Corn Laws. This 'cult of the individual' brought a sense of unity and purpose to Liberal politics which even the most unequivocally democratic party organisation could never have provided. Villiers and Gladstone symbolised the historic Liberal victories of earlier decades, and thereby reinforced the idea that Liberalism was a dynamic political movement dedicated to securing the political, religious and social emancipation of working people.

In many respects Wolverhampton's trade union leaders epitomised this attitude: almost universally Radical, they were none the less distinctly reluctant to become entangled with organised party politics. If anything, the major political reforms of the 1860s and 1870s strengthened this reluctance, since the Second Reform Act, and the labour law reforms of 1871 to 1875 tended to reduce the scope for common political action within the working class. Increasingly, the issues which united workers

---

[10] *The Wolverhampton Chronicle*, 12 Dec. 1832 and 18 Nov. 1868.
[11] See *The Wolverhampton Chronicle*, 27 June 1866 and 8 May 1867 and *The Commonwealth*, 2 Mar. and 18 May 1867.

appeared less immediate and less important than those, social, religious and political, which divided them. And as party politics became more intrusive in working-class life in the wake of the 1867 Reform Act, so local trade union leaders became more determined than ever to defend the political integrity and independence of their organisations. It is in this light that one should understand Wolverhampton Trades Council's constitutional commitment to remain 'non-political'. For Council leaders, as for most trade unionists in the 1870s, 'non-political' meant non-party rather than 'unpolitical'.

During the summer of 1875 the distinction between 'non-political' and 'unpolitical' became the subject of considerable controversy on Wolverhampton Trades Council when a group of delegates proposed to pass a resolution expressing sympathy for Samuel Plimsoll in his recent expulsion from the House of Commons (Plimsoll had been expelled for refusing to exempt fellow MPs from his stinging attack on British merchant ship owners). A delegate from the genuinely unpolitical Steam Engine Makers' Society objected to the resolution, stating that it 'contravened the rule preventing the introduction of political matters into their proceedings'. In reply Oliver of the tailors' union pointed out that 'if they were to exclude this subject, and were not in any way to interfere in so-called politics, then for ever more must they hold their peace with relation to the Labour laws, and all other obnoxious Acts which might affect the operative classes'. But it was Marshall, like Oliver a survivor from the short-lived Trades Council of the late 1860s, who best captured the mood of post-reform trade unionism when he declared that, 'of course it was not for them to meddle in the differences as between Liberals and Conservatives, but they were fully allowed to interfere as to any legislation affecting labour in any shape or form'.[12]

Most delegates agreed with Oliver and Marshall, and the resolution passed with only two against. Thus, far from being a sign of the labour movement's *embourgeoisement*, 'non-political' trade unionism reflected the determination of labour leaders to protect the independence of their organisation. It was merely one more manifestation of a deep-seated popular suspicion of party.

III

The first signs that Liberalism might be losing favour with the Wolverhampton populace came during the general election of 1874, the first

---

[12] *The Miner and Workmen's Examiner*, 7 Aug. 1875.

election to be held under the new householder franchise.[13] Four days before the poll Wolverhampton's Irish and Roman Catholic leaders summoned a mass meeting to declare their support for the Conservative candidate, Walter Williams, in recognition of his commitment to defend voluntary religious education.[14] On the day after this meeting a group of Irish working men disrupted a large Liberal rally in the town centre, heckling Rednall, the Birmingham republican leader, and smashing windows in the Liberal committee rooms.[15]

Election day itself began quietly and it seemed as though the town would escape major disturbance, but by 1.30 pm large crowds had begun to form as rumours spread that Liberal rioters were disrupting the poll in nearby Wednesfield, Willenhall and Sedgley. Within minutes the crowd, which according to a local paper stood at between 2,000 and 3,000, had commenced a series of bloody assaults on anyone sporting Liberal colours. For at least the first hour the rioters directed their wrath almost exclusively at well-to-do Liberals. With the police quite unable to reestablish control, and the riot beginning to spread to the respectable western suburbs, the mayor closed the poll and announced that the declaration would be delayed until the following day.

Clearly the political culture of Wolverhampton had changed dramatically since the turbulent elections of the 1830s when political crowds had been unequivocally Radical. True, in the more outlying parts of the parliamentary borough Liberal ascendancy had hardly been challenged, but within Wolverhampton itself one local paper could now even question whether Liberalism was 'the popular cause' anymore.[16]

Four years later Wolverhampton witnessed further political disturbances which appeared to confirm the decline in Liberal fortunes. On the nights of 31 January and 1 February 1878 Wolverhampton witnessed two of the most impressive 'jingo' demonstrations seen outside of Tory south Lancashire, as thousands of local townspeople attempted to demonstrate their support for Disraeli's bellicose anti-Russian foreign policy by breaking up a planned Liberal peace meeting.[17]

Local Tory councillors undoubtedly played a part in orchestrating these demonstrations, for instance by hiring a local band to play outside the

---

[13] The local Conservatives had not felt strong enough to mount a challenge at the 1868 election.

[14] *The Wolverhampton Chronicle*, 4 Feb. 1874. Villiers and Weguelin were pledged to revoke clause 25 of Forster's Education Act which guaranteed public subsidy of voluntary religious education.

[15] *The Wolverhampton Chronicle*, 11 Feb. 1874; a large crowd again attacked the Liberal headquarters on the night before the poll.

[16] *The Wolverhampton Chronicle*, 4 Feb. 1874.

[17] *The Evening Express*, 31 Jan. and 1 Feb. 1878.

hall, but the event was at heart a spontaneous display of popular support for the government. The numbers involved defy any other explanation: besides the 1,500 or so 'jingos' who infiltrated the Liberal meeting in the Agricultural Hall, there were as many again outside and a further 3,000 to 5,000 at a mass rally on Snow Hill.[18] Moreover, after the success of this initial demonstration (the Liberals were forced to abandon the meeting without putting their resolution) the Tories organised a second, even larger demonstration the next day.[19]

Significantly, the Tory councillors who suddenly found themselves thrust into the unlikely role of popular demagogues continually insisted that their support for the government was the product of national, rather than party, feeling. Indeed, the Tories' position was not so much non-party as anti-party, since the main focus of their wrath was the secretive 'Liberal faction' which had presumed to speak on behalf of all townsfolk by holding its protest meeting in the Agricultural Hall. Echoing criticisms made by Sam Griffiths in 1861, they denounced the Liberal party machine for trying to 'dictate and rule the borough autocratically'.[20] The Tories' intention was simple: to equate party politics with Liberalism, whilst portraying themselves as the guardians of the national interest. In this they were doubtless aided by their own complete lack of organisation in 1878.

Liberal confidence was severely dented by the events of 1878. Even on the left of the party faith in democracy and the working class had clearly waned. For instance, William Owen's *Midland Examiner* argued that:

Mr Disraeli, now Lord Beaconsfield, knew what he was doing when he 'shot Niagara' as Carlyle has it, and, by his Reform Bill of 1867, plunged English politics into the whirlpool of a politically uneducated class, who know none of the sharp lines that ever must distinguish the great political parties into which England has been divided for generations.[21]

The jingo demonstrations underlined working-class indifference to the claims of party, forcing *The Midland Examiner* to ask, with some anxiety, '[i]s this the maiden borough that never yet soiled itself by electing a Conservative? Here is a transformation, a medley ...'[22] The great expectations of 1867 had been dashed; no longer would Radical–Liberals assume that the advance of political rights and freedom necessarily brought with it the advance of progressive or rational politics. Democ-

---

[18] *The Evening Express*, 1 Feb. 1878.
[19] *The Evening Express*, 2 Feb. 1878.
[20] *The Wolverhampton Chronicle*, 6 Feb. 1878 and *The Midland Examiner and Wolverhampton Times*, 9 Feb. 1878.
[21] *The Midland Examiner and Wolverhampton Times*, 2 Feb. 1878.
[22] *Ibid.*

racy, once the Radicals' guarantor of enlightened progress, now appeared as its greatest enemy.[23]

After the events of 1878 the Conservatives had expected to do well at the 1880 general election, but in the end their candidate, the local industrialist, Alfred Hickman, polled just 5,874 votes, barely half the total for Henry Fowler, his nearest Liberal opponent.[24] Hickman's vote showed a significant improvement on 1874, but the Tories continued to make little impression in the industrial towns and villages which stretched east towards Walsall. Even in Wolverhampton proper the Liberals remained dominant in the poor 'east end' and in the Stafford Street district with its mixed population of Radical artisans and Irish. Elsewhere, however, the Tories appear to have polled strongly, emerging as the dominant force in such diverse areas as the exclusive west end, the more plebeian mid-Victorian suburbs of Whitmore Reans and Blakenhall, and the central light-metal working districts of St John's and St Paul's.[25]

Thus, despite Hickman's convincing defeat, the 1880 general election confirmed the growing political gulf between Wolverhampton, 'the capital of the Black Country', and its industrial hinterland. It was a gulf which continued to widen over the next decade. At the 1885 general election the Tories polled 46 per cent of the vote in the Wolverhampton parliamentary borough. More importantly, they also returned their first MP, thanks largely to the provisions of the Redistribution Act which divided the old borough into three single-member constituencies: Wolverhampton South, East and West.[26]

Charles Villiers, now 83, was returned unopposed for the Southern division, formed out of the two sprawling and largely industrial parishes of Bilston and Sedgley, while his Liberal colleague, Henry Fowler, won an easy victory in the Eastern division which included the parishes of Willenhall and Wednesfield and the Wolverhampton wards of St Mary's, St James's and St Peter's. But in the western division, which included over 70 per cent of the Wolverhampton population along with the small industrial village of Ettingshall, Alfred Hickman defeated his Liberal opponent, albeit by the slender margin of 153 votes.[27]

[23] For a contrasting picture of the jingo demonstrations see H. Cunningham, 'Jingoism and the working classes, 1877–78', *Bulletin of the Society for the Study of Labour History*, 19 (1969), pp. 6–9.

[24] The full result was, Villiers (L) 12,197 Fowler (L) 11,606 and Hickman (C) 5,874 (two elected).

[25] Information on the geographic basis of party support is taken from *The Evening Express*, 31 Mar. 1880.

[26] For a detailed description of the constituencies created in 1885 see PP 1884–85, vol. IV, p. 38 (Parliamentary Elections [Redistribution] Bill: as Amended in Committee and on Re-commitment).

[27] Population figures derived from the 1891 Census of England and Wales.

From then on the divergent political fortunes of East and West Wolverhampton could hardly have been more pronounced. If anything the eastern constituency became more firmly Liberal after 1885; indeed in 1892 Henry Fowler was, for the first time, returned unopposed. In the west Hickman narrowly lost his seat at the 1886 election, thanks largely to tactical shifts amongst Irish voters, only to enjoy a remarkable victory at the 1892 election when he defeated the sitting Liberal, Sir William Plowden, by the substantial margin of 1,116 votes on an historically high turn out of 89.4 per cent.[28] Popular Conservatism had come of age.

IV

How are we to explain the Conservatives' steady advance during the 1880s and 1890s? Was it simply that Wolverhampton West was an uncharacteristically middle-class constituency where 'villadom' had gone overboard for Salisbury and Conservatism? This must have been a factor in a constituency which included large expanses of middle-class suburbia on its western outskirts, but it is important to remember two things. Firstly, that throughout the period Nonconformity continued to bind a signficant proportion of the middle-class electorate to Liberalism, especially since the powerful local Wesleyan and Congregational churches were dominated by members of the town's Liberal elite.[29] And secondly, that as the Boundary Commission Enquiry of 1885 revealed, there was no ward in Wolverhampton in which houses rated at under £10 per annum did not form a distinct majority. Even in the exclusive ward of St Mark's, where 450 houses were rated at £50 or more, there were more than twice as many (969) rated at under £10.[30]

The resounding Conservative victory of 1892 could not have been won without large-scale working-class support, but what lay behind that support? Some historians would point to the collapse of mid-Victorian prosperity and popular support for free trade, but there are strong grounds for questioning whether protection played any major part in the growth of specifically *working-class* Conservatism during the late nineteenth century. After all, the revival of Conservative fortunes can be traced back to the mid-Victorian period, to the 1861 by-election and the violent election of 1874, and therefore preceded the onset of serious

[28] The result was Hickman (C) 4,772, Plowden (L) 3,656. In Wolverhampton Conservative hegemony during the 1890s was clearly not the product of voter abstentionism.
[29] See G. W. Jones, *Borough Politics: a study of Wolverhampton Town Council, 1888–1964* (London, 1969), pp. 36–7, W. H. Jones, *The Congregational Churches of Wolverhampton, 1664–1894* (London, 1894) and A. C. Pratt, *Black Country Methodism* (London, 1891).
[30] *The Wolverhampton Chronicle*, 21 Jan. 1885.

economic recession in 1877–8. At the same time, the Tories' greatest triumphs occurred, not in 1880, 1885 or 1886, when trade was at its most depressed, but during the 1890s when new industries were already flocking to the town and many of its traditional staples (outside crude iron manufacture) were buoyant once more.[31]

Significantly, the local industry most closely associated with Conservatism was the brass trade, which was almost wholly unaffected by foreign competition during the late nineteenth and early twentieth century. As G. C. Allen observes, '[m]any of the chief branches of the trade were essentially "sheltered" industries, for foreign competition was practically non-existent in the home market, because other countries did not produce goods which accorded with English taste'.[32] The trade enjoyed almost uninterrupted growth after 1870, so that throughout the 'Great Depression' it 'showed an independence of the normal cyclical movement of trade which has ever since distinguished it'.[33] And yet at the same time brassworkers were not privileged 'labour aristocrats' unaffected by the harsh economic realities facing their fellow working men, for the dynamism of the late nineteenth-century brass industry was largely achieved through the transformation of work practices and the supersession of traditional craft skills.

Particularly severely affected were the brass casters, many of whom were thrown out of employment by the wholesale introduction of stamping and pressing machinery between 1875 and 1895.[34] Traditionally they had expected, and received, a great deal of control over the work process. As one local employer told the 1862 Children's Employment Commission, '[t]he men are all paid by piece-work. The shops are open to them between 7 am and 7 pm and they can come when they like between those hours. We have no more control over our men than if they worked for us in their own homes.'[35] All this changed in the 1880s and 1890s; wage levels remained good and work remained relatively plentiful, but new methods of production demanded a new, more disciplined, workplace ethos.

If one follows the arguments of historians who have stressed the 'deskilling' affects of new technologies, one might imagine that these changes would have radicalised the brass trade and produced a new generation of militant leaders committed to the anti-capitalist doctrines of

[31] Local trades experiencing boom conditions after the mid-1880s included brass manufacture, tin-plate working, electrical engineering, bicycle manufacture and, until the turn of the century, the galvanised and corrugated iron industries.

[32] Allen, *Industrial Development of Birmingham*, p. 217.

[33] *Ibid.*, p. 216.

[34] *Ibid.*, pp. 216–17, 228–31 and 250–2.

[35] PP 1864, vol. xxii, Cd. 3414, I, p. 20 (Appendix to the Third Report of the Children's Employment Commission, 1862).

the new socialist parties.[36] In fact it did nothing of the kind: in Wolverhampton the union became increasingly pro-Conservative, nationally it remained staunchly Gladstonian.[37] Even when a few brassworkers began to embrace the idea of independent labour politics during the 1890s they showed no sympathy for socialism: their understanding of labour politics was essentially defensive. Hence one finds Thomas Moore, brass finisher and Labour representative on the School Board from 1891 to 1900, telling the May Day demonstration of 1894 that there would always have to be employers and employed, because the workers would never be able to run firms themselves.[38]

It was this conservative, defensive attitude which underpinned brassworker Toryism during the 1880s and 1890s; just as it almost certainly underpinned the Toryism of many other working-class groups. Protection in the narrow sense of 'fair trade' or tariff reform may have had little direct relevance for Wolverhampton's brassworkers, but in its wider sense of the protection of labour and the defence of traditional values and a traditional way of life it was of vital importance at a time when Liberalism was still generally equated with the relentless pursuit of 'progress' and economic efficiency.

During the 1880s Wolverhampton witnessed the emergence of a new type of populist Tory politician. Conservative councillors like Levi Johnson, Jeremiah Mason and Joseph Lawrence used their unusual proximity to working-class life (all three ran substantial public houses in working-class districts) to identify themselves unequivocally with 'the pleasures of the people' in opposition to the interference of state or municipality. Unashamedly populist, they understood working-class political attitudes sufficiently well to play down their own involvement in organised party politics. Hence when Abiathar Weaver, a Tory shoemaker and close friend of Johnson, contested St Paul's ward in 1891 he made a point of stressing that he was 'independent of any party – political or otherwise (Applause). He was a working man's representative.'[39]

Pledged to defend the right of working people to carry on their lives untroubled by outside authority, these populist Conservatives might almost be thought of as the true *laissez-faire* liberals of late nineteenth-century politics. During a period when working people were increasingly the objects of intense political interest, much of it of the most

[36] See, for instance, R. Gray, *The Labour Aristocracy in Victorian Edinburgh* (Oxford, 1976), pp. 165–83 or G. Crossick, *An Artisan Elite in Victorian Society: Kentish London, 1840–1880* (London, 1978), pp. 248–9.
[37] Hence Maddocks' expulsion in 1885 and the re-appointment of W. J. Davis as General Secretary in 1889, Webb Trade Union Collection E, A, vol. xix, fol. 6.
[38] *Express and Star*, 7 May 1894.
[39] *The Midland Evening News*, 2 May 1891.

manipulative and intrusive kind, there was something strangely positive about working-class support for a popular publican or a Tory working man; it was, in a sense, the politics of self-validation.

By the mid-1880s Wolverhampton Conservatism possessed an elaborate political organisation with ward parties, district social clubs and a central Borough Conservative Association, and yet it still presented itself, with some success, as above 'mere party'. Where Liberalism was associated with the dry procedural debate of the branch meeting, Conservatism was associated with entertainment and spectacle. Tory working men's clubs, Primrose League branches and the party's fêtes and picnics all stressed the same theme: the importance of 'the social element' over formal party politics.

The Liberal response to these innovative forms of organisation was, to say the least, inconsistent. On the one hand they denounced the Conservatives for debasing politics; accusing them of ignoring their responsibility to educate the masses in favour of pandering to their vulgar instincts.[40] On the other hand, they tried, not usually very successfully, to imitate every new development in Tory party organisation; apparently recognising that they could not afford to surrender the field of 'social politics' to their opponents whatever their misgivings. Hence, during the 1880s, local Liberals tried to develop their own network of social clubs to rival the Conservative working men's clubs, although they found their efforts handicapped by the fundamental reservations of many Liberal activists, for whom class-based organisation and political drinking clubs were anathema. For instance, the Willenhall Working-men's Liberal Club was originally established as a teetotal social centre,[41] while the Wolverhampton Liberal clubs continued to insist that they were 'popular' rather than class organisations throughout the 1880s.[42]

As with the working-men's clubs, so with other forms of political organisation: the Tories introduced bold innovations during the early 1880s and the Liberals tried desperately to imitate their efforts later in the decade. For instance, during the spring of 1885 a group of Wolverhampton Tories, most of them working-class activists from a local Conservative club, formed a branch (or 'habitation' as it was known), of the Primrose League.[43] The organisation soon flourished and by 1888 it had over 1,000 members.[44] Significantly, the League appears to have been particularly

---

[40] For instance, see *The Wolverhampton Chronicle*, 31 Oct. 1888.
[41] See *The Wolverhampton Chronicle*, 6 May 1896 for a short history of the club.
[42] For the Villiers Reform Club, founded 1883, see *The Evening Express*, 16 Feb. 1884, for the Fowler Reform Club, founded 1884, see Villiers to McIllwraith, 16 Sept. 1887 (The Villiers/McIllwraith correspondence, Wolverhampton Reference Library).
[43] *The Wolverhampton Chronicle*, 22 Apr. 1885.
[44] *The Primrose League Gazette*, 20 Oct. 1888.

successful amongst working people, perhaps because its uninhibited love
of pageantry and ritual echoed the elaborate ceremonies of working-class
friendly societies, or because it vociferously denied all connection with
formal party politics.[45] By 1887 the Wolverhampton Liberals had established a rival organisation, the Women's Central Liberal Association.
Like the League, the Association was responsible for organising teas,
concerts and other social events in the poorer districts of the town, but it
was never quite able to abandon either its explicit identification with party
or its urge to 'educate' and 'improve' the working classes rather than
entertain them.[46]

Somewhat less inhibited were the Liberals' attempts to imitate the great
summer carnivals organised by their Tory opponents.[47] For instance, a
'Liberal demonstration' staged in June 1888 included tug-of-war, trapeze
acts, acrobatics, a massive firework display, and most startling of all a
tableau vivant reenactment of the capture of a Chinese fort featuring 200
local schoolchildren.[48] A 'fête and demonstration' held for 5,000 people
two years later was even more impressive featuring professional cycle
races, fireworks and numerous speciality acts including 'Zampi the one-
legged gymnast'![49]

V

Wolverhampton Liberalism had changed markedly in the decade or so
since the 1878 jingo demonstrations. Most Radicals agreed that it had
changed decidedly for the worse. Convinced that *tableau vivant* imperialism and one-legged gymnasts debased the party and undermined its claim
to be the natural vehicle for rational and progressive values, they none the
less lamented the party's estrangement from popular attitudes and aspirations. By the mid-1880s it was becoming apparent that popular Conservatism had made serious inroads into the traditional Liberal constituency: historic centres of plebeian Radical–Liberalism like St. John's and
Whitmore Reans were rapidly emerging as bastions of Conservatism.[50]

---

[45] See *The Primrose League Gazette*, 2 June 1888 and *The Wolverhampton Chronicle*, 15 July 1885.
[46] See *The Wolverhampton Chronicle*, 31 Oct. 1888 and *The Midland Counties Express*, 23 May 1896.
[47] For instance, see *Express and Star*, 30 June 1884.
[48] *The Wolverhampton Chronicle*, 27 June 1888.
[49] *Express and Star*, 1 July 1890.
[50] Both districts had played an important part in the Reform League agitations of 1866–67. For evidence of Conservative advance see *Express and Star*, 29 July 1890 and 16 July 1895 and *The Midland Evening News*, 5 July 1892.

Worse, the Liberal party, both locally and nationally, seemed quite incapable of arresting the Conservative advance.

It was against this bleak political background that some Radical trade unionists began to rethink their traditional non-political stance. Buoyed by the revival of trade union fortunes in the mid-1880s,[51] impatient young activists began to talk of direct labour representation and, perhaps more controversially, of the need for co-operation with the Liberal Caucus to check the Tory advance. Indeed in 1885 Fred Mee, the Radical carpenters' leader, managed to negotiate a secret electoral pact with the Liberal Association only to find it unceremoniously rejected by Trades Council delegates who still insisted on strict independence.[52] Thereafter the advanced Radicals steered clear of party politics; directing their energies towards securing fair wages for local government employees, independent labour representation on the School Board and an end to sweated labour.[53] These issues all won wide support within the labour movement, and yet by the close of the decade little of substance had been achieved. Calls for the introduction of a fair wages clause and minimum wage for Council employees had been consistently rebuffed, the labour candidates at the 1888 School Board election had gone down to an humiliating defeat (despite the cumulative voting system), and sweated labour remained endemic throughout the Black Country.[54]

There was little indication that Wolverhampton trade unionism would overcome this impasse until suddenly, in late 1889, the entire political climate was transformed by the impact of a strike which took place over 125 miles away: the great London dock strike of August and September 1889. As Sidney Pollard has recently argued, 'there was ... a powerful psychological element in the outburst of New Unionism which superimposed itself on a "normal" cyclical trade union revival'.[55] After a decade of political and industrial frustration the dam had suddenly broken. Impoverished, semi-casualised workers had proved themselves capable of sustaining a highly disciplined organisation and, equally importantly, of accepting artisan political activists like Mann and Burns as their leaders. At last it seemed as though organisation would transform the working classes into something like the rational, self-disciplined and progressive

---

[51] See R. Walton's comments on the revival of Wolverhampton trade unionism in The Webb Trade Union Collection E, A, vol. IV, fol. 299.

[52] *The Midland Evening News*, 8 July 1885.

[53] See *Express and Star*, 26 Sept. 1888 and 13 Mar., 30 Aug. and 27 Sept. 1889.

[54] *Express and Star*, 16 Nov. 1888 and 10 Apr. 1889 and PP 1889, vol. XIII (The Select Committee of the House of Lords on the Sweating System [Third Report]).

[55] S. Pollard, 'The New Unionism in Britain', p. 48, in W. Mommsen and H. Husung (eds.), *The Development of Trade Unionism in Great Britain and Germany, 1880–1914* (London, 1985).

force which Radicals had hoped would emerge automatically from the 1867 settlement.

The months after the dockers' victory saw the formation of many new trade societies in Wolverhampton, including a strong branch of the Birmingham gas stokers' union which soon won substantial wage rises and the eight-hour day.[56] The political impact of the strike was, if anything, even more impressive. Just two months before the strike Wolverhampton Trades Council had refused to support a resolution stating that, in principle, it would be desirable for no one to work more than eight hours per day; five months after the strike it was lobbying Henry Fowler in favour of immediate legislation on the question.[57] The legal eight-hour day, like the minimum wage and the right to work, had ceased to be purely abstract questions: they now formed part of a recognisable 'labour programme' designed to free all working people from want and insecurity.

It should be stressed, however, that Burns, Mann and Tillett were very much heroes in retrospect for most Wolverhampton trade unionists. During the strike itself few local trade societies or working-class organisations displayed any sympathy for the dockers' cause. The organisation of a strike fund was left entirely to a group of middle-class Radicals, and the only working-class groups to contribute were Mee's carpenters and the Fowler Reform Club.[58] But if it took time for trade union activists to recognise the political and industrial significance of the 'New Unionism', once they had done so they soon outstripped the middle-class Radicals in their support for the movement and the ideals of the labour programme.

By the autumn of 1890 Wolverhampton's plebeian Radical–Liberal clubs were mirroring the trades unions new-found commitment to labour politics. For instance, in September 1890 the Villiers Reform Club held a lengthy debate on the labour programme which culminated in a decision to invite Burns and Mann to address an open-air mass meeting in the town.[59] A few months later young members of the Villiers club played an important part in the formation of a Wolverhampton Fabian Society which in turn found both the Trades Council and local Radical–Liberal clubs eager to support its lectures on socialism and the labour programme.[60] Perhaps most important of all, however, the unprecedented excitement and optimism of these months persuaded the Trades Council

---

[56] *The Workman's Times*, 16 July 1890.
[57] *Express and Star*, 5 June 1889 and *The Wolverhampton Chronicle*, 12 Feb. 1890.
[58] *Express and Star*, 30 Aug., and 7 and 10 Sept. 1889.
[59] *The Workman's Times*, 5 Sept. 1890.
[60] *Fabian News*, Mar. and Apr. 1891; *Express and Star*, 22 Jan., and 5 and 20 Feb. 1891.

to form a Labour Representation Committee (LRC) specifically to secure the return of independent labour candidates.[61]

Clearly, interest in the ideas of the labour programme was now acute, but it should not be assumed that this interest reflected any strong desire to break free from the Liberal coalition. On the contrary, most trade unionists were drawn to the labour programme because they believed it would reinvigorate late-Victorian Liberalism. As the trade unionist and Liberal stalwart Z. Butler explained in 1890, no one could deny 'the grandeur and the beneficence of the aims of people who advocated the doctrine of socialism',[62] but for Radical activists the task was to infuse Liberalism with this idealism and moral purpose rather than to channel it behind a new and independent political movement.

Sentimental attachments to Liberalism remained strong, but whereas once Radicals had been bound to the Liberal Coalition by a profound admiration for the movement's national achievements (notably free trade, the free press, franchise reform and free trade unions) their faith in the 'forward march' of Liberalism had now largely evaporated. Gladstone was still immensely popular, but the national party as a whole no longer inspired great optimism. Even a staunch working-class Liberal like Butler could be heard complaining that '[h]e had never in his life felt more disgusted with the hypocritical professions of both sides of the House'.[63] James Stevenson, Wolverhampton's first Labour councillor, shared this attitude. Immensely loyal to his friends and colleagues on the Wolverhampton West Liberal Three Hundred, to whom he was greatly indebted for his election in July 1891,[64] he was at the same time deeply unhappy with the drift of Liberal politics nationally. Indeed in May 1892 he became one of the town's first established Radical leaders to break with the Liberal coalition and ally himself with the young, independent-minded activists of the Wolverhampton Fabian Society. (He simultaneously joined the *proto*-Independent Labour Party being organised by Joseph Burgess through the pages of *The Workman's Times*.)[65]

It is clear that the constant political agitation of the Wolverhampton Fabians played an important part in creating the climate for a large-scale Radical secession from organised Liberal politics,[66] but it would be wrong to imagine that activism alone can explain such a fundamental

[61] *Express and Star*, 19 Sept. 1890, *The Birmingham Workman's Times*, 12 Sept. 1890.
[62] *Express and Star*, 15 Jan. 1890.
[63] *The Wolverhampton Chronicle*, 20 Mar. 1891.
[64] See *Express and Star*, 12 May, and 13 and 15 July 1891, *The Wolverhampton Chronicle*, 31 July 1891.
[65] *Fabian News*, June 1892, *The Workman's Times*, 25 June 1892.
[66] For testaments to the Fabians' influence in the early 1890s see *The Wolverhampton Chronicle*, 13 Feb. 1895 and *Express and Star*, 14 Feb. 1906.

political shift. Rather, it was the emergence of a rival and self-consciously Conservative brand of labour politics after 1889 which ultimately forced plebeian Radicals to reassess their traditional loyalties. For within a year of the London dock strike the leaders of Wolverhampton's Conservative working-men's clubs were talking of running their own 'Labour' candidates and of securing fair wages for Council employees and greater municipal expenditure in working-class districts.[67]

Given the hostile political climate of 1890 – De Cobain's so-called Strikes Bill had recently been before parliament and the press was reacting strongly against the violence of recent strikes – Radical trade union leaders were in no mood to co-operate with Conservative social clubs in which non-union labour traditionally possessed a powerful voice. When, in April 1891, the North Street Conservative Working-men's Club nominated Abiathar Weaver, a non-union shoemaker, as its 'Labour' candidate for a by-election in St Paul's ward, the Trades Council immediately resolved to secure his defeat.[68] Unable to find a rival 'Radical–Labour' candidate from their own ranks, they nominated the local businessman and publican Patrick Connolly, apparently unaware that his political credentials as a staunch home ruler were seriously undermined by his record as a notorious employer of sweated labour.[69]

Weaver's candidature has been portrayed as a plot by the Conservative establishment to appease demands for working-class representation whilst simultaneously promoting the cause of non-union labour.[70] In fact it was almost entirely the product of spontaneous activity within the working men's clubs. Throughout the election Weaver received little support from the Conservative establishment. Only Johnson and Hamp spoke regularly on his behalf, while on polling day itself he was left almost completely without vehicles.[71] Despite these handicaps, Weaver was returned with a comfortable 82 vote majority, much to the delight of the large band of working-class Tories who attended the declaration and subsequently marched him shoulder high through the town centre.[72]

The Trades Council's furious opposition to Weaver surprised many on the left, including the Radical–Liberal solicitor George Thorne and many Fabians,[73] perhaps because they failed to appreciate the extent to which Weaver's candidature forced Trades Council delegates to face their own isolation within the working class. Like Weaver, the vast majority of

[67] *The Wolverhampton Chronicle*, 29 Oct. and 7 Nov. 1890, *Express and Star*, 16 Apr. 1891.
[68] *Express and Star*, 31 Mar. 1891.
[69] *Express and Star*, 22 Apr. 1891.
[70] For instance see Jones *Borough Politics*, pp. 84–5.
[71] *Express and Star*, 1 May 1891.
[72] *Express and Star*, 2 May 1891 and *The Midland Evening News*, 2 May 1891.
[73] *Express and Star*, 24 Apr. and 4 May 1891, *The Workman's Times*, 7 Nov. 1891.

working people were neither political Radicals nor trade unionists. As James Stevenson told council delegates after he had been suggested as a possible municipal candidate: 'they [the delegates] must remember that the large majority of working men in the town were non-unionists, and that if a *bona fide* working man were brought out agreeable to their views, who was not a trade unionist, they might support him against the nominee of the Trades Council'.[74]

By December 1891 the Trades Council was formally committed to a stance of strict political independence,[75] and yet it is clear that many delegates still sought a special relationship with the Liberal Caucus. Indeed, during the 1892 general election the Trades Council again agreed to endorse and campaign for Sir William Plowden, prompting disgruntled pro-Tory delegates to circulate a sharply critical petition around the pubs and workshops of Wolverhampton.[76] Once again Trades Council Radicals were charged with selling themselves to the 'party wire-pullers'.

This acrimonious affair appears to have deeply shaken the confidence of the trade union leadership. Speaking immediately after the contest Councillor Stevenson remarked that in future 'he hoped the working classes would . . . dispose of party politics – dismiss from their minds all that had hitherto agitated them and injured them, and recognise labour, and labour exclusively, as their motto'.[77] The Council agreed: henceforth its commitment to political independence became real rather than formal. For instance, at the 1894 School Board election the Trades Council and the ILP ran a joint independent labour slate in a bold attempt to win outright control of working-class education in the town,[78] while at the 1895 general election both remained stubbornly neutral despite the fact that the Liberal candidate, George Thorne, was a strong Radical sympathetic to the labour cause.[79]

VI

Unfortunately, it is all too often assumed that the world of working-class politics can be understood simply by deploying categories such as 'socialist', 'Lib.–Lab.' or 'Labourist' to divide the labour movement into its component ideological parts. In reality working-class politics was far

[74] *Express and Star*, 8 May 1891.
[75] *Express and Star*, 19 Dec. 1891.
[76] *The Workman's Times*, 16 July 1892 and *Express and Star*, 4 July 1892.
[77] *The Wolverhampton Chronicle*, 3 Aug. 1892.
[78] *Express and Star*, 22 Sept., 5, 16 and 29 Oct., 2 and 17 Nov. 1894.
[79] *Express and Star*, 15 July 1895 and 21 Nov. 1905 (which demonstrates that bitterness over 1895 lay behind the Liberals' reluctance to support a Labour candidate [Freddie Richards] in Wolverhampton West at the 1906 General Election).

more complex. Individuals frequently shifted between these supposedly discrete ideological positions, or, more revealingly, behaved as though they were completely ignorant of their existence. Thus Councillor Stevenson continually shifted between advocating strict political independence and calling for a progressive alliance between Radical-Liberalism and the labour movement. Having relied heavily on the Liberal party during two municipal election campaigns in 1891, he then rejected the party in 1892 in favour of Fabianism and the campaign to found a national Independent Labour Party. (Although this did not prevent him from playing a prominent part in the Trades Council's ill-fated campaign in support of Plowden at the July election.)[80]

Stevenson's position was only marginally clearer after the 1892 election. For while he quickly emerged as a staunch opponent of the Gladstone and Rosebery ministries, especially over the plight of the unemployed and the Featherstone massacre,[81] he was also a strong advocate of the essentially 'Lib.–Lab.' Labour Electoral Association (LEA), which he eventually persuaded the Trades Council to join in December 1892.[82] Stevenson supported the LEA, not because it was pro-Liberal, but because it was pro-labour and pro-trade union. Hence he was simultaneously arguing, along with fellow Fabians, for the formation of an ILP branch in the borough, and he became 'chairman' of the Wolverhampton ILP at its inaugural meeting in September 1893.[83] Once the Conservatives regained power in 1895, Stevenson became less sympathetic to strict political independence, and, like many ex-Radicals, began to argue that a *rapprochement* with mainstream Liberalism was essential if Salisbury's all-powerful government was to be defeated.[84]

Stevenson's political career underlines the fluidity of late nineteenth-century working-class politics, and reminds us that beneath the organisational divisions there was a great deal of common political ground. Like Stevenson, most Black Country socialists retained strong sympathies for the advanced wing of the contemporary Liberal party, which they hoped might yet restore Liberalism to its former glory. Independence from the Caucus gave them the opportunity to oppose right-wing and anti-trade union Liberals but it did not mean that they had made a fundamental break with Radical-Liberalism. Especially after the Conservative election

---

[80] See *The Wolverhampton Chronicle*, 6 July 1892 and *Express and Star*, 12 July 1892.
[81] See *Express and Star*, 11, 13 and 21 Oct. 1893 and *The Wolverhampton Chronicle*, 13 Sept. and 11 Oct. 1893.
[82] *The Wolverhampton Chronicle*, 21 Dec. 1892.
[83] *Express and Star*, 13 Oct. 1893.
[84] See *Express and Star*, 31 Oct. 1898 where he urges workers to support both ILP and Radical–Liberal candidates for municipal office.

victory of 1895, most labour leaders maintained cordial relations with left-wing Liberal politicians like George Thorne and Price Lewis, although there was never any prospect of full-scale reintegration.[85] Even some sections of the ILP welcomed broad political co-operation, for instance, in 1898 Samuel Hodgkiss defended Wolverhampton South ILP's decision to support George Thorne in a parliamentary by-election by pointing out that 'the members we have come chiefly from the advanced section of the Liberal party, and in that party we know as many earnest socialists as there are members of the Wolverhampton and Bilston branches of the ILP put together'.[86]

Clearly the world of late Victorian popular politics was more complex than many historians have allowed, but what should we conclude about the nature of its complexities on the basis of this short survey of political change in Wolverhampton? It is first important to stress that the political fortunes of Wolverhampton were quite different from those of, say, Northampton, where Radical-Liberalism remained predominant until the 1914–18 war, or of coalfields such as Yorkshire and Durham where strong, politically united trade unions had no need of independent labour politics because they already controlled the Liberal party machine. However, since most constituencies resembled Wolverhampton rather more than they resembled Bradlaugh's Northampton or the English coalfields, it seems reasonable to suggest that this study can shed considerable light on the dynamics of later nineteenth-century popular politics.

I would suggest that three main points can be drawn from this chapter. Firstly, that Victorian popular politics was dominated by a powerful suspicion of party organisation and the party 'wire-puller'. On the one hand, this suspicion held many plebeian Radicals back from full-scale acceptance of the Caucus, thereby reinforcing the dominance of the economically and socially powerful within local Liberalism. On the other hand, it led large numbers of their less highly politicised contemporaries to support populist Conservatism, with its emphasis on national rather than party interest, and its staunch defence of traditional ways of life. Secondly, that major political phenomena such as the emergence of independent labour politics are best understood by placing them in the context of long-term political developments rather than by focusing exclusively on short-term social and economic factors. Here it has been shown that the

[85] See *Express and Star*, 12 and 16 Nov. 1897, 2 May and 27 Oct. 1898 and *The Wolverhampton Chronicle*, 10 May 1899.

[86] *Express and Star*, 27 Jan. 1898. D. Howell, *British Workers and the Independent Labour Party, 1888–1906* (Manchester, 1983) stresses the influence of the Radical–Liberal tradition on the evolution of the ILP (see in particular pp. 163–6, 174–203, 277–82 and 363–88).

emergence of a robust independent labour tradition in Wolverhampton can only adequately be understood when one recognises that trade union leaders were responding to two interrelated political developments: the rise of popular Conservatism within the working class, and the parallel decline of Liberal faith in democracy and progress. Labour activists in 1900 retained broadly the same political outlook as their Radical forebears of twenty, or even thirty, years earlier; it was the political context within which they operated which had undergone a sea-change.

Finally, and rising out of this last point, the paper demonstrates that both plebeian Radicals and the Labour activists who succeeded them, represented a distinct, and, to some extent, an isolated section within the working class. Although Labour politics has often been presented as an organic product of changes affecting working class society as a whole, it would perhaps be more accurate to present it as the cause of a radical minority anxious to re-model a diverse, and partly recalcitrant, working class in its own image.

5   Nonconformity and trade unionism: the Sheffield outrages of 1866

Kenneth D. Brown

In a lecture delivered to the Baptist Historical Society in 1986 the Cambridge theologian, David Thompson, revealed that his grandfather had kept on his desk the busts of three noted contemporaries – those of W. E. Gladstone, Robert Blatchford, and John Clifford.[1] It is difficult to imagine three individuals who might better epitomise some of the diverse strands of which nineteenth-century popular radicalism was composed: the Evangelical and Liberal politician, the jingo and socialist journalist, the reforming, Nonconformist minister from a lace factory. There can be no doubt that Gladstone and Blatchford – or at least the forces which they represented – have tended to dominate the historiographical stage, pushing Clifford's Nonconformity somewhat into the shadows. With a history going back at least to the seventeenth century, trade unionism was certainly a major institutional forum of radical thought and activity. Yet Nonconformity had an equally long association with radical movements. Despite the hyperbole, there was some truth in the suggestion of one mid-Victorian writer that its entire history was 'a record of noble and often painful struggles for popular rights'.[2] A more recent, though not necessarily less partisan, observer has argued that the Evangelicalism with which Nonconformity was deeply imbued was nothing less than the religious expression of radicalism.[3]

In the course of the nineteenth century both trade unionism and Nonconformity grew numerically and acquired greater influence. Eminent Dissenting ministers enjoyed close friendships with leading political figures while the Nonconformist presence made itself felt throughout contemporary society by means of educational institutions, charitable works, a flourishing press, and the sermons and pastoral activities of

---

[1] D. Thompson, 'John Clifford's social gospel', *Baptist Quarterly*, 31 (1986), p. 199.
[2] 'Working men and religious institutions', *British Quarterly Review*, 45 (Apr. 1867), p. 515.
[3] This is the view of W. T. Ward, cited in D. Hempton, *Methodism and Politics in British Society, 1750–1850* (London, 1984), p. 75.

thousands of preachers. According to the religious census of 1851 roughly half of those attending worship on census day were to be found in Nonconformist meetings, and the number of chapels increased rapidly in the course of a mid-century building boom. Similar, if slower and more socially confined, processes of aggrandisement were also at work within the trade union movement. Precise figures are lacking but union membership rose through the century, as industrialisation and urbanisation made it easier and more necessary for workers to organise. Periodically, too, trade unions forced themselves into the public eye through strikes, campaigns for legal reform, or through some incident of violence. The most notorious case of the latter occurred at Sheffield in October 1866 when striking sawgrinders attempted to blow up the house of Thomas Fearnehough, a grinder who had not supported their strike. An official inquiry exposed a long history of such intimidatory violence in the Sheffield metal trades, much of it sanctioned and frequently organised by the sawgrinders' union. The potential for damage to the union movement as a whole was enormous. Reporting a stay he made at Bristol at this time Isaac Ironside noted the observation of a fellow guest that 'if there were a commission appointed to examine into all trade secrets, perhaps Sheffield would not look so bad'.[4] John Stuart Mill reckoned that the outrage did much to stimulate 'indiscriminate prejudice against trade unions'.[5]

Certainly these events attracted national attention and culminated ultimately in the establishment of a major royal commission whose findings did much to shape the subsequent pattern of changes in the legal status of trade unions.[6] For the historian of popular radicalism they provide a useful focus for an examination of the relationships which existed between Nonconformity and labour organisation. This is a theme which has been explored before but rarely in the context of the mid nineteenth century. There is an enduring debate about the allegedly debilitating effects of Methodism on the revolutionary potential of British workers during and immediately after the Napoleonic Wars; some discussion but few substantial studies of the churches and Chartism; and a well documented and long-standing recognition of the Nonconformist contribution to the development of the labour movement, both political and industrial, especially in the years after

---

[4] I. Ironside, *Trade Unions* (London, 1867), p. 17.
[5] Quoted in *Bee Hive*, 26 June 1869.
[6] The process of legal reform is traced in Kenneth D. Brown, 'Trade unions and the law', in C. J. Wrigley (ed.), *A History of British Industrial Relations, 1875–1914* (Brighton, 1982), pp. 116–34.

1870.[7] The third quarter of the nineteenth century, however, remains relatively neglected. With some few exceptions, including those who have investigated the Christian Socialists and the Positivists, historians of the working classes have generally had little to say about the relationship between Nonconformity and trade unionism in these years. Yet it was a crucial period for both movements. The legislation of the early 1870s established an apparently secure legal basis for unionism, while it has been suggested that the Evangelicalism with which Nonconformity was closely identified reached the peak of its influence in the 1850s and 1860s.[8] Furthermore, as already suggested, both movements were expressions of the radical tradition and had often provided vehicles in the past for the articulation of popular radical sentiment. It is clear, however, that they were not always so comfortably juxtaposed as their plaster representations appeared to be on Grandfather Thompson's desk. Nor, indeed, did Dissenters always speak with one voice on the matter of trade unionism.

Prior to the middle of the century Nonconformists as a body did not concern themselves overmuch either with the working classes or their unions. For one thing, the most influential ministers and leaders tended to be concentrated around London where labour combinations were certainly strong but generally very fragmented. Because of this the Dissenters were not always in touch with the economic and social changes which were occurring in the provinces and providing a spur to large-scale organisation. This was undoubtedly why one observer was able to suggest in 1858 that the great need of the London pulpit was 'men abreast of the age, who can sympathise with its pulsation ... respond to its wants ... permeate it with a living faith'.[9] Again, the primary concerns of early-nineteenth-century Nonconformists, whether from the old or new traditions, were evangelism, church building, and mission. Political involvement was

---

[7] The literature on these issues is considerable. The debate on the impact of Methodism can be followed in E. P. Thompson, *The Making of the English Working Class* (London, 1963); M. Hill, 'The Halévy thesis', in D. Potter and D. Sarre (eds.), *Dimensions of Society: a Reader* (London, 1974); E. Itzkin, 'The Halévy thesis – a working hypothesis', *Church History*, 44 (1974); A. D. Gilbert, 'Methodism, Dissent, and political stability in early industrial England', *Journal of Religious History*, 10 (1978–9). For religion and Chartism see H. Faulkner, *Chartism and the Churches* (New York, 1916); S. Yeo, 'Christianity in Chartist struggle, 1838–1842', *Past and Present*, 91 (1981). On the Nonconformist contribution to labour organisation the following are useful: R. F. Wearmouth, *Methodism and the Working Class Movements of England, 1800–1850* (London, 1937); R. Moore, *Pitmen, Preachers, and Politics* (London, 1974); K. D. Brown, 'Nonconformity and the British labor movement: a case study', *Journal of Social History* (Winter 1974). There is a sustained discussion of the period 1850 to 1880 in W. H. Fraser, *Trade Unions and Society. The Struggle for Acceptance* (1974), but only a page or so on Nonconformist attitudes.

[8] D. W. Bebbington, *Evangelicalism in Modern Britain* (London, 1988), p. 105.

[9] J. Ewing Ritchie, *The London Pulpit* (London, 1858), p. 101.

largely restricted to those aspects of contemporary life which impinged directly on the interests of Nonconformists as a body and which raised broad issues of theological and social principle: Catholic emancipation, slavery, disestablishment of the Church of England, and educational matters, for example. Although at the individual level Nonconformist ministers must often have found that their pastoral work entailed other political and social considerations, there was little official interest in such matters which were frequently dismissed as 'worldly'.[10] The major Congregational minister of the early nineteenth century was probably William Jay and he believed that those who became politically and socially involved were too often 'sadly drawn off from keeping their own vineyards'.[11] Joseph Entwisle, first governor of the Wesleyan Theological Institution, took the same view, refusing to address social issues from the pulpit on the grounds that it was 'sacred to better purposes'.[12] This opinion was apparently typical, judging by the sentiments expressed at meetings of the Wesleyan Conference. This annual gathering of ministers might well have provided a suitable central focus for the discussion of social and political subjects but the participants seldom broadened their deliberations beyond immediate matters of connexional government and development. Before the 1830s neither the Baptists nor the Congregationalists, the main representatives of the older Dissenting tradition, possessed any such formal centralised mechanism for the expression of denominational opinion. Indeed, the very idea of such a thing would have cut directly across their underlying theological conviction that ecclesiastical authority rested ultimately with each individual congregation of believers. This was why an early Baptist Union, created in 1813, achieved very little. Even when both Congregationalists and Baptists did establish more effective central unions in the 1830s their memberships were far from comprehensive and both lacked governmental power of the sort exercised by the Wesleyan Conference. All the same, they did provide some sort of forum for the exploration of social and political issues. From the 1840s onwards, the old Dissent at least showed every indication of becoming more socially aware and of grappling with public affairs. The Congregational minister, J. Guinness Rogers, later suggested that the start of this process was symbolised by the presence of over 450 Congregational and Baptist ministers at an Anti-Corn Law League meeting held in Man-

[10] Despite John Wesley's apparent reluctance to become involved in political controversy, his successors, notably Jabez Bunting, were by no means so reticent, despite an official line of non-involvement. The matter is sensitively discussed in Hempton, *Methodism and Politics*, pp. 43ff.

[11] G. Redford and J. A. James (eds.), *The Autobiography of the Rev. William Jay* (London, 1855), p. 113.

[12] J. Entwisle, *Memoir of the Rev Joseph Entwisle. By His Son* (Bristol, 1848), p. 91.

chester in 1843. This, he claimed, was the first time that the voice of Nonconformist ministers had been 'heard in such strength upon affairs which seemed to be outside their proper province'.[13] More recently, Hugh McLeod has concluded that from the middle of the nineteenth century onwards 'it becomes much more possible to see churches and chapels as politically cohesive forces'.[14]

Concern with the working class developed, albeit slowly, not least because the three main Dissenting churches each attracted quite a high degree of support from the labouring population. It has been estimated, for example, that by 1837 about 80 per cent of Wesleyans, and 69 per cent of Baptists and Congregationalists were artisans, labourers or miners.[15] Chartism drew some sympathetic response from individuals like Reverend Edward Miall, the Congregational minister whose election platform in 1845 included all six points of the Charter. But it was the findings of the 1851 religious census that compelled the chapels' attention since it was abundantly obvious that the mass of unskilled workers, particularly in the inner areas of the large industrial cities, remained unreached by the gospel. Chapel building programmes, evangelistic campaigns, and conferences with or about the proletariat, proliferated during the years following the census, although relatively few workers appear to have been convinced by these displays of concern.

If the Nonconformists' own interests and attitudes were thus changing significantly, so, too, was the general political context. For one thing, in the decades after 1850 the trade unions themselves were acquiring a higher public profile. In 1852 William Newton became the first trade unionist to fight a parliamentary election – as radical candidate for Tower Hamlets. With the establishment of the London Trades Council in 1860 something akin to a national union leadership began to emerge, much of its energy being directed into a campaign for changes in the unions' legal status. For another, many Nonconformists were actively engaged in the struggle for an extension of the parliamentary franchise to include a much larger proportion of the working classes. It was against this background that the Sheffield outrages occurred in 1866, raising the whole question of whether or not it was yet appropriate to grant the vote to working men. Earlier notorious episodes in the development of trade unionism involving the Tolpuddle Martyrs or the Glasgow vitriol throwers had gone largely unremarked by Nonconformists. By the 1860s its own broadening concern with social issues and the changed political context compelled chapel

---

[13] J. Guinness Rogers, *An Autobiography* (London, 1903), p. 80.
[14] H. McLeod, *Religion and the Working Class in Nineteenth Century Britain* (London, 1984), p. 52.
[15] A. D. Gilbert, *Religion and Society in Industrial England* (London, 1976), p. 63.

society to come to terms with trade unionism and to locate it within its mental framework. It was not an easy process.

Indeed, some did not even make the effort. According to its prospectus, the *London Quarterly Review* was established and edited by J. H. Rigg as the Wesleyans' periodical mouthpiece on 'topics of the day' and 'so far as they may be connected with great social interests, on important economic principles'.[16] Revealingly, it offered virtually no comment on either the Sheffield outrages or the subsequent official inquiry. Neither did the *Wesleyan Times* although it customarily carried leaders on matters of current interest. It is true that the *Methodist Magazine* did refer to events in Sheffield but it was only in passing, and, in commenting that the affair showed the urgency of dealing with the deteriorating relationship between labour and capital, it had nothing positive to suggest.[17] Thomas Nightingale, a Wesleyan minister stationed in Sheffield at the time of the outrages, evinced a fairly common connexional response when he tried to play the matter down. The people of Sheffield, he wrote to a friend, 'are not all righteous, still my circuit steward really has not followed me about for six weeks, air-gun in hand, seeking to do me grievous bodily damage, nor has one of our poor stewards blown up the houses of my colleagues by throwing gunpowder canisters down the chimneys'.[18] In one sense these attitudes were not surprising, since of all Nonconformist groups the Wesleyans had been the most reluctant to address social issues and their older representatives in particular showed little inclination to modify this stance. Ten months after the outrages occurred, the veteran Thomas Jackson could write that 'in these days of political excitement and of cheap newspapers there is a danger lest our attention should be diverted from our great work ... to save souls'.[19]

Members of other Methodist traditions were not so sure about this, however. An editorial in the *Methodist Quarterly*, a New Connexion publication which was directed at the entire Methodist community, urged Wesleyans to move away from the position adopted by leaders like Jackson that political and social issues were out of court because as Christians their aims and purposes should be essentially spiritual.[20] There were some signs at the Wesleyan Conference of a positive response to such injunctions but as trade union issues came more to the front in political debate those Wesleyans who did heed the *Quarterly*'s pleas displayed

[16] Quoted in *Wellesley Index to Victorian Periodicals*, 5 vols. (Toronto, 1966–89), 4, p. 374.
[17] *Methodist Magazine*, 89 (Nov. 1866), p. 1033. A similar lack of positive suggestions occurred in a subsequent article in *ibid.*, 90 (Mar. 1867), p. 268.
[18] T. Nightingale, *Some of the Reminiscences and Experiences of My Life* (London, 1891), pp. 145–6.
[19] In a letter to *The Times*, 12 Aug. 1867.
[20] *Methodist Quarterly*, 1 (1867), p. 317.

overwhelming hostility to the unions. Initially, it is true, a paper like the *Methodist Recorder* was unwilling 'to impute such diabolical wickedness to the Trades Unions as a whole', but as the full dimensions of Sheffield unfolded there was a noticeable hardening in its editorial tone.[21] The findings of the official inquiry were cited as self-evidently giving the lie to the defence that the outrages were the work of a few individuals unconnected with the union. Further outrages in the Manchester brick trades were claimed as clear proof that such abuses were by no means confined to Sheffield. Rather, they were 'but the culmination of those petty acts of tyranny which are resorted to in other trades than those centred in Sheffield . . . it is clear that some check must be put on'.[22] Trade unionism, asserted the editor, was nothing less than a 'gigantic evil' and reform would be a major concern of the new parliament.[23] When the legislature indicated in 1869 that it accepted the validity of the unions' demand for better legal protection of their funds, it was another Wesleyan paper, the *Watchman and Wesleyan Advertiser*, which took the opportunity to renew the attack, claiming that a system which had the interests of a trade at heart ought to produce an increase in its prosperity and a spirit of contentment within its labour force. In practice, the article continued, the reverse was the case. In setting themselves against their employers, unions were also working against the public interest. Rejecting the assurances of union sympathisers like Thomas Hughes and A. J. Mundella that legal protection for unions would diminish the amount of intimidation and unrest, the paper averred that the most likely outcome was that unions would 'assume the position of dictators to their employers, dictators to all employers of labour in the land. Should the workmen of England ever assume such a position, the event would be calamitous in the extreme.'[24] This view remained substantially unaltered, even when parliament sought in 1871 to clarify the legal position. In February of that year, for example, the *Advertiser* added 'secret, arbitrary, and irresponsible' to the list of epithets it had already directed at the unions in previous issues.[25]

Baptist attitudes were rather more temperate. It may be true, as has been suggested, that in Wales their leaders had 'nothing good to say of Trade Unions', and Reverend Thomas Price was virulent in his denunciations of Alexander McDonald's attempts to establish the Miners Natio-

---

[21] *Methodist Recorder*, 4 Jan. 1867.
[22] *Ibid.*, 28 June 1867.
[23] *Ibid.*, 20 Sept. 1867. It is illustrative of the paper's general attitude that in December 1866 it reported enthusiastically on the efforts of striking miners to form a non-unionist association at Stavely. *Ibid.*, 14 Dec. 1866.
[24] *Watchman and Wesleyan Advertiser*, 4 Aug. 1869.
[25] *Ibid.*, 1 Feb. 1871.

nal Union in the Principality in the 1860s.[26] It seems likely that this may
have been inspired more by nationalist than anti-union sentiment, however. More commonly, Baptists were not much encouraged to become
involved in political issues, certainly not before the 1880s. Local Baptist
pastors in Lancashire, for example, were warned by their local association
'to avoid all interference with civil matters'.[27] The greatest Baptist
preacher of the nineteenth century, Charles Haddon Spurgeon, was a
convinced Gladstonian Liberal but he clung firmly to the view that social
problems would be resolved only through the instrumentality of personal
salvation. Of collective action and institutional remedies 'Mr Spurgeon',
commented an obituarist later, 'made little.'[28] The presence of such
attitudes doubtless explains why the *Freeman*, the Baptists' main newspaper, got a very muted response when it tried early in 1867 to generate a
correspondence on the whole question of trade unionism.[29]

The periodical equivalent of the *Freeman* was the *Baptist Magazine*, and
its cautious and narrow approach exhibited perhaps a better understanding of its readers' priorities. Edited by Reverend W. Lewis, it was
predominantly concerned with theological and denominational matters.
His only concession to current affairs was a feature called 'Short Notes'
but Lewis did not use it to offer any comment on the activities of the
Sheffield unions. In the *General Baptist Magazine*, organ of the New
Connexion General Baptists, there was a similar column called 'General
Public Events'. The editor, W. C. Underwood, was similarly reticent
about Sheffield. Only when the findings of the official inquiry started to
appear did he express the hope that such 'horrendous revelations' would
not cause the public to conclude that unions were necessarily either wrong
in principle or evil in practice. Properly conducted, they were beneficial
both to the trade and the general public.[30] Once John Clifford took over
the editorship in January 1870, however, the journal began to comment
regularly and sympathetically on trade union issues. Clifford represented a
more vocal stream of Baptist social concern, which, despite official
injunctions of the sort imposed in Lancashire, had always been evident.
Almost 200 Baptist ministers had attended the 1843 Anti-Corn Law
League meeting in Manchester, for example. The *Freeman* was edited in
this same generous spirit and did not ignore events in Sheffield. Rather it
sought to play down their import. The bombing of Fearnehough's house

[26] T. M. Bassett, *The Welsh Baptists* (Swansea, 1977), p. 316.
[27] J. Lea, 'Baptists and the working classes in mid-Victorian Lancashire', in S. P. Bell (ed.),
Victorian Lancashire (Newton Abbot, 1974), p. 70.
[28] Quoted in R. Helmstadter, 'Spurgeon in outcast London', in P. Phillips (ed.), *The View
from the Pulpit* (Toronto, 1978), p. 179.
[29] *Freeman*, 25 Jan. 1867.
[30] *General Baptist Magazine*, 69 (July 1867), p. 218.

was described in six brief lines as 'an evil work . . . *supposed* to have been done by trades unionists'. The editor's motive in thus minimising the matter was clear, given the lengthy coverage provided by the same issue to 'a great meeting' of working men held at Leeds to press for parliamentary reform.[31]

The reluctance of Baptist ministers (except apparently the Welsh) to comment too freely on the issues raised by the outrages sprang no doubt from the denomination's tradition of voluntarism. Nothing could be undertaken, no opinion expressed, which might alienate part of the congregation. Similar pressures also operated to keep some Congregationalists relatively silent. Individuals like Joseph Parker and Alexander McKennal, who were well known as sympathisers with working-class aspirations, offered no public comment when the news from Sheffield broke. It is true that another of the denomination's radical ministers, Newman Hall, did refer to the matter when he spoke at the annual meeting organised for working men by the Congregational Union Assembly. But he could hardly have done otherwise, given that in 1866 the autumn assembly was actually being held in Sheffield and that the bombing occurred on the first day of its deliberations. At the next meeting of the Union, in May 1867, the chairman, Reverend J. R. Campbell, devoted his remarks to a detailed consideration of the relationship between the working classes and the church, but his discourse made no mention either of trade unionism or of Sheffield. The following year, in his speech from the chair on the subject of franchise extension, Dr Raleigh made an oblique reference to the unease roused by the activities of the sawgrinders when he claimed that the real question was what people would do with the vote.[32] He was succeeded as chairman of the Congregational Union by R. W. Dale, arguably the greatest of the denomination's political figures, and a man whose espousal of the civic gospel perhaps conferred impeccable radical credentials. His presidential address in May 1869 surveyed the social condition of the people but, again, he made no specific reference to trade unionism.

A similar reticence was noticeable in sections of the Congregational press as well. The sawgrinders' misdemeanours went unremarked in the columns of the *Patriot*. The reason became apparent early in December 1866. Reporting at length on the parliamentary reform demonstration held by London trade unionists it urged that 'their determined tramp through the mud and drizzle is allowed to be convincing proof that they want votes'.[33] As a long time campaigner for franchise extension, this

[31] *Freeman*, 12 Oct. 1866. My italics.
[32] *Congregational Year Book* (London, 1869), p. 59.
[33] *Patriot*, 6 Dec. 1866.

leading Congregational paper could not afford to raise doubts as to the suitability of working men for the right to vote. For a similar reason the *Nonconformist* initially also ignored the immediate furore of the outrages. However, as the subsequent commission of inquiry uncovered the full extent of the violence and intimidation in the Sheffield metal trades, so the editor felt it necessary to undertake an exercise in damage-limitation. It would, he suggested, be 'an extreme of injustice to cast in the teeth of the artisans of this country any insinuation that this is the sort of conduct which has their sanction, or that such is the kind of outcome which is encouraged by their trade organisations'.[34] A long article in the *British Quarterly Review*, edited by leading Congregational minister Henry Allon, also sought to dismiss the notion that such tactics were widespread. On the contrary, they were 'so exceptional as to provoke protests from the recognised representatives of other working men'.[35] Such attitudes were in marked contrast with some of the wilder statements emanating from Wesleyan sources.

It is clear, then, that the immediate Nonconformist response to the Sheffield outrages varied between and even within denominations, coloured often by the wider implications of trade union activity for franchise reform. As events proceded through the official inquiry to the royal commission of 1867 and the subsequent legislation, so the nature of the Nonconformist critique of trade unionism emerged more clearly. It was one which owed very little to economics. Only two economic arguments were brought to bear on the subject and neither was utilised at all frequently, being confined rather to single commentators. One writer in the *Wesleyan Times* argued that trade was being driven abroad by high wages in Britain, which in turn were due to the 'wire pullers of the trades unions'. Their actions had not been in vain, however, since 'it is something to have brought an industrious man who earned 32sh a week to breaking five bushels of stone for threepence and a small loaf of bread'.[36] A second Methodist writer suggested that one corollary of this was Britain's poor showing at the recent Paris Exhibition. The blame for failing industrial performance was laid firmly at the trade unions' door. 'If the doctrine of the Trades Unions is to be generally acted on – that men shall work upon an average ability, without giving free scope to the skill and ability which they may individually possess ... is there any reasonable prospect of maintaining even our present position as compared with other nations?', the writer asked.[37]

[34] *Nonconformist*, 26 June 1867.
[35] 'Working men and religious institutions', p. 508.
[36] *Wesleyan Times*, 14 Jan. 1867.
[37] *Methodist Recorder*, 31 May 1867.

Not surprisingly, the economist J. Thorold Rogers, used theoretical arguments in his survey of unions which appeared in the Congregationalist *British Quarterly Review*. He defended them on the grounds that they performed the useful function of organising the labour market and preventing labour from being idle. He then used the wage fund theory to demolish the idea that unions could ever succeed in their fundamental aim of raising wages in any permanent way.[38] But ideas such as these deriving from contemporary economic thought formed a very small part of his argument. The bulk of it – despite Rogers' own eminence as an economist and economic historian – was cast very firmly in terms of traditional radical values such as equity or fair play, morality and individual freedom. In this, his analysis reflected accurately the prevalent characteristics of the Dissenters' view of trade unionism, which in turn was rooted firmly in radical ideology. For example, such ideals, especially the notion of fair play, were the very ones to which the supporters of the Tichborne claimant appealed, as Rohan McWilliam shows elsewhere in this volume. In a similar way, the campaign for the reform of the labour laws, discussed by Jonathan Spain, rested essentially on considerations of equity before the law, a notion much used by Nonconformist defenders of trade unionism.

The arguments which defended the principle of workers' organisation on these grounds of equity took several forms. One writer pointed out that it was only reasonable for workers to combine, given that employers had been doing just that for so long. 'The retaliation of a wrong is not justified by the wrong which it imitates, but it must be admitted that the organisation of employers is 500 years older than that of labourers, and is far more capable of acting, in concert, on the offensive.'[39] He then proceeded to show that the practices of labour unions were identical with those freely utilised by other interest groups in society. Thus he described the Institute of Architects as a trade union because it dictated the terms of architects' commissions as surely as a union tried to determine wage levels. In similar fashion union attempts to restrict the number of apprentices in an industry were likened to the controls placed upon the number of clerks that solicitors were permitted to employ. Again, just as a skilled bricklayer did not carry his own bricks but was served by an unskilled labourer so a barrister could be approached only through a solicitor.[40] Implicit in all of this argument was the belief that what was permissible for middle-class professionals should, on the grounds of equity, be allowed to working men.

[38] 'The Trade Unions', *British Quarterly Review*, 46 (Oct. 1867), pp. 520–5.
[39] *Ibid.*, p. 517.
[40] *Ibid.*, p. 519.

It was on similar grounds that the Nonconformist community responded favourably to the union campaign for a change in the Master and Servant Law. Typically, only the Wesleyans were out of step. When legislation to protect union funds was mooted the *Advertiser* wondered whether it was wise to give legal protection to 'a system about which there is much dispute'.[41] Baptists and Congregationalists, however, took the view that it was fundamentally unfair for workers who breached contracts of employment to be liable to criminal proceedings whilst employers guilty of a similar offence were subject only to civil actions. 'The odium which surrounds an unfair and partial law', commented the *British Quarterly Review*, 'is not mitigated by the difficulties which are put in the way of its execution.'[42] Even this was a somewhat rosy view, given that on average the act was being invoked against employees 10,000 times a year in the 1860s.[43]

The issue, in the eyes of the reformers, was one of equity of treatment before the law, and much of the Nonconformist response to the Sheffield outrages was couched in similar terms. Thus the *English Independent* suggested that trade unions *per se* could not expect legal protection because that could only be extended to an individual. Significantly, though, the paper went on to assert that this principle should also be applied to employers' associations. All combination, whether of labour or capital, it contended, should be outlawed in the interests of social harmony and legal equity.[44] The *Freeman* also saw the matter as one of equality but reversed its application, suggesting that if workers had the right to organise in order to agree on wage rates so the masters should have the same freedom to agree on what rates they would pay. It was inequitable that a practice deemed legal for one social group should be illegal if adopted by another. Masters had 'as much right to agree with each other to refuse employment to men who injure them by striking to enforce rules made by Unions of which the masters are not members, as the men to agree not to work for masters who decline to comply with Union terms ... Both acts must be equally held either legal or illegal.'[45]

Others concentrated on the moral issues raised both by the outrages themselves and the subsequent revelations of the way that unions operated. There is no doubt that the unionists did a good job in presenting a favourable image to the royal commission of 1867, but Nonconformist opinion was disturbed at the open admission of restrictive practices.

---

[41] *Watchman and Wesleyan Advertiser*, 4 Aug. 1869.
[42] 'Trade unions', p. 518.
[43] The figures for prosecutions are cited in C. F. Brand, 'The conversion of British trade unions to political action', *American Historical Review*, 30 (1925), p. 257.
[44] *English Independent*, 3 Jan. 1867.
[45] *Freeman*, 23 Aug. 1867.

Attention was focused particularly on the reluctance of workers to undertake other men's tasks, and the notion that irrespective of individual skill and ability, all employees should work at the same pace for the same remuneration. The existence of such customs, suggested the *General Baptist Magazine*, was very painful to Christians because they manifested an 'intensely selfish unchristian spirit ... It is we fear this heartless selfishness, this want of honesty and moral integrity, which is the cancer eating into thy vitals'.[46] A few, it is true, made attempts to defend the unions even on this issue but their efforts were feeble. Thus the *English Independent* suggested that restrictive practices served to protect the weak even though they were 'not examples of a very exalted morality'.[47] Another Congregational writer emphasised that 'the worst villainies which men commit are planned and effected for corporate, not for personal ends'.[48] The *Freeman* agreed, claiming that in adopting restrictive codes of work trade unionists were thinking of others in their class and thus could not be charged with selfishness.[49] Yet the editor was not really convinced by his own arguments. A few weeks earlier he had described as 'one of the unions' cardinal errors' their insistence that all men should be paid the same regardless of individual merit, and he admitted that such a policy was barely defensible from the public point of view.[50] Subsequent revelations made before the royal commission further undermined his position and by 1869 he had completely changed his mind, describing the Stonemasons' rules as 'monstrously absurd as well as tyrannical'.[51]

A somewhat different, but equally traditional form of moralism informed the *English Independent*'s views that restrictive practices destroyed the sense of love of work for its own sake and pride in individual craftsmanship. It was simply ludicrous, claimed the paper, to maintain that the work of the idle and incompetent was equal to that of the most skilled and hardworking men.[52] A further moralistic element was introduced into the debate by those, mainly Methodists, who related the outrages to intemperance. Not all crime could be directly attributed to alcohol, admitted one temperance zealot, but it was obvious that the trade outrages at Sheffield and Manchester had been 'concocted and settled for chiefly at the public houses'.[53]

As for the outrages themselves, they provoked universal condemnation.

[46] *General Baptist Magazine*, 69 (May 1867), pp. 154–5.
[47] *English Independent*, 25 Apr. 1867.
[48] 'Trade unions', p. 513.
[49] *Freeman*, 26 Apr. 1867.
[50] *Ibid.*, 29 Mar. 1867.
[51] *Ibid.*, 13 Aug. 1869.
[52] *English Independent*, 25 Apr. 1867.
[53] *Methodist Times*, 23 Sept. 1867.

One writer confessed himself to be 'horrified ... at the cold blooded ferocity of Broadhead and his assassins'. The whole affair had been an example of 'excessive violence' and it could only be hoped that such incidents were confined to one or two localities, and even in these localities to one or two societies.[54] The same rhetoric of morality was also apparent in the *British Quarterly Review* which suggested that 'men *cheat* themselves into a belief that a crime is a necessity, or even an act of heroism, when they anticipate that they will benefit others by commiting it'.[55] On the Sunday after the bombing, a Sheffield minister, David Loxton, preached on the subject and interpreted it exclusively in a moral light. It made no difference, he argued, that no one had been hurt, since the intention was evident and scripture made no distinction between the intent behind an action and its outcome. The perpetrators might escape earthly justice, he warned, but would not evade the retribution of God for their immoral actions. His sentiments were echoed in the press. The whole inquiry, suggested one paper, was a moral process throwing the light of doom upon the bombers. Whatever happened on earth the criminals would be judged in heaven for 'verily, there is a God who judges in the earth'.[56] The writer went rather over the top, however, in comparing the outrages with the September days of the French revolution.

The moral outrage reached its highest pitch in the summer of 1867 by which time the official inquiry had uncovered the long history of the sawgrinders' unsavoury tactics. These included earlier murder bids sanctioned by William Broadhead and fellow union officers. The sawgrinders, however, resisted enormous public pressure when in August they refused to repudiate Broadhead, his associates and their actions. This, thundered the *Freeman*, was because long habit and moral complicity had deadened the members' consciences.[57] The Wesleyans were similarly appalled at the sawgrinders' moral cowardice. Their decision had been governed by 'strange moral obliquity and insensibility to shame'. Equally for the Wesleyans, however, the remedy lay in the direction of moral, rather than legal reform. Sheffield had been exposed as the seat of a system of organised violence – 'dark, cowardly, and murderous' – but nothing, suggested the *Methodist Magazine*, could be so effective 'as the grace which saves from all manner of selfishness and sin. We are glad to know that Methodism during the last few years has become increasingly aggressive in Sheffield and that there is a prospect of reaping a rich harvest.'[58] The

---

[54] 'Trade unions', p. 513.
[55] *Ibid.*, my italics.
[56] *English Independent*, 27 June 1867.
[57] *Freeman*, 23 Aug. 1867.
[58] *Methodist Magazine*, 90 (Sept. 1867), pp. 852–3.

Wesleyan Times similarly placed its hope only in the Cross and 'its blood-dyed banner'.[59]

The ethics of trade union violence brought into particularly sharp focus the fundamental question of individual freedom which was raised by the activities of the Sheffield sawgrinders. This was the issue which Noncon-formists found particularly difficult to sort out. The dilemma presented itself in this form: did the freedom of the individual, sacrosanct in all radical and Nonconformist thinking, include the liberty to act collectively against other individuals whose own freedom might thus be restricted? Predictably, the Wesleyans interpreted this in the most extreme way, arguing that the Sheffield unionists misunderstood the nature of freedom if they believed that it included the right to 'render up their private liberties to the despotic rulers of the Trades Unions'. Such a belief so confused the individual's sense of rectitude and justice that he was even prepared to kill at the arbitrary dictates of union officials.[60] For some the solution was pragmatic, but again shaped by considerations of equity. Labour should be rendered as legally free to organise as capital was. It could act collectively to get its way against employers but not at the cost of intimidating other individuals.[61] This was the line which Newman Hall took in addressing working men at the Congregational Union's Sheffield assembly in 1866. Workers, he declared, had every right to combine to strike and to ask for higher wages but not to demand that others join them. That was tyranny, and coming from those who were always denouncing tyranny was 'so despicable a thing that I can't find a word in the English language to describe it. I denounce such despotism.'[62] For others, it was more complicated because the very concept of a trade union was protectionist and thus impinged on other individuals' freedoms. As a contributor to the *British Quarterly Review* had it, 'there is no error so inveterate as that which believes in the benefit of protection'.[63] Yet the author could not simply leave it at that because notions of equity and morality were also woven into his argument. Thus, as we have already seen, he believed that union practices were no different in principle to those adopted by others in contemporary society. Nor, he went on, bringing into play a moral dimension, was it any 'marvel that working men are and have been protectionists. After many centuries of cruel and insolent oppression on the part of protectionists, they were partially freed. It would have been an act of astonishing generosity if they had forborne to

[59] *Wesleyan Times*, 22 Apr. 1867.
[60] *Methodist Recorder*, 20 Sept. 1867.
[61] *English Independent*, 12 Sept. 1867.
[62] *Sheffield Daily Telegraph*, 12 Oct. 1866.
[63] 'Trade unions', pp. 510–11.

retaliate.'[64] He felt secure enough, however, to suggest that organised labour had no right to call upon the general public to assist it against employers. 'We, at least, must bid them abandon their sentimental phrases about the tyranny of capitalists, and so forth.'[65] Similar criticisms of the protectionist ethic of unionism appeared frequently in other parts of the Nonconformist press. They were, for example, condemned as 'an interference with trade, an application on a large scale of the principle of protection. The only protection which the law ought to afford is that of persons, not of trades.'[66] Elsewhere it was admitted that while unions performed useful functions they were only at their 'most effective when they most glaringly violate personal rights'. If they could not be made compatible with the freedom of the subject they should not be allowed to survive.[67] Others were more moderate, placing their hopes in a suitable legislative solution.[68]

Yet more than one contributor to the debate pointed out that to prohibit the freedom of association and joint action within the law just because the limits of legality had been transgressed as they had at Sheffield, would be to confess the failure of liberal institutions.[69] Clearly this was an insoluble ideological dilemma – it was one about which jurists were still arguing in 1911 – and even those who acknowledged the dubious nature and morality of restrictive practices doubted that they could be controlled by means of legislation.[70] This was why so many Nonconformists found themselves advocating arbitration and conciliation schemes as the way forward to a new era of industrial relationships in which unions would be unnecessary. Liberal minded Methodist writers, for example, took this view, arguing that the labour–capital conflict was but a temporary phenomenon paving the way for a social system that would combine their respective interests.[71] John Clifford had been advocating just such an approach for a long time in the pages of the *General Baptist Magazine* and he continued his campaign when he took over as editor.[72] The *Freeman* agreed: 'It is clear that we are to look to co-operation in

---

[64] *Ibid.*, p. 525.
[65] *Ibid.*, p. 526.
[66] *English Independent*, 3 Jan. 1867.
[67] *Methodist Times*, 16 Sept. 1867. See also the *Nonconformist*, 28 Aug. 1867.
[68] E.g., see *English Independent*, 20 June 1867.
[69] *Nonconformist*, 26 June 1867.
[70] E.g., *Freeman*, 17 Feb. 1871. For later legal uncertainties see J. H. Greenwood, 'Trade unions and the law', *Westminster Review*, 176 (1911), p. 613. 'Trade unionism as a distinct and fundamental conception has never found its true place in our political and juridicial systems.'
[71] *Wesleyan Methodist Magazine*, 94 (Oct. 1871), p. 931.
[72] For example, see his remarks in *General Baptist Magazine*, 69 (July 1867), p. 218. See similar arguments advocated in *ibid.* (Feb. 1867), p. 57: (Mar. 1867), p. 90.

some form.'[73] In similar vein a writer in the *Nonconformist* reckoned that the struggle between capital and labour represented nothing more than a passing phase in which unionism had been necessary in order to even up the balance between the two. Once industrial harmony was established the need for union organisation would disappear.[74] By October 1871 the paper was a total and enthusiastic supporter of the co-operation and arbitration line. Alarmed by the pronouncements of, and English involvement in, the International, that 'vortex of secret conspiracy', it urged employers to imbue workers with moderation by being conciliatory themselves.[75] Such schemes had a further advantage in Nonconformist eyes. In granting recognition to the unions as equal negotiating partners with employers they embodied the principle of equity which was such an important feature of the Dissenters' approach to unionism.

In the late 1860s the major Nonconformist concerns centred on issues arising from the American Civil War, the appearance of ritualistic tendencies in the Church of England, and the proposed reforms of parliament and the educational system. The fact that so much comment on trade union affairs appeared when their main interests thus lay elsewhere, is testimony to the seriousness with which Dissenters approached the issues opened up by the Sheffield outrages. In so far as the utterances made at annual assemblies or in the columns of denominational papers may be taken as expressions of prevailing attitudes it is clear that Nonconformist reaction to the trade unions, like that of the public at large, was very mixed. It was certainly sufficiently complex to throw some doubt on Patrick Joyce's claim that organised religion generally supported the employers.[76] From the evidence surveyed above, his suggestion appears to be true of Wesleyanism but far less so of the other main Nonconformist denominations which frequently displayed sympathy for workers' efforts to protect themselves and further their own interests.

It is, however, also worth pointing out that in mid-century, despite the evidence of official hostility towards unionism, Wesleyanism was the most strongly entrenched of all the large Nonconformist churches in the main manufacturing regions of Britain. In contrast, the Congregationalists, so much more sympathetic to the unions, had their main areas of strength in a predominantly rural belt of southern counties running from Devon to Essex. They were relatively weak in the industrial areas of the north and west midlands. If any correlation existed between areas of strength and

---

[73] *Freeman*, 8 Sept. 1871.
[74] *Nonconformist*, 13 Nov. 1867.
[75] *Ibid.*, 4 Oct. 1871.
[76] P. Joyce, *Work, Society and Politics. The Culture of the Factory in Later Victorian England* (Brighton, 1980), p. 178.

attitudes towards trade unionism, it would appear to have been an inverse one, with the most sympathetic responses coming from the denominations probably least familiar with modern unionism. Only among the Baptists does there appear to have been a positive correlation. The sympathetic New Connexion drew its main support from the industrial counties of the east midlands. The more cautious mainstream Baptists predominated in the more agrarian south.[77]

In most cases, however, the prevalent sentiments of a particular denomination appear to have owed less to its regional distribution than to its wider political stance. John Wesley's advocacy of an a-political approach had developed, in the hands of his descendants, into a pro-establishment position. While there was still a strong desire on the part of some Wesleyans to ignore the issues raised by the growth of trade unionism, the majority was consistently suspicious of it. At first sight, this is perhaps difficult to reconcile with the high proportion of Wesleyans who were themselves members of the working classes, but it points up the fact that neither the connexion's press nor its leadership accurately represented the views or interests of the rank and file.

A pietist or 'other-worldly' streak was also discernible among Baptists but in general they did evince more sympathy for the unions than did the Wesleyans. Support, however, was strongest of all among the Congregationalists and this is consistent with a number of aspects of that connexion's development in the mid nineteenth century. Congregationalists had always regarded themselves as possessing a special mission to the middle class but this rather faded after 1850 and working-class issues came more to the fore in their thinking. More particularly, Congregationalists played a prominent part in the campaign for franchise reform and thus perhaps had to face more squarely the issues raised by Sheffield as to the suitability of working men for the vote. Again, the Congregationalists as a denomination were the first to experience the serious questioning of the old Evangelical verities. The subsequent search for a meaningful Christian message led them ultimately to the social gospel, but, already in the third quarter of the nineteenth century, social concern was becoming a more prominent feature in their theology than it yet was in that of any other denomination. It is important, too, to notice the language in which the Nonconformist debate was conducted. It owed virtually nothing to contemporary economic theory. This must bring into question Henry Pelling's long-standing assertion that trade unionism became more accep-

---

[77] These remarks on the dissenters' geographical distribution are based on the analysis of the 1851 census made by J. D. Gay, *The Geography of Religion in England* (London, 1971), pp. 118–48.

table as the wage fund theory was progressively abandoned, following the publication of W. T. Thornton's book, *On Labour*, in 1869.[78] If the Nonconformists were, as seems likely, representative of middle-class opinion, few of them thought about the issues in strictly economic terms at all. Nor was the Nonconformist assessment very often expressed in directly scriptural language. Superficially this may appear to offer some support to Edward Norman's contention that 'the social attitudes of the Church have derived from the surrounding intellectual and political culture and not, as churchmen themselves always seem to assume, from theological learning'.[79] On the other hand, if the rhetoric was not scriptural the notions on which Nonconformists rested their judgements clearly were. Terms such as 'equality', 'liberty', 'justice', 'despotism', and 'tyranny' were freely deployed in the discussions while the issues raised were seen in similar terms as ones of equity, morality, freedom and fair play. If these had a biblical origin they were also, of course, key elements in popular radical ideology.

It is true that the Nonconformist opinion-makers used such concepts both to defend and to attack the principles and actions of trade unionism. This illustrates just how elastic were the purposes to which radical rhetoric could be turned and how flexible and self-contradictory it could often be. It sometimes proved very difficult, for example, to provide a consistent and intelligible basis for trade unionism within the parameters of these radical notions. Perhaps only a socialist analysis of economics and society could do that. Yet the very attempt to locate unionism in such a traditional framework had important and beneficial side effects for the unions themselves. It is clear that during the debates raised by the Sheffield outrages Congregational and to a lesser extent Baptist opinion began to move more firmly towards the same idea of voluntarist collective action which informed the thinking of union leaders like Robert Knight, himself a deacon in a Congregational chapel.[80] This expressed itself both in the contention that individual workers should be free to join unions if they wished and also in the growing advocacy of arbitration and conciliation schemes. In this way the Old Dissenting elements of Nonconformity provided a means of intellectual convergence between Liberalism and trade unionism, reinforcing the existing institutional ties between them. It is suggested in Graham Goodlad's chapter that Gladstone's record as a radical reformer enabled him to win the loyalty of Nonconformists for an Irish Home Rule policy which was not necessarily consistent with their theological or historical position. In a reciprocal way and for similar

[78] H. Pelling, *History of British Trade Unionism* (London, 1963), p. 70.
[79] E. Norman, *Church and Society in England, 1770–1970* (London, 1976), p. 10.
[80] See Alastair Reid, ch. 10 in this collection.

reasons – they all spoke in the same radical language – the Nonconformist community was able to encourage sympathy for trade unionism among the Liberal leadership. The protective nature of trade unionism meant that it was a suspect concept to *laissez-faire* Liberals. Yet, as Jonathan Spain argues, the Liberal Party, contrary to received historical wisdom, made an important and positive contribution to the legislation of 1875. That measure, along with the acts of 1871, did much to establish a secure basis for future union development. Undoubtedly, both the legislation and the concurrent change in public perceptions owed much to the sophisticated way in which the unions handled themselves before the royal commission of 1867. But some part was also played by an immensely influential Nonconformity which debated the issues in familiar radical terms. In so doing it did much to offset the potential damage done to the union movement by the Sheffield sawgrinders and paved the way for the significant legislative change of the early 1870s.

Part II

The Liberal party and the people

6   Trade unionists, Gladstonian Liberals and the labour law reforms of 1875

Jonathan Spain

I

There has been surprisingly little modern research on the passage of the labour law reforms of 1875,[1] and that which has been published has emphasised the importance of Disraeli and R. A. Cross, the Conservative Home Secretary, in bringing about a final and comprehensive settlement of the question.[2] The picture which emerges from a reading of general histories of the period is therefore that Gladstone's first ministry, after the ambivalent reforms of 1871, became neglectful or even hostile to the claims of the trade union movement.[3] Then, following the 1874 general election, Disraeli entered office mindful of the opportunity of weakening the electoral base of Liberalism still further; sensitive also to the need to prove the capability of the new Conservative administration by finding solutions to thorny social questions, with the more general intention of wooing the masses away from constitutional and political reform. One result of this was the labour law reforms of 1875, the centrepiece of the social reform 'initiative' pushed through by the Conservative government during its first two years in power.

In fact, the passage of the labour law reforms of 1875 was a truly bi-partisan effort. As Colin Matthew has indicated,[4] by the autumn of 1873, the previous Liberal administration had moved significantly towards the

This chapter is, in part, the result of research towards a Ph.D.; 'Parliamentary radicalism, 1874–80' (Kings College, Cambridge), as yet unfinished. I would like to thank the editors, Dr A. J. Reid and Dr E. F. Biagini, and my supervisor, Professor D. E. D. Beales, for their helpful comments and criticism.

[1] Since writing this chapter, it has come to my attention that Dr Mark Curthoys of Oxford University is publishing a general study on trade unions and the labour laws.

[2] See R. Blake, *Disraeli* (London, 1966), pp. 550, 553–5. Also P. R. Ghosh, 'Style and substance in Disraelian social reform', in P. J. Waller (ed.), *Politics and Social Change in Modern Britain*, Essays presented to A. F. Thompson (Sussex, 1987, pp. 59–90). For a more detailed discussion see P. Smith, *Disraelian Conservatism and Social Reform* (London, 1967), pp. 215–18.

[3] E. J. Feuchtwanger, *Democracy and Empire, Britain 1865–1914* (London, 1985), pp. 72–4, 86; R. C. K. Ensor, *England 1870–1914* (Oxford, 1966, reprint), pp. 35 and 132–3.

[4] H. C. G. Matthew, *Gladstone 1809–1874* (Oxford, 1986), p. 214.

trade union position. Under the stimulus of the new Home Secretary, Robert Lowe, the Home Office conceded in principle what became the basis of the settlement of 1875.[5] Moreover, my own research has shown that during the passage of the parliamentary bills of 1875 the Liberal opposition significantly amended and extended Cross's legislation, transforming an honest though, in certain key areas, a limited attempt at reform into a comprehensive and final settlement. During the course of 1873–5 the Liberal leadership (spurred on by the advanced wing of the party) was therefore far more positive in its support of the legal rights of trade unions than historians have hitherto recognised. This reflected a sympathetic regard for the aims and objectives of the 'new model' craft unions who dominated the trade union movement during this period.

The Liberal contribution to the settlement of 1875 was fully understood and recognised by the trade union leadership and, I would argue, explains in part the political commitment of the late Victorian trade union movement to the Liberal party. The labour law reforms of 1875 should not be considered solely as an example of Disraelian opportunism, or perhaps the working out of the social aspects of Peelite Conservatism – although these were undoubtedly important factors. We must also consider the Liberal background and contribution to the reforms of 1875. This chapter will therefore deal more specifically with three neglected elements of the reforms of 1875, namely: the nature of the political alliance which developed between the trade union leaders and the 'Gladstonian' or 'advanced' Liberals following the legislation of 1871, with the intention of securing further reform; the evolving response of the Liberal administration to this pressure between 1872 and the general election of 1874; and finally, the contribution of the Liberal 'front bench' and the 'advanced' wing of the party to the legislative settlement of 1875.

II

Hitherto, the historiography of the trade union reforms of 1871–5 has emphasised the role of the Positivist intellectuals: Beesly, Harrison, Crompton and Lushington.[6] This has led to a neglect of the relationship which evolved between the trade union leaders and the 'friends of labour' in the House of Commons.[7] This political alliance was of crucial

[5]   H. C. G. Matthew, (ed.), *The Gladstone Diaries, 1871–4*, vol. 8 (Oxford, 1982), pp. 417–9.
[6]   See R. Harrison, *Before the Socialists* (London, 1965), 'The Positivists: a study of labour's intellectuals', pp. 286–305.
[7]   The exception is H. W. McCready, 'Britain's labour lobby, 1867–75', *Canadian Journal of Economics*, 22 (1956), pp. 141–60.

importance. Having no direct representation, the trade union leaders were dependent upon the *indirect* representation provided by this group to lead the parliamentary campaign and maintain pressure upon the Liberal administration. Their chief spokesmen in the parliament of 1868–74 were Thomas Hughes and A. J. Mundella.[8]

This political alliance evolved in the late 1860s with the dual aims of firstly, establishing legal protection of trade societies' funds following the judicial decision of 1867 in Hornby v. Close, which highlighted the inability of the unions to protect their funds from embezzlement because of their extra-legal status in common law; and secondly, defending the skilled craft unions from further legal restrictions in the aftermath of the 'Sheffield outrages', an episode which revealed widespread terrorism within the Sheffield saw grinders' trade.

During this crisis the leadership of the trade unions was assumed by the heads of the major craft unions, the so-called 'Junta' in which Applegarth and Odger played a prominent role.[9] With the passage of the Trade Union Act of 1871, political leadership passed into the hands of the Parliamentary Committee of the newly established Trades Union Congress, itself the product of the legal battles of 1868–71. The principal forces within the Parliamentary Committee were its secretary, George Howell[10] and chairman, Alexander McDonald.

The trade union legislation of 1871 had gone some way towards meeting the union grievances. Bruce's act gave trade unions legal status in law and protection of their funds. By clause 2 of the act Bruce rendered trade unions exempt from conviction under the law of conspiracy by reason of their merely being in 'restraint of trade'. However the trade unions were critical of the 1871 Criminal Law Amendment Act (hereafter referred to as the CLA Act), which retained penal sanctions against 'coercion', 'intimidation' and 'molestation'. In the House of Lords the Tory peer Lord Cairns amended the bill making the molestation sub-clause more stringent; in the first instance, by making the definition of 'molestation' open-ended; and in the second, by removing the test of numbers applied to the definition of 'watching and besetting'. The trade union leaders argued that the CLA Act imposed unfair restrictions on peaceful picketing and constituted discriminatory class legislation; viol-

---

8   W. H. G. Armytage, *A. J. Mundella 1825–97. The Liberal Background to the Labour Movement* (London, 1941); E. C. Mack and W. H. G. Armytage, *Thomas Hughes, the Life of the Author of Tom Brown's Schooldays* (London, 1952).
9   See A. Briggs, *Victorian People* (Middlesex, 1982, reprint), ch. 7, 'Robert Applegarth and the trade unions', pp. 184–99.
10 F. M. Leventhal, 'George Howell 1833–1910. A career in radical politics', Ph.D. Thesis, Harvard (1967).

ence or intimidation by trade unionists should be dealt with by the general criminal law.[11]

Bruce's legislation of 1871 was designed specifically to deal with the legal status of trade unions; the wider working-class grievance against the Masters and Servants Act was left to one side. In the post-1871 period the trade union leaders linked their specific trade union grievances against the CLA Act with the reform of the law governing contracts between employers and workmen. Again, the theme of their criticism was the discriminatory nature of the law which was seen to favour employers, particularly with regard to the penalties for breach of contract. The amending legislation of 1867 had gone some way towards meeting their criticism by making both masters and men subject to the same legal process and penalties, and by drawing a distinction between 'civil' and 'criminal' breaches of contract. However, in practice, the law still fell heavily on the side of employers. The levying of fines in 'civil cases' and the retention of the penalty of imprisonment in 'aggravated cases' was seen as an excessive punishment which bore disproportionately upon workmen, for very few employers were convicted for unfair dismissal.[12]

These separate grievances all came to a head during the celebrated 'Gas Stokers' case of December 1872.[13] During the course of the strike at the Beckton gas works in late 1872 all 500 gas stokers were summoned before magistrates, and 24 were imprisoned for six weeks with hard labour for 'aggravated' breach of contract, under the Masters and Servants Act. Six ringleaders of the strike were subsequently imprisoned for one year upon the charge of conspiracy to organise this aggravated breach of contract (the maximum penalty laid down by the 1867 act for aggravated breach of contract was three months). The leaders of the strike were indicted, though acquitted by the jury, on a second charge of conspiracy – namely, by threats and obstruction to force the company against its will to alter its

---

[11] 'Mr Lowe and the trade unions'. Report of delegation to Home Secretary . *The Bee Hive*, 6 Nov. 1873, p. 5. See also the Memorial of the Parliamentary Committee of the TUC to the subsequent Tory Home Secretary, R. A. Cross. *The Bee Hive*, 1 May 1875, p. 10.

[12] Regarding the masters and servants act, see D. Simon, 'Master and servant', in J. Saville, *Democracy and the Labour Movement, Essays in honour of Dona Torr*, (London, 1954), pp. 160–200. Also C. J. Kaufman, 'Lord Elcho, trade unions and democracy', in K. D. Brown (ed.), *Essays in Anti-Labour History* (London, 1974), pp. 183–207. See also, Return of persons convicted and imprisoned under the Masters and Servants Act, 1867; distinguishing between employers and employed (under section 14 of the act dealing with aggravated cases) 1. 1868–72; PP, 1873. vol LIV, pp. 229–35, 2. 1873–4; PP, 1874, vol. LIV, pp. 395– . See, 'Mr Lowe and the Trade Unions', *The Bee Hive*, 6 Nov. 1873, p. 5; Memorial to the Conservative Home Secretary, R. A. Cross in *The Bee Hive*, 1 May 1875, pp. 12–13.

[13] The gas stokers' dispute and the subsequent legal proceedings were given comprehensive coverage by *The Times*. See the following reports; 4 Dec. 1872, p. 5. col. c; 10 Dec. 1872, p. 11 col. a; 11 Dec. 1872, p. 8 col. f; 20 Dec. 1872, p. 11 col. a; 21 Dec. 1872, p. 5 col. b.

mode of business (by the forced reinstatement of a dismissed colleague). In his ruling to the jury, the presiding judge, Justice Brett, stated that such a conspiracy was not

held to be an offence on the grounds that it was in 'restraint of trade', within the meaning of the proviso in the Criminal Law Amendment Act. It was an offence on the grounds that it was an intentional attempt to interfere with another man's freedom by threats or obstruction, which is as much an offence when practised by Servants against Masters as when it happened between any other persons.[14]

The successful use of the Masters and Servants Act and the law of conspiracy in a trade dispute was seen as outflanking the whole basis of the 1871 Trade Union Act. Moreover Justice Brett's ruling that the organisation of a withdrawal of labour could in itself be regarded as an unlawful conspiracy undermined the very legality of 'combination' recognised by the 1871 legislation.

As a result of this sudden and dramatic threat to the legality of strike action the Trade Union Congress at Leeds in January 1873 endorsed a threefold reform of the law including abolition of imprisonment for breach of contract, specific legal immunity for trade unions from prosecution under the law of conspiracy and repeal of the special CLA Act.[15] During the course of 1873 a series of public demonstrations was organised at which the reform of the labour laws was established as a test question for candidates in the forthcoming general election. This 'pressure from without' reached its peak in the late summer with a mass meeting of trade unionists at Edinburgh.[16]

Given the prevailing interpretation of mid to late nineteenth-century trade unionism as cautious – driven by middle-class notions of respectability[17] – it should be pointed out that the trade unionists' grievances against the labour laws and the judicial system which enforced them, fuelled a general distrust of the legal system which was interpreted in classical early-nineteenth-century radical terms as oppressive,

[14] *The Times*, trial report, 20 Dec. 1872, p. 11 col. a-; see also Justice Brett's report to the Home Secretary on the trial, 25 Jan. 1873, HO 45/9326/18243/24, and Lushington's (Home Office Legal Counsel) memorandum on Justice Brett's ruling. 4 Feb. 1873. HO 45/9362/18243/30.

[15] See Henry Crompton's programme of legal reforms outlined at the Leeds conference of the TUC *The Bee Hive*, 18 January 1873, pp. 7–10.

[16] *The Times*, report on Edinburgh meeting, 15 Aug. 1875, p. 4, col. d; see also report on Blackburn meeting, 18 Aug. 1873, p. 10, col. d and reports on meetings of the London Trades Council, 11 Sept. 1873, p. 10 col. d and 9 Dec. 1873, p. 10 col. e.

[17] For example, S and B Webb, *The History of Trade Unionism* (London, 1920) pp. 239–40 and pp. 361–74; also Harrison, *Before the Socialists*, pp. 5–6, 17–19 and 133; G. Claeys, 'The triumph of class conscious reformism in British radicalism, 1790–1860'. *Historical Journal*, 5 (1983), pp. 969–85; and finally T. R. Tholfsen, *Working Class Radicalism in Mid-Victorian Britain* (London, 1976), pp. 9–13 and 124.

discriminatory and unjust. This general radical critique of the judiciary and the law illustrates an important strand of ideological continuity between the supposedly more radical early-nineteenth-century trade union movement, and the 'new model' craft unionism of the 1860s and 1870s.[18] This continuing radical critique of the judicial system was reflected in the campaigns by trade union leaders such as Henry Broadhurst, during the 1870s and thereafter, for the diversification of the social composition of the magistrates' bench, removal of the property qualification for jury attendance, as well as general codification of the criminal law.[19] This continuity in working-class radical politics does, however, need to be qualified. For whereas the Chartists in particular believed that it was impossible to bring about desired reforms (say, of the law and the judiciary) without fundamental constitutional and political reform, the later campaign for the reform of the labour laws, and Broadhurst's wider programme of legal reform, were based on the assumption that specific reforms could be accomplished through the contemporary political structure of government. This is partly explained by the achievement of instalments of the Charter – most notably, the extension of the borough franchise in 1867 and the secret ballot in 1871. At the level of political strategy the campaign for the reform of the labour laws therefore revealed a discontinuity with radical working-class politics during the Chartist period; a discontinuity which implied a less alienated and more optimistic outlook regarding the responsiveness of contemporary political institutions. This political outlook was reflected in the commitment of both the 'junta' and the Parliamentary Committee which succeeded it, to the strategy of alliance with the 'advanced wing' of the Liberal party, and as such was the forerunner of 'Lib.–Labism.'. The emphasis on parliamentary politics, on working through the established political system, was a central feature of the labour laws reform agitation; it was the *lobby* of the House of Commons which became the trade union leaders' primary theatre of operations.[20]

The cornerstone of the trade union argument for the reform of the labour laws was the assertion of the right of equal treatment under the law for both masters and men. This emphasis on the importance of law and

[18] See H. Pelling, *Popular Politics and Society in Late Victorian Britain* (London, 1979, 2nd edn), ch. 4, 'Trade unions, workers and the law', pp. 62–81.

[19] The Broadhurst Papers, British Library of Political and Economic Science, vol. 1 (Correspondence 1873–82). Correspondence with J. F. Stephen on the Codification of the Criminal Law, Oct. 1876, f8–10; Jan. 1877, f15–20, TUC resolution in favour of Codification, f21. See also correspondence between Lord Coleridge and Broadhurst, 23 Apr. 1877, concerning a delegation on the jury laws, f22.

[20] McCready, 'Britain's labour lobby, 1867–75'. The exception to the general Lib.–Lab. position of the trade union leadership was Alexander McDonald; see Kaufman, 'Lord Elcho'.

the principle of legal justice (rather than a class analysis based on social and economic causes) was of crucial importance to the trade union campaign. Politically, it enabled the trade unions to muster a broad-based coalition of supporters, both at Westminster and among political journalists and intellectuals in the country at large. The trade unions and their 'advanced Liberal' allies in parliament effectively highjacked the Whig/ Liberal creed of 'civil equality before the law', deploying it on behalf of trade unionists and workmen in general as a discriminated grouping. Philosophically, this was an argument which the liberal establishment, in both its 'Whig' and 'Liberal–Conservative' variants, could not ultimately ignore.

In the aftermath of the 1871 legislation, support for the trade union demands in parliament therefore stemmed from three interconnected groups: first, the semi-independent 'Radicals', who constituted the core of the advanced wing of the Liberal party; second, a group of progressive Liberal industrialists who espoused a more pragmatic 'advanced Liberalism'; and third, a small number of 'young Whigs' or career minded moderate Liberals.

The Radicals – for example, Sir Charles Dilke and Henry Fawcett, P. A. Taylor and R. M. Carter, P. Rylands and latterly Edward Jenkins, Joseph Cowen and Joseph Chamberlain – supported trade union rights as part of a general platform of political emancipation and the removal of unjust and discriminatory laws. The labour laws agitation fitted neatly into the general radical critique of an unrepresentative parliament legislating for the benefit of narrow vested interests. Thus, in a pamphlet published in 1874 and inscribed by the author 'to the Radical Party and the workmen of Great Britain ... for the election of 1874' Edward Jenkins castigated the CLA Act as 'a gross instance of special legislation aimed at and effecting in almost all its particulars only one portion of the community.'[21] Joseph Chamberlain criticised the labour laws on similar grounds in a series of articles for the *Fortnightly Review*.[22] However, the Radicals, despite their sympathy for and attachment to the trade union case for legal equality, did not provide the parliamentary leadership of the campaign.

Prior to 1871 the most prominent parliamentary spokesman had been the idiosyncratic 'advanced Liberal' Thomas Hughes, whose defence of the legal rights of trade unionism stemmed from his association with Christian socialism and concommitant involvement with the Co-operative

---

[21] *Glances at Inner England. A lecture delivered in the United States and Canada, By E. Jenkins MP* (London, 1874), p. 32.
[22] J. Chamberlain, 'The Liberal Party and its leaders', *The Fortnightly Review*, 1 Sept. 1873, pp. 287–302.

movement. Hughes viewed trade unionism as an adjunct to the Co-operative movement; at most, as a step towards the Co-operative millennium. A threat to trade unionism was therefore a threat to the ultimate success of Co-operation. After the 1871 Trade Union Act Hughes became gradually detached from the trade unions. Their legal position was, he considered, now secure. Moreover Hughes became disenchanted with the demand for outright repeal of the CLA Act.[23] His acceptance of a seat on Disraeli's royal commission of 1874, set up to consider possible reforms of the labour laws, was seen by the union leaders as an act of open betrayal.

The parliamentary leadership of the labour laws reform campaign in the post-1871 period continued to come from within this second grouping of 'advanced' or 'Gladstonian' Liberals, many of whom were now industrialists who had been elected for the newly enfranchised northern provincial boroughs in 1868; men such as Sir Thomas Brassey, Samuel Morley, William Rathbone, the Bass Brothers, J. Hinde Palmer, J. J. Colman, Samuel Plimsoll, and, in particular, A. J. Mundella.

The 'advanced Liberal' manufacturers[24] were wholehearted in their endorsement of the aims and objectives of the 'new model' craft unions and the trade union leadership of Applegarth, Howell and Broadhurst. This positive attitude was exemplified by A. J. Mundella who, after his election for Sheffield in 1868, became the parliamentary spokesman for the London based trade union leaders. Mundella expressed the wider social vision of the Liberal manufacturers and their awareness of the growing threat of social conflict between capital and labour. He stressed economic interdependence and preached the gospel of industrial arbitration as a mechanism to by-pass industrial disputes and institutionalise the relationship between employers and trade unions.[25]

Because of the politically damaging image of trade unionism evoked by the 'Sheffield outrages', Mundella, as the champion of industrial arbitration, was the ideal candidate for Robert Applegarth to approach on behalf of the Sheffield trades council for the election of 1868. His selection

[23] Hughes to Mundella, January 1872, quoted in Mack and Armytage, *Thomas Hughes*, p. 197.

[24] The political involvement of this group with the grievances of the labouring classes was extraordinary; for example, Samuel Morley, the Nottingham textiles magnate, who in 1872 became a member of the 'Consulting Committee' of Joseph Arch's agricultural labourers' union, E. Hodder, *The Life of Samuel Morley* (London, 1887, 2nd edn), pp. 354–61; consider also the brewer and MP for Derby, M. T. Bass, who was the chief patron and parliamentary spokesman for the Amalgamated Society of Railway Servants, G. W. Alcock, *Fifty Years of Railway Trades Unionism* (London, 1922), pp. 31–2, 37, 42, 51 and 85; finally, Samuel Plimsoll, the coal merchant and fellow MP for Derby who led the campaign to secure better safety regulations for merchant seamen. See D. Masters, *The Plimsoll Mark* (London, 1955). See also S. Plimsoll, MP, *Our Seamen. An Appeal* (1873).

[25] Speeches in Sheffield by Mundella on arbitration reported in the *Sheffield Independent*. 23 Sept. 1868, p. 3, and 22 Oct. 1867, p. 3.

represented a direct attempt by Applegarth to present a new public image of trade unionism – law abiding, peaceful and conciliatory.[26]

Mundella's support for trade unionism was wholehearted. His justification of the right of 'combination' in accordance with the canons of political economy – declaring, in 1868: 'Combination was the only way, in the absence of positive laws to place the workmen on an equality with the masters'[27] – mirrored in full the intellectual defence of trade unionism articulated by its own leaders.[28] Mundella asserted the positive and moral value of 'combination' which he interpreted as a virtuous example of political education and collective self-help.[29] His acceptance of a high-waged and 'organised' labour force[30] was complemented by a commitment to state education, in particular to the extension of technical education. Mundella's support for trade unions and industrial arbitration, factory legislation and education reform therefore constituted a wide ranging and coherent programme aimed at the improvement of the condition of the labouring classes.

In the election of 1868 Mundella appealed to the Sheffield electorate 'as a working man's candidate ... to send a man to Parliament who knew something about working men'.[31] Between 1868 and 1874 he was an indispensable representative of the labour movement, working hand in hand with the trade union leaders, first Robert Applegarth, and then later George Howell. In 1869 Mundella sponsored, with Thomas Hughes, the original trade union bill drafted by Crompton, Lushington and Harrison.[32] In 1871 he played an important role in the passage of Bruce's Trade Union Act; advocating the separation from the bill of the contentious third clause dealing with violence and intimidation – an important compromise which secured trade union support for the bill,[33] but which led to the separate CLA Act.

In 1872 Mundella secured George Howell's support for a policy of moderate opposition to the CLA Act, concentrating upon repeal of the

---

[26] On Applegarth's role in Mundella's nomination for Sheffield see A. W. Humphrey, *Robert Applegarth* (London, 1913), pp. 34, 63–9. Also, Applegarth to Mundella, November 1868, Mundella papers, Sheffield University library, 6P/1/9/1–iii.

[27] 'Mr Mundella on Capital and Labour', The *Sheffield Independent*, 5 Nov. 1868.

[28] On this point see E. F. Biagini, 'British trade unions and popular political economy'. *The Historical Journal*, 30, 4 (1987) pp. 811–40.

[29] 'Mr Mundella on capital and labour', *Sheffield Independent*, 5 Nov. 1868.

[30] *Ibid.*

[31] Mundella's speech at Attercliffe. The *Sheffield Independent*, 19 Sept. 1868, p. 8. See also M. Higginbotham. 'A. J. Mundella and the Sheffield election of 1868'. *Trans. of the Hunter Archaeological Society*, 5 (1939), pp. 285–93.

[32] See Armytage, *A. J. Mundella*, pp. 67–72.

[33] Mundella to R. Leader, editor of the *Sheffield Independent*, 11 Mar. 1871. Mundella–Leader correspondence; Sheffield University Library, 6P/58/9.

Lords' amendments[34] to the molestation clause rather than the act in its entirety. Following the failure of this stratagem[35] and the outrage generated within the trade union movement against the imprisonment of the gas stokers in December 1872, he fell in line behind the policy adopted by the 1873 Trades Union Congress – total repeal of the CLA Act, reform of the law of conspiracy and of the Masters and Servants Act.[36] In 1873 Mundella successfully pressed for a remission of the gas stoker's sentences.[37]

As a large and successful employer himself, Mundella's position on the repeal of the CLA Act was finely judged. Speaking before an audience of employers at the Sheffield chamber of commerce in January 1874, Mundella fully acknowledged the duty of parliament to protect, in equal manner, the non-unionist in the free sale of his labour, and the unionist in his right to combine. However, Mundella denounced the statutory instrument, the CLA Act, as so 'partial in its operation' and 'so confused in its definition that it was made applicable to cases to which it ought not to apply'. Ultimately the 'question of Capital and Labour' could not be resolved by 'repressive laws . . . They must lean upon something better . . . at any rate they must mete out to them just laws.'[38]

At the core of Mundella's outlook was the notion that the labour laws as they stood – one-sided and discriminatory – were the root cause of hostility between capital and labour; jeopardising the benevolent influences of education, industrial arbitration and good will. This concentration upon the legal grievances of labour, instead of an analysis based on structural economic inequalities, was perhaps the most important ideological element underpinning the alliance of trade unions and the 'advanced Liberal' manufacturers.

The third element of support within the parliamentary Liberal party came from two young and politically ambitious lawyers, Vernon Harcourt and Henry James, both of whom were to become front bench politicians of the moderate or 'Whig' centre. However, during the early 1870s both Harcourt and to a lesser extent, James, identified themselves, on certain well-chosen issues, with the advanced wing of the party. Harcourt's and James' association with the labour laws campaign reflected the trade union leaders' willingness to couch their demands in terms sensitive to the

---

34 Mundella to Leader, 18 Jan. 1872. Mundella papers, P/62/6.
35 Armytage, *A. J. Mundella*, pp. 113–14. See also Mundella to R. Leader, 18 Jan. 1872, 6P/62/6. Mundella's Bill to amend the C.L.A. Act, removing Cairns' amendments, failed on second reading when Lord Elcho moved to adjourn the debate. *Hansard*, 3rd series, vol. 212, 5 June, 1872, pp. 459–60, 750, 752.
36 Mundella to Leader, 30 May 1873, Mundella papers, 6P/62/41.
37 Mundella to R. Leader, 30 Jan. 1873, Mundella papers, 6P/63/11.
38 The *Sheffield Independent*, 29 Jan. 1874, p. 3.

precepts of mainstream Liberalism; for, it should be emphasised, the overtly legal and constitutional framework within which the trade unionists' demands were articulated was indistinguishable from the language which guided Liberal attitudes regarding the proper basis and direction of reform.

In 1872 both Harcourt and James supported Mundella's unsuccessful bid to repeal the Lords' amendments to the CLA Act.[39] During the parliamentary session of 1873 Harcourt and James were the prime parliamentary movers for the reform of the law of conspiracy following the imprisonment of the gas stokers' leaders.

Harcourt's bill was designed to ensure that the 1871 legislation was not outflanked by Justice Brett's ruling that an agreement among workmen to strike could constitute an unlawful conspiracy. Harcourt proposed three guarantees: prosecutions for conspiracy involving labour disputes should be restricted to existing statutory offences such as intimidation and coercion; the penalties for conspiracy in such cases should be limited to the penalty for the principal offence – thereby meeting the trade union grievance that the gas stokers had been imprisoned for twelve months whereas the maximum sentence under the CLA Act was three months; and finally Harcourt proposed the specific exemption of trade unionists from prosecution under the law of conspiracy solely by reason of their being members of a trade organisation.[40] This met the trade union demands in full.

In the House of Commons Harcourt defended the exceptional nature of his bill on the grounds that there was an exceptional grievance, and declared: 'If parliament was to keep faith with the working classes in respect of the pledges it had given to secure the freedom of labour, it was bound to protect it against the practical suppression of its will by this sort of judge made law.'[41] In such a manner did the trade union critique of 'judge made' anti-union law march hand in hand with Harcourt's essentially 'Whig' espousal of the primacy of parliament as a law-making body.

During the session of 1873 Harcourt also raised a discussion on the Masters and Servants Act. He fully endorsed the trade union grievance with the law governing contracts between labour and capital, particularly with regard to the gas stokers' case where the law of conspiracy had been applied to breach of contract. By making breach of contract a purely civil and not a criminal matter the law of conspiracy would not apply. Harcourt also accepted in full their more general criticism, asserting:

[39] *Hansard*, 3rd series, vol. 212, p. 750, 5 June 1872.
[40] See Harcourt's explanation of the bill on second reading, *Hansard*, 3rd series, vol. 216, pp. 1889–90, 7 July 1873.
[41] *Hansard*, 3rd series, vol. 217, p. 1535. 4 Aug. 1873.

'They took one class of contracts out of the whole category – contracts which affected alone one class of individuals, and they enforced their observance by the penalty of imprisonment.'[42] He contended that either all contracts should ultimately be enforced by such a penalty or none. This was the classic Liberal, and for that matter Whig, position of civil equality before the law. Harcourt, like Mundella, argued that 'coercive' legislation would not solve the difficult problems between capital and labour. The role of the legislature was to secure equal treatment under the law; but ultimately: 'the solution to these problems could be found only in absolute freedom ... freedom between master and men'.[43] Harcourt had effectively hitched the 'rights of labour' to the grand theme of nineteenth-century liberalism – civil and legal emancipation. The campaign had become a test case of the Liberal administration's ability to put liberal principles into action.

III

Historians have, in general, neglected or misinterpreted the response of the Liberal administration to the labour laws agitation in the post-1871 period. As Colin Matthew has pointed out, between 1871 and 1873 there was in fact a transformation in the position of the government, from a belief that the legislation of 1871 represented a general settlement of the question, to a recognition of the case for further wholesale reform.

The architect of the 1871 legislation was the Home Secretary, H. A. Bruce. The penal clauses of the CLA Act relating to 'molestation' had been made more stringent by the Tory peers led by Lord Cairns. Bruce had attempted to throw out the Cairns' amendments, and to reintroduce the test of numbers to be applied to the definition of 'watching and besetting'. Bruce argued that Cairns' redefinition of molestation would prevent 'peaceful persuasion' and 'the seeking of legitimate information', but was defeated by a sizeable majority in the House of Commons.[44] He had then retreated to a defence of the status quo. In November 1872, armed with the experience of the operation of the act at Bolton and Newcastle where there had been long strikes, Bruce informed Gladstone:

---

[42] *Hansard*, 3rd series, vol. 216, p. 580. 6 June 1873.
[43] *Ibid.*, p. 583.
[44] *Hansard*, 3rd series, vol. 207, p. 282, 19 June 1871. Mundella noted 'The employers in the House went over to the Tories making it penal for one man in the street to watch a building or workshop ... Forster kept the Government right and remarked to me that the masters in the House were "A pack of fools".' Mundella to Leader, 20 June 1871, Mundella papers, 6P/58/24.

'except in the Bolton case where the justices and not the act, had been at fault, there seems to have been no decision to which any reasonable man could object'.[45]

When Mundella and Harcourt brought in their bill of 1872 repealing the Lords' amendments to the 'molestation' sub-clause, Bruce argued that the concession of a day would 'be a useless waste of time'. Mundella's attempt at modification of the CLA Act, which the Parliamentary Committee of the Trade Union Congress were then prepared to countenance, was left in abeyance. To Gladstone Bruce wrote that out of the hundred or so decisions made under the act, a small number were open to objection, on the grounds that the punishments were not wrong but excessive.[46] This Bruce described as 'a necessary consequence of discretion, which is just as common with judges as with justices'. It was precisely this anti-union bias which the union leaders wished to counteract by a narrower definition of intimidation and molestation. Bruce was on firmer ground when he added that the Commons supported the Lords' amendments by a large majority, arguing that the Commons would not reverse that decision, nor the Lords, on such short experience of its working.

Following the conviction of the gas stokers in December 1872, Bruce's position became more flexible, particularly on the law of conspiracy, though during the parliamentary session of 1873 he still discounted further alterations of the CLA Act or the Masters and Servants Act. When the cabinet met in January 1873 the gas stokers' sentence was the second item on the agenda.[47] Earlier in December Bruce had requested the opinion of the law officers, Sir James Coleridge and Sir George Jessel, on the gas stokers' case, covering all aspects of the law.[48]

In their report to the Home Secretary, delivered in February 1873, the law officers provided an important though limited push in the direction of reform;[49] legislation would be necessary to prevent Justice Brett's ruling, that there was a common law offence of interfering with the free will of an employer from overturning the intention of clause 2 of the 1871 Trade Union Act. The law officers added that the chief evil with the law of conspiracy was 'its obscurity in reference to questions that occur between employers and employed, and that if its vagueness and obscurity were put an end to in reference to these questions, the most pressing necessity for the amendment of this part of the criminal law would cease'. On the

[45] Bruce to Gladstone, 21 Nov. 1871. BL Add MS 44087, f34.
[46] Bruce to Gladstone, 14 July 1872. BL Add MS 44087, f52–.
[47] Gladstone papers, minutes of cabinet meeting; 22 Jan. 1873. BL Add MS 44641, f2.
[48] Memoranda from Bruce to the law officers; December 1872. PRO HO 45/9326/18243/30a.
[49] Legal officer's opinion, 7 Feb. 1873. HO 45/9326/18243/30a.

Masters and Servants Act, Coleridge and Jessel left the matter in Bruce's hands, stating that it 'was a question of policy only'.

The immediate question for Bruce and the cabinet, at the start of 1873, was the twelve months imprisonment of the gas stokers, which in effect overturned the maximum sentence of three months laid down in the legislation of 1871. Following a memorial from the presiding judge, Justice Brett, defending the legal sanctity of the sentence but suggesting that the Home Secretary was in a position to consider 'mitigating circumstances',[50] and a memorial from the imprisoned stokers, organised by Mundella, expressing their sorrow at having, as they put it, 'unintentionally' broken the law,[51] the prisoners were released after four months of their sentence.

In the House of Commons, Bruce lent the weight of the front bench to Harcourt's conspiracy bill, but not without reservation. To Gladstone, Bruce wrote, 'the law of conspiracy may be improved, possibly during this session, so as to remove the main grievance of the workmen. But the question is difficult and requires careful treatment.'[52] On the second reading Bruce declared that the government had no objection 'to fixing more definitely . . . the punishment applicable to offences of this nature',[53] thereby removing the trade unionists' grievance against the severity of the sentences passed on the gas stokers. During the committee stage, control of the bill was taken out of Harcourt's hands, as the government introduced a series of amendments which transformed the character of the bill, making it one dealing more generally with the law of conspiracy.[54] This was fatal to the success of the bill so late in the session. In the House of Lords, the Tory peer, Lord Cairns, again pressed amendments which proved unacceptable to both Harcourt and the government.[55] As a result the bill was dropped. In the meantime, Bruce gave a rather vague promise that the government would reconsider the whole question during the recess.[56]

[50] Report of Mr Justice Brett in favour of a mitigation of sentence. 25 Jan. 1873. HO 45/ 9326/18243/24. See also Lushington's memorandum on Justice Brett's ruling. 4 Feb. 1873, HO 45/9362/18243/30.
[51] Memorial from the gas stokers, presented by Mundella. Jan. 1873, HO 45/9326/18243/28.
[52] Bruce to Gladstone, 6 July 1873. BL Add MS 44087, f92.
[53] *Hansard*, 3rd series, vol. 216, 7 July 1873, p. 1890.
[54] As amended the bill specified a schedule of more general common law offences to which the law of conspiracy would henceforth apply: affray, common assault etc. PP, 1873, vol. 1, p. 221.
[55] Cairns accepted the anomaly in the sentence of the gas stokers, between the conviction for conspiracy and the original breach of contract. However Cairns rejected the amended bill, arguing that the schedule of common law offences to which the law of conspiracy was to apply, was too restrictive. *Hansard*, 3rd series, vol. 217, 1 Aug. 1873, pp. 1419–21.
[56] *Hansard*, 3rd series, vol. 217, 4 Aug. 1873, p. 1541.

The parliamentary campaign would seem to have faltered, however the close of the parliamentary session was in fact a turning point; the whole question was transformed by events of a wider political nature. During the late summer of 1873 Gladstone turned towards the forthcoming election and the need to resurrect the political popularity of the party in the country. A ministerial reshuffle was part of this process. The subsequent change of personnel shifted the whole position of the government towards the reform of the labour laws. The replacement of Bruce by Robert Lowe at the Home Office was perhaps the most important factor. The return of Bright to the cabinet, and the appointment of Harcourt and James as law officers, strengthened the position of established supporters of further reform within the government, such as Forster and Stansfeld.

By their acceptance of non-political offices Harcourt and James disqualified themselves from an independent parliamentary role. Nevertheless in August Harcourt corresponded with Bright, urging him, on his return to the cabinet, to 'get the government to address itself to the grievances of the criminal law amendment act, the masters and servants act and the conspiracy laws', adding, 'they are the sort of things the mass of people do care about and which have been strangely neglected'.[57] In September Bright privately expressed his anxiety to Gladstone 'about the laws affecting the condition of the working men'; a view which Gladstone passed on to Lowe, suggesting that Bright, Bruce (now Lord Aberdare) and Lowe communicate on the matter and present their views to the cabinet.[58] At the end of August, on his appointment to the Home Office, Lowe had written independently to Gladstone on the matter. Drawing attention to a recent trades' demonstration in Edinburgh, Lowe proposed careful inquiry to see 'if we cannot make some concession', particularly with regard to labour contracts.[59]

Thus it can be seen that Gladstone's new cabinet added a sense of urgency to the whole question. Picking up this concern, Gladstone replied to Lowe, noting the resolutions passed at the Edinburgh meeting and concluding rather ominously; 'For my part I have no fear of the labouring classes ... except the fear of being embarked against them in a bad cause.'[60] Lowe, unleashed from the burdens of the exchequer, set his mind to consider the legal complexities of the labour laws in general. The result

[57] Harcourt to Bright, 8 Aug. 1873. Bright MS BL Add. MS 43388, f5–12.
[58] Gladstone to Lowe, 27 Sept. 1873, BL Add. MS 44542, f189. Quoted in H. C. G. Matthew (ed.), *The Gladstone Diaries, 1871–74*, vol. 8 (Oxford, 1982), p. 394.
[59] Lowe to Gladstone, 29 Aug. 1873, BL Add. MS 44302, f151.
[60] Gladstone to Lowe, 3 Sept. 1873, BL Add. MS 445542, f170. Quoted in Matthew, *The Gladstone Diaries, 1871–4*, p. 382.

of Lowe's endeavours was a memorandum to the cabinet in late October 1873.[61]

It is clear that Lowe's prime concern was the question of legal principle, and on these grounds the demands of the trade unionists were broadly endorsed. With regard to the law of conspiracy, Lowe repudiated Harcourt's bill, simply because it made trade unionists a special case, and proposed instead a general reform of the law of conspiracy which would abolish the class of conspiracies to commit minor offences, punishable by summary jurisdiction before magistrates. Lowe concluded, 'by this means we should much improve the general law and get rid of a cause of irritation and discontent among the working classes, which I, at least admit to be just.'

With regard to the 1867 Masters and Servants Act, Lowe was particularly critical of the retention of the power of imprisonment. If breach of contract was made penal for workmen, Lowe argued, 'You must extend it to all contractors, a conclusion for which I think, we are hardly prepared.' He called for the repeal of the act, and the transfer of jurisdiction to county courts:

It would be very impolitic now that attention has been drawn to this act, to enter into a contest with the working classes in a matter in which they appear to be so entirely right. I hold that there is no sound distinction between contracts to buy and sell labour and contracts to sell any other commodity, and the sooner this absolute equality between all persons contracting irrespective of the subject matter of the contract, is recognised, the better.

With regard to the CLA Act Lowe distanced himself from the objections of the trade unions, arguing that parliament was bound to protect workmen and their masters from 'the tyranny of the majority'. 'But this act', Lowe continued, 'is limited to the tyranny of working men and masters ... This is class legislation ... I would suggest that the law be made general.' Lowe concluded that such a change would be well received, even though the same powers were retained, on the grounds that 'the working classes are very reasonably jealous of legislation pointed only at them'.

Lowe's memorandum marked a wide ranging concession to the arguments put forward by the trade unions and their parliamentary allies. Neither a Whig nor a Radical, Lowe's position within the Liberal party was unique. His memorandum reflected a commitment to rational utilitar-

---

[61] Memorandum by Mr Lowe, 31 Oct. 1873. Printed for the cabinet, 7 Nov. 1873. Gladstone papers, BL Add. MS 44621, f130. Referred to in Matthew, *The Gladstone Diaries, 1871–74*, pp. 417–18.

ian government based upon equal treatment under the law, conceived in the long-term interest of the propertied middle classes.[62]

Lowe's proposals received general acceptance by the cabinet on 26 November, two changes being made at the behest of the Lord Chancellor, Lord Selborne. Firstly, conspiracies to commit minor offences would not be abolished as Lowe recommended, but would continue to be dealt with by summary jurisdiction, though the penalty would not exceed that for the principal offence. Secondly, the power of imprisonment was to be retained in certain cases where wilful breach of contract would have a direct tendency to endanger life or property, such as the public utilities.[63] Thus it should be noted that, although the gas stokers' case had prompted a general reevaluation of the labour laws, their position as employees of public utilities was still to be hedged by legal restrictions. On 27 November the Home Office instructed the parliamentary counsel to draft a bill, 'dealing with certain points relating to conspiracy, the masters and servants act and the criminal law amendment act'.[64] When the cabinet met on 1 December, it was affirmed that 'Lowe's Conspiracy Bill' would be made ready for the next session of parliament.[65]

During the autumn and winter of 1873–4 it became quite common knowledge within the circle of trade union leaders, and their supporters at Westminster, that the government was considering further wholesale changes in the law. At Bingley Hall, in Birmingham on 22 October, in a speech widely regarded as setting out the future Liberal programme, Bright declared that with regard to the labour laws 'alteration may be made which would be just to all classes of the community and will be satisfactory to all reasonable and thoughtful men among the working classes'.[66] On 6 November *The Bee Hive* published a report of a meeting between Lowe and a delegation of trade unionists, including George Odger, Alexander McDonald and George Howell accompanied by the parliamentarians, Mundella, Hughes, Hinde Palmer and Wedderburn. Lowe made it fairly plain that he was contemplating further reform, assuring the delegation that 'this subject has engaged my very serious attention, and the subjects brought before me are very well worth the consideration of the government'.[67] Both Joseph Cowen, at a public

---

[62] See J. Winter, *Robert Lowe* (Toronto, 1976), pp. 300–6.

[63] Lord Selborne's amendments were framed as an appendix to Lowe's memorandum of 31 Oct. 1873; quoted above. For the cabinet discussion of Lowe's proposals on 26 Nov. see Matthew, *The Gladstone Diaries, 1871–4*, p. 417.

[64] Liddell, Secretary to the Home office, to the Secretary to the Treasury, 29 Nov. 1873, PRO HO 34/33. Letter books, 1873–4, p. 307.

[65] Mintues of cabinet meeting on 1 Dec. 1873. Matthew, *The Gladstone Diaries, 1871–4*, p. 419.

[66] Printed in T. Rogers (ed.) *Public Addresses of John Bright* (London, 1879).

[67] *The Bee Hive*, 6 Nov. 1873, 'Mr Lowe and the trade unions', p. 5.

meeting at Newcastle in late December, and A. J. Mundella, at the TUC's conference in the following January, gave much weight to the meeting with Lowe, stressing the certainty of legislation in the coming session.[68]

However, this was not to be. Gladstone called a snap election and the central theme of his campaign, as Eugenio Biagini has pointed out in ch. 7, was fiscal reform. The labour laws were merely earmarked as a subject requiring the attention of the new parliament.[69] It was left to the Radicals and 'advanced Liberals' to flesh out and make bold the Liberal party's actual intentions. However Gladstone's decision not to make the labour laws a national question left the trade unions' parliamentary supporters on the Liberal benches isolated and floundering.

The Liberal party actually polled more votes than the Conservatives in the 1874 election – 756,000 to 690,000 – but the Conservatives ended with a comfortable and secure majority of seats. Perhaps one of the most striking turn arounds was in the English boroughs, where the Liberals lost 54 seats.[70] In the north east the Liberals retained their electoral predominance: there the labour movement was strong and well organised, and Thomas Burt's election for Morpeth testified to the political cohesiveness of the mining communities. In such a heavily unionised region, it can be argued, the labour laws question was less significant than in other areas where the unions were weaker, more dependent on statutory legal protection and often inclined to voice their discontent against sitting Liberals. This seems to have been the case particularly in Yorkshire and Lancashire where Conservative candidates took up the labour laws question to defeat sitting Liberals; Frederic Harrison, the Positivist ally of the trade unions, informed John Morley that in those regions the Conservative candidates represented 'the working men's causes', even 'criminal law amendment act abolition'.[71]

Tory peers, led by the incoming Lord Chancellor, Lord Cairns, had consistently opposed concessions to the trade unions between 1871–3. Moreover, Disraeli, in his election address, offered no specific pledges on the question. Yet at the level of individual borough contests, Conservative candidates were more willing to compete for working-class votes. This was typified by R. W. Callender, the successful Tory candidate at Manchester,

---

[68] See *Speeches of Joseph Cowen on Public Questions* (Newcastle, 1874), pp. 19–20; speech on 30 Dec. 1873. Mundella's address to the Sheffield Congress, reported in the *Sheffield Independent*, 14 Jan. 1874, p. 3.
[69] The Manchester Guardian, 24 Jan. 1874, p. 7, Gladstone's manifesto to the electors of Greenwich.
[70] See C. Cook and B. Keith, *British Historical Facts 1830–1900* (London, 1975), see p. 144; numbers of votes recorded, 1874–1900. See also pp. 140–1.
[71] Frederic Harrison to John Morley, 10 Feb. 1874; Library of Political and Economic Science, Harrison papers, 1/59, f37. Quoted in McCready, 'Britain's labour lobby', p. 156.

where the Radical, Jacob Bright, was defeated. After the election Callender wrote to Disraeli confirming Frederic Harrison's view that in Yorkshire and Lancashire the election had largely focused upon the nine-hours bill and the labour laws. 'On both points', Callender stated, 'every candidate for a borough constituency has had to promise compliance. My promise only being in accordance with views expressed long ago.'[72]

There is a need for a detailed study of individual constituency contests, to provide a more accurate picture of the impact of the labour laws question on the election of 1874. Nevertheless it is apparent that the failure of the outgoing Liberal administration to offer little more than general promises of reform, despite the existence of detailed legislative proposals, allowed Conservative borough candidates to compete effectively for working-class votes. The 1874 election was quick and sudden, little time was given for the trade unions to mount a campaign on the labour laws. Nevertheless the points of law involved were raised as 'test' questions for candidates, and many Tories as well as Liberals vowed support for some measure of reform. Moreover eleven 'Workmen's' candidates stood for election, often splitting the Liberal vote.[73] Two were elected, Alexander McDonald and Thomas Burt. Burt, like Howell and the other workmen's candidates, stood as an 'advanced Liberal'. McDonald, it must be stressed, did not share the general trade union commitment to 'Lib.–Labism.' and had previously been prepared to negotiate with notable Tory figures such as Lord Elcho.[74] All in all, when the new parliament met the labour laws question had emerged as an issue 'ripe' for settlement.

IV

The new Home Secretary, R. A. Cross, came into office with the materials already prepared for further reform of the labour laws. His immediate action, perhaps because of this, was to announce the setting up of a royal commission.[75] However the trade unions refused to co-operate. The Parliamentary Committee regarded the commission as a blocking device.

[72] R. W. Callender to Corry, Disraeli's Private Secretary; 16 Feb. 1874. Hughenden papers, B. XXI/C (11). Microfilm collection, Cambridge University Library. Of course religion and sectarian issues were a prominent factor in Lancashire politics, and Bright's defeat at Manchester requires further study.
[73] The labour laws question was an undoubted catalyst in the running of workmen's candidates; Labour Representation League Minute Book 1873–8, record of meetings during 1873–4. Library of Political and Economic Science, 'Archives; R (SR) 61'.
[74] See Kaufman 'Lord Elcho'.
[75] Smith, *Disraelian Conservatism and Social Reform*, pp. 214–15.

The new chairman, Henry Broadhurst, expressed the opinion that it was nothing more than an attempt 'to bamboozle the working men of the country.'[76] This distrust was further enhanced by the devious means by which Cross pressured Thomas Hughes and Alexander McDonald into sitting on the commission.[77]

However, there is no doubt that the trade unions and their parliamentary allies were caught off balance by the extent of Cross's proposals, when they were introduced at the start of the 1875 parliamentary session. The first of these measures, the Conspiracy and Protection of Property Bill, reaffirmed the legality of peaceful picketing by amending the law of conspiracy, which, henceforth, would not apply to trades disputes unless the action was itself criminal. However clause 4 of the bill stipulated that 'malicious' and 'wilful' breach of contract by workmen employed in the supply of gas or water was a criminal offence, liable before a court of summary jurisdiction to a fine of £20 or a maximum of three months imprisonment, with or without hard labour. Under clause 5, Cross retained the same penalties for breach of contract (in this instance 'by an employer or workman') involving wilful damage to property.

The second measure, the Employers and Workmen Bill, replaced the Masters and Servants Act. By this measure Cross limited the penalty for breach of contract to payment of civil damages. Moreover, in cases where damages claimed were in excess of £10, jurisdiction passed over to the county courts. However a maximum penalty of one month's imprisonment was retained as an ultimate power to enforce the court's authority. Cross proposed only slight alteration of the 1871 Criminal Law Amendment Act, establishing the right of trial by jury (recommended by the royal commission).[78]

Henry Crompton, the Positivist legal adviser to the Parliamentary Committee, informed George Howell that he thought very well of the proposals although this would not prevent criticism of 'the secondary and financial proposals'. Crompton concluded, 'It is a very important fact to note ... these bills do not re-enact the CLA Act. If they were to pass into law we can still keep up the demand for the repeal of the act.'[79] This was the line adopted by the Parliamentary Committee at a series of meetings, at which Mundella, Harrison and Crompton attended. On 24 June, a few days before the second reading of Cross's bills, the committee voted in

[76] Reported in *The Times*, 20 Jan. 1875, p. 10, col. a.
[77] Mundella to Leader, 21 Mar. 1875; quoted in Armytage, *A. J. Mundella*, p. 148–9.
[78] *The Times*, 23 Feb. 1875, p. 9, col. e. Report of royal commission.
[79] Henry Crompton to George Howell, 15 June 1875. Howell papers, on microfilm at Cambridge University Library (the Howell papers are held at the Bishopsgate Institute).

favour of supporting the legislation with a view to amendment during the committee stage.[80]

In the House of Commons, the dynamic of inter-party rivalry now emerged, with Lowe and Forster on the Liberal front bench, and Mundella acting as an unofficial Liberal Whip, pressing for further improvements to Cross's bills in line with the principles laid down in Lowe's memorandum of November 1873. On the second reading of the Employers and Workmen Bill, Lowe signalled the Liberal initiative.[81] They would give general support to the government's measure, yet look to improve the bill by relaxing the conditions under which workmen were liable to civil damages, and to remove the power of imprisonment for non-compliance with the court's order, thereby removing the last vestige of imprisonment for breach of contract. In the committee debate on the Conspiracy and Protection of Property Bill[82] Lowe urged the amendment of clauses 4 and 5, replacing the explicit references to 'workmen' with 'any person', thereby eradicating a move towards a new class of penalties aimed specifically at workmen. On the CLA Act Lowe announced the Liberal opposition's intention to repeal those aspects of the act already covered by the general law, and introduce a new clause on coercion and intimidation, not exclusively applicable to workmen.[83] Thus Lowe remained true to the principles laid down in the memorandum of October 1873.

During the brief parliamentary hiatus between the second reading and the committee stages of Cross's two bills the Liberal opposition regained the initiative. In late June a conference of trade unionists in Manchester voted for the outright repeal of the CLA Act, before a final settlement of the question could be achieved.[84] On 30 June *The Times* published Lowe's amendment to the 1871 Act, repealing section 1 and introducing a new clause to be incorporated in Cross's Conspiracy and Protection of Property Bill, which redefined coercion and intimidation in general terms.[85]

80 *The Times*, 25 June 1875, p. 12, col. b; See also Crompton's article in *The Bee Hive*, 26 June 1875, pp. 1–2.
81 *Hansard*, 3rd ser., vol. CCXXV, 28 June 1875, pp. 658–64.
82 See Lowe's speech on the conspiracy and protection of property bill, *Hansard*, 3rd series, vol. CCXXV, first night in committee, 28 June 1875, pp. 1341–2.
83 *Ibid.* 28 June 1875, pp. 662–4.
84 *The Times*, 28 June 1875, p. 7, col. f.
85 The text of Lowe's new clause ran; 'Any person who, with a view seriously to annoy or intimidate any person, persistently follows such a person about or hides any property owned or used by such a person, or deprives him, or hinders him in the use thereof, or watches or besets the place where such person resides ... or with one or more person follows such person in a disorderly manner through any street ... shall on summary conviction before two magistrates be imprisoned with or without hard labour, for a term not exceeding two months', *The Times*, 30 June 1875, p. 5, col. f.

That Lowe's initiative went far beyond what Cross had so far offered was quickly recognised. In a letter published in *The Times* on 1 July, Frederic Harrison urged the government to adopt Lowe's clause and grasp the opportunity presented for a final settlement of the question. Harrison concluded:

It may be asked ... why should the workmen be satisfied by a change which repeals the obnoxious section only to re-enact it in practically identical words? The answer, Sir, is simple, and in it lies the whole gist of the standing quarrel. The striking point of Mr Lowe's proposal is that it would turn special class law into general law applying to all persons in all occupations alike.[86]

At a full meeting of the Parliamentary Committee on 5 July, with Mundella, Crompton and Harrison in attendance, it was decided to support Lowe's new clause, 'as the recognition of a principle for which we have long contended, namely the abolition of special class legislation'.[87]

Whilst pressure was now mounting for Cross to repeal the CLA Act, the Home Secretary showed no outward sign of concession. Just prior to the committee stage Mundella and a delegation of trade unionists were informed by Cross that 'nothing would induce him to touch this act'.[88] Within the next day or so Cross reversed his whole position, repealing the 1871 CLA Act and signalling his acceptance of a general clause along the lines of Lowe's amendment. It would appear that Cross's volte-face was the consequence of events which transpired on the first night in the committee stage. Mundella's amendment on the Employers and Workmen Bill (removing the ultimate power of imprisonment on non-performance of the Court's order),[89] and Lowe's amendment of the Conspiracy and Protection of Property Bill (making general the penal sanctions for breach of contract by workmen employed by the public utilities)[90] reduced the government's majority to twenty and nineteen respectively.

This reduction of the government's support in the voting lobby forced Cross to bow to a series of minor amendments on the Employers and Workmen Bill. The most significant concession was the reduction of the maximum term of imprisonment for non-compliance with the court's

---

[86] *The Times*, 1 July 1875, p. 12, col. f.

[87] *The Times*, 6 July 1875, p. 5, col. d.

[88] See Mundella to Leader, 15 July 1875. Quoted in Armytage, *A. J. Mundella*, p. 151. However discussions between Cross and the law officers revealed that repeal of the Cairns amendments to the molestation sub-clauses of the 1871 CLA Act was under consideration, PRO HO 45/9384/45462. Law Officer's legal opinion, 2 July 1875.

[89] *Hansard*, 3rd series, vol. CCXXV, pp. 1331–40. 12 July 1875. Mundella's amendment allowed the defendant to raise one or more sureties subject, on non-performance, to repayment rather than imprisonment. The vote was 162 for, 182 against the amendment.

[90] Lowe's amendment replaced the words, 'where a workman is employed' with, 'where a person is legally bound and is able to perform his duty'. *Hansard*, 3rd series, vol. CCXXV, 12 July 1875, pp. 1341–51. The vote on Lowe's amendment was for: 108, against: 127.

order from one month to fourteen days.[91] Several amendments were also conceded on the Conspiracy and Protection of Property Bill. Following the closeness of the vote on Lowe's amendment, Cross accepted McDonald's request that clause 5, dealing with imprisonment for breach of contract resulting in damage to property, should be altered so as to apply 'to any person', enabling Cross to rebuff an attempt at outright repeal.[92]

These concessions were, in part, the result of Mundella's effectiveness in getting a high Liberal turn out, including a maximum turn out of the advanced section of the party, as well as the ex-Liberal front bench: Gladstone, Hartington, Lowe, Forster and Harcourt, and a sizeable cluster of moderate Liberals in their wake.[93] The Liberal amendments were undoubtedly aided by Conservative abstentions. Many Tory MPs had pledged themselves to reform of the labour laws in the recent elections.

In such a fluid climate of opinion, with Lowe's amendment on the CLA Act waiting to be brought in and the government's majority falling, Cross went down to the lobby of the House of Commons to discuss the position with George Howell. According to Howell, Cross informed him that he could not accept Lowe's amendment. Howell then suggested that Cross put down one of his own covering the same ground – 'He partially explained, and then returned to the House to move his now historic amendment.'[94]

Whilst Cross was straining to maintain the initiative, the underlying victory went to the opposition, Lowe and Mundella in particular. Commenting on the unexpectedly close divisions and the Liberal success in forcing amendments, Mundella reported: 'at 12 o'clock Cross dared not face Lowe's amendment to repeal section 1 of the Criminal Law Amendment Act. He proposed to remodel the act himself by words not on the paper, and he had to yield to report progress ... Tonight he has been forced to reopen the whole question, and you may look out for fun on Friday.'[95]

Cross returned to the House with his two bills on 16 July. On the Employers and Workmen Bill, Cross accepted the principle of Mundella's amendment, proposing a new clause allowing one or more sureties to be

[91] *Ibid.*, pp. 1337–9.
[92] *Hansard*, 3rd series, vol. CCXXV, 12 July 1875, pp. 1352–3.
[93] House of Commons Division Lists; Mundella's Amendment, 12 July 1875, no. 170, p. 425. Lowe's Amendment, 12 July 1875, no. 171, p. 428.
[94] G. Howell, *Labour legislation, Labour Movements, Labour Leaders* (London, 1902), pp-. 374–5.
[95] Mundella to Leader, 15 July 1875. Mundella papers, 6P/104/168. Quoted in Armytage, *A. J. Mundella*, p. 151.

raised for a person against whom damages were given, thus replacing imprisonment for non-performance of the contract with repayment of the surety. The last vestige of penal servitude for breach of contract had thereby been removed.[96] On the Conspiracy and Protection of Property Bill Cross introduced a new general clause on coercion and intimidation, a composite of Lowe's clause and a clause drafted by the law officers. The Criminal Law Amendment Act was finally repealed.[97] However, subsequent attempts by Mundella, Harcourt and Forster to amend the new clause, with the effect of defining the terms 'intimidation' and 'annoyance' more narrowly, were rebuffed by sizeable majorities.[98]

Cross still faced a fight on clause 4, dealing with imprisonment for breach of contract by workmen employed in public utilities. The committee stage on the Conspiracy and Protection of Property Bill reconvened on 20 July. By then Cross had accepted the principle of Lowe's amendment, making the clause applicable not solely to workmen but any 'person' employed by a public utility. Nevertheless, on an amendment pressed by J. Holms extending the penal sanctions to all 'contractors', the government's majority was reduced to twelve.[99] By these amendments the Liberal opposition attempted to ensure that Cross's legislation did not once again single out breach of contract by workmen for exceptional treatment.

In forcing the repeal of the CLA Act and by the amendment of Cross's legislation it can be seen that the Liberal opposition had transformed the character of Cross's original proposals, contributing towards a final and comprehensive settlement. That the settlement of the labour laws question was due to the Liberal opposition as much as the Conservative government, was widely recognised by the trade union leaders and the Positivist intellectuals. In an article for *The Bee Hive* Frederic Harrison wrote:

It would be unjust to deny that the government had shown a sincere desire to grapple with the question in a fair spirit ... At the same time we must remember that the abolition of the special Criminal Law Amendment Act is the work of Mr Lowe and that the greatest improvements which have been effected in both bills have been due to him with the assistance of Mr Forster and Mr Mundella.

Harrison concluded:

No one can speak of the virtual settlement of these inveterate disputes without feeling how much the settlement is the work of the untiring and almost single

---

[96] *Hansard*, 3rd series, vol. CCXXV, 16 July 1875, pp. 1589–91.
[97] *Ibid.*, pp. 1581–3. This new clause, clause 8, stipulated a maximum penalty of three months hard labour.
[98] *Ibid.*, pp. 1584–7.
[99] *Ibid.*, pp. 1738–9. 20 July 1875. For the amendment, 88, against, 100.

handed labours of Mr Mundella for many years, and also for the tact and patience with which he has managed the protracted transformation of the bills.[100]

This view was reiterated by Henry Broadhurst when he wrote to Mundella on behalf of the Parliamentary Committee; 'We owe more to you than any other single man in the House of Commons, but in addition to what you have done publicly we owe to you perhaps more for what you have done quietly for our own relief and benefit.'[101]

Mundella's role in the labour laws campaign was crucial. He and the small band of Radicals and 'advanced Liberals' provided a line of communication between the trade union leaders and the Liberal leadership. Prior to the autumn of 1873 they operated more or less in a vacuum. After the general election of 1874, Mundella and the advanced wing of the party operated in concert with the Liberal front bench to secure a comprehensive and final settlement. Historians have remarked upon the apparent paradox of the reforms of 1875, commenting that a Conservative administration, in passing the labour law reforms, itself brought about a *rapprochement* between the trade unions and the Liberal party by removing the main source of trade unionist discontent. In fact the ground had already been prepared by the previous Liberal administration and the reforms of 1875 were a genuinely cross bench effort.

For Howell, Applegarth and the trade union leaders of the mid-to late-Victorian period, the labour laws campaign of 1871–5 was a vindication of the strategy of alliance with the 'Gladstonian' or 'advanced Liberals', revealing the underlying compatibility between the trade unions and the Gladstonian Liberal party.[102] As a Durham Miners' Association pamphlet was to argue in 1884:[103]

If anyone looks through the discussions of these measures they will see that the best portions of the acts ... were amendments prepared by the Liberals, and incorporated into the acts as the result of their labours. With these facts before me ... I cannot see any inducement to make working men endorse Conservative politics, but on the other hand, there is much to make them ... have some respect for Liberals and Liberalism.

---

[100] Frederic Harrison, 'The new labour laws', *The Bee Hive*, 7 Aug. 1875, pp. 1–2. It is interesting to note that R. A. Cross, in his privately printed memoir, *A Political History 1868–1900*, 1903, referred only briefly to the labour law reforms of 1875, mentioning the support given by Lowe and Forster, but not Mundella, see pp. 34–5.

[101] Quoted in Armytage, *A. J. Mundella*, p. 152.

[102] See G. Howell, 'Labour politics, policies and parties, A striking indictment', *Reynolds Weekly*, 4 January 1905. See also the contributions by Alastair Reid, ch. 10, and John Shepherd, ch. 9, in this collection.

[103] William Crawford, 'Conservative working men' (Durham Miners' Association, 1884), Durham County Record Office, D/DMA7, pp. 7–8.

7 Popular Liberals, Gladstonian finance and the debate on taxation, 1860–1874

Eugenio F. Biagini

It may be said of Mr Gladstone that he found the people who live in cottages hostile to political parties, and that he had succeeded in uniting them with the rest of his countrymen.[1]

I

Historians of the labour movement have generally undervalued the importance of the Gladstonian finance and fiscal system in the making of the 'liberal consensus' in Victorian Britain. Yet there is little doubt that the point of view expressed by 'Ironside' in the passage quoted above would have been endorsed by many contemporaries of Ernest Jones and Thomas Burt, and that nineteenth-century historians and politicians were well aware of the social and political impact of the financial work of Peel and Gladstone.[2] Even in the early twentieth century the legacy of free trade finance remained so important in popular politics that its preservation constituted one of the 'causes' on which parties supported by a majority of the working-class electors won the general elections of 1906, 1910, and 1923. Therefore the inconspicuous role of this factor in modern historiography is not easy to explain. Recently, however, after the publication of H. C. G. Matthew's article on the policy of mid-Victorian budgets, the tide has changed, with G. Stedman Jones' and R. McKibbin's important revisions of the history of the left.[3] However, there has not as

I would like to thank all the scholars who took part in the Churchill College conference of 1989 for their comments on early drafts of this paper. In particular, I am indebted to Prof. D. E. D. Beales, Dr H. C. G. Matthew, Dr A. J. Reid, Mr J. Spain, Dr P. Thane and Dr J. Zeitlin for their helpful criticism and valuable references.

[1] 'Ironside' [alias W. Adams], 'Mr Gladstone', *Newcastle Weekly Chronicle*, 7 Aug. 1880, p. 4.
[2] J. Noble, *National Finance*, London 1876, p. 62; J. Morley, *Life of Gladstone* vol. 1 (London, 1903), p. 459.
[3] H. C. G. Matthew, 'Disraeli, Gladstone, and the policy of mid-Victorian budgets', *Historical Journal*, 22 (1979), p. 616; G. Stedman Jones, *Languages of Class* (Cambridge, 1983), pp. 177–8; R. McKibbin, 'Why was there no Marxism in Britain?', *English Historical Review*, 99 (1983), pp. 322–4. See also N. Kirk, *The Growth of Working Class*

yet been a detailed study of the relationship between plebeian radicalism and Gladstonian finance.

In this chapter, I will begin to explore this territory, extending the path opened up by the three aforementioned scholars, and focusing on the heyday of the 'liberal consensus', and more particularly on the years of the first Gladstone administration. My purpose is to show why free trade and retrenchment were really popular financial policies. Moreover, I suggest that the Liberal management of the Exchequer in the early 1870s had a much wider social and political perspective than is generally accepted, and that working-class radicals considered it as basically adequate to the needs of the time. Finally, I will try to illustrate how and why the 1874 programme of financial reforms – including the repeal of the income tax and the reduction of the rates – was consistent with this policy, and aimed at striking a balance between the interests of the various sectors of society and of the Liberal electorate in the new conditions generated by the 1870 Education Act.

II

In the second half of the nineteenth century the two foundations of popular views of taxation and expectations of financial politics were free trade and hostility to central government intervention. Free trade as a plebeian creed had a long tradition going back to the Levellers[4] and Thomas Paine – who had worked out a sort of pre-Cobdenite philosophy of history based on peace, retrenchment, international free trade, and disarmament.[5] In similar ways the protest against the fiscal system became part of the platform of the radical artisans both in London and in the industrial north between the 1810s and the 1840s: Henry Hunt, John Gast, and Francis Place campaigned for the repeal of the Corn Laws and of the taxes on the necessities of life, often using arguments which were to be developed further by the Anti-Corn Law Leaguers in the 1840s.[6] By then free trade was becoming the kernel of a sort of new 'moral economy'

Reformism in Mid-Victorian England (London, 1985), p. 154, for the acceptance of this new perspective.

4 E.g., *To the Supream Authority of England, the Commons Assembled in Parliament. The Earnest Petition of Many Free-Born People of This Nation* (London, 1648), in D. M. Wolfe (ed.), *Leveller Manifestoes of the Puritan Revolution* (London, 1967), pp. 268–70.

5 T. Paine, *Rights of Man*, in Paine, *The Complete Works of Thomas Paine*, ed. by M. D. Conway, (New York, 1945), pp. 371, 358–9, 416, 424.

6 J. Belchem, *'Orator' Hunt* (Oxford, 1985), pp. 110–11; I. Prothero, *Artisans and Politics in Early Nineteenth-Century London* (London, 1979), p. 77; F. Place, 'National political union, on the pledges to be given by candidates', in D. J. Rowe (ed.), *London Radicalism 1830–43* (London, 1970), p. 104.

of working-class consumers, supported with great earnestness and an almost religious fervour.

Chartism did not represent a break in this development. The arguments between the Chartists and the Anti-Corn Law League were not about the desirability of the repeal of the Corn Laws, but about the necessity of first obtaining 'manhood' suffrage and the other 'five points'. The Chartists' attitude could be summarised with the words which a shoemaker addressed to John Buckmaster, a League lecturer:

> Give us the Charter, and we will take off the tax; and we can get the Charter as easily as you can get the repeal of the Corn Laws. ... Look at your House of Commons and your House of Lords, made up of landlords, or men sent there to protect the interests of landlords who sit in the House of Lords. They will never repeal the Corn Laws without a revolution ...[7]

Hostility to the Corn Laws was reinforced by the political implications of the repealers' campaign: the platform of the League was anti-aristocratic and anti-clerical (since the Church of England was a great landowner),[8] and was accompanied by anti-militarism and by internationalism: all four characteristics being common features of popular radical movements in Britain and the rest of Europe.[9]

The repeal of the Corn Laws in 1846 became one of the turning points in the history of British radicalism in the nineteenth century. What Buckmaster's Chartist friend had thought impossible did happen, and the psychological impact of the event was very great, particularly because it had been prepared for by important measures like the Mines Act and the budget of 1842. 'All this proved fatal to the conviction and self-certainty of the language of Chartism.'[10] Many working-class biographies published in the second half of the century register the repeal as a great liberation,[11] and there were ex-Chartists who tried to reinterpret the history of the movement of which they had been members, over-stressing its commitment to free trade.[12]

---

[7] J. Buckmaster, *A Village Politician* (Horsham, 1982), p. 186; cf. T. Cooper, *The Life of Thomas Cooper*, ed. by J. Saville, (Leicester, 1971), p. 182. Cf. L. Brown, 'The Chartists and the Anti-Corn Law League', in A. Briggs (ed.), *Chartist Studies*, (London, 1978), esp. pp. 349–51, 359, 361, 370.

[8] N. McCord, *The Anti-Corn Law League* (London, 1968), pp. 22–3, 26.

[9] *Ibid.*, p. 32.

[10] Stedman Jones, *Languages of Class*, p. 177.

[11] J. Arch, *The Story of His Life* (London, 1898), pp. 6, 10, 151; J. Wilson, *Memories* (Firle, 1980, 1st edn 1910), pp. 42–3; J. Hawker, *A Victorian Poacher, James Hawker's Journal* (Oxford, 1979), pp. 72–3, 95.

[12] J. B. Leno, *The Aftermath* (London, 1892), pp. 18–19; G. Howell, 'The autobiography of a toiler ...', p. 116, in G. Howell Collection, I, 3. I would like to express my gratitude to the Librarian of the Bishopsgate Institute, London, for allowing me to quote and cite from papers in the invaluable Howell Collection.

If the repeal of the Corn Laws was seen as a great victory for the 'left' as a whole, the fact that it brought with it the widespread conviction that the cause of 'cheap food' needed thoroughgoing free trade, and that protectionism was synonymous with taxation of the necessities of life, was Cobden's personal triumph. For generations after 1846 free trade was to the labouring people a 'bread and cheese' question, the question of the 'free breakfast table'.[13] Hatred for the very word 'protectionism' was such that it remained in the political vocabulary only as a term of abuse.[14] Even when cyclical crises led to requests for 'fair trade' and 'tariff reform', the reactions of the labour movement and the mass press showed that under no circumstances would a departure from free trade have been tolerated.[15]

Another facet of popular views of finance and politics was commitment to retrenchment in central government expenditure. This was closely linked with anti-state, anti-authoritarian and semi-anarchist attitudes which, together with the ideal of a society of independent producers, characterised plebeian movements both in Europe and America during the eighteenth and nineteenth centuries.[16] Most radicals tended to consider the state an appendage of the upper classes and shared Adam Smith's view that it was inherently oppressive, incompetent, inefficient, and corrupt.[17] In Britain this atavistic anti-statism had been strengthened by the experience of the New Poor Law of 1834, which met with such intense hostility that in many areas its implementation was not possible without major concessions to local customs and the rights of self-government.[18] Thus, self-government as an ideology and as an inveterate practice also contributed to popular hostility to the expansion of the powers of the state. Both at the level of institutions (through municipal 'democracy' and the parish vestries), and at the level of religion and

---

[13] (Leading article (LA)), 'The story of free trade', *Lloyd's Weekly*, 28 Oct. 1866, p. 1.

[14] (LA), 'Free trade and the revivers', *Weekly Times*, 7 Nov. 1869, p. 4. Cf. B. Semmel, *Imperialism and Social Reform* (London, 1960), p. 108.

[15] T. J. Dunning, 'Emigration as an imperial question', *Bee Hive*, 8 Jan. 1870, p. 7; (LA), 'Answers to Reciprotarians', *Lloyd's Weekly*, 9 Jan. 1870, p. 1; (LA, no title), *The Daily News*, 27 Apr. 1871, p. 4.

[16] Cf. for a few examples: A. Soboul, *Les Sans-culottes parisiens en l'an II* (Paris, 1962), pp. 471–2; M. D. Peterson, *The Jefferson Mind in the American Image* (New York, 1960), p. 80; W. Hugins, *Jacksonian Democracy and the Working Class*, (Stanford, 1960), p. 143; Stedman Jones, *Languages of Class*, p. 111; I. Prothero, *Artisans and Politics*, p. 78; A. Romano, *Storia del movimento socialista in Italia*, vol. 2, (Bari, 1966), p. 251.

[17] R. D. Freeman, 'Adam Smith, education and *laissez-faire*', *History of Political Economy*, 1, 1 (1969), p. 173; G. Crossick, 'Shopkeepers and the state in Britain, 1870–1914', in G. Crossick and H.-G. Haupt (eds.), *Shopkeepers and Master Artisans in Nineteenth Century Europe* (London 1979), p. 258.

[18] M. E. Rose, 'The anti-Poor Law agitation', in J. T. Ward (ed.), *Popular Movements c. 1830–1850* (London, 1978), p. 92; Rose, 'The anti-Poor Law movement in the north of England', *Northern History*, 1 (1966), pp. 81–2.

culture (through congregationalist Nonconformity, trade unions, the co-operative movement and friendly societies) the ideal was one of local autonomy, community politics, and to some extent a nineteenth-century version of the direct democracy of the Athenian *ekklesia*.[19]

A further consideration behind the 'minimalist' attitudes of the sub-altern classes was the extent of army, navy and national debt in central government expenditure: put together they accounted for an average of more than 70 per cent, between 1861 and 1880.[20] On top of that there was the cost of the police, the diplomatic service, the Civil List and other establishments which were also favourite targets for radical criticism. Thus central government expenditure appeared mainly aimed at provid-ing 'fuel' for a 'class' machinery whose purposes were war abroad, repression and economic exploitation at home, and the general preserva-tion of a system based on privilege and injustice. In their attempt to force retrenchment on the Exchequer, plebeian radicals also aimed at reducing the exploitation allegedly exercised by rentier bond-holders through their receipt of interest on the national debt.[21] In their view, 'The great art of taxation in a well governed State [was] to spend as little as possible, and to collect that little from the people better able to pay.'[22] 'Light taxation – other things being equal – implies unfettered industry, enterprising and profitable trade, a well-fed, well-clothed, and well-educated people.'[23]

Like Painite radicals and Chartists,[24] plebeian Liberals of both the 'old' and the 'new' schools prided themselves on their sturdy 'independence',[25] and assumed that if society was at peace and in a generally healthy condition, the services of the state were hardly required, and its branches should virtually be disbanded; if, on the other hand, society was in an unhealthy condition, then it was political reform and democracy which were required, rather than government patronage of an impoverished population. They were very receptive to the Jeffersonian and almost

---

[19] On this issue cf.: E. Biagini, '"La liberta' degli antichi paragonata alla liberta' dei moderni": John Stuart Mill e la democrazia ateniese, 1832–1861', *Critica storica*, 22, 4 (1985), pp. 469–501.

[20] Compiled from H. C. G. Matthew, *Gladstone 1809–1874* (Oxford, 1986), p. 111.

[21] Significantly, this policy went along with the typical left-wing request for popular control of the diplomatic service; cf. the Petition of the Financial Reform Union presented to parliament by Samuel Morley on 12 March 1869, in *Papers on Taxation and Expenditure issued by the Financial Reform Union*, no. 6, London nd (but 1869), p. 16.

[22] Northumbrian, 'The money value of the people', *Reynolds's Newspaper*, 28 Oct. 1877, p. 3.

[23] (LA), 'John Stuart Mill on the Malt-Tax and the national debt', *Reynolds's Newspaper*, 22 Apr. 1866, p. 4.

[24] Stedman Jones, *Languages of Class*, p. 168.

[25] A. J. Reid, 'Intelligent artisans and aristocrats of labour: the essays of Thomas Wright', in J. Winter (ed.), *The Working Class in Modern British History* (Cambridge, 1983), pp. 180–4.

anarchist part of Paine's thought, and took over both his model of a self-governing, self-helping, libertarian society, and his concept of a cheap state. However their interest did not extend to Paine's social security programme, which was rejected as a 'Trojan horse' of state social repression: theirs was a demand-side 'moral economy', accompanied by a negative attitude towards central government intervention. This attitude was strengthened by the conviction that all taxes interfered more or less directly with 'the perfect freedom of trade' and tended in one shape or another to limit expenditure and diminish the demand for labour.[26]

In this way working-class radicalism found itself close to Cobden – who had accepted Paine's heritage of financial reform as well as of foreign policy[27] – and to the thoroughgoing free traders of the Liverpool Financial Reform Association[28] and the London Financial Reform Union. These organisations stood for 'bold retrenchment' and a more or less complete abolition of indirect taxation as the first step towards real social reform.[29] Their financial ideal was basically like Cobden's proposed 'National Budget' of 1848–9, which was built on a reduction of 45 per cent of the military estimates and on massive reductions in taxation.[30]

III

If Cobden was the closest interpreter and advocate of popular views of finance and taxation in mid-Victorian England, it was Gladstone who reaped the benefits of his work. By the 1860s Gladstone enjoyed an established reputation as the 'liberator' of British trade and the workman's 'breakfast table', the author of the emancipation of the popular press from the 'taxes upon knowledge', and as the man who placed a duty upon the succession of the estates of the wealthy.[31]

According to Schumpeter's classic analysis, Gladstonian finance was based on three principles: retrenchment and rationalisation of state

---

[26] (LA), 'Tory extravagance and working class indulgence', *Reynolds's Newspaper*, 10 May 1868, p. 4; and (LA), 'John Stuart Mill on the Malt Tax and the national debt', 22 Apr. 1866, p. 4.

[27] E. Royle, *Victorian Infidels* (Manchester, 1974), p. 147.

[28] Especially in the 1880s: W. N. Calkins, 'A Victorian free trade lobby', *Economic History Review*, 2nd series, vol. 13 (1960–1), p. 91 and note; however, it seems that the situation was different in the late 1840s, see pp. 97–8.

[29] Cf. Noble, *National Finance*, pp. 126–8.

[30] J. Morley, *The Life of Richard Cobden* (London, 1920, 1st edn 1879), pp. 498–9. The 'wasteful expenditure' of money which had unjustly been obtained through 'the taxation of the humblest classes' by the Liberal government was one of the reasons why Cobden declined to enter Palmerston's last Cabinet in 1865 (p. 929).

[31] Northumbrian, 'Mr. Gladstone for premier', *Reynolds's Newspaper*, 10 May 1868, p. 2; J. Noble, 'Taxation, imperial and local', *Bee Hive*, 12 Sept. 1876, p. 3; Noble, *The Queen's Taxes* (London, 1870), p. 104.

expenditure; a system of taxation which would interfere as little as possible with industrial and commercial operations; and the production of balanced budgets with surpluses to allow for fiscal reforms and the reduction of the national debt.[32] This scheme, however, does not account for Gladstone's sensitivity to the political importance of the distribution of taxation, and tends to confuse the attempts to minimise central government's expenditure with a 'minimalist' approach *tout court*. In fact his financial strictness was compatible both with non-expensive forms of state intervention (like factory legislation),[33] and with an expanding scope for local government, the responsibilities and budget of which continued to grow throughout Gladstone's parliamentary career. Thus, while *laissez-faire* and retrenchment were preached at Nos. 10 and 11, Downing Street, the organisation of social services was methodically carried out by 'municipal socialists' in town councils and local school boards, under the supervision of central government inspectors and with the help of the loans and 'grants in aid' which Gladstonian surpluses made available.[34] At any level *laissez-faire* was applied in a pragmatic way and with due attention to what economists called the 'exceptions' to its principles. The latter were quite wide and included the establishment of public hospitals, the organisation of a national system of education,[35] and the nationalisation of 'natural monopolies' like the telegraphs – a bipartisan measure prepared by the Disraeli government in 1868 and ratified and implemented by the Gladstone administration between 1869 and 1870 with the blessings of the orthodox *Economist* and of W. Stanley Jevons.[36]

However, it was neither on occasional great measures of state intervention, nor on the spending of public money that Gladstone's popularity was based: rather, as Colin Matthew has shown, it was his work on the public revenue side which brought much credit to him, generating psychological

---

[32] J. Schumpeter, *History of Economic Analysis* (London, 1954), pp. 403–5.

[33] B. Hilton, *The Age of Atonement*, (Oxford, 1988), p. 268. Mine and factory inspection was in fact very cheap; in 1868–9, when the total estimates for the 'civil services' stood at £15,169,369, the cost of factory inspection was £12,356, of mine inspection £10,500, and of inspection of alkali works £3,300 (H. Mann, 'On the cost and organization of the Civil Service', *Journal of the Royal Statistical Society*, 32 [1869], pp. 39, 43).

[34] As happened in 1892, when a former Liberal minister, Goschen, provided the money to make primary education free: P. Marsh, *The Discipline of Popular Government* (Hassocks, 1978), p. 171. Cf. E. T. Stokes, 'Bureaucracy and ideology: Britain and India in the nineteenth century', *Transactions of the Royal Historical Society*, 5th series, 30 (1980), pp. 138–43.

[35] Cf. J. S. Mill, *Principles of Political Economy*, in J. S. Mill, *Collected Works*, vol. 3, 2 (Toronto and London, 1977), pp. 936–71. See also R. L. Crouch, '*Laissez-faire* in nineteenth-century Britain', *Manchester School*, 35 (1967), pp. 209–15.

[36] Cf. I. J. Cohen, 'Toward a theory of state intervention: the nationalization of the British telegraphs', *Social Science History*, 4 (Spring, 1980), pp. 176, 183; T. W. Hutchison, 'Economists and economic policy in Britain after 1870', *History of Political Economy*, 1, 1 (1969), p. 237.

expectations of balance, social equity and political justice.[37] Gladstone had occupied a strategically central position in the debate on finance and politics, in contrast to Disraeli and the 'left-wing' Cobdenites.

Gladstone's political and intellectual triumph over Disraeli was complete and crushing. The Conservative leader was also aiming to reduce the pressure of taxation, but without Gladstone's sensitivity towards those who were poor and less able to pay, and without his zeal for retrenchment and reorganisation.[38] In 1852 Disraeli had tried to reconstruct the income tax, to make it a permanent source of revenue by removing some of its most socially objectionable features – which Gladstone valued as electoral inducements to retrenchment.[39] Later, and especially between 1874 and 1880, Disraeli's government adopted the course of an elastic approach to the national debt and showed that it was ready to borrow as an alternative to both retrenchment and increase in taxation.[40] Gladstone defeated the former strategy in the House in 1852 and 1853, and the latter in the country, with the general elections of 1880.

Gladstone's handling of the 'left-wing' alternative was more tactful. He managed to obtain the support of the Cobdenites by presenting his approach as the only politically feasible way to financial reform. In the process he conquered working-class opinion as well. One of the most important steps in the latter part of this operation was the remission of paper duties, which, together with stamp duties, had been the source of much strife for generations. Not only did the reform itself bring credit to Gladstone, but also the spectacular way in which it was achieved.[41] Following his victorious fight with the Lords in 1860 and 1861 Gladstone became 'the idol' of working-class radicals,[42] who saw the budget as a powerful vindication of the 'Saxon constitution', as well as a measure of social justice and popular education.[43] Therefore the budget coupled a symbolic component with a degree of material relief. The 'people' were thankful for both, as suggested by Janet Hamilton's 1865 'Rhymes' – one of the very few working-class poems ever dedicated to a Chancellor of the Exchequer:

> That gleg birkie, Gladstone, has weel dune his part;
> Exchequer's big pouches o' siller are fu',
> An' mony's the taxes that's duna awa' noo,

[37] Matthew, 'Mid-Victorian budgets', pp. 615–18.
[38] P. R. Ghosh, 'Disraelian Conservatism: a financial approach', English Historical Review, 99 (1984), p. 293.
[39] Matthew, 'Mid-Victorian budgets', pp. 620–2, 639.
[40] Ghosh, 'Disraelian Conservatism', pp. 284, 286–7.
[41] Matthew, Gladstone, 1809–1874, pp. 113–14.
[42] Royle, Victorian Infidels, p. 265.
[43] J. Wilson, Memories, pp. 134–7.

An' labour's weel paid, an' the flour an' the meal
At a wanworth – an' sae we micht fen unco weel.[44]

But the most significant demonstration of the sentiments of the working classes was that which Gladstone received in radical Northumberland in 1862. Recalling the event in 1865 Holyoake wrote:

When Mr Gladstone visited the North, you well remember when word passed from the newspaper to the workman that it circulated through mines and mills, factories and workshops, and they came out to greet the only British minister who ever gave the English people a right because it was just they should have it . . . and when he went down the Tyne, all the country heard how twenty miles of banks were lined with people who came to greet him. Men stood in the blaze of chimneys; the roofs of factories were crowded; colliers came up from the mines; women held up their children on the banks that it might be said in after life that they had seen the Chancellor of the People go by. The river was covered like the land. Every man who could ply an oar pulled up to give Mr Gladstone a cheer. When Lord Palmerston went to Bradford the streets were still, and working men imposed silence upon themselves. When Mr Gladstone appeared on the Tyne he heard cheer that no other English minister ever heard . . . the people were grateful to him, and rough pitmen who never approached a public man before, pressed round his carriage by thousands . . . and thousands of arms were stretched out at once, to shake hands with Mr Gladstone as one of themselves.[45]

From the viewpoint of political success with plebeian radicals it was important also that the central tenets of Gladstone's finance were easy to understand. His businesslike mottoes of 'small profits and quick returns' and of leaving 'the money to fructify in the pockets of the people' effectively summarised two of the reasons why his finance was admired: as George Howell wrote, Gladstone was believed to have been 'the first to discover how to increase the receipts by reducing the burthens, the remission of taxation being one of his greatest achievements'.[46] The related endeavour of encouraging employment by making trade and investment easier basically constituted the only kind of employment policy devised by financiers[47] and asked for by plebeian radicals[48] in

[44] J. Hamilton, 'Rhymes for the Times, 1865', in Hamilton, *Poems and Ballads* (1868), cited in Matthew, *Gladstone 1809–1874*, p. 132. For a very different poem on another Chancellor of the Exchequer see 'A. Syntaxis', 'EX LUCE Lucellum', *Bee Hive*, 10 June 1871, p. 14 (a satirical composition on Robert Lowe).

[45] G. J. Holyoake, 'The Liberal situation, or the parliamentary treatment of the people. II.', *Newcastle Weekly Chronicle*, 18 Mar. 1865, p. 4.

[46] G. Howell, 'Taxation, how levied and how expended', *Industrial Review*, 12 Jan. 1878, p. 3.

[47] Sir S. Northcote, *Twenty Years of Financial Policy* (London, 1862), p. 69; S. Buxton, *Mr Gladstone as Chancellor of the Exchequer* (London, 1901), p. 45; Matthew, *Gladstone 1809–1874*, p. 213.

[48] (LA), 'Tory extravagance and working class indulgence', *Reynolds's Newspaper*, 10 May 1868, p. 4; Noble, *National Finance*, p. 144.

times of economic expansion. Even Gladstone's stress on the need for balanced budgets was easy to understand, and – as an assimilation of national finance to that of a well-managed family – seemed rational and verifiable. Finally the classical principles of taxation which the 'People's Chancellor' applied were also deeply rooted in popular expectations through readings and popularisations of Adam Smith.[49]

Given the tone of popular reactions to Gladstone's finance, it is not surprising that before 1867 the Liberal leader hoped to be better able to achieve retrenchment with an enlarged electorate which included a section of the working classes.[50] And it is notable that working-class radicals were of a similar opinion, seeing the repeal of the paper duty and franchise reform as steps in the march of 'democracy' towards 'real economy': as *Lloyd's Weekly* put it immediately after the passing of the Reform Act, 'thanks to cheap press and cheap literature . . . [the workman's] voice will never cease to be raised in the reformed House of Commons against the least squandering of the public money'.[51] Financial enthusiasm ran high during the months that led to the general elections of 1868, and Liberal candidates managed to fill huge lecture halls with thousands of people eager to listen to their Philippics against Tory profligacy,[52] or to praise free trade and its 'progress'.[53]

As a consequence the 1869 'popular' parliament was expected to be the harbinger of an era of unprecedented economies. However, the financial millennium was not at hand. Robert Lowe as Chancellor of the Exchequer produced two brilliant and celebrated budgets in 1869 and 1870,[54] with spectacular reductions in expenditure and in both direct and indirect taxation. But by 1870 it became apparent that the reduction of the military estimates involved a cost to the working classes, since thousands of soldiers and artisans were discharged from the army and government dockyards. Although Gladstone claimed that the relevant decisions had been taken by the previous Tory administration,[55] these measures counterbalanced the popularity of the budgets, and working-class critics

[49] Cf. for an example 'A working man', 'The ABC of Social Science' in twenty lessons – taxation', *Bee Hive*, 12 Sept. 1868, p. 1.

[50] Matthew, *Gladstone 1809–1874*, p. 128; J. Vincent, *The Formation of the British Liberal Party 1857–68* (Harmondsworth, 1972), p. 250.

[51] (LA), 'Next year's question', *Lloyd's Weekly*, 2 Dec. 1867, p. 1.

[52] [Report], 'Mr. Leatham, MP, on expenditure and the Irish Church', *Leeds Mercury*, 5 Nov. 1868, p. 3.

[53] [Rep.], 'West Riding – Eastern Division – Mr. Thompson and Mr. Holden, M.P., at Selby', *Leeds Mercury*, 13 Oct. 1868, p. 5.

[54] (LA), 'Public opinion and the budget', *Weekly Times*, 18 Apr. 1869, p. 4; (LA), 'The budget', *Bee Hive*, 16 Apr. 1870, p. 4; (LA), 'The budget', *Newcastle Weekly Chronicle*, 16 Apr. 1870, p. 4. See also Noble, *National Finance*, pp. 154, 164, 171–2.

[55] W. E. Gladstone, 'Speech on administrative economy at Blackheath, October 1871', in A. Tinley Basset (ed.), *Gladstone's Speeches* (London, 1916), pp. 406–8.

were adamant in pointing out that the cuts in the defence establishment had begun at the wrong end. Moreover, in the context of a critical situation in the labour market, the resulting large surpluses and the prospect of more forthcoming, stimulated popular requests for a more energetic social policy, which would have been viable without increasing taxation. For example, *Reynolds's Newspaper*, regretting the 'misemployment' of almost £9 million in the Abyssinian expedition, maintained that the same amount of money would have provided 'the establishment of a complete system of national education, and an equally national emigration scheme, to say nothing of the difference being a sufficient capital sum to provide interest on the payment of, say, a perfect system of colliery inspection, by which 500 lives might be saved every year'.[56]

These ideas were not revolutionary, however, and actually went little beyond what the government was actually doing: the Education Act was passed in that year, and the disbanded artisans of the government dockyards were offered free passages to Canada on board Royal Navy ships;[57] moreover, two years later the Mines Act went a long way towards meeting the requests of the miners.[58] The programme of the Financial Reform Union – based on further cuts in military expenditure and the repeal of the duties on sugar, tea and corn – was radical, but in a classically Cobdenite sense.[59] In fact, working-class criticism remained substantially within the limits of financial orthodoxy, and aimed at improving the lot of the 'common people' without upsetting the Gladstonian 'social contract' or interfering with the policy of retrenchment.

One of the most interesting cases for a test of radical attitudes in these years is provided by the debate on the 1871 budget. In 1870–1 the Chancellor of the Exchequer had to interrupt his systematic efforts to reduce public expenditure because the threatening developments of the Franco-Prussian war had called for increased military estimates. Lowe thought it necessary to augment taxation, but instead of taking Gladstone's advice that he should resort to a simple increase in the income tax, he presented a much more elaborate project. He proposed to raise the supplementary revenue through three different channels: (1) a marginal increase in the income tax; (2) an increase in the succession and legacy

[56] (LA), 'The budget for 1870', *Reynolds's Newspaper*, 17 Apr. 1870, p. 1.

[57] Cf. (rep.), 'The 'Woolwich emigrants', *The Times*, 7 June 1870, p. 12. Between 1869 and 1870 thousands of British and Irish workers emigrated 'at the expense of colonial and public funds' ([rep.], 'Government emigration', *The Times*, 11 Oct. 1870, p. 5).

[58] C. Fisher and C. Smethurst, '"War on the law of supply and demand": the Amalgamated Association of Miners and the Forest of Dean Colliers 1869–1875', in R. Harrison (ed.), *Independent Collier* (Brighton, 1978), pp. 132–3.

[59] Cf. 'A Budget for 1869, based on Mr. Cobden's National Budget proposed in 1849', in *Financial Reform Union – Papers on Taxation and Expenditure*, no. 3 (London nd [but 1869]), pp. 2–5.

duty; and (3) match duties of 1/2d on each box of 100 matches, and 1d on each box of 100 wax matches. The increase in the income tax would have been paid mainly by the middle classes, the higher succession and legacy duties would have fallen especially on the upper classes, and the match tax would have struck the working classes. In this way Lowe's 'revenge' against what he considered the party of rearmament and 'profligate expenditure' would have been complete, and every social class would have had to realise the consequences and costs of a warlike foreign policy. Lowe hoped that in the long run his fiscal policy would have stimulated public opinion to a new sense of responsibility and a more peaceful attitude.[60]

Unfortunately the abstract logic of this plan was totally out of touch with the political realities of the day. Both the increased death duties and the match tax were highly divisive and were likely to generate an anti-government coalition of the right and the extreme left: the former opposed the death duties, while the latter rejected the match tax as a grievous imposition on the necessities of life, a duty which would have obstructed trade and caused unemployment.[61] Outside parliament, in the year of the Paris *Commune* republican sentiments ran high, and working-class radicals were exasperated at the proposal of the match tax. This duty looked like a treason against the sacred canons of Cobdenite and Gladstonian taxation[62] committed by a notoriously anti-democratic Chancellor in order to compensate aristocratic officers for the abolition of the purchase system, and to provide Princess Louise with a dowry.

To heighten the drama a demonstration of the London matchmakers intervened: on 24 April – while the Liberal ministers were arriving in Parliament Square – 3 or 4,000 people, 'principally working girls and working boys' from Bryant and Mays protested energetically against the new tax.[63] The situation was very embarrassing for a government which claimed to be 'popular', and was made even more so by the brutal intervention of the police. The fact that the budget was promptly amended by Gladstone himself possibly gave the impression that this demonstration by the 'common people' had given it the *coup de grâce*: but it is questionable whether the matchmakers' action would have been as

---

[60] [LA, nt], *The Times*, 21 Apr. 1871, p. 9.
[61] See especially the speeches of H. Fawcett (20 Apr. 1871, cols. 1429–31), Sir Charles Dilke (21 Apr. 1871, cols. 1528–30) and Jacob Bright (24 Apr. 1871, cols. 1631–2), in *Hansard P.D.*, 3rd series, vol. ccv. On the contrary, the strongest supporter of this tax was W. Stanley Jevons, see his pamphlet *The Match Tax: a Problem in Finance* (London, 1871), esp. pp. 38–60.
[62] (LA), 'The miserable match tax farce', *Potteries Examiner*, 28 Feb. 1871, p. 2.
[63] [Rep.], 'Demonstration against the match tax', *The Manchester Guardian*, 25 Apr. 1871, p. 5; according to the *Times* the demonstrators were 'several thousands' ([rep.], 'The government and the matchmakers', 25 Apr. 1871, p. 10). For the matchmakers' protest see also (rep.), 'The matchmakers', *The Times*, 24 Apr. 1871, p. 10.

effective without the strong opposition met by the government in the House. It must have been especially significant to Gladstone to realise that many of the MPs who spoke against the budget had entered parliament for the first time in 1868,[64] and therefore could be supposed to be the chosen representatives of the town workers who had been enfranchised in 1867.

The resulting reshaped Financial Bill replaced the match tax, and – to appease the right – also the increased death and succession duties, with a substantial increase in the income tax. Lowe's experiment had been a political mistake due to lack of consultation with his colleagues, and to his determination to implement what he intended to be a sort of 'finance of chastisement'. In the end it had been only the government who was 'chastised', since the crisis was avoided at the price of a serious humiliation. Its solution had stressed the strength of the working-class lobby and the fact that the payers of the income tax had become the only 'soft target' from a fiscal viewpoint.

This situation could not be satisfactory since it was likely to encourage the migration of middle-class electors into the Conservative fold, a phenomenon which had already begun in 1868 and which the Liberals had to stop if they wanted to preserve their position as the party of the centre. On the other hand, in spite of the 1871 'incident', the working classes were not moving away from the Liberal party: Gladstone kept receiving labourers' demonstrations of support and appreciation for the way in which the Liberals had managed the Treasury since 1869,[65] and even an ultra-radical newspaper like *Reynolds's* had to grudgingly acknowledge that as a result of the Liberal budgets many important and beneficial reforms had been achieved since 1853:

We released the people from the charges of the Customs upon articles of food, and we abolished some fetters of the excise upon the production of industry. We even made some slight approach towards treating realised property as a fund for taxation and imposed an income tax upon rent and a small charge upon real property in the form of a succession duty. We went so far as to declare that licenses upon industry were iniquitous, and last year the Chancellor of the Exchequer, in a fit of enthusiasm, removed the oppressive charges upon hawkers.[66]

The reason why *Reynolds's* was nevertheless dissatisfied was the old obsession with retrenchment and remission of taxation, an obsession

---

[64] W. Fowler, E. A. Bowring, R. A. McFie, Sir C. Dilke, P. Rylands, A. J. Mundella, J. Holms, G. Osborne Morgan, H.Richard, and W. Vernon Harcourt, cf. *Hansard P.D.*, 3rd series, vol. ccv, cols. 1433–997. I am grateful to Miss Elizabeth Norman who brought this fact to my attention.

[65] Cf. for instance the address of the Whitby Working Men's Liberal Club in (rep.), 'The premier at Whitby', *The Leeds Mercury*, 4 Sept. 1871, p. 3.

[66] Northumbrian, 'The Chancery of Luciferus', *Reynolds's Newspaper*, 30 Apr. 1871, p. 3.

which was still widespread, and in fact had been strengthened – both in parliament and among rank-and-file radicals[67] – by the reaction to the match-tax budget. Even before the increase of the military estimates the TUC declared:

That this Congress desires to record its solemn conviction that the present Taxation of this country, both Imperial and Local, is enormous and burdensome especially to the great mass of the working classes; and this Congress earnestly calls upon the Representatives of the People to support a complete readjustment of the excessive national burthens, so that incomes and property shall bear its fair share, and that the burthen of labour and the necessaries of life, shall be proportionally decreased.[68]

In a similar mood George Howell – writing to William Owen of the *Potteries Examiner* – wondered: 'What has become of our Economists? We are off into Palmerstonian expenditure. No one to check it, no one to take the matter into their hands from our point of view.' And concluded: 'Let us combine for Labour representation regardless of all the old cliques and parties.'[69] Thus the demand for retrenchment was becoming one of the incentives to independent labour representation: but it is remarkable that if Gladstone's administration of finance was criticised it was because it was considered not Gladstonian enough – a contention with which Gladstone himself fully concurred.[70]

IV

Discontent was voiced with increasing energy in 1872. In June the representatives of 'Trade Unionism in all its branches', of the Labour Representation League and of the ultra-radical Land and Labour League met in London to discuss several proposals for radical reform. Under the heading of 'Finance questions' they required:

1. Reduction of expenditure in all departments of the State. 2. Taxation, as far as possible, to be direct. 3. National Debt to be diminished. 4. Readjustments of Income-tax, so as to relieve incomes derived from industrial or professional pursuits from the same percentage as income derived from real property. 5. Changes of incidence of rating, so as to diminish local in favour of national rates.[71]

---

[67] Cf. *Hansard P.D.*, 3rd series, vol. ccv, esp. 1428–35, 1585–93, 1631–5; (LA), 'Mr. Lowe's budget', *Bee Hive*, 29 Apr. 1871, p. 9; (LA), 'Our political prospects', *Lloyd's Weekly*, 7 Jan. 1872, p. 1.

[68] 1871 TUC Minutes, 6th Day (11 Mar. 1871), in G. Howell Coll. TUC Parl. Cttee, p. 46.

[69] G. Howell to W. Owen, 19 Feb. 1871, Howell Coll., Letter Books, 445.

[70] W. E. Gladstone to R. Lowe, 27 Nov. 1871, in H. C. G. Matthew (ed.), *The Gladstone Diaries*, vol. 8 (Oxford, 1982), p. 65.

[71] (Rep.), 'A new political alliance', *The Times*, 24 June 1872, p. 13.

It is significant that even the income tax posed problems to plebeian radicals, to the extent that the Land and Labour League – which R. Harrison has described as a 'proletarian' organisation[72] – was ready to join in the request for its reform. This was not an unusual demand either: working-class newspapers contained articles complaining that the tax weighed heavily on those who 'were struggling against poverty',[73] and letters by well-paid artisans pressing for a reconstruction of the tax so as to make it more just in its application,[74] or at least to obtain the complete exemption of incomes between £100 and £200.[75] The latter request reflected the fact that several categories of artisans[76] and some trade union leaders and officials – besides the small shopkeepers who often held key position in labour organisations – came within reach of the tax as it then stood. Moreover, there were plebeian radicals who did not ask simply for its reconstruction, but indeed for its complete abolition: they objected to it in principle, complaining that it was 'a tax levied to cover extravagant expenditure' and that it was assessed and collected in an inquisitorial way.[77] In any case, at this stage the income tax was no longer seen as the best means of forcing the wealthy to pay their share of the national expenditure, and in fact one of the radical arguments for its abolition was that it would have been more just and more economic to replace it with some special tax on landed property and the 'unearned increment' of its value.[78] As for the opposite solution – the extension of a reconstructed income tax and the repeal of all indirect taxes, the policy advocated by the Financial Reform Association – though popular at a later stage, it was not recommended by labour spokesmen in the early 1870s, and in any case it posed difficult political and technical problems.[79]

Another serious fiscal question was posed by the increase of local government costs through the implementation of urban 'improvement' schemes and the national education system, which while solving old social

---

[72] R. Harrison, *Before the Socialists* (London, 1965), pp. 210–46.

[73] (LA), 'Our financial difficulties', *Weekly Times*, 7 May 1871, p. 1; see also (LA, nt), *The Daily News*, 28 Apr. 1871, p. 4.

[74] (LA), 'The budget and the income tax', *Newcastle Weekly Chronicle*, 6 May 1871, p. 4.

[75] (Letter by) 'Quevedo', 'Parliament and the people', *Reynolds's Newspaper*, 5 Mar. 1871, p. 4; (letter by) 'A Bristol joiner', 'The income tax and the working man', *Bee Hive*, 28 Feb. 1874, p. 8; Northumbrian, 'The weight of taxation', *Reynolds's Newspaper*, 14 May 1871, p. 3.

[76] Evidence given by J. G. Waldson [17 Mar. 1892], *Royal Commission on Labour*, PP 1892, xxxvi, q.20, 185.

[77] Cf. the remarks of *Lloyd's Weekly* on the meeting between a delegation of the Income and Assessed Property Tax Payers' Association in December 1866: (LA), 'Where the income tax shoe pinches', 30 Dec. 1866, p. 6.

[78] (LA), 'Comments on the budget', *Lloyd's Weekly*, 23 Apr. 1870, p. 1.

[79] O. Anderson, 'Wage earners and income tax: a nineteenth-century discussion', *Public Administration*, 41 (1963), pp. 189–92.

problems created new ones. In particular, the load of taxation on the working and lower-middle classes became increasingly heavy because of the rising incidence of the rates, which were paid even by the very poor.[80] In view of this, the renewal of popular pressure for retrenchment in central government expenditure after 1870 becomes easily understandable; as a mass phenomenon it was stimulated not by an ideological commitment to the abstract ideals of *laissez-faire*, but by the practical necessity of making up for the increased costs of social services by saving on national taxation and reducing the charges for the army, navy and national debt. And yet the Liberal administration had worked wonders, managing to keep the cost of central government in 1873 within the levels of 1861 – despite the increased cost of shipbuilding due to the introduction of ironclads, and the always increasing grants for education.[81] At this stage fiscal reform required redistribution, for which both Radicals and Conservatives had been pressing since 1869, and which became inevitable after parliament passed Sir Massey Lopes' 1872 resolution on rate relief.[82]

However, Conservatives and Radicals had sharply contrasting views because they had different problems at heart. Lopes and the Conservatives were worried about the growing local burdens on the propertied classes and especially on the landowners in the countryside, and sought a 'compensation' for the losses that the landed interest claimed to have suffered from the repeal of the Corn Laws. In contrast, the Radicals were concerned with the costs of their schemes for municipal improvement and with the difficult situation existing in London. In 1866 the Select Committee on Metropolitan Local Government – of which J. S. Mill had been an active member – had highlighted the peculiar problems of the capital: what happened was that, because of the lack of a central municipality and a system of equalisation of the rates, there was a wide divergence of resources between authorities expected to fulfil the same statutory duties. Because of lower property values, a substantially higher rate in the pound was required to raise a given sum in a poor parish – where expenditure for poor relief etc. was also higher – than in a rich one: hence the amounts and incidence of London rates were highly regressive.[83] Moreover the rates

[80] Noble, *National Finance*, p. 300. Therefore it is not correct to say – as Matthew does ('Introduction', *Gladstone Diaries*, 7 [Oxford, 1982], pp. lxxxiv–lxxxvi) – that the rates were a question concerning only the propertied classes, though it had been their spokesmen who raised the question more forcibly (almost to the point that the relief of local taxation was a Tory cause in the early 1870s; Noble, *National Finance*, pp. 142–3, 287; S. J. Chapman, *Local Government and State Aid* [London, 1899], p. 89).

[81] The grants for 'education, science and art' grew from £1,380,962 in 1869 to £2,426,250 in 1874 (Noble, *National Finance*, p. 167).

[82] Cf. Matthew, *Gladstone 1809–1874*, pp. 215–16.

[83] 'First Report from the Select Committee on Metropolitan Government ...', PP (1866), xiii, p. xi.

weighed on the occupiers only, not on the owners as such, despite the fact that any urban improvement increased both the commercial and rateable value of the property and hence benefited the owners at the expense of the tenants. The Select Committee recommended equalisation and redistribution, so that 'a portion of the charges for permanent improvements and works should be borne by the owners of property'.[84] In this way the reformers wanted to bring relief to 'the small struggling tradesmen . . . and others who might be described as the working classes', who 'patiently' paid an amount of local taxation out of all proportion to their means.[85]

Therefore, though the policy of the progressive remission of duties on the necessities of life had to be continued, the real questions in the early 1870s were posed by the income tax and local taxation, which – in different ways and degrees – were both impinging unfairly on the lower-middle classes and on the working classes. In fact the number of persons subject to income tax under schedule (D) had increased impressively year after year during Gladstone's administration. But what is most important is that the category which had increased more than any other had been that of the taxpayers assessed at the lowest level:

1869	1870	1871	1872	1873	1874
75,577	195,296	209,752	218,098	257,103	273,554[86]

By 1874 their number was equivalent to about 10 per cent of the total number of registered electors, and it was likely to keep increasing as an effect of inflation, pushing new and wider social groups beyond the limit of the £100 exemption. This was of particular political relevance because income tax payers were concentrated in towns, and especially in London, where the Liberals had been losing votes from 1868.[87] Moreover, observers maintained that the effect of the tax on low incomes was to reduce social mobility and in this way aggravate the problems of the poor.[88]

In 1872 Lowe began to deal with this tax by increasing the abatement on incomes between £100 and £300 from £60 to £80, a reform which was

---

[84] *Ibid.*, p. xii.
[85] *Ibid.*, 99. 614–17. Evidence given by Sir J. Thwaites, Chairman of the Metropolitan Board of Works (15 Mar. 1866).
[86] Income Tax Returns, PP, 1873, xxxix, p. 297; and 1878–9, xlii, p. 234.
[87] In fact as early as 1859–60, 36.56 per cent of all adult males in London earned £100 or more: W. D. Rubinstein, 'The size and distribution of the English middle classes in 1860', *Historical Journal*, 61 (1988), p. 79.
[88] T. Cliffe Leslie, 'The incidence of imperial and local taxation on the working classes', *Fortnightly Review*, 15, new series (1874), p. 253.

expected to be popular.[89] Yet to Gladstone this was only a temporary solution, and it is well known that he was still thinking of abolishing the tax altogether, though the emergencies of the previous years had shown that it was an instrument difficult to dispose of.

Local taxation was much more delicate and difficult to settle because the old system of the rates was also invested with growing social importance; with political significance in relation to the concept of full citizenship and the autonomy of local communities; and it played a crucial role in the apportionment of fiscal burdens because it was a form of direct taxation which reached most householders and lodgers. Given the chaotic state of the system of local government – afflicted by a multitude of elective authorities with conflicting and overlapping competence and jurisdiction, raising different rates for their special projects – the amount and distribution of local taxation could not be altered without a major reform of local government itself.

The state of local government and taxation was also a major hindrance to social reform. Since occupiers and not owners were taxed and had to pay for improvements, during the 1870s popular radicals were less favourable than middle-class ones towards improvement schemes. More-over, the fact that a property qualification debarred the poorer ratepayers from all local elective positions meant that they had little control over local government, and were generally suspicious as to how public money was spent: working-class radicals had no time for the aesthetic ambitions of municipal patricians, which often resolved themselves into rate-financed slum clearances without any provision of cheap housing for the evicted proletarians.[90] As an indignant ratepayer expressed himself:

They launch into extravagant schemes of so-called improvement, build themselves palatial town-halls, purchase sites for public parks at absurdly high prices, and indulge in other feats of reckless expenditure – borrow money at high rates to cover that expenditure, utterly regardless of the wants or wishes of the ratepayers, and, instead of diminishing the rates, increase them to such an extent as to rouse the hatred and hostility of the overburdened and struggling class of persons who have to pay the piper.[91]

Without direct representation on town councils working-class radicals were unable to prevent municipal corporations from giving too generous compensation to private companies, or from starting enterprises of

---

[89] The measure was accompanied by a reduction of 50 per cent on the duties on coffee and chicory: S. Buxton, *Finance and Politics*, 2 (London, 1888), p. 144. For positive popular reactions see: (LA), 'Mr. Lowe's Little Bill', *Lloyd's Weekly*, 31 Mar. 1872, p. 1; and (LA), 'A popular budget', *Reynolds's Newspaper*, 31 Mar. 1872, p. 1.

[90] H. Pelling, *Popular Politics and Society in Late Victorian Britain* (London, 1968), pp. 3–4.

[91] (Letter by) G. Humphries, newspaper cutting, nd, in G. Howell Collection, 'Community envelope'.

doubtful social usefulness. Concern for the heavy financial burdens generated by many municipal enterprises was well-founded: for instance, a radical newspaper in the north observed in 1876 that the municipalisation of the water companies of Middlesborough and Stockton had cost 'a sum of money amounting to five times the total rateable value of the property of the two towns'.[92] In the end municipal reforms were popular only when they were not financed through the rates, as in Birmingham. Chamberlain's motto, 'High Rates and a Healthy City', was misleading: Birmingham 'municipal socialism' was financed mainly from the profits of the municipalised gas company, whereas the attempts to increase the rates in 1855 and 1874 provoked ratepayers' revolts.[93] But, in general, local administrations were less fortunate than in Birmingham, and local reformers had to choose between giving priority to reform or safeguarding the ratepayer's purse.

There were two viable solutions to this standstill situation. First, it was possible to ask the Exchequer for ever-increasing 'grants in aid' for local finance. Second, it was possible to pursue a reform of the system of local taxation. The two solutions were reciprocally compatible, and the former was in fact also inevitable because of the growing complexity of the public services and the technical skills they required, which meant growing co-operation and interdependence between local and central government.[94] Though 'grants in aid' were resorted to increasingly after the 1870 Education Act,[95] this form of state 'interference' was not always reconcilable with the widespread passion for local autonomy[96] – especially cherished by some working-class leaders[97] – and generated the fear that the increase of Exchequer grants and loans would eventually

---

[92] (LA), 'Middlesborough and Stockton Joint Board', *Northern Echo*, 21 Aug. 1876, p. 2; cf., for another instance 'Littlejohn', 'Housing the poor: who is to pay?', *Weekly Times*, 9 Mar. 1884, p. 6.

[93] E. P. Hennock, 'Finance and politics in urban local government in England, 1835–1900', *Historical Journal*, 6, 2 (1963), pp. 218–20, 221; cf. A. Briggs, *History of Birmingham*, vol. 2 (London, 1952), pp. 72–3. Briggs writes that 'In 1882, during an inquiry held on the Birmingham Corporation Consolidation Bill, it was conclusively shown that during the seven years' working of the scheme, after allowing for considerable reserve, a sum of £182,500 had been set aside for the borough improvement fund. *This meant a reduction of the rates by over 4 d. in the pound.*' (*ibid.*, p. 73, my italics).

[94] R. Lambert, 'Central and local relations in mid-Victorian England: the Local Government Act Office 1858–1871', *Victorian Studies*, 6, 2 (Dec. 1962), pp. 133–4, 148–50.

[95] H. Page, *Local Authority Borrowing* (London, 1985), pp. 146–51.

[96] *Vigilance Association for the Defence of Personal Rights, Report*, 1872, pp. 4–7, in Cambridge University Library, 'Secondary Material'; cf. J. Row-Fogo, *An Essay on the Reform of Local Taxation in England* (London, 1902), pp. 284–5; D. Fraser, *Power and Authority in the Victorian City* (Oxford, 1979), p. 169.

[97] K. D. Brown, *John Burns*, (London, 1977), p. 200.

cause an increase in Imperial taxation.[98] Moreover, subsidisation without reform would mean perpetuating the uncontrolled waste and inequalities by rendering them more tolerable to the local ratepayers.

A reform of the system of local taxation was in theory much more agreeable, but in practice very difficult to pursue because of the technical difficulties involved, which prevented many working-class radicals from fully understanding the problem, and anyway made it arduous to start a popular agitation. For instance, George Howell, one of the most learned of the labour leaders, had been intermittently active in organisations for the reform of local taxation since 1869: but one of the main points in his programme was 'the greatest possible economy compatible with efficiency'.[99] Even in the 1870s – when he prepared the programme for a London-based 'Ratepayers' National Protection League' – he asked for a revision and redistribution of the fiscal load, but his priority was the reduction of the rates and retrenchment in all unnecessary expenditure.[100] Howell was not alone, since as late as 1882 the TUC – voting for a resolution in favour of a parliamentary inquiry into the Poor Law – especially stressed the necessity of reducing expenditure.[101] In fact, retrenchment came to be the only clear-cut, easily understandable criterion, the only one which could be resorted to to provide the rallying point for a popular movement.

If this was the state of the problem with 'organic intellectuals' and labour leaders, it is hardly surprising that the rank and file were passive. This issue was very different from the campaign for reform of imperial taxation: while free trade and the 'free breakfast table' were unequivocally radical causes, retrenchment in local government was a much more tricky business. In spite of pressure to reduce local expenditure, a serious reduction in the rates would not have been possible or, in the end, popular, because they were the most important financial engine for social reform, the only impost whose social usefulness was apparent.

The only alternative was the 'Chartist' one: that is, the radical democratisation and rationalisation of the whole system of local government in order to give 'to any resident Householder a more direct and practical control as to the mode of levying and expending our vast local income and

98 (LA), 'Local taxpayers' grievances', *Weekly Times*, 30 May 1875, p.1; (LA), 'The clever foot of Tory taxation', *Reynolds's Newspaper*, 22 Apr. 1883, p. 1.
99 G. Howell, 'Ratepayers' Association Dinner, July 13th/[18]69 – Toast of the Evening. – Success to the Ratepayers' Association of St. Mary's Newington', MS. in G. Howell Coll., Letter Books. 151.
100 G. Howell, 'The Ratepayers' National Protection League', MS in *ibid.*, 294.
101 *Report of the 15th Trade Union Congress* (Manchester, 18–23 Sept. 1882), p. 37.

expenditure'.[102] Many were convinced that the problems of social reform would become less difficult once the competent authorities were unified and democratically elected.[103] But it took a long time before popular opinion was stirred up even about this platform, because the problems of the reform of local government were different in different parts of the country. Moreover, in some regions where the need for reform was greater, popular apathy was prevalent: this was the case in London, where – in spite of the report of the Select Committee of 1866, the commitment of J. S. Mill and the radicals, and the campaigns of A. S. Ayrton, Tower Hamlet's Liberal MP, in favour of the equalisation of the rates[104] – the cause of municipal reform for a long time interested almost exclusively the middle classes.[105] Even Howell's attempts to start a ratepayers' movement died out for lack of support and funding in the late 1870s.[106] It was necessary to wait until the 1890s before the working classes became involved at a mass level.[107]

V

Gladstone, however, was not insensitive to these problems, and in 1869 he asked Goschen to prepare a scheme for the reform of both local government and local taxation.[108] In the resulting proposal Goschen had three objectives: he wanted to consolidate all the rates into a single general rate; he intended to give the power of raising local taxation to unified local authorities, responsible to the taxpayers; and he proposed to levy part of the burden of the rates on the landlords. Moreover, he intended to offer substantial relief to ratepayers by turning the existing house tax into a

---

[102] 'Report of the Sub-Committee appointed by the Financial Committee [of the Labour Representation League], at its meeting on Aug. 12th [18]75, to inquire into the Report upon the Conditions and Future Prospects of a Number of Parliamentary Boroughs to be selected by the Committee', *Labour Representation League Papers*, 'Appendix', p. 26. Cf. also the *Report of the 15th Trades Union Congress* (1882), p. 13.

[103] This was the platform of mass newspapers both in London and the north: cf. (LA), 'Mr. Goschen's "Astounding Totals"', *Lloyd's Weekly*, 9 Apr. 1871, p. 1; (LA), 'Local taxation', *Newcastle Weekly Chronicle*, 4 Mar. 1871, p. 4; (LA), 'Local and less taxation', *Lloyd's Weekly*, 27 Apr. 1873, p. 1.

[104] 'First Report from the Select Committee on Metropolitan Local Government', PP, 1866, xiii, pp. xi–xii; G. Stedman Jones, *Outcast London* (London, 1984), p. 250; for a contemporary plebeian comment see Northumbrian, 'The equalization of the Poor Rates', *Reynolds's Newspaper*, 18 Oct. 1868, p. 3.

[105] J. Davis, *Reforming London* (Oxford, 1988), pp. 28–9, 73.

[106] Cf. the appeal for money in G. Howell, 'The Ratepayers' Protection League', nd (but June 1879), MS, in G. Howell Coll., Letter Book, pp. 415–7.

[107] Davis, *Reforming London*, p. 168; the equalization became a point in Will Crooks' programme in 1892: G. Haw, *Will Crooks* (London, nd), p. 91.

[108] W. E. Gladstone to G. J. Goschen, 17 Jan. 1869, in *Gladstone Diaries*, vol. 7, p. 12.

local one.[109] Along these lines a still-born Rating and Local Government Bill was drafted and introduced in 1871, but was criticised in the House for being too favourable to urban dwellers.[110] In 1873 Goschen's successor, Stansfeld, tried again with three bills, none of which was successful.[111] In any case a remarkable degree of interest was shown by the premier, who, after giving a lead to his cabinet in the attempts to find a permanent solution, reiterated his involvement in 1872, when he introduced a 'much prolonged' cabinet 'conversation' 'on the question of Local Taxation'.[112] It was an interesting parallel to the radicals' view that he intended to distinguish between the urban and rural facets of the problem; regarding the latter, he expressed his hostility to giving relief to the landowners for grievances which he considered imaginary, without increasing imperial taxes on the land.[113] However he intended to solve the problem after settling the question of Irish university education; but on that issue the government fell in 1873.

When Gladstone resumed power after Disraeli's refusal to form a government, he took upon himself the additional duties of Chancellor of the Exchequer, a decision which reflected his growing concentration on financial reform as the most important need of the time, and which generated widespread expectations in public opinion.[114] But the disintegration of his majority and the difficulties in the cabinet convinced the premier that the only way to meet these expectations was by a renewal of the House and of his personal mandate.

Gladstone's programme for the elections of 1874 mentioned both the reform of local government and the relief of local taxation;[115] one of his letters to his eldest son shows that for him local government reform had become a priority,[116] and this is confirmed by the amount of preparatory work he had done during the months before the dissolution. After asking Goschen to publish the results of his work of 1869–71 as a sort of Liberal

[109] See G. J. Goschen, *Reports and Speeches on Local Taxation* (London, 1872), pp. 173–6, 189–216.

[110] Matthew, 'Introduction', *Gladstone Diaries*, vol. vii, p.lxxviii.

[111] The Rating (Liability and Value) Bill, the Valuation of Property Bill, and the Consolidated Rate Bill: the former was rejected by the Lords after a bitter fight in Committee, and the other two were withdrawn: cf. J. Noble, *Local Taxation: A Criticism of Fallacies* (London, 1876), pp. 50–1.

[112] Cabinet Minute 14 Oct. 1872, in *Gladstone Diaries*, vol. 8, p. 222.

[113] *Ibid.*; cf. W. E. Gladstone to G. J. Goschen, 17 Jan. 1869, *ibid.*, vol. vii, p. 12.

[114] Buxton, *Finance and Politics*, vol. ii, p. 164.

[115] W. E. Gladstone, 'Dissolution of parliament', *The Times*, 21 Jan 1874, p. 8.

[116] Listing the points of his programme Gladstone wrote: '1. Pecuniary aid to local taxation, but with reform of it. 2. Repeal of the income tax. 3. Some great remission in the class of articles of consumption. (This last remission probably means sugar, but nothing is to be said by any member of the government as to choice of articles.)' (W. E. Gladstone to W. H. Gladstone 24 Jan. 1874, cited in Morley, *Life of Gladstone*, vol. 2, p. 487).

manifesto,[117] in November 1873 Gladstone obtained a memorandum from Stansfeld, and discussed it with the cabinet.[118] Early in 1874 he wrote a long letter to J. Lambert, the secretary of the Local Government Board, discussing another memorandum.[119] The measure which he envisaged was to be drafted along Goschen's lines, at least in the sense that relief on local taxation was to be achieved through the house tax, and to be preceded by a reform of local government (including London)[120] 'to allow ratepayers ... a control over county expenditure',[121] by a unification of the local government authorities and a consolidation of the rates.

Therefore, Colin Matthew's assessment of the 1874 manifesto as devoid of anything like the ambitious social outlook of the great reforms of the 1860s seems ungenerous. Certainly relief on local taxation with increased death duties was not 'something of a "tit-for-tat"'[122] offered to the propertied classes, because in fact Gladstone did not have the propertied classes in mind – though on this issue he was trying to disarm Sir Massey Lopes and the Tories once and for all. At the same time – through the spectacular retrenchment it proposed – the programme represented Gladstone's boldest attempt to give an almost Cobdenite 'fiscal constitution' to the country,[123] with a view to forcing permanent economies on the army and navy establishments; and in this case too he intended to settle in a definitive way a question which had troubled him for decades and which was one of the causes of the sudden dissolution of 1874.[124]

Some of the details of the plan will never be available because, after the defeat of the Liberal party, there was no further need to develop the electoral platform into a working programme. However, in a secret memorandum dated 19 February 1874 Gladstone stated that he needed a surplus of more than £7,500,000 to repeal the income tax and sugar duty, and to relieve local taxation to the extent of £800,000. He already had a

---

[117] W. E. Gladstone to G. J. Goschen, 18 Sept. 1872, in *Gladstone Diaries*, vol. 8, pp. 212–3. See Goschen, *Reports and Speeches on Local Taxation*.

[118] Matthew, 'Introduction', *Gladstone Diaries*, vol. 7, p. lxxix n.; Cabinet minute 28 Nov. 1873, in vol. 8, p. 418.

[119] W. E. Gladstone to J. Lambert, 2 Jan. 1874, in *Gladstone Diaries*, vol. 8, p. 435.

[120] W. E. Gladstone, 'Dissolution of Parliament', *The Times*, 21 Jan. 1874, p. 8.

[121] Cited in F. W. Hirst, *Gladstone as Financier and Economist* (London, 1931), p. 255.

[122] Matthew, 'Introduction', *Gladstone Diaries*, vol. 8, p. lxxxiv.

[123] On this concept see B. Baysinger and R. Tollison, 'Chaining the Leviathan: the case of Gladstonian finance', *History of Political Economy*, 12, 2 (1980), pp. 206–13; and C. G. Leathers, 'Gladstonian finance and the Virginia school of public finance', *ibid.*, 18, 3 (1986), pp. 515–21. Baysinger and Tollison's application of the 'fiscal constitution' theory to Gladstonian finance in the 1850s and 1860s is inappropriate, but can usefully be applied to describe both the alternative Cobdenite model and the Gladstonian programme for 1874.

[124] W. H. Maehl, 'Gladstone, the Liberals, and the election of 1874', *Bulletin of the Institute of Historical Research*, 93 (May 1963), p. 63 and more generally pp. 61–9; Matthew, *Gladstone 1809–1874*, p. 225.

surplus of £5,000,000, which he was going to increase by saving some £600,000 on the army and naval estimates; moreover, he intended to 'venture upon opening new sources of revenue to the extent of 2m[illions]'.[125] In this memorandum Gladstone did not specify what kind of charges he meant by 'new sources', but it is known that an increase in indirect taxation was ruled out,[126] and that he intended to replace the easily expandable income tax by some other taxes on property[127] characterised by a less flexible revenue. As for the nature of these taxes it must be remembered that as early as 1853 Gladstone had made it clear that the alternative to income tax was a tax on 'visible property', with increased legacy duties and a licence duty for all trades.[128] In fact in 1874 his programme included increased legacy and succession duties, which he had discussed with Cardwell and Stephenson in 1873 when he first planned the repeal of the income tax,[129] and which he had supported when they were proposed by Lowe in 1871.[130]

It is true that by this programme Gladstone wished to appeal first of all to those social groups which formed the rank-and-file of the Liberal party before 1867, and which continued to form a very important section of popular liberalism – the lower middle and middle-class electorate. But it was by no means a purely middle-class programme. If his proposed budget 'was intended to ensure retrenchment without upsetting class relationships'[131] and to restore the unity of the party via a non-controversial issue,[132] it is interesting to find that a similar appeal was launched by the *Bee Hive* in 1873,[133] and voiced by leading trade unionists at public demonstrations.[134] Moreover, the 1874 programme included a number of reforms which were very important for the working

---

[125] Cf. *Gladstone Diaries*, vol. 8, pp. 442–3.
[126] Gladstone told Childers that 'You cannot provide for the means for abolishing Income Tax, either whole or in part, out of new indirect taxation' (cited in Matthew, *Gladstone 1809–1874*, p. 222).
[127] W. E. Gladstone to H. C. E. Childers, 2 Apr. 1873, in *Gladstone Diaries*, vol. 8, p. 312.
[128] J. H. Clapham, *An Economic History of Modern Britain, Free Trade and Steel 1850–1886* (Cambridge, 1932), pp. 404–5.
[129] *Gladstone Diaries*, vol. 8, entry for 11 Aug. 1873, p. 368; W. E. Gladstone to Sir W. H. Stephenson, 12 Aug. 1873, in *ibid.*, p. 370; cf. Matthew, 'Introduction', *ibid.*, vol. 7, pp. lxxxiv, lxxxvi.
[130] *Hansard P.D.*, 3rd Series, vol. ccv, col. 1662 (21 Apr. 1871); cf. Matthew, *Gladstone 1809–1874*, p. 222; Buxton, *Finance and Politics*, vol. 2, p. 167.
[131] Matthew, 'Introduction', *Gladstone Diaries*, vol. 8, p. lxxxvi.
[132] See W. E. Gladstone to J. Bright, 14 Aug. 1873 and 10 Oct. 1873, *Gladstone Diaries*, vol. 8, p. 372 and p. 399 respectively. See also W. E. Gladstone to the Duke of Argyll, 17 Jan. 1874: 'I am very far indeed from sanguine about the position of the party & the Government generally, & I see no chance anywhere but in finance of mending the position . . .' (*ibid.*, p. 442).
[133] (LA), 'Mr Gladstone's Guildhall Speech', *Bee Hive*, 15 Nov. 1873, p. 7.
[134] Cf. *Ibid.*, (rep.), 'Free breakfast table', 25 Oct. 1873, p. 3.

classes. Besides the repeal of the sugar duty and the relief for ratepayers, there was the reform of local and London government, county franchise, the game laws, the laws on the 'transfer, descent, and occupation of land', and on the relations between employer and employed.[135] It was also apparent that Gladstone shared the concern of the artisan radicals for a peaceful foreign policy: his programme committed the Liberal party to a foreign policy which would avoid 'the first entrance into equivocal and entangling engagements',[136] like the Ashanti war that the defence ministers had started almost against the premier's will. But these issues were not stressed in the manifesto, because Gladstone wanted public opinion to 'mature' before pressing them, and because, in the end, he felt quite confident that he would have been able to retain the allegiance of the working classes on the basis of their trust in the 'People's William'.[137]

At first Gladstone's strategy seemed to be quite successful with all shades of Liberal opinion. *The Times* and *The Daily Telegraph* reaffirmed their unconditional support for the government:[138] for years *The Times* itself had been maintaining the classical Gladstonian viewpoint that the income tax was a temporary measure and that 'its continuance [was] a standing encouragement to lavish expenditure'.[139] Even the radical *Daily News* declared that 'it cannot be doubted that Mr GLADSTONE chose wisely when he selected economy and sound finance as the motto of the Liberal party in the present crisis . . . here undoubtedly his position and that of the Liberal party is strong and almost unassailable'.[140]

The reactions of the plebeian press were not so enthusiastic, but the most controversial points were those concerning education and religious matters,[141] while the government's fiscal proposals were generally well received. Relief in the rates had been a popular demand as early as April 1873.[142] Even the abolition of the income tax met with no serious objection: the real concern of radical critics was that all the surviving taxes on foodstuffs and the necessities of life should be abolished with it.[143]

---

[135] On the latter question see J. Spain, chapter 6, in the present collection.

[136] W. E. Gladstone, 'Dissolution of parliament', *The Times*, 21 Jan. 1874, p. 8.

[137] *Ibid.*, col. 3. The manifesto itself contained a request to working-class voters to trust the premier on the issues on which his address was not clear or explicit.

[138] (LA, nt), *The Times*, 24 Jan. 1874, pp. 8–9; (LA, nt), *Daily Telegraph*, 26 Jan. 1874, p. 4.

[139] (LA, nt), *The Times*, 8 Apr. 1864, p. 2; it is interesting that the Financial Reform Association maintained the opposite view, that 'Extravagant expenditure in every department of the State has only been rendered possible because the great bulk of the revenue is raised indirectly by taxes on the necessaries and comforts of life' ([rep.], *The Times*, 14 Oct. 1864, p. 7).

[140] (LA, nt), *The Daily News*, 29 Jan. 1871, p. 4.

[141] Cf. M. Hurst, 'Liberal versus Liberal: the general election of 1874 at Bradford and Sheffield', *Historical Journal*, 15, 4 (1972), pp. 669–713.

[142] Gracchus, 'Mr. Lowe's Triumph', *Reynolds's Newspaper*, 6 Apr. 1873, p. 3.

[143] (LA), 'Sir C. Dilke on retrenchment', *Weekly Times*, 18 Jan. 1874, p. 1.

Moreover, its proposed repeal was welcomed by those who saw it as a threat to small employers and a detraction from the 'wages fund' of the country. However, popular support for direct taxation was strong, and the introduction of some new tax on property was considered essential to fiscal and social justice: therefore the fact that Gladstone's manifesto said little about his real intentions on that issue was a weak point in the Liberal platform. On this point working-class electors were asked to sign, as it were, a blank cheque.

In fact, a great number of them were ready to do even that for the 'People's William'. In many regions as soon as the electoral campaign began, popular Liberals came round to the 'good old cause' without questioning, and in any case radical candidates took upon themselves the business of filling the gaps in the premier's manifesto and 'interpreting' it, so that it would look more attractive. At Gildersome, for instance, A. Illingworth said that the reduction of indirect taxation and the abolition of the income tax would have been followed by an increase in the taxation of realised property: at that stage the public applauded.[144] But in most cases no radical 'cosmetics' were necessary: at Newcastle-upon-Tyne Joseph Cowen addressed large meetings of factory workers, artisans and miners amidst great cheers, speaking of the virtues of Gladstonian retrenchment and the wickedness of Tory profligacy, and praising the 'clear, definite, and powerful lines' of the 'magnificent and luminous appeal to the patriotism and intelligence of the people' contained in the premier's manifesto.[145] At Morpeth Thomas Burt, the miners' leader, speaking in front of 'crowded and enthusiastic meetings', expressed himself in a similar vein.[146] At Bradford the 'Labour' candidate J. Hardaker included the abolition of the income tax in his manifesto.[147] George Potter of the *Bee Hive*, candidate for Peterborough, offered a programme including 'the strictest economy in the National Expenditure by the reduction of every item not absolutely necessary for the conduct of the Nation's affairs';[148] the message of George Howell, who tried to

[144] (Rep.), 'Liberal meeting at Gildersome – Mr. A. Illingwoth on the political situation', *The Leeds Mercury*, 10 Feb. 1874, p. 8.

[145] (Rep.) (Cowen's speech), *Newcastle Weekly Chronicle*, 31 Jan. 1874, p. 3. On the other hand it must be remembered that in another speech Cowen found it necessary to justify the remission of £7 millions of direct taxes with the remission of another £7 millions of indirect taxes (a point which did not appear in Gladstone's manifesto): cf. (rep.) *Newcastle Weekly Chronicle*, 7 Feb. 1874, p. 8.

[146] (Rep.), 'Morpeth, *Newcastle Weekly Chronicle*, 31 Jan 1874, p. 3 (speeches by Burt in the Assembly Room and in the Market Place).

[147] (Rep.) (J. Hardaker), *The Leeds Mercury*, 28 Jan. 1874, p. 8.

[148] G. Potter, 'To the working men electors of the Borough of Peterborough', *Bee Hive*, 31 Jan. 1874, p. 11.

conquer Aylesbury, was similar.[149] Alfred A. Walton, Lib.–Lab. candidate for Stoke-on-Trent, speaking to 'a large and enthusiastic meeting', said that he was 'anxious to make them understand the taxation question, because it formed a very important part of Mr Gladstone's programme of the future'. To him the central issue of future politics was the reduction of expenditure, and Gladstone was fully justified in choosing financial reform as the crucial point of the Liberal programme.[150] At another meeting in support of Walton's candidature the leaders of the Staffordshire miners maintained that 'if Mr . Gladstone's Government is returned to power . . . many grievances will be removed, which has [sic] and which does [sic], give a great anxiety to large numbers of Englishmen', whereas a Tory victory would mean 'woe to national progress, national life, and working men'.[151] Even the Labour Representation League's manifesto declared that the working classes 'have yet to struggle for . . . a sound economy in the national expenditure'.[152]

Other Radicals popular with the labour movement, like A. J. Mundella,[153] Sir Charles Dilke, and Thomas Hughes, also supported the 'the abolition of the Income Tax and of the sugar duties, and the affording of a measure of relief to the overburdened taxpayer'.[154] It is a significant measure of the level to which popular enthusiasm for financial reform could be whipped up that a sort of 'choral dialogue' occurred frequently between the public and Liberal candidates. A good example is offered by a meeting at Barnsley, where a Liberal speaker almost 'conversed' with an enthusiastic 'crowd which numbered several thousands':

They were well aware that the issue raised at this election was whether they would or would not retain in office Mr. Gladstone – (cheers) – who had promised the repeal of the obnoxious income-tax, and a thoroughly Liberal programme. (Applause.) Were they prepared to transfer the management of the finances of the country from Mr. Gladstone to Mr. Disraeli? – (No, no.) – who had never introduced a budget without committing some great financial blunder. (Hear, hear.) They were told by the Conservative leaders that the Abyssinian war would cost two millions, but they carried it up to $8 \frac{1}{2}$ millions – ('Shame') – the consequence of which was a considerable increase in the income-tax (Hear, hear). The traditional policy of the Conservatives was to maintain taxation . . . if they wanted

[149] G. Howell, 'To the Electors of the Borough and Hundreds of Aylesbury', *Bee Hive*, 31 Jan. 1874.
[150] (Rep.), 'The representation of Stoke-on-Trent', speech by A. A. Walton, *Potteries Examiner*, 31 Jan. 1874, p. 4.
[151] (Rep.), 'Meeting of miners at Bream', speech by W. Brown, *Potteries Examiner*, 30 Jan. 1874, p. 4.
[152] 'The Labour Representation League to the working classes of Great Britain', *Forest of Dean Examiner*, 30 Jan. 1874, p. 4.
[153] W. H. G. Armytage, *A. J. Mundella 1825–1897* (London, 1951), p. 139.
[154] C. W. Dilke and H. A. Hoare, 'To the electors of the Borough of Chelsea', *Bee Hive*, p. 9; T. Hughes, 'To the electors of the Borough of Marylebone', p. 11.

this policy to be re-established they should return the Conservatives – (No, no) – but if they wished for a continuance of Liberal measures they must vote for Beaumont and Leatham. (Loud cheers.)[155]

Even the *Bee Hive* – which was a strong supporter of direct taxation – came round to the Gladstonian platform: its leading articles proclaimed that 'The abolition of the Income Tax is very important, so is the adjustment of taxation on articles of general consumption; so, in fact, is every question stated by Mr. Gladstone in his Greenwich address.'[156]

Therefore the reactions of the popular electorate to Gladstone's financial proposals were more favourable than might be expected given the fact that they were presented as the most important part of what turned out to be an unsuccessful electoral programme. In fact the Liberal programme was considered threatening and offensive not by the poor, but by 'the monied interest'.[157] It is significant that, though the Liberals were defeated, they obtained clear majorities in the popular vote in each of the kingdoms, and 189,451 votes more than the Conservatives in the country as a whole.[158] But their majority in the polling booths was turned into a minority in the House of Commons because of the peculiar unfairness of the distribution of seats. Moreoever, it seems likely that the Liberal electoral majority could have been even greater had there not been so much disorganisation and fragmentation in the party at constituency level. Those regions such as the mining north-east, where the labour movement was stronger, better organised, and not split by sectarian hatred, remained Liberal. Elsewhere – as working-class Liberal activists complained – party disorganisation, the decay of the Liberal electoral registers,[159] and the lack of mobilisation due to the brevity of the electoral campaign,[160] – played a more important role than rational

[155] (Rep.), 'The General Election – West Riding – Southern Division', *The Leeds Mercury*, 3 Feb. 1874, p. 7.

[156] (LA), 'The Franchise', *Bee Hive*, 31 Jan. 1874, pp. 8–9.

[157] In Edward Baines' words after the Leeds election: cited in Vincent, *The Formation*, p. 160.

[158] That is, 1,281,159 votes (52.7 per cent), against 1,091,708 for the Conservatives (43.9 per cent). The Home Rulers obtained 90,234 votes, mainly from electors who had previously voted Liberal. In 1868 the Liberals had obtained 1,428,776 votes (61.5 per cent), against 903,318 (38.4 per cent) for the Conservatives: F. W. S. Craig (compiler and ed.), *British Electoral Facts 1832–1980*, Parliamentary Research Service (Aldershot, 1989), pp. 10–11, 67.

[159] J. R. Williams, *Quarryman's Champion* (Denbigh, 1978), p. 100.

[160] 'Ironside', 'Political ignorance', *Newcastle Weekly Chronicle*, 3 Apr. 1875, p. 4. Cf. Mahel, 'Gladstone, the Liberals', pp. 67–8. Not only did the dissolution take both friends and foes of the government by surprise, but coming – as it did – at the end of the week, it did not allow time for the mass-circulation, popular Liberal newspapers to enter into the fight before the end of January; by then the first MPs had already been returned, and within two weeks the Tories had already obtained a clear majority. It is useful to remember that the campaigns for the elections of 1868 and 1880 lasted for a very long time and were preceded by radical agitation in the previous years.

arguments for or against the income tax and reform of local taxation, or in fact any other point in the programme.[161] It must also be remembered that the most dramatic decline suffered by the Liberals took place in Ireland, where they lost forty-five seats to the Home Rulers,[162] a reversal which clearly had nothing to do with Gladstone's financial proposals.

The fact that Gladstone's analysis of the needs of the time was right was demonstrated by Northcote's budget later in the year. This included – besides repeal of the sugar duty – local taxation relief to the amount of £1,250,000 (a figure which roughly corresponded to Goschens' 1870 proposal), without reform of local government; and an important reshaping of the income tax: 'raising the exemption limit from £100 . . . to £150, the deduction being increased from £80 to £120 for incomes between £150 and £400. It was generally agreed "that between 200,000 and 300,000 persons would obtain entire remission, and about 200,000 would receive benefit from the exemptions".'[163]

The Liberals regarded it as 'a crude bribe to the new borough voters enfranchised in 1867': they were basically correct, though the word bribe was inappropriate. Very simply, both with relief to ratepayers and with income tax reform Northcote offered a short-term solution – relief through unconditional remission of taxation – to the problems to which Gladstone intended to offer a more thorough-going one – relief through Cobdenite retrenchment, increased death duties and reorganisation of local government.

As a result, Northcote's policy implied slowing down the redemption of the National Debt,[164] and from 1875 and 1876 was accompanied by growing taxation and ever-increasing deficits, for which he was no longer able to offer credible solutions by 1880. At the general election of that year the Tories were beaten on finance first and foremost. This result further confirmed the correctness of Gladstone's analysis of 1874, though his proposed reforms were delayed for some fifteen or twenty years until 1888–94. By then, however, the other part of Gladstone's programme – retrenchment – was no longer really viable as a Liberal policy, though Lib.–Labs. and diehard Cobdenites still abode by it for decades to come.[165]

[161] H. J. Hanham. *Elections and Party Management* (Hassocks, 1978) p. 221; R. Blake, *Disraeli* (London, 1966), pp. 534–7.
[162] G. Morton, *Home Rule and the Irish Question* (London, 1980), p. 15.
[163] Matthew, 'Mid-Victorian budgets', p. 639.
[164] Buxton, *Finance and Politics*, vol. 2, p. 182.
[165] Cf. W. Leigh Bernard and A. Reid (eds.), *Bold Retrenchment* (London, 1888), esp. George Howell's contribution, pp. 43–8; and Brown, *John Burns*, pp. 177, 197.

8 Gladstone and his rivals: popular Liberal perceptions of the party leadership in the political crisis of 1885–1886

Graham D. Goodlad

I

This chapter has evolved from a wider study of the first Home Rule crisis, undertaken in reaction to the exclusively 'high political' perspective of Dr A. B. Cooke and Professor John Vincent's *The Governing Passion*.[1] Its starting point is an observation made by Dr Peter Marsh in an essay on Joseph Chamberlain's role in the Liberal schism, that 'the passions aroused by that crisis among politicians in Britain had little to do with Ireland and an extraordinary amount to do with loyalty among leaders, friends and followers'. He argues that, notwithstanding the title of their study, Cooke and Vincent tended to underplay the element of 'passion' which the crisis generated. Marsh's own analysis of the part played by Chamberlain's tempestuous personality goes some way to redrawing the picture.[2] By drawing on a wide range of manuscript, pamphlet and newspaper sources, this chapter aims to show that the personal attachments and enmities which were so powerful a force in the world of Westminster were no less real in the constituencies. Indeed, though rank-and-file radicals were often very conscious of the peculiarity of the problems of Ireland and some of the Lib.–Labs. had been supporting devolution for years, many Liberal supporters were unfamiliar with Home Rule as a question of practical politics; and given the uncertainty and the conflicting emotions which its adoption as party policy aroused, it might be argued that the personalities of the leading figures assumed a proportionately greater influence at local level than they did even at Westminster.

For it has to be borne in mind that Irish Home Rule was not a policy which automatically commended itself to the average Liberal. The Parnellites' record of obstruction in the 1880–5 parliament and their opportunism in directing Irish voters to reject the Liberals in the 1885 general election;

[1] A. B. Cooke and J. R. Vincent, *The Governing Passion: Cabinet Government and Party Politics in Britain, 1885–86* (Brighton, 1974).
[2] P. T. Marsh, 'Tearing the bonds: Chamberlain's separation from the Gladstonian Liberals, 1885–6', in B. L. Kinzer (ed.), *The Gladstonian Turn of Mind: Essays Presented to J. B. Conacher* (Toronto, 1985), p. 123.

the long-standing anti-Catholic strain in English Nonconformity; the association of Nationalism with violence and illegality in Ireland: these factors scarcely predisposed rank and file Liberals in favour of such a policy departure. Moreover, quite apart from downright hostility, there is considerable evidence of uncertainty, doubt and often, real confusion over the new Gladstonian crusade. The *Birmingham Daily Post* commented in December 1885 on the widespread ignorance, below the level of the party leadership, of what the Home Rule question entailed:

> There is much unreality – we do not, and will not say, insincerity – about this talk of maintaining the unity of the empire, and the supremacy of Parliament or of the Crown. Many men are saying this, and believing themselves to mean it, when they have never looked at the subject closely, and have certainly not realised either the means of maintaining unity and supremacy, or even the kind of unity and the degree of supremacy which are to be maintained.[3]

Home Rule had never before received serious consideration at a British general election; in 1885, the main topics for debate were disestablishment, allotments and smallholdings, and local government reform. In these circumstances, it was not surprising that Liberal parliamentarians and, even more, provincial activists and followers, should turn for guidance to the party's great national figures. This chapter seeks to explain why it was Gladstone – rather than Lord Hartington, John Bright or Joseph Chamberlain – who remained, for the majority of party supporters, unquestionably the most influential of those figures. Wherein lay the source of the immensely powerful hold which the Grand Old Man continued to exert over provincial Liberal loyalties in 1886?

II

I propose now to explore the public image of each of these individuals in turn and to attempt an assessment of their strengths and weaknesses as potential leaders of Liberal opinion. Let us begin with a character whose role in the politics of the mid-1880s was, until relatively recently, virtually ignored by historians: John Bright. The publication in 1985 of an article by Roland Quinault, however, made it clear that Bright exercised an influence on the national political scene quite out of proportion to his actual activity.[4] If anything, his public profile was enhanced by the sudden prominence of the Irish question in the first half of 1886. Dr Quinault quotes *The Times* as saying in November 1885 that Bright

---

[3] *Birmingham Daily Post*, 30 Dec. 1885.
[4] R. Quinault, 'John Bright and Joseph Chamberlain', *Historical Journal*, 28 (1985), pp. 623–46.

'ignores nearly everything except what happened between the Corn Law agitation and the Crimean War; consequently, he scarcely counts as a force in the politics of the day'.[5] Yet it considered the veteran campaigner sufficiently influential to call upon him the following April to lend his voice to the Unionist cause:

Is it vain that his countrymen look to Mr Bright to repeat at this crisis the manly words he has often spoken on this subject? ... We have often differed from Mr Bright, but we have never called in question the sincerity of his desire to do justice to Ireland and ... we hope he may now speak out, in his own way, against measures he knows to be fraught with danger and possibly with disgrace to his country.[6]

Bright was widely regarded as a force to be reckoned with. His support was repeatedly solicited by Gladstone,[7] Chamberlain,[8] and Hartington;[9] and a deputation of Ulster Liberals sought an audience with him.[10] Bright's disinclination to become actively involved in the political struggle in fact enhanced his authority when he finally descended into the arena. As the *Nonconformist and Independent* observed:

Mr Bright has, in days gone by, been the trusted leader of a large section of the Liberal party. He has had a reputation for political sagacity. No one has supposed that his political judgment in regard to the Irish question has been warped by personal ambition and feeling, and he has always taken a deep interest in the welfare of the Irish people. His final utterance was likely to affect those who might have remained unaffected by the sober criticisms of Lord Hartington, the passionate logic of Mr Goschen, or the calculating invective of Mr Chamberlain.[11]

Bright's one speech of the election campaign, delivered to his Birmingham constituents, was widely acknowledged by the Gladstonians as having played a crucial role in their eventual defeat in the 1886 general election. Sir B. Walter Foster. chairman of the Committee of the National Liberal Federation, wrote bitterly that Bright 'probably did more harm in this

5 *The Times*, 21 Nov. 1885.
6 *The Times*, 20 Apr. 1886. *The Times* again called on Bright not to stand aloof in an editorial on 20 May 1886.
7 Gladstone to Bright, 19 Mar. 1886, London, British Library (BL), Bright papers, Add. MS 43,385, fol. 342; J. M. Carmichael to Bright, 11 Apr. 1886, fols. 344–5; Gladstone to Bright, 12 May 1886, fols. 346–7.
8 Chamberlain to Bright, 15 May 1886, Birmingham University Library, Chamberlain papers, JC5/7/44; Chamberlain to Bright, 30 May 1886, JC5/7/45; Chamberlain to Bright, 2 June 1886, JC5/7/47.
9 Hartington to Bright, 5 Mar. 1886, Bright papers, Add. MS 43,387, fol. 238; Hartington to Bright, 11 Apr. 1886, fols. 242–3.
10 *Ibid.*, Hartington to Bright, 26 Mar. 1886, fol. 240.
11 *Nonconformist and Independent*, 7 (8 July 1886), pp. 651–2.

election to his own party than any other single individual'.[12] A Liverpool Gladstonian wrote to the prime minister: 'I wait on a hundred persons a week and I know that thousands were waiting for Bright's speech before they finally made up their minds.'[13] Most dramatic of all, perhaps, was the evidence of P. W. Clayden, who stood for Islington North as a Gladstonian. Clayden repudiated the unpopular Land Purchase Bill and took a copy of the Home Rule Bill round to the homes of the leading dissentient Liberals in this, a constituency where they were numerous and influential:

Going through the Bill with some of them clause by clause, I was able to answer all their objections, and in many cases to get their promise of support. Mr Bright's speech, however, at once undid all my work. In the whole country it probably kept many thousands of Liberal voters from going to the polls, and did more than all the other influences put together to produce the Liberal abstention which gave the Coalition its decisive victory.[14]

It was significant that *The Times* should stress Bright's fondness for reminiscing about the politics of the early Victorian era. For, in large part, he owed his standing to his long service in the cause of liberalism. Indeed, his influence seems to have been strongest with Liberals of the older generation. Herbert Gladstone was informed by his private secretary, Sir Guy Fleetwood Wilson, that 'John Bright's speech has done much harm in London. It has decided a great number of oldish folk who, like him, do not keep pace with the times.'[15] Although his governmental experience had been limited, Bright had been intimately involved in the great reform agitations of the previous fifty years and he had been unwavering in his advocacy of conciliatory policies for Ireland. He had come to be regarded as something of a guardian of the liberal faith. Francis Schnadhorst, writing from Birmingham, saw trouble early on in the rumour that the Home Rule Bill would grant the Irish control of the customs and excise: 'It will raise the Free Traders. It will offend Mr Bright – a very serious thing – Mr Bright's decision will probably determine our policy here and it will greatly influence a lot of the new members. I hope rumour on this point is wrong.'[16] In the heat of the battle, some Liberal Unionist spokesmen could not resist pointing out that Gladstone's liberalism was of much more recent date and had not always been in step with that of the rank and

---

[12] Quoted in Andrew Reid, *The New Liberal Programme; Contributed by Representatives of the Liberal Party* (1886), p. 158.

[13] Alfred Boggis to Gladstone, 2 July 1886, Hawarden, St Deiniol's Library, Glynne–Gladstone papers, General Correspondence of W. E. Gladstone, Box 3, fol. 40.

[14] P. W. Clayden, *England Under the Coalition, 1885–1892* (1892), p. 104.

[15] Sir G. Fleetwood Wilson to H. J. Gladstone, 3 July 1886, BL, Viscount Gladstone papers, 1st series, 45,990, fol. 133.

[16] *Ibid.*, F. Schnadhorst to H. Labouchere, 4 Apr. 1886, 46,016, fol. 23.

file. The *Scotsman* hailed Bright's Birmingham speech as the work of 'the Nestor of the Liberal party', and argued that he was a steadier liberal than Gladstone, who had been converted at a late stage on a number of issues, including free trade, franchise reform, the Crimean and the American Civil Wars, and the secret ballot.[17]

The Liberal Unionists used Bright's great prestige to the full. Extracts from his past speeches on Ireland were reprinted in pamphlet form, as were his electoral address and the letter in which he announced his intention to vote against the second reading of the Home Rule Bill.[18] In Newcastle-upon-Tyne Albert Grey, who had 30,000 copies of Bright's Birmingham speech printed and distributed, expressed the hope that 'five-sixths of the electors will lie in bed and read John Bright tomorrow instead of going to church'.[19] At the same time, Bright's passivity for much of the first half of 1886 made possible some attempts by supporters of Home Rule to use his name to their own advantage. A rumour in late June that Bright, unwilling to trust the Tories, intended to vote for the Gladstonian candidate at Rochdale, was seized upon in the popular press. A regular contributor to the *Northampton Mercury* urged that the news about Bright, 'the patriarchal patriot, the pet of the paper Unionists, the "awful example" of turbulent Tories' should be widely advertised. 'Liberal Unionists have been most persistent publishers. Extracts from the Bright letters have been sown broadcast throughout the land. One fact is, however, worth pounds and pounds of theory; and that fact I now repeat – John Bright will himself vote for a Gladstonite in the coming contest.'[20] When Herbert Gladstone repeated the claim at an election meeting in Leeds, Bright issued a denial in the press.[21] There were, in addition, innumerable attempts to show, by means of quotations from Bright's earlier speeches, that he had changed his mind about Home Rule. For example, William Summers, MP argued that although Bright now took Gladstone to task for condemning the Union, he had done this himself in the House of Commons in February 1886.[22]

Bright's stand nevertheless caused real sadness to many Liberals who had persuaded themselves of the rightness of Home Rule. So high was

[17] *Scotsman*, 3 July 1886.

[18] Liberal Unionist Association leaflets: *Irish Question, no. 31. Mr John Bright on Home Rule, 1872–1886; No. 33. Mr Bright and Mr Spurgeon on the Home Rule Bill; No. 36. Principles Before Party* (Bright to W. S. Caine, 22 June 1886); *No. 37. Mr Bright's Election Address* (1886).

[19] Albert Grey to the 3rd Earl Grey, 3 July 1886, Durham University, Dept. Palaeography and Diplomatic, 4th Earl Grey papers.

[20] *Northampton Mercury*, 26 June 1886.

[21] *Leeds Mercury*, 1 July 1886.

[22] W. Summers, MP, *The Liberal Unionists and their Leaders* (National Liberal Federation, Birmingham, c. 1886), pp. 9–10.

their regard for his liberalism that some Gladstonians assumed that he must have been subject to unfair pressure. Harry Jeffs, who served on the editorial staff of the *Christian World*, considered that 'it was the Chamberlain and Dale influence that drew Bright into the Liberal Unionist camp'.[23] The old man was treated in the Gladstonian press, often with great regret, as hopelessly behind the times. The *Northampton Mercury* characterised his acceptance of an honorary degree from the 'notoriously Tory' University of Oxford as 'a testimony to the John Bright with the Conservative tendencies of today and not to the John Bright, the orator of many a progressive movement in past days'.[24] His position on Home Rule was frequently placed in the context of a growing conservatism of outlook on a range of issues. The organ of the Primitive Methodists, the most pronouncedly working class of all Nonconformist denominations, found indications of Bright's Unionist stance in his opposition to the repeal of the Criminal Law Amendment Act in 1874, and in his cautious attitude towards the franchise and the 'residuum' of society.[25] More simply, his stand was seen as the product of advancing age which had bred an unimaginative attitude to reform. The *Leeds Mercury*, quoting a speech delivered by Bright twenty years earlier, urged electors to 'listen to Mr Bright in his prime rather than to Mr Bright in his enfeebled age'.[26] An equally exasperated *Bristol Mercury* told its readers that 'we are driven to the theory that age has clouded the judgement and dimmed the perception of the once popular tribune'.[27]

Bright's influence over the party as a whole was in the end circumscribed because he had lost the sense of liberalism as a dynamic creed which constantly questioned the assumptions of the previous generation. Liberals who were able to see Home Rule as Gladstone presented it – as another stage in the march of progress and enlightened government – for the most part treated him with respect on account of his past reputation and the manifest honesty of his position; but they could not follow him. Many appeals were addressed to him to see Home Rule in this broader context, including the one made by one of his closest correspondents, W. H. Northy of Newquay:

I have been daily thinking for some time past that you and you alone can put an end to this political deadlock. No one possesses your influence and power, and rightly too, because of your past glorious services. Having given the people bread, and a cheap Press, the franchise, and mainly instrumental in the disestablishment

[23] H. Jeffs, *Press, Preachers and Politicians: Reminiscences, 1874–1932* (1933), p. 39.
[24] *Northampton Mercury*, 10 July 1886.
[25] *Primitive Methodist*, 8 (8 July 1886), p. 442.
[26] *Leeds Mercury*, 3 July 1886.
[27] *Bristol Mercury*, 25 June 1886.

of the Irish Church, to add Freedom to Ireland by giving her an Irish Parliament for Irish affairs only! What a crowning this would be of your career.[28]

Yet Bright remained impervious. In this way he isolated himself from what was to be the mainstream of Liberal politics for the remaining three years of his life.

III

That Bright, an old and unambitious figure, reluctant to play a prominent role in the crisis, should have retained the high regard of Gladstonians is not necessarily surprising. That the Marquess of Hartington, an active politician and the heir to a great dukedom into the bargain, should also have been excepted from the general condemnation of Liberal Unionists is perhaps more worthy of comment. Certainly the prominent Congregationalist divine and Gladstonian loyalist, J. Guinness Rogers, thought so: 'For myself, indeed, I fail to understand why so marked a distinction is made between his lordship and the other seceders. Is it that even Liberals feel that a certain reverence is due to a lord?'[29]

Undoubtedly much of Hartington's political strength derived from his aristocratic rank and territorial power. For example, there is some truth in Henry Labouchere's claim, that the Cavendish influence in W. S. Caine's Barrow constituency was a major factor in his defiance of the Gladstonian whips in 1886, since it removed the danger of defeat in a conflict with a Liberal loyalist.[30] As Dr John Lea has pointed out, only Caine's local security separated him from his friend Samuel Smith, member for Flintshire, who had similar reservations about Gladstone's bill, but who ultimately supported the government.[31]

A discussion of Hartington cannot, however, ignore perceptions, both within and without the political elite, of his qualities of character. It is not my intention here to take issue with the portrait of Hartington as an actor in the Westminster arena which emerges from the work of Cooke and Vincent. Yet it has to be stressed that the calculating politician of *The Governing Passion*, deliberately standing aloof in order to inherit the premiership with the support of a broadly based majority party,[32] was not the Hartington of the rank and file. The flexibility on matters of policy,

---

[28] W. H. Northy to Bright, 15 June 1886, BL, Miscellaneous papers, Add MS 44,877, fol. 104.

[29] J. G. Rogers, 'The coming election', *Congregationalist*, 15 (July 1886), pp. 499–500.

[30] Henry Labouchere to Joseph Chamberlain, 26 May 1886, quoted in A. L. Thorold, *The Life of Henry Labouchere* (1913), p. 318.

[31] J. Lea, 'W. S. Caine and Irish Home Rule. A study of the Radical opposition of 1886', *History Studies*, 1 (1968), p. 62.

[32] Cooke and Vincent, *The Governing Passion*, pp. 88–97, 106–9, 112.

which these authors see as underpinning his conduct in the first half of 1886, was not a prominent feature of his image in the country at large. On the contrary, as we shall see, Hartington's reputation for uncomplicated straight-forwardness earned him much higher regard in Liberal circles than did Chamberlain's qualified opposition to the government policy. The Whig leader's initial coolness, in the spring of 1886, towards approaches from the Conservatives was approved by those newspapers which were soon to become identified with the Liberal Unionist cause. The *Scotsman*, for example, praised his refusal to spare the Tories for their recent opportunistic flirtation with the Irish Nationalists.[33] It described a speech delivered by Hartington in Edinburgh on 30 April as 'an emphatic and influential expression of Liberal opinion', which did not indicate any leaning towards Tory principles.[34]

Hartington saw himself as standing in the mainstream of liberalism: cautiously progressive, ready to rethink earlier positions if the need arose, but knowing where to draw the line. Here, for example, is an extract from a speech at Crawshawbooth, in his Rossendale constituency:

I have on former occasions given expression to much doubt whether, in the present condition of Ireland, a large extension of self-government will be for the good of Ireland herself . . . but I have long ago acknowledged that on that point I was not in agreement with the bulk of the Liberal party, and I am perfectly willing to admit that any reasonable desire for the extension of self-government must now be considered by the Imperial Parliament.[35]

Hartington was concerned to distinguish his own brand of mild reformism from the more clear-cut opposition of the Conservatives. In his election address, published in June 1886, he declared his readiness to consider a measure of devolution on certain clearly defined conditions. 'In advocating the policy which I have attempted to define', he insisted, 'I deny that I have seceded from the principles or traditions of the Liberal party. I contend, on the contrary, that I am maintaining them, and with them the best security for freedom and justice in every part of the United Kingdom.'[36] He was, moreover, keen to stress that his collaboration with the Tories was purely a matter of short-term expediency; in his own words, 'an alliance which is distinctly limited as to time and as to extent'.[37]

By and large his Gladstonian opponents, too, agreed that Hartington continued to speak as a liberal. There were some, of course, who attempted to rationalise his stand in 1886 as the logical culmination of a

[33] *Scotsman*, 6 Mar. 1886.
[34] *Scotsman*, 1 May 1886.
[35] *The Times*, 6 July 1886.
[36] *The Times*, 17 June 1886.
[37] *The Times*, 25 June 1886.

gradual alienation from the party. Lord Eversley (the former Gladstonian MP, George Shaw-Lefevre) considered that 'with him it was not only a breach with the Liberal party on the Irish question, but along the whole line of Liberal measures. He had worked half-heartedly in a Liberal team.'[38] Few, however, were prepared to write him off as utterly lost to liberalism. His services as interim party leader in 1875–80 were not wholly forgotten. Even those radical elements who welcomed the passing of the old Whig section frequently made an exception for Hartington. Although the *Bristol Mercury* regarded his election address as deeply distrustful of the Irish people and marking 'a long stride in the direction of Toryism', it repented of this view at the end of the campaign:

The gibe that if you scratch a Whig you will find a Tory does not apply to the Dissentient leader. Throughout his political career Lord Hartington has been a steadfast Liberal, and he is not going to abandon the convictions of a lifetime for the purpose of consolidating Lord Salisbury's power.[39]

He was rarely charged with desertion, but frequently accused of slowness and negativism. His opponent in Rossendale, Thomas Newbigging, considered that 'the retina of his political eye required time to become familiar with any sudden light that was projected upon it'; whilst Newbigging's chairman, the Reverend Richard Heyworth, drew an interesting distinction between the 'consistency of standing still' and the 'consistency of moving on'.[40] Yet if Hartington's stance led relatively few to give him support, it aroused Liberals' respect. He was universally credited with disinterested motives. A *Pall Mall Gazette* correspondent found that Newcastle-upon-Tyne Liberals recognised his honesty even if his proposals received little support; whilst in Edinburgh he was respected for his honesty, frankness and stolidity, 'but that is all'.[41]

Integrity, consistency, steadiness: these were the qualities most commonly remarked upon in popular appraisals of Hartington. It was an image to which his public pronouncements lent weight. These were always sober, balanced, reasonable, even slightly ponderous productions which conveyed the impression of a man who had carefully weighed the merits of an issue and had reached a conclusion without reference to private self-interest. As the *Scotsman* commented after his appearances at Glasgow and Paisley in June 1886:

The difference between his relation to the democracy and Mr Gladstone's is that he addresses himself to the intelligence and judgement of the whole people, while

---

[38] Lord Eversley, *Gladstone and Ireland: The Irish Policy of Parliament from 1850 to 1894* (1912), p. 306.
[39] *Bristol Mercury*, 17 June, 21 July 1886.
[40] *Manchester Guardian*, 9 July 1886.
[41] *Pall Mall Gazette*, 28, 29 Apr. 1886.

the Prime Minister speaks to the feelings and prejudices of the most numerous class. Lord Hartington's speeches are therefore calm, sober and weighty appeals to the national judgement . . . his courage and resolution are as unquestionable as his sense of duty, and his sincerity of speech, if it fail to awaken passionate devotion, cannot but inspire public confidence.[42]

Confidence was the crucial word. As his biographer expressed it, 'Lord Hartington was sanity itself; and, having good reason to be satisfied with life, was singularly free from any domination by ambition, vanity or jealousy.'[43] Even the Gladstonian *Nonconformist and Independent* observed in March 1886 that his example of caution and independence would be a good one to follow if the prime minister proved too sanguine in his approach to the Irish problem.[44] His stolid yet pragmatic attitude won the approval of the Unionist press while retaining for him the respect of his Gladstonian opponents. It was significant that he alone of the leading Liberal Unionists was seriously mooted as a possible alternative prime minister. There was, for a brief period, a belief in some quarters that he would be called upon to act as a unifying force amidst party and factional strife. The *Scotsman* argued for a Hartington ministry even after Salisbury's notorious 'Hottentots and Hindoos' speech of 15 May had effectively polarised the competition for power between the Conservatives and the Gladstonians.[45] Only in July did it accept the concept of a Conservative government, enjoying Liberal Unionist support on Irish issues, as a means to eventual reunion.[46] Of course, only a minority of Liberals were willing to see Gladstone set aside to be replaced by the heir to the Devonshire dukedom. With all his *gravitas*, relatively few were prepared to follow where he led.

IV

Gladstonians frequently drew contrasts between Hartington and our third character, Joseph Chamberlain; and, significantly, these were almost invariably to the disadvantage of the latter. Although Chamberlain retained some radical support and earned the grudging regard of the centre-right, the real significance of 1886 lay in the revelation of his essential isolation in the world of liberal-radical politics.

[42] *Scotsman*, 28 June 1886.
[43] B. Holland, *The Life of Spencer Compton, Eighth Duke of Devonshire*, vol. 2 (London, 1911), p. 135.
[44] *Nonconformist and Independent*, 8 (11 Mar. 1886), p. 227.
[45] *Scotsman*, 19 May 1886. For a brief analysis of the significance of Salisbury's speech, see Cooke and Vincent, *The Governing Passion*, p. 422; also M. Pugh, *the Making of Modern British Politics, 1867–1939* (London, 1982), p. 56.
[46] *Scotsman*, 14 July 1886.

This is not to say that Chamberlain faced monolithic hostility from the rank and file of the party. Delegates at a meeting of south London working men, held at the Walworth Radical Club, distinguished between Gladstone's scheme – characterised by one of them as meaning 'the destruction of Imperial unity . . . the dismemberment of the Empire' – and Chamberlain's local self-government proposals.[47] The Birmingham leader's influence is manifest in a memorial to the prime minister, signed by nineteen Nonconformist ministers at Nottingham, professing support for the principle of Irish autonomy, but calling for a bill:

that will establish National Legislation in Ireland on lines that will make it possible for Parliaments or Assemblies possessing equal rank and influence to be established in England, Wales, Ireland and Scotland; and that will ensure the permanent possession by Irishmen of their equal rights as citizens of one Commonwealth – the symbol and instrument of whose unity shall be one supreme and sovereign Parliament.[48]

Indeed, a letter in the Chamberlain correspondence, reporting that the preparation of the memorial was under way, and asking for advice on publishing it, reveals that the idea must originally have come from Highbury.[49]

There was, moreover, considerable resentment of Home Rule in some sections of the party as an unwarranted diversion from domestic reforms. Peter Rylands, Radical member for Burnley, spoke for many when he declared regretfully that the parliament elected in 1885 had been 'practically an abortion . . . a barren parliament'.[50] Such feelings did not, however, produce a nation-wide groundswell of support for Chamberlain's radical Unionist alternative. More commonly, they resulted in abstention or in reluctant acquiescence in Home Rule. The Rev. W. Tuckwell, the famous 'radical parson' of Warwickshire, bitterly criticised Gladstonian priorities in his lively memoir of this period: 'Workingmen would find that their devotion had been thrown away, their confidence abused, the promised reforms to which they gave their votes postponed indefinitely, if not altogether sacrificed, to a measure of which no one amongst them had ever heard.' Yet, at the Home Rule election, Tuckwell spoke in favour of H. P. Cobb, Gladstonian candidate for the Rugby division, and wrote a leaflet arguing the case for Home Rule.

It seemed to me (1) that the retention in power of the existing Government was vital to all our aims; (2) that Home Rule, though forced on us unwisely and even

47 *The Times*, 12 Apr. 1886.
48 *Nonconformist and Independent*, 8 (27 May 1886), p. 511.
49 Rev. J. B. Paton to Chamberlain May 1886, Chamberlain papers, JC8/5/3/40.
50 L. G. Rylands, *Correspondence and speeches of Mr Peter Rylands, M.P.*, vol. 2 (London, 1890), p. 245.

iniquitously, to the postponement of far more important and pledged reforms, was righteous in itself, and by Gladstone and Parnell acting in concert, was practicable. While therefore confessing deep disappointment, I declared *faute de mieux* for the Home Rule policy.[51]

Even in Birmingham, Chamberlain's position was far from secure in the spring and summer of 1886. A *Pall Mall Gazette* correspondent who visited the city in mid-May found that 'the people of Birmingham are not yet Montagues and Capulets, but the feeling of the town is pretty evenly divided between Chamberlainism and Gladstonism.'[52] Although Chamberlain managed to retain the confidence of the caucus, a large section of liberal and radical opinion was clearly reluctant to side unequivocally and irrevocably with him. Francis Schnadhorst told him in mid-April that

if it were not for the personal loyalty to yourself an overwhelming majority of Birmingham Liberals would support the Government. I have no doubt that your influence will carry the 'two Thousand' but it will leave us a divided party. An Elector from North Birmingham has just asked me 'Cannot the breach be healed?' This is the question in many minds. I cannot describe to you the distress which many of those who have followed you loyally for years are in.[53]

Party unity was the overriding concern, too, of two men whose influence was to be of crucial importance in Chamberlain's continued ascendancy in Birmingham politics: R. W. Dale, the minister of Carr's Lane Congregational chapel, and J. T. Bunce, editor of the leading Radical newspaper, the *Birmingham Daily Post*. Dale, whose handling of the caucus on Chamberlain's behalf in April 1886 has been superbly analysed by Michael Hurst,[54] was more than a tool of the Radical chief. Before the elections, he worked for an arrangement for the return of the seven sitting Liberal members, regardless of their views on the Irish question. The only one for whom he spoke was Alderman Cook, the Gladstonian candidate in Birmingham East.[55] Similarly, the myth that the *Birmingham Daily Post* was simply Chamberlain's mouthpiece is by now thoroughly exploded. As H. R. G. Whates explained in a little noticed survey of the paper's history, published some thirty years ago, although it eventually followed him into the Unionist camp, 'the choice was made reluctantly and with much heart-searching'.[56] Although its editor rendered vital

[51] Rev. W. Tuckwell, *Reminiscences of a Radical Parson* (London, 1905), pp. 59–61.
[52] *Pall Mall Gazette*, 13 May 1886.
[53] Schnadhorst to Chamberlain, 15 Apr. 1886, Chamberlain papers, JC5/63/15.
[54] M. C. Hurst, *Joseph Chamberlain and West Midland Politics, 1886–1895*, Dugdale Society Occasional Papers, no. 15 (Oxford, 1962), pp. 16–19.
[55] A. W. W. Dale, *The Life of R. W. Dale of Birmingham* (London, 1898), pp. 463–4.
[56] H. R. G. Whates, *The Birmingham Post, 1857–1957: A Centenary Retrospect* (Birmingham, 1958), p. 40.

assistance to Chamberlain by winning for him the opportunity to put his case to the 'Two Thousand',[57] it is clear that relations between the two were not uniformly smooth. In mid-May we find Chamberlain complaining to his brother that Bunce should have waited for an explanation before criticising his appearance at a meeting of Hartington's supporters: 'The fact is that he (i.e.: Bunce) is hedging and at any moment may go over to the Home Rule camp.'[58] In fact, as Whates points out, the *Post*'s line throughout the crisis was that the margin of disagreement between Liberal Unionists and Gladstonians was very narrow: from December 1885 to the summer of 1887 it sought consistently for compromise and reconciliation.[59] Whilst hoping for a concession from Gladstone on the question of Irish representation at Westminster,[60] the *Post* declared in late May that Liberals should return all seven members for Birmingham, regardless of their position on Home Rule.[61] The Chamberlainite's rejection of the compromise over representation, announced by Gladstone on 27 May, was seen by the *Post* as a disaster since it meant that the Liberal party would face the election disunited.[62] The only alternative to support for the principle enunciated by Gladstone was the return to power of a Tory government: 'thus we come to the main question now before the electors – conciliation or coercion in Ireland, Gladstone or Salisbury as the head of government in Great Britain'.[63] It was to take almost another year for the *Post* to shift to an unambiguously Unionist position.

If Chamberlain's position in the world of Birmingham politics was far from assured, in the country at large he was positively isolated. Perhaps the most telling indicator is the response of the Liberal press to his resignation from the cabinet, together with G. O. Trevelyan, in March 1886. In general, reaction can best be described as sanguine. The agricultural labourers' leader, Joseph Arch – whose election to parliament had been celebrated barely two months earlier, at a dinner at which Chamberlain presided[64] – clearly did not regard the pair as indispensable. Arch told a meeting at Diss, Norfolk that 'while he should be extremely sorry to lose the services of Mr Chamberlain and Mr Trevelyan, he had no doubt that the right honourable gentleman at the head of the Government would be able to find two good men to fill their places'.[65] Most Liberal papers

[57] Hurst, *Joseph Chamberlain and West Midland Politics*, p. 16.
[58] Chamberlain to Arthur Chamberlain, 15 May 1886, Chamberlain papers, JC5/11/8.
[59] Whates, *The Birmingham Post*, p. 122.
[60] *Birmingham Daily Post*, 8 May 1886.
[61] *Birmingham Daily Post*, 20 May 1886.
[62] *Birmingham Daily Post*, 1 June 1886.
[63] *Birmingham Daily Post*, 4 July 1886.
[64] See the *Daily News*, 19 Jan. 1886.
[65] *English Labourers' Chronicle*, 27 Mar. 1886.

were simply prepared to put their trust in Gladstone's proven experience and capacity. The *Bristol Mercury* commented that 'until we have their views before us, it is impossible to decide between Mr Gladstone and Mr Chamberlain, but the drafting of a measure of Irish government is a test of statecraft, and the presumption in such a case is in favour of the old Parliamentary hand'.[66]

The real weakness of Chamberlain's national position was revealed by the reception of his qualified opposition to Gladstone's scheme. Outside Birmingham and Scotland – where the issue had a more direct interest for supporters of devolution – his insistence on continued Westminster representation was viewed with incomprehension or worse. The more charitable Gladstonians looked on Chamberlain's estrangement as an inexplicable inconsistency, a temporary aberration from which he would soon recover. George Leveson Gower likened his action to that of 'a man who, wishing to go on a railway journey over a certain line, might object to get into the train because the engine was painted a particular colour'. However, he did not doubt that 'the master engineer would be able to get a paint pot more to his liking ... and they would find Mr Chamberlain travelling along in the same carriage again'.[67] In many cases, however, a marked note of hostility crept into appraisals of Chamberlain's action. Especially was this the case in May and June as the political battle became more acute and the survival of the Home Rule principle – and therefore of the government – increasingly became the priority for most Liberals. The *Manchester Guardian*, for example, agreed that representation should be tied to taxation, asserting after the announcement of Gladstone's scheme that 'a common Parliament is the pledge and bond of national unity'.[68] However, it welcomed Gladstone's declared readiness to consider amendments as evidence of a genuine desire for reconciliation,[69] and with growing stridency blamed the persistence of the rift on Chamberlain. The real danger to the bill, it asserted on 13 May, came not from those who rejected the Home Rule principle, but from those who, whilst accepting the principle, insisted on giving it their own interpretation or on applying it in their own way.[70] After the defeat of the second reading came a comprehensive attack on Chamberlain's position on Ireland. He had helped to undermine the old system of coercion by bringing down W. E. Forster in 1882 but, unlike John Morley, had not drawn the logical conclusion, that a new system must be tried. He had failed to see that

[66] *Bristol Mercury*, 29 Mar. 1886.
[67] *Home Rule Address by Mr George Leveson Gower, delivered in the Imperial, Hanley, May 27 1886* (1886), p. 2.
[68] *Manchester Guardian*, 10 Apr. 1886.
[69] *Manchester Guardian*, 19 Apr. 1886.
[70] *Manchester Guardian*, 13 May 1886.

Ireland required exceptional treatment, and in his espousal of the Protestant minority cause had attempted to defend the indefensible.[71]

Unlike Bright or Hartington, Chamberlain was widely assumed to be acting from unworthy personal motives. The allegation was made in so many quarters that it necessarily attracts our attention. After the 'Committee Room fifteen' meeting of 31 May, at which the Chamberlainites decisively repudiated the bill, the *Bristol Mercury* castigated their leader as 'the spoilt child of politics'. It was clear, now, that 'he objects to the scheme because it is Mr Gladstone's and not his and that no concessions will satisfy him unless Mr Gladstone will surrender and accept Mr Chamberlain's dictation'.[72] The *Pall Mall Gazette*'s travelling correspondent found many Liberals in both Newcastle-upon-Tyne and Birmingham who believed that Chamberlain's hostility was due to chagrin at the prime minister's neglect to consult him, and at the promotion of Morley over his head in the cabinet.[73] His position was unaccountable and unacceptable to Liberals who could not conceive of politics except in terms of the old Liberal–Conservative divide. For the *Primitive Methodist* the issue was highlighted by Salisbury's 'Hottentots and Hindoos' speech: 'the feeling growing in the country is not favourable to Mr Chamberlain as a consistent Radical. We had hopes concerning his future career, but . . . if after the speech of Lord Salisbury he continues to oppose the Government, our hopes will be entirely blighted.'[74]

Chamberlain was widely acknowledged to have been the object of a much more intense animosity than any other prominent Liberal Unionist. Gladstone reported to Spencer that at a meeting in Edinburgh, 'I could manage pretty well with the names of Hartington and Salisbury but nothing could induce them to tolerate the name of Chamberlain, invariably followed by the bitterest hooting and groaning'.[75] Years later the veteran Bradford Gladstonian, Alfred Illingworth, gave as his opinion that Bright had 'acted honestly, though not wisely', but that the same could not be said of Chamberlain: 'he has been true to nothing, except the advancement of his own vulgar ambition'.[76] 'Asmodeus', a regular columnist in the *Tyneside Echo*, wrote that, unlike Hartington, who 'represented the great historic Whig party and Whig principles, the

[71] *Manchester Guardian*, 21 June 1886.
[72] *Bristol Mercury*, 2 June 1886.
[73] *Pall Mall Gazette*, 28 Apr. 13 May 1886.
[74] *Primitive Methodist*, 8 (20 May 1886), p. 314.
[75] Gladstone to Spencer, 19 June 1886, quoted in P. Gordon (ed.), *The Red Earl: The Papers of the Fifth earl Spencer, 1835–1910*, Northamptonshire Record Society, 34,2 (Northampton, 1986), p. 123.
[76] A. Illingworth, *Fifty Years of Politics: Mr Alfred Illingworth's Retrospect, Recollections and Anecdotes* (Bradford, 1905), p. 30.

Glorious Revolution of 1688, and the predominance of the Protestant religion', Chamberlain had 'no moral force behind him'.[77] There was the rub: 'no moral force'. It is a theme to which I shall return during my discussion of Gladstone. Chamberlain's failure to realise that radicalism must aspire to satisfy the heart as well as the stomach meant that such hold as he had on the affections of Liberal Nonconformists disappeared when he chose to stand apart from the party leader. As an article in the *Pall Mall Gazette* explained:

He is deficient of imagination and curiously lacking in the capacity of rousing the better nature of those whom he addresses . . . With all his zeal for the amelioration of his fellow-countrymen, Mr Chamberlain has never mastered that elementary truth so well expressed by Mrs Browning when she says 'It takes a soul to move a body; it takes a high-souled man to move the masses, even to a cleaner style.'[78]

V

Chamberlain himself had a more prosaic explanation for the Grand Old Man's continued popular strength: the inherent advantages, in a time of increasingly formal and disciplined party organisation, of the leader's position. His acidic comment on the prospect of political isolation which lay before a cabinet minister who resigned was that 'there is little backbone in politics and the great majority are prepared to swallow anything and to stick to the machine'.[79] On the Home Rule side, the *Pall Mall Gazette* acknowledged that

the keen party man, who takes sufficient interest in politics to get elected on the local caucus and to run the Liberal machine, is of all others the citizen whose mind is dominated by party discipline. The caucus exists in a large measure to win elections, and anything and everything which threatens success at the next electoral combat is hateful in the eyes of the thoroughgoing Liberal Association.[80]

Yet there was more than merely formal deference to Gladstone as the ultimate head of the party machine. By virtue of the length of his service and his involvement in much of the progressive legislation of the last thirty years, the Grand Old Man had become synonymous with the whole tradition of British liberalism. In voting for Home Rule, men were voting for the past record of a man who had come to symbolise the historic struggle between the principle of popular liberty and the forces of reaction. In their enthusiasm some Liberals slipped into distortions of recent history. Addressing a meeting of delegates of the South Molton

[77] *Tyneside Echo*, 10 May 1886.
[78] *Pall Mall Gazette*, 23 June 1886.
[79] Chamberlain to Arthur Chamberlain, 8 Mar. 1886, Chamberlain papers, JC5/11/5.
[80] *Pall Mall Gazette*, 3 May 1886.

division of Devon, Edwin Hanford, vice-president of the Torrington district Liberal Association, ventured the opinion that

They did not wish to take any rash measures, but they believed in Mr Gladstone as the man most able to grapple with the great question of the day. For fifty years Mr Gladstone had led the party to victory, and it was not the first time he had attempted Irish legislation.[81]

Gratitude for benefits conferred in the past was a recurrent theme in working-class and Nonconformist utterances during the crisis. The speeches delivered at a meeting in support of Home Rule, held during the Primitive Methodist conference at Derby in June 1886, make interesting reading in this respect. Significantly, the mover of the resolution of sympathy with Gladstone, one Mr Lawrence of Leicester, declared that its intentions were, firstly, 'to express their admiration of the greatest statesman of the age, whether living or dead – (cheers) – and secondly, to approve of the policy which that statesman had now launched upon the nation'. The following extract gives something of the flavour of the speech, and of its reception by the meeting:

The services which Mr Gladstone – (cheers) – had rendered to the nation and to the cause of humanity at large had no parallel in the history of the country. As a scholar he had enriched the library with productions which would have been no disgrace if he had spent his whole time in the seclusion of his study. (Hear, hear.) As a Parliamentary orator and debater, he had no compeer, and as a philanthropist he had always been on the side of the down-trodden and oppressed. (Cheers.) They did not forget his sympathies with struggling nationalities in their endeavours to assert their national freedom, and as a Christian patriot they remembered that he had never plunged the nation into the war with a light heart. (Cheers). As a financial reformer Mr Gladstone had completely revolutionised our financial system, and had freed from taxation 1,200 of the necessaries of life. (Cheers.) He had been instrumental in passing the Education Act of 1870, had liberated the Irish from the domination of an alien Church, and last, but not least, had given to two or three millions of our fellow-subjects the franchise – (cheers) – which had enabled them to exercise the rights and duties of citizenship. To his intellectual qualities were added great moral qualities, which had challenged their admiration most of all. (Cheers.) He certainly could wear the 'rare white flower of a blameless life', he had laid his intellectual and moral qualities on the altar of the nation for the country's good, and if he (the speaker) had a voice like a trumpet he would ask them if such a man's life was to be allowed to go down in gloom at this crisis. (Cheers.)

The remainder of the speech consisted of an attack on Gladstone's opponents, especially Chamberlain – whom he described as 'but "small dust in the balance, less than nothing" and vanity' – and an expression of

[81] *Western Morning News*, 4 June 1886.

hope that the Irish question would soon be settled so that legislation on the Church, the land laws and the liquor traffic could pass.[82] At no point did the speaker make anything more than a passing reference to the merits of the Home Rule Bill.

By 1886 this kind of hero-worship of the Grand Old Man was already well-rooted in popular political culture. In his seminal work, *The Formation of the British Liberal Party*, John Vincent charted the growth of Gladstone's relationship with the masses – initially more enthusiastic on their side than on his – through his popular oratory during the 1860s.[83] The strength of Gladstone's hold on the popular imagination at this early stage, especially in northern England, is richly suggested by the leading Newcastle-upon-Tyne liberal, Robert Spence Watson:

Returning from Grasmere with my wife, I got a copy of *The Times* at Oxenholme station, and on the platform, waiting for our train, I began to read her Mr Gladstone's 'flesh and blood' speech. A few porters gathered around, and asked to be allowed to listen, and so I sat up on the back of the seat and read a little more loudly. Then one went and told some men who were working outside the station, and soon I had an audience of some thirty persons. And when we got to the passage 'Time is on our side' – the subject was household enfranchisement – and the assertion that the men sought to be enfranchised were flesh of our flesh and bone of our bone, my audience cheered and cheered as if they had been listening to the speaker himself.[84]

Richard Shannon's masterly study of the Bulgarian agitation of 1876 shows how this rapport deepened in the succeeding decade. Unlike the situation in 1886, the initiative in this case was not Gladstone's; rather he became associated with an already existing movement in the country. In particular, Shannon argued, 1876 was crucial for the development of relations between Gladstone and Nonconformity. Through the experience of co-operation in the atrocities campaign, 'the two greatest forces in English public life asserting the moral obligation inherent in political action at last came together in full sympathy'.[85] Here is surely the crucial point of contact between Gladstone and grassroots liberalism. It shows through in the emphasis of the Primitive Methodist speaker, Lawrence, on the moral qualities of the Liberal leader. This theme was taken up by the president of the conference, the Rev. J. Atkinson:

---

[82] *Primitive Methodist*, 8 (24 June 1886), p. 419.
[83] J. R. Vincent, *The Formation of the British Liberal Party, 1857–68* (London, 1966), pp. 260–7.
[84] Aaron Watson, 'Modern influences, XLI. The Right Hon. Robert Spence Watson', *Millgate Monthly*, 4 (1909), pp. 337–42.
[85] R. T. Shannon, *Gladstone and the Bulgarian agitation, 1876* (London, 1963), pp. 110, 163.

He could not hide from himself that Mr Gladstone was a profoundly religious man and was governed in his political action by principles of religious conviction. He believed that a religious man always felt stronger when he realised that other religious men were in sympathy with him, and therefore their leader would be strengthened by a knowledge of that resolution.[86]

In such remarks, perhaps, we see the impulse which lay at the heart of popular Gladstonianism: the regard for an evidently deeply religious man felt by men whose whole view of the world was coloured by the Christian ethic. More especially in the light of Jonathan Parry's stimulating study of *Democracy and Religion*,[87] we cannot afford to judge the nineteenth century by the criteria of the secular twentieth. Thus, a *Primitive Methodist* editorial after Gladstone's defeat in July 1886 declared frankly that 'we are politicians because we are Christians, and our politics are determined by our conception of the teaching of the New Testament; and we dread the advent of a Tory government'.[88] The equation between radical–liberalism and Christianity was made at greater length in the *Congregationalist*. An editorial positively welcomed the charge made by W. H. Hall, that the Liberal Unionists had been defeated in Cambridgeshire East because the area was 'dominated by Nonconformist ministers in the case of some of whom religion and radical politics are inseparably connected'.

One qualification only do we supply. For themselves, and those who agree with them these ministers regard religion and Radical politics as identical. They do not judge other men, but they hold that the great law of the Gospel can only be carried out in national affairs by the adoption of what are described as 'Radical politics'. It is this which gives them their strength and influence. That religion begets in them popular sympathies, teaches them to believe in the triumph of justice, inspires them with a trust in God which enables them to contend that, at whatever cost, right should be done.[89]

For such men, Gladstone, with his ability to impart a moral imperative to every major political question which he took up, was the natural leader. The *Baptist* – which was itself highly critical of the Home Rule Bill – commented in mid-June that:

Baptist opinion has been fairly foreshadowed at association meetings held within the last week or two. There is a seeming preponderance in favour of Mr Gladstone, as he was, as he is, and as he shall be, and to avoid the committal either of voting for a man rather than a measure, or of supporting and defending a legislative

---

[86] *Primitive Methodist*, 8 (24 June 1886), p. 419.
[87] J. P. Parry, *Democracy and Religion: Gladstone and the Liberal Party, 1867–1875* (Cambridge, 1986), pp. 1–6.
[88] *Primitive Methodist*, 8 (29 July 1886), p. 497.
[89] *Congregationalist*, 15 (Aug. 1886), p. 603.

bubble, a compromise by way of thunderous applause for the Grand Old Man and 'his heroic efforts to settle the Irish question' has very *prudently and harmlessly* been adopted.[90]

Home Rule thus took its place in an essentially clear-cut world-view which saw history as a struggle between liberty and tyranny, progress and reaction, light and darkness. The details of the legislation were of comparatively little interest at the side of the great principles which were at stake. Even if Gladstone failed in his enterprise, declared the *Leeds Mercury*,

at least, as he rides forth today to battle, there is no man who will not admit that it is against hideous forms of old world evil that his sword is raised, and that if he can but conquer them, he will have done better for the common-wealth than did Theseus of old when he slew the fabled monster.[91]

The *Pall Mall Gazette*'s roving correspondent, after meeting Liberals in Manchester, concluded that 'the Premier satisfies their aspirations after liberty, justice and righteousness, as neither Mr Chamberlain nor any other man can, and in according Home Rule to Ireland they may be relied upon to support him both staunchly and substantially'.[92] There was between Gladstone and large numbers of Nonconformists what D. W. Bebbington, in a perceptive essay, has termed a shared 'vital Christianity', which transcended differences over the Church establishment and over attitudes to Rome and denominationalism.[93] In his memoirs Samuel Smith, MP, remarked upon the devotion of Protestant Dissenters in north Wales to Gladstone the High Anglican: 'the bond that united them was something deeper than church connexion; it was a common devotion to the Christian religion, taught in different forms, but one in essence'.[94] If the bond was sufficiently deep to make differences of denominational allegiance between leader and followers of no account, it was also strong enough to override doubts about Irish Home Rule as a policy. Gladstone's moral rhetoric made it possible to see Home Rule as another stage in the march of freedom and progress, as part of the seamless web which was the history of the liberal cause. Thus the Liberal Unionists could be portrayed as the real deviants from liberalism; as having, in the words of Guinness Rogers, only 'an enlightened opportunism, without any element

---

[90] *Baptist*, 28 (18 June 1886), pp. 392–3, my emphasis.
[91] *Leeds Mercury*, 8 Apr. 1886.
[92] *Pall Mall Gazette*, 10 May 1886.
[93] D. W. Bebbington, 'Gladstone and the Nonconformists: a religious affinity in politics', in D. W. Baker (ed.), *Church, Society and Politics: Studies in Church History*, 12 (Oxford, 1975), pp. 381–2.
[94] S. Smith, MP, *My Life-work* (London, 1902), pp. 232–3.

of daring and not infrequently coloured by selfishness'. Theirs was a failure to see politics as an 'organic whole'; they had a 'general disposition to introduce necessary reforms', but 'not necessarily the grasp of any ruling idea on which reform was to be worked out'.[95] It was a measure of Gladstone's moral standing that in 1886 he was able to remain, for the majority of Liberals, the unique interpreter of that 'ruling idea'.

[95] J. G. Rogers, 'Mr Gladstone and the Nonconformists', *Nineteenth Century*, 44 (1898), p. 33.

Part III

Radicals, Liberals and the Labour party

Labour and parliament: the Lib.–Labs. as the first working-class MPs, 1885–1906

John Shepherd

I

In 1898 Henry Broadhurst, MP, the first workman to be appointed a government minister, was present at the state funeral of William Gladstone. On leaving Westminster Hall, the former stonemason remembered with pride an earlier time he had laboured at the Houses of Parliament:

> my eye involuntarily sought the clock tower, on whose tall flanks I had worked, chilled to the bone, nearly thirty years before; and my memory recalled one bitter cold, wet day in the winter of 1858–59 when, almost barefoot, I had crossed the Palace Yard ... The contrast was almost overwhelming: then unknown and penniless; today in a place of honour, the sorrowing colleague of the greatest Englishman of the century.[1]

In the late nineteenth century Broadhurst held the distinction of being one of the first of a small group of working-class MPs, known as Lib.–Labs., who sat in the House of Commons as labour members but were ardent Gladstonian Liberals in politics. For after Chartism, the dominant feature of English working-class politics was not the emergence of an independent working-class movement, but the rise of an influential group of Victorian trade union and labour leaders who broadly accepted the tenets of liberal capitalism. For this new elite of working-class politicians, parliament was often the culmination of a professional career as a trade union leader and labour organiser.

In 1897, Herbert Samuel, of the National Liberal Federation, urged Gladstone to support Sam Woods, the miners' leader and Lib.–Lab. secretary of the Parliamentary Committee of the Trades Union Congress (TUC) as the official Liberal nominee in the Walthamstow by-election. Samuel stressed 'the great importance at the present moment of a hearty alliance between the party and the more sober section of the Labour politicians',[2] a well-directed reference to the long-established links in Victorian politics between the Gladstonian Liberal party, its mass support

---

[1] H. Broadhurst, *Henry Broadhurst M. P. Told by Himself* (London, 1901), p. 312.
[2] Samuel to Gladstone, 23 Jan. 1897, BL, Gladstone papers, Add. MS 44,525, fol. 64.

amongst workmen, and the political allegiance to Liberalism of trade union and labour leaders. For despite the challenge of independent labour and socialist politics, in the late nineteenth century this Lib.–Lab. elite continued to dominate the Trades Union Congress and the organised labour movement and remained virtually unshakeable in its connections with Gladstonian Liberalism and the Liberal party.

Even before the advent of the modern British Labour party, the labour presence at Westminster had therefore been represented for over twenty-five years by the Lib.–Lab. MPs. Their role as the first working-class representatives at Westminster has often been ignored or dismissed as detrimental to the growth of democratic politics:

Broadhurst's career marks the ultimate landmark on the road taken by the labour elite of the 'new Model' period . . . His view of his own story is an expression of this mentality, which made the labour elite of his time the most submissive towards the ruling class and the most conservative in relation to the aspirations of its own stratum in the history of the British labour movement.[3]

Moreover, in emphasising the parliamentarianism of the Labour party, greater attention has been paid to the foundation of the Labour Representation Committee (LRC) in 1900 as an alliance of trade unionists and socialists with the primary purpose of securing an increased number of Labour members in the next parliament. But direct workers' representation was nothing new; a point readily acknowledged by many later Labour party stalwarts, such as J. R. Clynes: 'Thomas Burt and Alexander McDonald, the forlorn hope of the mighty army of British workers, flung upon the gates of St. Stephen's; and those gates have never been shut against us since.'[4]

This chapter attempts to reappraise the contribution of the Lib.–Lab. MPs in first establishing a strong labour tradition at Westminster, continued by most of the later LRC/Labour MPs. As working-class members, the Lib.–Lab. MPs belied the image of self-satisfied upward mobility often attributed to them by their opponents. Instead, in consistently representing the working-class and labour movement, they retained a strong sense of their own proletarian origins and direct practical experience of industrial life. Thus Randal Cremer in 1885 predicted that the first group of labour representatives would enter parliament 'to prove to the landlords, to the squires, to the lawyers, and to the men who had in the past been exclusively their legislators, that they too knew something about the making of the laws, and were capable of holding their own'.[5]

[3] Z. Bauman, *Between Class and Elite* (Manchester, 1972), p. 131.
[4] J. R. Clynes, *Memoirs 1869–1924* (London, 1937), p. 21.
[5] *English Labourer's Chronicle*, 19 Dec. 1885.

Paradoxically, though they remained staunch opponents of independent labour representation, the Lib.–Labs. thus laid the basic pattern of a parliamentary tradition (albeit restricted to men in the late nineteenth century), based on the representation of a social class hitherto excluded from parliament. As a result the Labour party was to inherit this non-revolutionary tradition of working-class politics, stretching back to the Labour Representation League, the Reform League and beyond, which focused on parliament for the redress of social and economic grievances.[6]

Indeed, as a parliamentary group, the Lib.–Labs. actually saw themselves as the first 'Labour party', a term in use by the 1890s. At the foundation conference of the Labour Representation Committee, John Burns reminded the delegates: 'There was a distinct Labour group in Parliament organised for the past four or five years, of which Mr Woods and himself were whips. They had not called themselves independent, they had not worn trilby hats and red ties but they had done the work.'[7] In a similar vein, the Miners Federation of Great Britain (MFGB) established an electoral fund, in effect a second 'Labour party', to finance mining candidates at the next election. At the MFGB annual conference in 1899, president Ben Pickard had made the classic Lib.–Lab. rebuttal of the notion of a general association of labour representation with his well-known declaration: 'I should like to ask why we as a Federation should be called upon to join an association to find money, time or intellect to focus the weaknesses of other Trade Unionists to do what you are doing for yourselves and have done for the last fourteen years.'[8]

II

During the late nineteenth century the Lib.–Labs. formed a small, but distinct, group of MPs in parliament. After the 1885 election the twelve new labour members met together at Broadhurst's TUC office in Buckingham Street, near the Strand, before walking proudly as a group to Westminster for the state opening of parliament.[9] By this action, this small band of representatives demonstrated their common identity and class pride shared by their humble origins, lack of formal education, and experience of working at a trade from an early age. As self-educated workmen, in the main, they had progressed from manual occupations to influential positions as professional trade union officials and labour organisers. In 1874 the two miners' officials, Thomas Burt and Alexander

[6] D. Coates, *The Labour Party and the Struggle for Socialism* (Cambridge, 1975), pp. 5–6.
[7] *Ironworkers' Journal*, Apr. 1900.
[8] Quoted in H. Pelling, *Origins of the Labour Party, 1880–1900* (Oxford, 1954), p. 194.
[9] *English Labourer's Chronicle*, 30 Jan. 1886.

McDonald were elected as the first Lib.–Lab. MPs, with Broadhurst, secretary of the Parliamentary Committee of the TUC, joining them in 1880. In 1885 the group increased in size to twelve members, and firmly established the new pattern of parliamentary representation with its numbers never falling below eight or nine members. In all, although the composition of this parliamentary group altered at times, between 1874 and 1906 some twenty-four members of working-class parentage and background, and generally described as Lib.–Labs., were returned to the House of Commons.[10] (See the table in the appendix, pp. 211–13, for details on the backgrounds and careers of the individual Lib.–Labs.).

There has never been a generally accepted definition of the political name Lib.–Lab., despite its common use since the late nineteenth century. As MPs, the Lib.–Labs.' own perception was that they regarded themselves, and were acknowledged, primarily as labour representatives. At the same time, Broadhurst, Burt and their colleagues saw nothing incompatible with this view in being sound Liberals and members of the Gladstonian Liberal party. These working-class representatives, therefore, proudly called themselves Liberal–Labour members or spoke of a Labour party in parliament. Like other party political labels, the description appears to have originated as a term of political abuse (by socialist opponents), being abbreviated to 'Lib.–Lab.' in the 1890s. As the 'Liberal–Labour' members, *The Labour Leader* roundly castigated them as 'no more parliamentary men to the class they are supposed to represent than would be an equal number of whipped and toothless poodles'.[11]

Thomas Burt gave his own definition of a labour member: 'The House of Commons has itself practically decided the point. Those whom it has accepted as labour members are, without exception, men who worked at their respective trades, and who still maintain a close connection with large associated bodies of workmen, such associations selecting and recognising them as their representatives and spokesmen.'[12] Burt's description reveals the psychological importance these former workmen attached to earning a living by working with their hands, the essential *raison d'être* for their role as labour representatives. In terms of occupation, about half the Lib.–Lab. MPs were former miners, since no other occupational group, including the powerful cotton unionists, was able to secure representatives to the same extent at municipal or parliamentary

---

[10] Published lists often include Radical and middle-class MPs whose claim to the title 'Lib.–Lab.' would have been considered dubious by their contemporaries. See, for example, A. W. Humphrey, *A History of Labour Representation*, (London, 1912); G. D. H. Cole, *British Working Class Politics* (London, 1941); T. Boyle, 'The Liberal imperialists, 1892–1906', *Bulletin of the Institute of Historical Research*, 52 (1979), pp. 48–82.

[11] *Labour Leader*, 2 Apr. 1898.

[12] Thomas Burt, 'Labour in parliament', *The Contemporary Review*, 55 (May 1899), p. 679.

levels.[13] The remainder of the Lib.–Lab. MPs were drawn from a number of crafts and trades, as shown in the appendix (pp. 211–13).

In the mining contingent of Lib.–Lab. MPs, there was a quartet of representatives before 1900 from the north-east coalfield; Thomas Burt, William Crawford, Charles Fenwick and John Wilson. Besides Alexander McDonald, who represented Stafford, a non-mining constituency, until 1881 the other Lib.–Lab. miners' MPs were Ben Pickard of the Yorkshire coalfield and William 'Mabon' Abraham from the Rhondda, south Wales. In addition, from 1892 to 1895 Sam Woods was returned for the Ince division of Lancashire.[14] Almost as important as the miners' desire to be directly represented in parliament, on such matters as safety in mines legislation, was the social and political distinction bestowed on the miners' leader and his union by membership of the Commons, echoed in the well-known poem by Robert Elliot celebrating Burt's victory, 'The Pitman gan te Parliament'. As a result, nearly all these miners' MPs had long tenures at Westminster, with Burt in December 1918 becoming the 'father of the House of Commons' and completing forty-four years and ten months continuous service in parliament.

The nature of the miners' parliamentary representation indicated the regional character of the coalfields and the partial democratisation of the local political institutions. In the late nineteenth century the large concentration of colliers in certain constituencies often gave the mining communities the electoral power to return their own representatives to Westminster. As early as 1874, the economic and political bargaining power of Thomas Burt's union forced the retirement of the sitting MP:

3,000 more [electors] than in 1871, the addition being almost entirely pitmen, all members of their union bound to support a candidate from their own body ... they will not, I might say dare not under the shelter of the ballot vote against the nominee of their union. Nor is this all, the union is ... threatening their influence with the small tradesmen ... it will not be a question of principle but of class which will weigh with the great majority of electors.[15]

In south Wales and the north east miners' MPs like 'Mabon' Abraham enjoyed extremely long parliamentary careers based on miners' support.

---

[13] In Lancashire, with its tradition of working-class Conservatism, cotton workers' leader James Mawdsley became a rare example of a 'Con.–Lab.' candidate by unsuccessfully contesting the 1899 by-election with Winston Churchill for the two-member constituency of Oldham. I am indebted to Dr Henry Pelling for this reference.

[14] For biographical details of the following Lib.–Lab. MPs, Arch, Broadhurst, Burns, Burt, Crawford, Cremer, Fenwick, Howell, Maddison, Rowlands, Steadman, Havelock Wilson, Wilson and Woods, see J. Bellamy and J. Saville (eds.), *Dictionary of Labour Biography*, vols. 1–6 (1972–82).

[15] Woodman to Grey, 3 Oct. 1873, Grey papers, Northumberland Record Office ZAN M16B40.

In the Rhondda constituency, where nearly 80 per cent of the electorate were miners, 'Mabon' was only opposed twice between 1885 and 1910.[16]

The election of miners' leaders to local school boards, county councils and parish councils and, in some cases, parliament was a clear expression of the miners' developing political consciousness during the period. Local standing was the important factor in marking them out as miners' leaders for a parliamentary career. Besides McDonald and Burt, who had also established themselves as well-known leaders of the labour movement by the time they entered parliament, the Lib.–Lab. miners' MPs usually gained reputations as community leaders and pioneer trade unionists. Membership of their local chapel, and in most cases their role as lay preachers gave them experience in administration, organisation and public speaking. Scottish miners' leader and Labour MP, Robert Smillie, revealed the power the seventeen-stone Mabon held over his Welsh colliers:

> It was at these [outdoor] gatherings that I discovered the secret of 'Mabon's' vast influence over his Welsh miners. If any friction arose and pandemonium threatened – so easy to rouse, and so difficult to quell – 'Mabon' never tried to restore order in any usual way. He promptly struck up a Welsh hymn, or that magical melody, 'Land of my fathers'.
> Hardly had he reached the second line when, with uplifted arms, as though drawing the whole multitude into the circle of his influence, he had the vast audience dropping into their respective 'parts' and accompanying him like a great trained choir. It was wonderful, almost magical, and the effect was thrilling. When the hymn or song was finished he raised a hand, and instantly perfect silence fell. The storm had passed.[17]

As trade union leaders, they had usually been instrumental in building their unions, often by leadership of an important strike in the formative years, by well-won reputations in mining rescue work or as expert witnesses on behalf of their mining communities at colliery accident inquiries and court cases.[18] Above all, by holding in turn key positions, such as checkweigh men, miners' agents and secretaries of the union, the first Lib.–Lab. MPs had established an unchallengeable claim to be sent to Westminster as the local miners' representatives.

After 1885, in addition to the miners, about half the Lib.–Lab. parliamentary group were usually leading working-class politicians connected with trade unions and labour organisations. In 1886 these non-

[16] For 'Mabon', see L. J. Williams, 'The first Welsh "Labour" M.P.', *Morganwg*, 6 (1962). For the miners in Lib.–Lab. politics, R. Gregory, *The Miner in British Politics* (Oxford, 1968).

[17] R. Smillie, *My Life for Labour* (London, 1924), pp. 62–3.

[18] J. Saville, 'The ideology of labourism', in R. Benewick, R. N. Berki and B. Parekh (eds.), *Knowledge and Belief in Politics* (London, 1973), pp. 214–5, 217.

mining labour MPs in the group were Henry Broadhurst, secretary of the Parliamentary Committee of the TUC; Joseph Leicester, secretary of the Glassblowers; Joseph Arch, the agricultural workers' leader; and three London working-class radicals, Randal Cremer, James Durant and George Howell. Broadhurst was arguably the most prominent Victorian labour leader and a close associate of the Liberal party manager, Francis Schnadhorst. Arch's parliamentary career owed as much to his links with middle-class radicals as to the support of his fading National Agricultural Labourers' Union. Changes in the registration of voters, coupled with the effects of Reform Acts, 1883–5, created opportunities for labour candidates in a number of predominantly single-class urban constituencies with increased working-class electorates. In London, Cremer, Durant, Howell and Leicester were adopted by the local Liberal associations, in part as a result of these changed circumstances as well as the popular support expressed for labour candidatures in the local political and radical clubs. Durant and Leicester had short-lived parliamentary careers but Cremer and Howell, who had served their political apprenticeships as officials in organisations such as the Reform League and the Labour Representation League, became well-known figures amongst the Lib.–Labs. in the Commons.

Durant and Leicester were not reelected in 1886, but James Rowlands then joined the labour group in parliament. Rowlands, educated at the Working Mens' College and night school in Shoreditch Town Hall, was a former apprentice to a watchcase maker and had built up his own business. Though Durant and Rowlands had established themselves on a small scale as self-made businessmen, by the time they became MPs both men were regarded as labour members and, along with Howell and Cremer, were fêted at an official Liberal banquet for this reason.[19]

Thus the pattern was broadly set for labour representation until, in the 1890s, five other new figures joined the Lib.–Lab. parliamentary group: John Burns, a former engineer and celebrated London political activist; Joseph Havelock Wilson, the seamen's leader; Frederick Maddison, a former compositor and labour journalist; Will Steadman, secretary of the Bargebuilders' union and a prominent working-class figure in London progressive politics; and John G. Holburn, president of the Edinburgh Trades Council. All had gained experience in local radical politics before entering parliament. Burns and Havelock Wilson had entered parliament

---

[19] For Joseph Arch, see P. Horn, *Joseph Arch* (Kineton, 1971); for Randal Cremer, H. Evans, *Sir Randal Cremer* (London, 1909); For George Howell, F. M. Leventhal, *Respectable Radical: George Howell and Victorian Working Class Politics* (London, 1971); for James Durant, *The Weekly Dispatch*, 31 May 1885, *The Daily News*, 27 Nov. 1885; for James Rowlands, *The Star*, 29 Apr. 1891, *The Labour Tribune*, 13 Nov. 1886.

under the banner of being socialist or independent labour MPs, but later joined the Lib.–Lab. group. Steadman and Maddison had also been unsuccessful parliamentary candidates at the general elections in 1892 and 1895. Though in business as a tinsmith, Holburn was of working-class origin and continued to work at his trade while an MP. He was clearly counted by the Liberals as a Labour MP.[20]

During the last two decades of the century there was a growing desire to see more members of parliament recruited from the working-class, and labour representation became a crucial issue in English working-class politics, however the number of Lib.–Lab. members did not improve substantially. By 1901, Broadhurst was disappointed that 'there were not at least fifty labour members in the present House of Commons in spite of financial obstacles'.[21] As this implied, the main reason that the Lib.– Labs. were unable to increase their parliamentary representation was the attitude of the Liberal party towards working-class candidates, and the lack of finance needed to meet heavy election expenses and pay parliamentary salaries.[22] While the miners' union generally paid their members a salary and travel expenses, the other Lib.–Labs. normally had to find other sources of income from paid employment. Cremer worked for the International Arbitration League, Maddison was a journalist and Steadman needed a small wages fund established by his union. In 1885 Leicester's election had exhausted his life savings and put him in debt.[23] By contrast, though secretary of the TUC Parliamentary Committee, Woods' candidature and surprising by-election victory in 1897 was heavily dependent on money from wealthy Liberal sympathisers.[24]

In the 1880s and 1890s the electoral fortunes of these workmen with aspirations to enter the House of Commons could easily be destroyed by the response of the Liberal party to the claims of organised labour for increased parliamentary representation. In theory, the party leaders were in favour of more working-class MPs as maintained by Arnold Morley, the chief whip, in 1886:

I am strongly impressed with the advantage of not only retaining but of increasing the numerical representation of labour in the House of Commons and although I

---

[20] For John Holburn, see *The Leith Pilot Annual for 1900*; for Herbert Gladstone's lists of 'Labor' (sic) candidates, which included Holburn's name, see 'Labour M.P.'s' (1905), BL, Viscount Gladstone papers, Add, MS 46,107, fol. 66.

[21] Broadhurst, *Henry Broadhurst*, p. 286.

[22] On the financing of working-class MPs, see W. B. Gwyn, *Democracy and the Cost of Politics* (London, 1962), ch. 6.

[23] Bargebuilders' Trade Union, *Annual Report* (1889); Leicester to Chamberlain, 24 Nov. Chamberlain papers, Birmingham University Library, JC/5/76/39.

[24] J. Shepherd, 'A Lancashire miner in Walthamstow: Sam Woods and the by-election of 1897', *Essex Journal* 24 (1987), pp. 11–14.

am bound to recognise that the question of selection of candidates is mainly if not entirely a matter for the local association without interference from headquarters, I shall not fail where the circumstances warrant it, to use my influence in the direction I have indicated.[25]

Outside mining constituencies, where electoral pacts and agreements with local Liberals were negotiated by the miners' unions, the Liberal associations, controlled by middle-class elites, often refused to adopt labour parliamentary candidates on the grounds of social class and finance. The conflict within provincial Liberalism over working-class claims for labour representation, particularly in the selection of official Liberal candidates in the 1880s and 1890s, provided bitter experience for working-class politicians. In joining the Independent Labour Party in 1894, Ramsay MacDonald publicly gave as his reason the rejection by the local Liberal party of Charles Hobson, president of the Sheffield Federated Trades Council, for the Liberal nomination at the Attercliffe by-election.[26] From 1886 to 1895 former compositor Thomas Threlfall worked hard, but in vain, to develop the Labour Electoral Association (LEA) into a fully fledged working-class party with a paid secretary, political agents, annual congresses and a mass circulation newspaper. Originally founded by the TUC, the LEA met with little success in attempting to promote workmen candidates at municipal and parliamentary elections under Liberal auspices.[27] After the 1892 election, Threlfall complained:

Of the thirteen labour MPs in the present House, four ran in opposition or without recognition of the caucus, five represented constituencies where organised miners absolutely dominated the position and where the shop-keeping and employing class are so small in number as to have comparatively little power, and only four either captured or out generalled it . . .[28]

And in 1895 Threlfall, who was a loyal Liberal and the first labour councillor in Southport, was again complaining bitterly, this time to Thomas Ellis, the Liberal chief whip:

I am sure you will excuse my speaking frankly but the opinion of my political friends is that after fighting two hopeless seats the very least that could be done

[25] Arnold Morley to Champion, 8 Feb. 1888, quoted in H. Pelling, *Origins of the Labour Party, 1880–1900* (Oxford, 1965), p. 59.
[26] J. Brown, 'Attercliffe 1894: how one local Liberal party failed to meet the challenge of Labour', *Journal of British Studies*, 14 (1975), p. 75.
[27] Labour Electoral Association, *Annual Reports* (1888–93, 1895); *The Leader*, 12 Sept. 1891; F. Walmsley to J. S. Purcell, 13 Oct. 1892, PRO B7/31/4983/333/9.
[28] T. R. Threlfall, 'The political future of Labour', *Nineteenth Century*, 35 (Feb. 1894), pp. 213–4.

was to find me a safe seat. The ILP and the Socialists frequently parade my case as an illustration of how little the Liberal party will do even for those who fight forlorn hopes for it.[29]

However, with the rise of mass politics, the Liberal party leadership did see the electoral value in promoting the parliamentary careers of a small number of prominent Victorian labour leaders who gave unflagging support to Gladstonian Liberalism. In over twenty years, Broadhurst contested six seats and represented four constituencies, out of the many possibilities offered to him.[30] In Joseph Arch's case, John Morley admitted to Joseph Chamberlain that he was willing to 'go without dinner for a fortnight to subscribe to his going to the House of Commons'.[31] The Liberal whips tried hard to recruit John Burns, at a time when he was still a socialist, promising him assistance if he came 'forward as the supporter of the Liberal programme plus of course such fads of his own as he thinks indispensable'.[32] Even in 1895, during the depths of defeat and discord within the Liberal party, considerable sums of money were spent from official party funds on litigation to retain Randal Cremer's Haggerston seat in parliament.[33]

III

Socialists accused the Lib.–Lab. MPs of having divided loyalties in political life. According to their critics, they were not truly representative of the labour movement, but subservient to a Liberal party dominated by the capitalist class. In a famous incident at the 1887 Bradford Trades Union Congress, Hardie attacked Broadhurst for his political connections with the Liberal employer, J. T. Brunner, most notably his failure in parliament to question the death of a worker at the Brunner chemical works, in which Broadhurst owned shares.[34] For similar reasons Hardie later turned his invective on Sam Woods, whom he likened to 'a hooded falcon, guaranteed to return to rest when ordered by his master'. Joseph

[29] Threlfall to Ellis, 5 June 1895, Ellis papers, University of Wales Library, 1348.
[30] Schnadhorst to Broadhurst, 29, 30 Aug. 13 Sept. 1892, Broadhurst papers, British Library of Political and Economic Science; Broadhurst, *Henry Broadhurst*, pp. 67, 172–3, 235–7.
[31] Morley to Chamberlain, 11 Jan. 1877, Chamberlain papers, JC5/54/149.
[32] Marjoribanks to Gladstone, 15 Sept. 1889, BL, Gladstone papers, Add. MS 44,332, fols. 207–8.
[33] Haggerston election petition, Accounts and Papers (1895–6); Ellis papers, 182.
[34] Dona Torr, *Tom Mann and His Times* (London, 1956), pp. 273–5; Stephen Koss, *Sir John Brunner, Radical Plutocrat* (Cambridge, 1970), pp. 61, 105, 146–7. Tom Ellis (Brunner's secretary, and later Liberal MP and chief whip) asked Thomas Forgan (the company manager): 'Will you kindly send the original transfer of shares from Mr Brunner to Mr Broadhurst and oblige', Ellis to Forgan, 11 Mar. 1889, Brunner papers, University of Liverpool Library, IV, 187.

Chamberlain, previously an old friend of the Lib.–Labs., denounced them in 1894 as 'mere fetchers and carriers for the Gladstonian Party'.[35]

These criticisms revealed a conflict of views over the role of the Lib.–Labs. in parliament. By the nineteenth century the generally accepted tradition, derived from Burke, held that members of parliament were elected representatives who promoted the interests of the nation as a whole according to their personal judgement. But from the early twentieth century the Labour party, by returning its own representatives to the House of Commons, sought to promote directly the interests of the working-class. As members of parliament, the Lib.–Labs. were caught somewhere between these two different concepts of political representation. As a result, there were often tensions in the different, sometimes overlapping, roles of the Lib.–Labs. as Liberal MPs, labour representatives and members of a parliamentary group.

On being elected to parliament, the first labour members sat on the Liberal benches in the House of Commons and took the Liberal whip, a demonstration of their enduring belief in liberalism as a political faith and in the Liberal party as the means to achieve social and political reform. For these Victorian labour leaders Lib.–Lab. politics appeared to work: labour representation was for the first time achieved with workmen appointed as factory inspectors, magistrates, members of royal commissions and elected to municipal authorities, as well as to parliament. From the outset in 1886 the inclusion of Broadhurst as a junior minister in the Liberal government, albeit briefly, was symbolic of the presence of the labour group within parliament and the Liberal party's relations with Victorian labour leaders. A similar position as parliamentary secretary to the Board of Trade was found for Burt by the party managers in the 1892–5 Liberal government, and by 1905 only a post of cabinet rank was considered suitable for John Burns:

the confidence of the labouring class in the next Liberal government will be enormously promoted by the inclusion of John Burns in the Cabinet. He carries much weight among a large section of the working classes throughout England. An exclusion from the Cabinet would . . . loose [sic] the Liberal party thousands of votes in the election . . . Labour attacks would be accentuated especially on Liberal candidates . . . in the interests of the future identification of Labour and Liberalism, I venture to record my view.[36]

As a result Burns' appointment as the first working man to become a cabinet minister, as President of the Local Government Board, consoli-

[35] ILP Annual Report (1897); H. Clegg, A. Fox and A. F. Thompson, *A History of British Trade Unions Since 1889*, vol. 1, *1889–1910* (Oxford, 1964), p. 279.

[36] Pease to Gladstone, 6 Dec. 1905 (rough draft), Gainsford papers, Nuffield College Library, 82.

dated half a century of the Liberal–Labour alliance by which the Liberal party attempted to secure working-class votes and the allegiance of the labour movement.

Amongst working men and their leaders, the practice of Lib.–Lab. politics was the formal expression of a genuine attachment to Gladstonian Liberalism, embracing different social classes in a common political culture and community of interests. In the 1880s and 1890s, labour formed one of a number of the interest groups along with the Nonconformists, nationalists, liberals, radicals and temperance reformers which sheltered under the umbrella of Gladstonian Liberalism and were held together by the moral and political leadership of William Gladstone.[37] As a staunch Gladstonian Liberal, Joseph Arch expressed the universal respect and loyalty of Victorian labour leaders for their Liberal chief:

I think no man has stronger claims upon my sympathy, and affection than Mr Gladstone ... Although I was twitted by weak-kneed Liberals and Tories that he would never concede the franchise, my faith in his honesty, in his sense of justice, and his love for the people, was not shaken in the slightest degree by these jeers.[38]

After the defection of Chamberlain and the Liberal Unionists split the Liberal party in 1886, within the Liberal ranks there were no more loyal supporters of Gladstone than the labour members on the supreme issue of Home Rule for Ireland. Lib.–Lab. sympathy for Irish nationalism predated Gladstone's conversion to Home Rule. As early as 1874, McDonald and Burt were two of a small group of about ten to fifteen Radical MPs who had promised during the election campaign to support the Irish demand for an inquiry into Home Rule, a pledge also made in 1880 by Broadhurst. In the late nineteenth century the Lib.–Lab. working-class politicians consistently supported Irish nationalism and displayed an identity of interest in opposing landlordism as the root evil of the Irish social and political condition.[39]

From 1885 to 1905 the Lib.–Labs. spent most of their parliamentary careers in opposition to Tory governments, apart from the Gladstone and Rosebery administrations of 1892–5. In the House of Commons they were normally ready to unite against the Tories when in opposition and to defend the Liberals when in office. In 1893, for example, on the Queen's Speech the Lib.–Labs. solidly supported the Liberal government's propo-

---

[37] J. Vincent, *The Formation of the British Liberal Party, 1857–1868* (Harmondsworth, 1972), p. 116; D. A. Hamer, *Liberal Politics in the Age of Gladstone and Rosebery* (Oxford, 1972), *passim.*

[38] J. Arch, *The Autobiography of Joseph Arch* (London, 1966 edn), p. 143.

[39] T. W. Heyck, *The Dimensions of British Radicalism in the Case of Ireland, 1874–1895* (Urbana, Illinois, 1974), pp. 24–7; See also House of Commons, *Divisions*, 20 Mar. 1874; 23 Mar., 11 June 1875; 30 June 1876; 24 Apr. 1877.

sals, including voting against Keir Hardie's amendment concerning unemployment. Cremer defended the Liberal government against Hardie's criticisms with appropriate rhetoric: 'his impression was that the present was one of the best and most honest governments that ever existed'. In a fierce exchange Cremer warned Hardie, whom he described as 'a catspaw of the Tories', that 'hon. Member would not find any of the Labour Members following him into the lobby in support of the Amendment'.[40] In 1894 Fenwick regarded his selection by the new Prime Minister, Rosebery, to second government proposals in the Queen's Speech as 'a guarantee ... that as far as this House is concerned equality of privilege and opportunity should no longer be limited by consideration of birth or social distinction'.[41]

The Liberal orientation of the Lib.–Labs. was derived from the three-fold source of Victorian Liberalism: Nonconformity, temperance and radicalism.[42] The majority of the Lib.–Lab. members came from areas with a strong religious tradition of Dissent, such as the coalfields, or had backgrounds or upbringings which were heavily Nonconformist in some way. On entering the House of Commons, Mabon made his maiden speech on the resolution for the disestablishment of the Church of England in Wales. He claimed that 'the Church of England ... has entirely failed to meet the religious requirements of the [Welsh] people'. To emphasise his view that 'the Church had neglected to provide the means to teach the people the word of God in the language that they understand', he concluded his speech by uttering the Lord's Prayer in his native Welsh.[43] In terms of an active religious commitment, the Lib.–Labs.' Nonconformist connections must be studied with care, since in later adult life it is evident that there were individual variants in their religious belief, practice and knowledge. Of some twenty-three Lib.–Labs. in 1906, for example, who claimed a denominational allegiance, only twelve were acknowledged as members of their respective faith by the religious press.[44] And, though a staunch Nonconformist, Joseph Arch was married a second time in an Anglican church. Nevertheless, in parliament the Lib.–Labs. undoubtedly played an active role in the Nonconformist campaign to achieve religious equality in social and political life.

With the Liberal–Nonconformist alliance, it was clearly an electoral advantage for the Lib.–Labs. to stress any Nonconformist attachments. In the early twentieth century a Nonconformist revival united the Liberals in

[40] *Hansard*, 4th series, vol. 8, 7 Feb. 1893, cols. 764, 766, 767.
[41] *Ibid.*, vol. 22, 12 Mar. 1894, col. 42.
[42] See also Alastair Reid, ch. 10, in this collection.
[43] *Hansard*, 3rd series, vol. 303, 9 March 1886, cols. 345–6.
[44] See K. D. Brown, 'Nonconformity and the British labour movement: a case study', *Journal of Social History*, 8 (1975), pp. 113–20.

response to the Tory government's policies on education, licensing and tariff reform. The opposition of the labour movement to the 1902 Education Bill became part of a wider Free Church or Nonconformist crusade. Broadhurst, who led the Lib.–Lab. members' challenge in the Commons spoke as much in the terms of a representative of political Nonconformity as a labour member. He denounced the Tory measure as 'a School Board killing bill', which would

> resuscitate the whole demand for the disestablishment and disendowment of the Church of England. The contentions raised by it were such as had not been experienced since the days of the old church rate system. He remembered those days, for his father was one who suffered persecution and loss. The spirit which animated Nonconformists in those days was not yet dead . . . The Government was going, by public funds, to teach principles of religion to which probably half the nation did not subscribe.[45]

In addition, connected with Nonconformity, many of the Lib.–Lab. members had life-long associations with the temperance movement and the parliamentary lobbies for measures such as the control of the liquor trade. Burt, for example, was a resolute supporter of Sir Wilfrid Lawson and other temperance reformers in parliament, but on temperance measures was opposed by his fellow Labour MP, McDonald.[46] Though an MP only in 1886, two of Joseph Leicester's four speeches were on the liquor trade. In his maiden speech he spoke forcibly in favour of the restriction of the sale of liquor on Sundays. Identifying himself at once as the representative of 'a thorough working man's constituency', he told the Commons that 'he went in for Sunday Closing and every other kind of closing if he could get it; and if they left the question to the workingmen of England, they would very soon make short work of the whole liquor traffic'.[47] In his speech, Leicester claimed overwhelming popular support amongst the working-class for temperance reform.

The case against sabbatarianism clearly divided the Lib.–Lab. Nonconformist conscience in terms of religious and class loyalties. Baptist lay preacher Sam Woods, who opposed the Sunday opening of the Wigan Free Library, and Ben Pickard, a staunch member of the Lord's Rest Day Association, were both resolute defenders of the sabbath.[48] Broadhurst defended sabbatarianism on the TUC line that any erosion of the principle would result in an extension of Sunday working in other areas. Acknowledging that his fellow labour member, Burt, did not share his view, Broadhurst argued 'it is in the interests of labour that we should keep the

[45] *Hansard*, 4th series, vol. 8, 17 June 1902, 21 July 1902, cols. 830–1, 896.
[46] *Hansard*, 3rd series, vol. 225, 7 July 1874, col. 1901.
[47] *Hansard*, 4th series, vol. 138, 10 Mar. 1886, cols. 627–34, 648–55.
[48] *Wigan Observer*, 6, 20 Apr. 1878.

seventh day as free and as fully relieved from all associations of labour as it is possible for us to do'.[49] On the other hand, Holburn chose his maiden speech to support Sunday opening as a working man himself who 'had worked at the bench not only until the last election, but all through the last Recess'. He was supported in the same debate by Burns, who pointed out that the majority of the working class were in favour of Sunday opening.[50]

In addition to Nonconformity and temperance, as working-class politicians the Lib.–Labs. were closely identified with late Victorian radicalism and the middle-class pressure groups inside and outside parliament. In the 1880s and 1890s, Howell, Cremer and Rowlands were members of the London group of Radical MPs at Westminster. Broadhurst became president of the Leasehold Enfranchisement Association, a largely middle-class organisation. In the House of Commons, this radicalism on the part of the labour members was often channelled into calls to abolish the House of Lords and to oppose the payment of royal grants and expenditure on embassies abroad. In 1889, in a characteristic broadside, Mabon opposed a grant of £30,000 to the children of the Prince of Wales:

What is the work His Royal Highness performs in return for this ample wage? I will quote from the *Daily News*. 'The Prince of Wales had a hard day's work on Saturday. In the afternoon besides holding a formal reception he unveiled a statue of Sir Rowland Hill at Cornhill, and in the evening he dined with the Lord Mayor at the Mansion House and afterwards witnessed part of the performance of the *Marriage of Figaro*' and that is a hard day's work![51]

Mabon's attack was typical of the radical assaults on privilege in Victorian society in which the labour members participated, often with middle-class allies in parliament on a range of political issues: disestablishment, land law reform, temperance and education. In this way, radical Nonconformity lay at the heart of their liberalism: the Gladstonian Liberal party provided the opportunity for these former workmen to participate in politics and to achieve individual liberty and progress.

IV

From the outset, the first Lib.–Lab. MPs set the pattern of labour representation within parliament as working-class politicians who aspired to lead, and to speak for, the whole of the labour movement. At Westminster they established the *ouvrieriste* tradition of working-class

[49] *Speech of Mr Broadhurst on the Closing of Museums on Sundays* (19 May 1882).
[50] *Hansard*, 4th series, vol. 38, 10 Mar. 1896, cols. 634, 648–9, 651.
[51] *Hansard*, 3rd series, vol. 338, 25 July 1889, cols. 1337–8.

politics, that working-class interests in parliament could only be directly represented by members who had worked at a trade. As in the case of nearly all the Lib.–Lab. members, the first labour representatives, Burt, McDonald and Broadhurst, had ceased manual work some time before entering parliament as full-time salaried officials of trade unions or labour organisations. Nevertheless, the first labour members continued to stress their working-class connections and personal experience of working-class life, often choosing for their maiden speeches a subject of radical or labour concern. Though Burt was a member of the House of Commons, seen as an exclusive upper-class parliamentary club, the *Bee Hive* defended this former pitman as an archetypal working-class leader of impeccable proletarian credentials who:

in every sense of the term is a working man. He was a working miner until his fellow-workers took him out of the pit, and gave him a post in their midst as secretary and agent. His elevation, if such it may be called, did not separate him from them. It did not lead him into action opposed to them as he might have been led had he risen to be an employer of labour; but it so united his interests with theirs as to make their welfare the business and study of his life.[52]

In this way, the first labour members regularly displayed in parliament their right to speak for the working class based on their own direct experience of the hard, physical labour of industrial life. As a political elite, the Lib.–Labs. still took pride in remaining members of the working class they represented. As a result, in a House of Commons dominated by upper-class and middle-class members, the first labour MPs formed a fascinating paradox. Whilst they were often characterised as having pretensions to the middle class in terms of manners, dress and social values, their working-class origins and backbrounds provided abundant material for the parliamentary commentators. Style of dress clearly identified the first labour members many sessions before Keir Hardie's celebrated arrival and appearance at the Commons in 1892.[53] Six years earlier, the headgear of Broadhurst drew the comment that

Mr Broadhurst, whose proud boast is that from the position of a working mason he made his way to become a Minister of the Crown . . . Returned to the House as a member for Stoke, he adopted Mr Cowen's expedient of coming down in his ordinary gear, but refrained from wearing it in his place below the gangway. When he was invited to take a seat on the Treasury bench he felt something – a topper to wit – was due to his exalted position. He accordingly bought a silk hat, but kept it exclusively for House of Commons use. He might be seen any day the House was sitting hastily crossing the lobby, crowned with a billy cock, presently to return at

---

[52] *The Bee Hive*, 1 Nov. 1873.
[53] F. Reid, *Keir Hardie – The Making of a Socialist* (London, 1978), pp. 140–1.

a more leisurely pace with a shiny hat on his head. This he kept in his locker, returning it when the business of sitting was over and he was free to walk home.[54]

On the occasion of Broadhurst becoming a junior minister, Gladstone found it necessary to assist in his presentation at court. He asked the Queen's secretary, 'if her Majesty would kindly permit him to take a little time before getting his Court Dress, so that he may grow more accustomed to what is for him a very novel situation'. The official reply noted that 'Mr Broadhurst may be excused but his writing shows his origin.'[55] From the start, therefore, there was little mystery about the social class to which the Lib.–Labs. belonged, a point the individual members continued to acknowledge and emphasise in their parliamentary careers.

Usually the labour member's parliamentary career was an extension of his period in office as a trade union official. As labour representatives, nearly all of the Lib.–Lab. MPs claimed some close connection with an individual trade union or the trade union movement, often as pioneers and officials. During their later careers in parliament, Cremer, Maddison, Howell and Broadhurst no longer held direct links in this way, but valued their association with the trade union movement, often keeping up individual membership subscriptions. Originally associated with Marx's First International, Cremer was a founder member of the Amalgamated Society of Carpenters and Joiners and the London Trades Council and was 'still a Trade Unionist' in his last years. On his retirement from parliamentary life after twenty-six years, Broadhurst received an allowance of 9 shillings from the Operative Society of Stonemasons' superannuation fund he had founded many years before, as he had held an uninterrupted membership of the society for forty-nine years. Broadhurst also possessed a medical certificate, declaring him unfit to take up his trade as a stonemason.[56]

As trade union members in parliament, the Lib.–Labs. have often been portrayed as the guardians of a particular sectional interest, rather than the representatives of the labour movement as a whole. The classic example usually cited of such parochialism was during the campaign by the Miners' Federation of Great Britain for the legal eight-hour day, when the opposition of Northumberland and Durham representatives Burt, Fenwick and Wilson, not only prevented a common front but also provided opportunities for the coal owners to exploit the divisions

[54] H. W. Lucy, *A Diary of the Home Rule Parliament, 1892–1895* (London, 1896), pp. 217–18.
[55] Gladstone to Ponsonby, nd (Feb. 1886), BL, Gladstone papers, Add MS 45,724, fols. 187–8.
[56] TUC *Souvenir* (1902); Amalgamated Toolmakers' *Monthly Record* (Apr. 1906).

amongst the miners' MPs.[57] In 1894 Sam Woods replaced Fenwick as the secretary of the Parliamentary Committee of the TUC after he had been heavily censured for voting against the measure in the Commons. Fenwick's defence uncovered an interesting conflict of loyalties to his constituency and the TUC. Even though his vote was against the direct instructions of the TUC, he maintained a greater loyalty to his Wansbeck constituents, in the main Northumberland miners opposed to the introduction of eight-hours legislation.[58]

But the divisions over the eight-hours question did not impede the Lib.–Labs.' role as the first working-class MPs on a wide range of labour matters, inside and outside parliament. Often the Lib.–Labs. took up issues not directly connected with their union's affairs. Even Hardie's journal, *The Miner*, openly admitted the value of Burt's presence and stature in parliament.

Mr Burt is the recognised authority on all Labour questions. Men have come to learn that he is not a gad-fly, to be driven hither and thither by every political wind that blows ... He has great faith in the doctrines of Political Economy, and capitalists knowing this, and trading on his honesty, feel that they are quite safe in following his lead. A kind of set phrase with politicians, when being asked to support measures affecting the interests of the working class, is – I will follow Mr Burt's opinion on the matter. No greater compliment could be paid than this.[59]

Outside parliament, Burt, the exemplar of Liberal–Labourism, supported the unskilled workers establishing the new Tyneside and National Labour Union. Though secretary of the Bargebuilders' Union, Steadman became closely identified with the Post Office workers, raising over fifty grievances on their behalf alone in two years. On first entering the Commons, Howell fought the dismissal of workmen at the Woolwich Arsenal and in the same session defended socialists accused of provoking riots during the unemployed demonstrations in London.[60]

In parliament, the labour members regularly took collective action on trade union and labour measures, such as workmen's compensation and factory reform. Pickard and Woods led a long campaign on the miners' legal eight-hour day issue and raised the issue of the use of police and troops in labour disputes, such as the 'Coal War' in 1893. As a result, Rosebery's appointment as mediator to resolve the greatest industrial

---

[57] For the miners and the 8-hour day, see B. McCormick and J. E. Williams, 'The miners and the eight-hour day, 1863–1910', *Economic History Review*, 2nd series, 12 (1959–60), pp. 225–6.

[58] TUC *Annual Report* (1894).

[59] *The Miner* (Feb. 1897).

[60] For Steadman, see *Hansard*, 4th series, vol. 72, 1 June 1899, cols. 99–104; for Burt, see Clegg, Fox and Thompson, *History of British Trade Unions*, vol. 1, p. 57; for Howell, see *Hansard*, 4th series, vol. 302, 26 Feb., 4 Mar. 1886, cols. 1043, 1911.

dispute to date was the first direct intervention by a government in nineteenth-century industrial relations. TUC concern at the lack of labour justices, with its adverse effects in industrial disputes, had prompted Broadhurst's action in pressing in Westminster and Whitehall for the appointment of the first working-class magistrates.[61] On the payment of parliamentary salaries, Fenwick gained a reputation within labour circles as the specialist within the group on electoral and registration reform. The resolutions in the House of Commons in favour of this reform were supported solidly by the Lib.–Labs. in the late 1880s and 1890s inside and outside parliament, to the extent, for example, that in 1888 Gladstone caused surprise amongst his colleagues with a more favourable response.[62]

As labour representatives, the Lib.–Labs. clearly saw themselves as constituency MPs, as well as the parliamentary agents of individual trade unions and the trade union movement in general. Often these roles were combined, though their function as elected representatives of their constituency sometimes included community interests beyond the working class. As a self-styled labour leader, Broadhurst did not neglect his middle-class constituents of Stoke. He claimed that his achievement in pressing for Hanley in his constituency to be designated a Quarter Sessions town, 'entirely disproves the theory that a Labour representative could be of no service to the general and commercial interests of his constituency, and would confine his attention to voicing the desires of the working classes only'.[63]

Clashes of interest between working-class and middle-class communities were less likely to occur in mining constituencies, where as we have seen, owing to sheer weight of numbers the miners normally dominated the electorate. Burt had no difficulty in making his maiden speech on the Household Franchise (Counties) Bill to expose the anomalies of geography which disqualified some of his union from voting in parliamentary elections:

The borough that I represent [Morpeth] ... extends about ten miles, and is bounded by Morpeth on the one side, and Blyth on the other. It goes through the chief part of the Northumberland coalfield; it embraces some of the largest collieries in the county, and very large bodies of colliers are excluded from the franchise simply from the fact that they live beyond – it may be a few yards – a privileged line.[64]

[61] For the appointment of the first working-class JPs, see J. Shepherd, 'James Bryce and the recruitment of working-class magistrates in Lancashire, 1892–1894', *Bulletin of the Institute of Historical Research*, 52 (1979), pp. 155–69.
[62] See Edward Hamilton's Diary, 7, 11 July 1888, BL, Gladstone papers, ADD MS 48,649, fols. 6, 11–12.
[63] Broadhurst, *Henry Broadhurst*, p. 105.
[64] *Hansard*, 3rd series, vol. 219, 13 May 1874, col. 222.

Besides the miners, other Lib.–Lab. MPs had strong connections with constituencies where they had been born or lived for a considerable time. Steadman was well known in Stepney, where he was president of the local Liberal and Radical Association. During the debate on the Metropolitan Water Company's Bill in 1899 he attacked the East London Water Company for its failure to provide a proper water supply to his constituents in the East End.[65] As the new member for Finsbury East, Rowlands in his maiden speech, criticising government foreign policy in Burma, also warned the Commons that 'with the knowledge I possess of the condition of the working classes ... something should be done to relieve them of some of the burdens which they bear already. I represent an industrial population, and I know what they had to suffer in the past'.[66]

Above all, John Burns as the member for Battersea for over twenty years had the closest identification with a constituency and a reputation built on his political activity in the capital in the unemployed demonstrations and the London Dock Strike. As the most prominent working-class leader in London, and later in the country, Burns enjoyed the political and financial support in parliament and on the London County Council of the Battersea Labour League, established to return and maintain its celebrated municipal and parliamentary representative.[67]

V

Though at times the Lib.–Labs. held strong individual views, as the first working-class members they co-operated increasingly in the labour interest in parliament. In particular, as trade union representatives they enjoyed a special relationship with the Parliamentary Committee of the TUC and served more and more as its political arm in parliament during the period of industrial conflict and adverse legal decisions culminating in the Taff Vale judgement in the late nineteenth century.[68] As a result, in carrying out this role the Lib.–Labs. formed the first parliamentary Labour party at Westminster. As early as 1886, Cremer declared:

I wish it were possible to have a labour 'party' in the House, and by and by I believe we may have one. We tried in the early part of the last Parliament, and we have had appointed Mr Fenwick as the whip; and although we have had no formal

---

[65] *Hansard*, 4th series, vol. 69, 18 Apr. 1899, cols. 1493–4.
[66] *Hansard*, 3rd series, vol. 308, 30 Aug. 1886, cols. 856–7.
[67] For John Burns, see K. D. Brown, *John Burns* (London, 1977).
[68] R. M. Martin, *T.U.C.: Growth of a Pressure Group, 1868–1976* (Oxford, 1980), pp. 48–50, 56–7, 76–81.

meeting in the present Parliament, where our ranks are somewhat thinned, Mr Fenwick acts in that capacity still.

In the House of Commons, Fenwick was acknowledged by contemporaries as 'the Parliamentary "Whip" of the Labour Party'.[69] In his autobiography, Broadhurst recalled that in 1886 he had attended a dinner, with Gladstone, Morley and other prominent Liberal party members, given by Rosebery 'as a compliment to the Labour party'.[70] Three years later, Burt confirmed the existence of a parliamentary Labour party: 'These members now consult and act together on all matters that specially affect the workmen. On purely Labour questions they are actually, as they ought to be, a party.'[71]

Before 1880, the TUC had relied heavily on the good offices of its 'Parliamentary friends', usually sympathetic middle-class Liberal and Radical MPs, for assistance in the House of Commons with legislation affecting trade unions. Broadhurst's election to parliament provided the TUC with its most distinguished parliamentary spokesman. More so than Burt or McDonald, he handled the TUC lobbying work, arranged deputations to ministers and actively tabled questions or intervened in debates as the direct representative of the TUC on industrial issues. By the late 1890s the Parliamentary Committee was no longer slow to participate in direct political action. As secretary of the Parliamentary Committee, Sam Woods was its main servant and parliamentary spokesman in the House of Commons. He claimed to represent 1,200,000 workers:

I write from two to three thousand letters every year, and dictate almost as many more ... I suppose there is not a single trade in which I am not more or less concerned in the course of a year ... working men are calling upon me at the House – as many as thirty in the course of one day sometimes.[72]

Woods co-ordinated the labour members' response to Chamberlain's Workmen's Compensation Bill and took initiatives on industrial matters in the Commons.[73] In consequence, by 1899 it was reported at the TUC that the eight Lib.–Lab. MPs had formed a distinct labour group 'to watch closely the agenda paper of the House of Commons in order to be prepared when labour questions were likely to be under discussion'.[74]

Though the Lib.–Labs. were stern opponents of independent labour politics, they did little to defeat the historic resolution at the 1899

[69] *The Labour Tribune*, 30 Oct., 11 Dec. 1886.
[70] Broadhurst, *Henry Broadhurst*, p. 301.
[71] Burt, 'Labour in parliament', p. 686.
[72] *Walthamstow Reporter*, 16 Mar. 1900.
[73] Trades Union Congress, *Minutes*, 11, 12, 13, 24, 25 May, 12 Oct. 1897, 7 June 1898.
[74] Trades Union Congress *Annual Report*, 1899.

Plymouth TUC which led to the foundation conference of the LRC. Some old hands at labour representation, like Durham Miners' leader John Wilson who ignored the event in his monthly circular, deliberately stood apart.[75] But at the TUC, the strategy was to maintain control of the new organisation and prevent socialist domination of its affairs. Therefore, as chairman of the foundation conference, Steadman declared that he 'gave way to no man in his desire to see labour better represented in the House of Commons than it was today'.[76]

The advent of the LRC introduced a new concept of parliamentary representation of the microcosmic kind, which stressed that the member was typical of, and acted for a social class or category of persons. As a result, the new Labour party threatened the positions of Lib.–Labs. as labour representatives. In the Commons, Fenwick directly challenged Hardie's claim for Labour party representation on parliamentary committees on this issue:

> What special right had his hon. friends [Hardie] on the other side to be considered as representatives of labour that they [the Lib.–Labs.] who had sat on the Ministerial side of the House had not an equal claim to? They were the trade unionists, they stood at the head of large labour organisations which they had built up. Their claim in both respects was infinitely superior to the claim of some of those who claimed to be members of the Labour party. They had worked in the mine and in the factory side by side with those who had sent them to this House.[77]

By and large, after some initial difficulties in their relations, the Lib.–Lab. members co-operated with their new LRC, and later Labour party, colleagues in various attempts to secure trade union legislation. During this time the Parliamentary Committee of the TUC was also concerned with questions of housing, unemployment and old age pensions, and organised major campaigns, including large demonstrations against the 1902 Education Bill and tariff reform. As a result, the years 1902–5 were a period of strong Lib.–Lab. politics, symbolised in the growing *rapprochement* of the Parliamentary Committee and Liberal politicians in support for the TUC programme and the Lib.–Lab./LRC electoral agreement reached in the Caxton Hall 'concordat' in 1905.[78]

The attempt to establish the LRC as a political and parliamentary organisation, by the narrow definition of its candidates' nomenclature and the delimitation of the role of labour representatives at the 1903 Newcastle

---

[75] Durham Miners' Association, *Monthly Circular*, March 1900 in John Wilson Papers, Durham County Record Office, DX/188/15.

[76] *Ironworkers Journal*, Apr. 1900.

[77] *Hansard*, 4th series, vol. 156, 8 May 1906, col. 1275.

[78] F. Bealey and H. Pelling, *Labour and Politics 1900–1906* (London, 1958), pp. 134–5, 187–8; Clegg *et al.*, *Trade Unions*, pp. 379–80.

LRC conference, however, did result in conflict with certain labour members with strong Liberal connections, such as John Ward, Will Steadman and especially Richard Bell, who consistently refused to sign the LRC constitution and did not receive LRC endorsement. Bell, LRC MP and former chairman, was at the centre of a long struggle by the LRC executive committee to discipline him.[79] After 1906, the Lib.–Lab. group at Westminster was soon diminished by retirements, defeats at elections and other losses. In 1909 the affiliation of the Miners' Federation of Great Britain to the Labour party effectively reduced the size of the remaining Lib.–Lab. parliamentary group at one stroke. By this stage, the dominant question in English political and parliamentary history during the years before the First World War (and beyond) was the relationship between the Liberal and Labour parties.[80] In reality, the term Lib.–Lab. was now largely an anachronism, a relic of the Gladstonian past. Among the old guard, particularly the miners' leaders, Liberal loyalties died hard; to the point that Burt, Fenwick and Wilson were unshakeable in their allegiance to Liberalism and were generally regarded as conventional Liberal MPs. Similarly, in their attitudes, political ideology and activities, the MFGB leaders who joined the Labour party revealed that, in the main, they remained sound Liberals who had simply switched political parties.

VII

The Lib.–Labs. who entered parliament in 1886 for the first time had an average age of forty-seven, compared to forty-six for the new Labour party members in 1906. By this time they represented an older generation of labour leaders. However, in conducting his well-known inquiry into the books that had been influential in their early lives, W. T. Stead did not distinguish between the Lib.–Labs. and Labour MPs he surveyed. His published survey produced similar results, with references to the Bible, Shakespeare, Dickens and writers such as Ruskin and Carlyle.[81] In

---

[79] For Bell and his relations with LRC, see Labour Party files LP CAN/06.
[80] For different interpretations of the relationship of the Liberal and Labour parties in the early twentieth century, see P. F. Clarke, *Lancashire and the New Liberalism* (Cambridge, 1971), T. Wilson, *The Downfall of the Liberal Party 1914–1935* (London, 1968); H. Pelling, *Popular Politics and Society in Late Victorian Britain* (London, 1968), ch. 6; R. McKibbin, *The Evolution of the Labour Party* (London, 1974), K. O. Morgan, 'The New Liberalism and the challenge of Labour: the Welsh Experience 1885–1929', in K. D. Brown (ed.), *Essays in Anti-Labour History* (London, 1974); D. Howell, *British Workers and the Independent Labour Party 1888–1906* (Manchester, 1983); M. Savage, *The Dynamics of Working-Class Politics* (Cambridge, 1987).
[81] W. T. Stead, 'The Labour Party and the books that helped to make it', *Review of Reviews*, 33 (1906).

seeking his electoral understanding with Ramsay MacDonald, the Liberal chief whip, Herbert Gladstone, saw little new in the LRC, apart from its £100,000 election fund. He regarded the LRC, in the context of labour representation, as being a natural evolution in the long tradition of popular radicalism, a faction which could still be accommodated within Liberalism.[82] In this respect, Gladstone continued to use the parliamentary experience of Broadhurst and other prominent Lib.–Labs. as political intermediaries in his various electoral negotiations.[83] If, for a new generation of men and women an independent position in party politics was the future strategy, the Labour party in the next decade or so was still to develop, as Pat Thane and Duncan Tanner show in their contributions (chs. 11 and 12) to this collection, as much from an inheritance of liberalism and radicalism as from socialist theory and organisation. The Labour party's parliamentary leaders, MacDonald, Hardie, Henderson and Shackleton had all been shaped and influenced in their early careers in popular politics by contact with radical liberalism. Within the mythology of labour history, the Lib.–Labs. are now little remembered as labour pioneers. But, as former workmen representing working-class interests in parliament for the first time, they contributed directly to the growth of the tradition of radical and democratic politics in the late nineteenth and early twentieth centuries.

[82] Undated memorandum (probably 1903) Viscount Gladstone Papers BL Add. MSS 46, 106, f.27.
[83] Diary entries, 18 July 1900, 12, 17 Nov. 1902, 24 Feb. 1903, 19 Jan. 1904, *ibid.*, BL Add. MSS, 46484.

Labour Members of Parliament 1874–1900

Name	Birthplace	Religion	Education/ Age at work	Occupation Father	Occupation Own	Parliament MP	Parliament Maiden Speech	Estate
William Abraham 'Mabon' 1842–1922	Cwmarvon Glamorganshire	Calvinist Methodist Connexion	Elementary school; self-educated, Eisteddfod (10)	Miner and coppersmith	Miner	1885–1918	Disestablishment of Church of England in Wales	£32,777
Joseph Arch 1826–1919	Barford Warwickshire	Primitive Methodist	Village school (9)	Farm labourer	Agricultural labourer	1885–6 1892–1900	Agricultural allotments	£349
Henry Broadhurst 1842–1911	Littlemoor Oxford	Methodist	Local private school (12)	Stonemason	Stonemason	1880–92 1894–1906	Employers liability	£7,046
John Burns 1858–1943	Lambeth London	Secularist	National school	Engineer	Engineer	1892–1914	Registration of Electors Amendment Bill	£15,137
Thomas Burt 1837–1922	Murton Row Northumberland	Not known	Village schools (10)	Miner	Miner	1874–1918	Extension of household franchise	£5,017
William Crawford 1833–90	Whitley Northumberland	Primitive Methodist	Elementary (10)	Miner	Miner	1885–90	No maiden speech	£204

Labour Members of Parliament 1874–1900 (cont.)

Name	Birthplace	Religion	Education/ Age at work	Occupation		Parliament		Estate
				Father	Own	MP	Maiden Speech	
William Randal Cremer 1828–1908	Fareham Hampshire	Agnostic 'Broad-minded Christian'	Elementary (12)	Coach painter	Carpenter	1885–95 1900–8	Metropolitan Police Force	£9,656
John Durant 1846–1929	Fordingbridge New Forest Hampshire	Christian Socialist	Not known	Tinplate worker	Printer	1885–86	No maiden speech	£8,349
Charles Fenwick 1856–1918	Cramlington Northumberland	Primitive Methodist	Elementary (9)	Miner	Miner	1885–1919	Tenure of Town Houses Ireland Bill	£1,419
John Holburn 1843–1899	Edinburgh	Not known	Self educated	Not known	Tinplate worker	1895–99	Sunday opening of national museums	Not known
George Howell 1833–1910	Wrington Somerset	Wesleyan Methodist	Village (10)	Mason	Shoemaker/ bricklayer	1885–95	Metropolitan Police Force	£210
Joseph Leicester 1825–1903	Warrington Lancashire	Not known	Elementary (10)	Glass-blower	Glass-blower	1885–86	Sale of intoxicating liquor on Sunday	£1,164
Alexander McDonald 1821–1911	Dalmacouter New Monkland Lanarkshire	Pres-byterian	Elementary (8)	Sailor	Miner	1874–81	Extension of household franchise	£3,487
Frederick Maddison 1856–1937	Boston Lincolnshire	Unitarian	Elementary	Hotel worker	Compositor	1897–1900 1906–10	Workmens' trains	£1,578

Name	Place	Religion	Education	Father's occupation	Own occupation	Years in Parliament	Main interest	Estate
Ben Pickard 1842–1904	Kippax Yorkshire	Wesleyan	Grammar school (12)	Miner	Miner	1885–1904	Coal Mines Amendment Bill	£2,019
James Rowlands 1851–1920	East Finsbury London	Free Thinker	Working Mens' College	Not known	Watchcase maker	1886–95 1906–10 1910–20	British colonial policy in Burma	£4,636
William Steadman 1851–1911	Poplar London	Anglican?	National (8)	Shipwright	Barge-builder	1898–1900 1906–10	Vaccination	£622
Joseph Havelock Wilson 1855–1929	Sunderland	Methodist	Elementary (13)	Foreman Draper	Seaman	1892–1900 1900/6–10 1918–22	Destitute aliens (immigration)	£428
John Wilson 1837–1915	Greatham, Co Durham	Primitive Methodist	Dame schools (10)	Labourer	Miner	1885–86	Coal Mines Amendment Bill	£4,888
Sam Woods 1846–1915	St Helens, Lancashire	Baptist	Elementary (9–13)	Miner	Miner	1892–95 1897–1900	Labour questions	£235

10 Old Unionism reconsidered: the radicalism of Robert Knight, 1870–1900

Alastair J. Reid

I

The established trade union leadership of the late nineteenth century has perhaps the least impressive reputation of its kind among British labour historians. Like most of their counterparts in other generations they have been condemned by Marxists for their commitment to gradual and constitutional change, or 'reformism', but they have had the additional misfortune of being seen as not particularly innovative even in this respect. This is in some contrast both to the trade union leaders of the mid nineteenth century, who have at least been presented as pioneers of a new form of industrial and political pragmatism, and to the parliamentary leaders of the early twentieth century, who have at least been credited with the construction of a distinctive brand of socialist political argument.[1] For their part the leaders of the 1880s and 1890s have generally been seen not only as unoriginal followers of already established trade union practices but also as active opponents of the rise of socialism, and for historians writing between the 1940s and the 1970s it was difficult not to see this as obstructive and backward-looking whatever their own particular political viewpoints. The result has been that the Old Union leaders and their colleagues among the Lib.–Lab. MPs have come to be regarded largely as a collection of ageing Victorian has-beens whose only role in history was to vacate the stage in favour of the next generation.

In so far as there has been a discussion of their political attitudes it has generally been agreed that they were unthinking and conservative. John Saville, for instance, in his influential article on 'The ideology of labourism', took the miners' leaders of these years as his central example of the

I have benefited a great deal from the comments both of the authors of the chapters in this collection and of the other scholars who attended the conference at which they were originally presented, and would like to thank in particular Dr Eugenio F. Biagini and Dr John Shepherd for the generosity of their suggestions and references.

[1] F. M. Leventhal, *Respectable Radical. George Howell and Victorian Working Class Politics* (London, 1971); B. Barker, editor's 'Introduction' to *Ramsay MacDonald's Political Writings* (London, 1972), pp. 1–50; S. Macirtyre, *A Proletarian Science. Marxism in Britain 1917–1933* (Cambridge, 1980), pp. 47–65.

limited nature of British working-class consciousness after 1850.[2] This he characterised above all as a 'fractured comprehension' of the world they inhabited, which led them into a combination of partial independence and broader collaboration, in the mistaken belief that it was possible to achieve a genuinely fair deal within the framework of bourgeois society. In industry their aims were therefore summed up in the limited slogan 'A Fair Day's Wage for a Fair Day's Work'; in their social attitudes their adherence to Nonconformity led them to be fundamentally individualistic; and in politics they were prepared to accept the handicaps of 'parliamentarianism'. Their overall outlook was therefore presented as 'economistic', limited, and fatally dependent on bourgeois Liberalism. Even when it was conceded that organised labour did make measurable economic and political gains in these years, it was asserted that its attitudes were still 'basically defensive' and that it merely 'reacted to, and provided safeguards against, the gross insecurities of industrial society'.[3]

Henry Pelling's account in *Popular Politics and Society in Late Victorian Britain* was both more sympathetic and considerably more detailed, so much so that it still remains the pioneering treatment of the subject.[4] In contrast to Saville, Pelling placed more weight on the significance of improvements in the position of working people in these years, as well as recognising the independence and the appropriateness of their political responses to the world they inhabited. Yet even he at times fell back on similar language to describe the outlook of the late Victorian labour leadership. In stressing that the early Labour party was not a socialist organisation, for example, Pelling not only pointed to the loyalty of union leaders to the Liberal party but also argued that 'their interests were in the status quo, rather than in social change; they were politicians from fear of adversity, rather than through hope of improvement'. He emphasised their 'complete freedom from commitment to ideas or programme', pointed to 'strong forces of conservatism' within the party, and even referred to 'a sort of undogmatic "Labourism"' . . . which consisted of little more than the opinion that the Labour Party, and not the Liberal, was the party for working men to belong to'.[5]

---

[2] J. Saville, 'The ideology of labourism', in R. Benewick *et al.*, *Knowledge and Belief in Politics* (London, 1973), pp. 213–26.

[3] Saville, 'Ideology of labourism', pp. 217, 222. It should be said that the detailed life histories collected under Saville's editorship in the *Dictionary of Labour Biography* are an invaluable resource for work in this field, and that his own contributions to these volumes are usually more nuanced than these Marxist generalisations might suggest.

[4] H. Pelling, *Popular Politics and Society in Late Victorian Britain* (London, 1968). My indebtedness to Pelling's work will be clear in the references to it throughout the rest of this chapter.

[5] Pelling, *Popular Politics*, pp. 15, 80, 118.

Thus it seems that, despite differences in their own outlook, there has been some agreement among historians that the established labour leaders of the late nineteenth century were a dull lot, unable to see beyond their immediate concerns, and lacking both in significant ideas and in progressive aspirations.[6] This has come about largely as a result of a shared assumption that political attitudes after the 1880s should be measured primarily in terms of their relationship to socialism, which has made it more difficult than it might have been for labour historians to recognise that other types of popular politics might still be considered as intelligent and progressive in their own right.[7] In order to contribute to the revision of thinking in this area, the rest of this chapter has been devoted to a study of the attitudes of Robert Knight (1833–1911) who, as general secretary of the Boilermakers' Society between 1871 and 1898, was one of the leading craft unionists of the period and has generally been regarded as an arch-conservative of the type already described: interested only in narrow trade union affairs, and actively opposed to new trends in labour politics.[8] Even though Knight was scrupulously careful not to mention party politics in his role as a trade union leader, enough emerges from his *Annual Reports* to his members, from his interventions at the Trades Union Congress (TUC), and from his evidence to Royal Commissions, to permit a reconstruction of his basic outlook on broader affairs, paying particular attention to the religious and political influences which can be detected in it. From this reconstruction it will become evident that the standard description of Knight's outlook is unhelpful: he may have been a moderate but that did not require him to be unthoughtful, he may have been an anti-socialist but that did not mean he was in favour of an unchanging status quo, he may have been primarily concerned with particular reforms but that did not mean he lacked a coherent tradition on which he could draw for inspiration.

---

[6] This has also generally been the view of those working on the social history of the period, see, for example, G. Stedman Jones, 'Working-class culture and working-class politics in London, 1870–1900: notes on the remaking of a working class', *Journal of Social History*, 7 (1974), pp. 460–509 (reprinted in *Languages of Class. Studies in English Working Class History 1832–1982* [Cambridge, 1983], pp. 179–238); R. McKibbin, 'Why was there no Marxism in Great Britain?' *English Historical Review*, 99 (1984), pp. 297–331.

[7] This has, however, been increasingly recognised in the case of the middle-class liberalism of the period, above all as a result of the work of P. Clarke in *Lancashire and the New Liberalism* (Cambridge, 1971), and *Liberals and Social Democrats* (Cambridge, 1978).

[8] H. A. Clegg, A. Fox and A. F. Thompson, *A History of British Trade Unions Since 1889*, vol. 1 (Oxford, 1964) pp. 258, 297, 303; J. E. Mortimer, *History of the Boilermakers' Society*, vol. 1 (London, 1973) pp. 169–70, 180–1, 185, 195–7; *Dictionary of Labour Biography*, vol. 6 (London, 1982), pp. 155–6.

II

As a trade unionist who was not a socialist it would be surprising to find that Robert Knight was in favour either of abject collaboration with management or of extensive public ownership of productive resources. Indeed, in clarifying his own position it is helpful to define it in terms of a clear rejection of, on the one hand, the *laissez-faire* individualism still being asserted by many employers and, on the other hand, the extensive state intervention in the economy increasingly proposed by some younger trade unionists after 1888. Knight pursued something of a middle way between these two poles which, if it can be captured in one phrase, might be defined as collective self-organisation to regulate the market, for, as he commented in his *Annual Report* for 1892, 'Thomas Carlyle once said that freedom was a divine thing sometimes, but that when it was freedom to die of starvation it was not so divine. And yet that is what freedom of contract and freedom of competition has led to, and must inevitably lead to, when unrestrained.'[9]

The most detailed discussion of the practical implications of this point of view for trade unionism is to be found in Knight's evidence to the Royal Commission on Labour in May 1892, where he argued that the intensity of unregulated fluctuations in shipbuilding production led to unacceptably large swings in the levels of employment and wages experienced by his members. Since these cycles of output were only possible because there was enough skilled labour available to supply requirements at the peak of production, the first major plank in Knight's strategy to regulate the market was the restriction of entry to the skilled trades.[10] It was expected that this would not only inhibit huge booms in output but that, by enforcing a more even response to the demand for ships, it would also reduce the severity of slumps in the industry. Later in 1892 Knight went so far as to put a figure on this issue, aiming ideally for a 30 per cent smaller workforce in continuous employment.[11] Something along these lines had already been indicated in his *Annual Report* for 1885 when, reflecting on the deep depression in trade, Knight had mentioned such remedies as further reductions in the length of the working day, encouragement of emigration, and schemes for returning labour to the land, all of which were calculated to reduce the effective supply of skilled labour.[12] Eventually he settled on the unilateral control by the union of the ratio of

[9] United Society of Boilermakers and Iron and Steel Shipbuilders, *Annual Report* (hereafter USBISS), 1892, p. vii.
[10] Royal Commission on Labour, *Minutes of Evidence, Group A* vol. 3 (1893 c. 6894) (hereafter RC Labour 1893), Q 20,681–3.
[11] USBISS 1892, p. vi.
[12] USBISS 1885, pp. vi–vii.

apprentices to journeymen, as the revival of trade from 1888 led to a corresponding revival in the strength and confidence of his own organisation. At the same time as acting to enforce this policy, Knight also attempted to find some acceptable argument to justify it in public, and he settled on an analogy with the government dockyards' budgets for labour being based on a planned programme of warship-building, rather than on *ad hoc* responses to market forces.[13]

This was very much in the tradition of mid-nineteenth-century trade unionism, accepting the logic of supply and demand and attempting to turn these forces in a favourable direction by controlling the supply of skilled labour.[14] However, Knight went one step further by advocating a second major plank to his strategy based this time on collective bargaining. He proposed that unions and employers should come to agreements to reduce fluctuations in wages by limiting the extent of each change in rates and limiting the frequency with which they could occur, in fact the opposite of a sliding scale with which it has sometimes been confused.[15] The intention behind this proposal for regulated collective bargaining was that, by preventing large wage reductions in slumps, it would become more difficult for employers to survive through periods of excessive competition, thus putting strong pressure on them to find a way of spreading contracts more evenly across the trade cycle. Moreover, given the greater predictability of wage costs which would be provided by this type of collective agreement, employers ought to be better able to price their contracts in all phases of the cycle and this would hopefully contribute to better planning of work and less under-employment in the industry.[16] Again, something along these lines had already been suggested by Knight some time before, in this case during the tenuous boom of 1881 when he was hoping that moderation in union pressure for advances might be matched by moderation in employers' pressure for cuts once the depression set in again.[17]

So far this might be dismissed as a classic case of narrow 'labourism',

---

[13] USBISS 1888, pp. 9–10; also RC Labour 1893, Q 20,788–792.
[14] See E. F. Biagini, 'British trade unions and popular political economy 1860–1880', *Historical Journal*, 30 (1987), pp. 811–40 especially pp. 816–9; E. J. Hobsbawm, 'Custom, wages, and work-load in nineteenth-century industry', in A. Briggs and J. Saville (eds.), *Essays in Labour History*, vol. 1 (London, 1960), pp. 113–39 (reprinted in *Labouring Men* [London, 1964], pp. 344–70, especially p. 350); and for the success of the strong craft unions in restricting access to their trades see H. Pelling, 'The concept of the labour aristocracy', in *Popular Politics*, pp. 37–61, especially pp. 50–1.
[15] For an account of a sliding scale in coal mining, and the moves by miners towards wage regulation by collective bargaining in the 1900s, see E. W. Evans, *Mabon (William Abraham 1842–1922). A Study in Trade Union Leadership* (Cardiff, 1959), pp. 13–4, 71–3.
[16] RC Labour 1893, Q 20,698.
[17] USBISS 1881, pp. xii–xiii.

with trade unions advancing their own members' short-term interests within a broader framework already established by their employers. However, it is not in fact clear that this would be an adequate characterisation of Knight's industrial strategy, for employers were rather sceptical about the idea of controlling wage fluctuations and were openly hostile to the idea of union restraints on the supply of skilled men, which offended their *laissez-faire* approach to the labour market. Thus, as Knight was gradually able successfully to enforce both of the main planks of his strategy in the course of the 1890s, he was not only justifying his preference for collective self-organisation without state assistance, but also demonstrating that it was possible by this method to shift the framework of industrial relations against the resistance of capital in a direction distinctly more favourable to labour.

There are a number of other aspects of this position which ought also to be considered to throw light on its wider significance. In the first place, at the Royal Commission on Labour itself Knight argued forcefully that, although platers' semi-skilled helpers could not be admitted to the Boilermakers' Society because it would not be financially viable to do so, they were in fact already enjoying many of the advantages of membership simply because the craftsmen's union was strong enough to alter the conditions of labour in the industry in general. For example, helpers usually gained wage increases parallel to those won by the platers for themselves, and, in so far as limitation on apprenticeships really could even out the fluctuations in industrial activity, this would naturally also benefit semi-skilled and unskilled labour.[18] Similarly, by keeping up the rates of pay and the levels of skill, the Boilermakers' Society would be preventing the construction of cheap and sub-standard vessels and thus contributing to the convenience and safety of both their passengers and their sailors, and it is significant in this context that Knight had been one of the major trade union supporters of the Plimsoll campaigns of the early 1870s.[19] Moreover, there are a number of scattered comments in Knight's public statements which indicate a firm grasp of demand-side economics and thus an understanding of the wider benefits of full employment and high wages for his own members. For example, in 1876 objecting strongly to employers' pressure for further wage reductions, he wrote 'they are no friends of their country who advocate starvation wages. Not only are the working classes affected by low wages, but the whole retail trade of the nation suffers most severely, because it mainly depends upon working-

---

[18] RC Labour 1893, Q 20, 814–7.
[19] RC Labour 1893, Q 20,681; USBISS 1873 p. 5; *Bee Hive Labour Portrait Gallery*, volume 2 (London, 1874), entry for Robert Knight pp. 4–6, especially p. 6; Trades Union Congress *Annual Report* (hereafter TUC), January 1875, pp. 18–20.

class custom.'[20] This was later elaborated in a more sophisticated form in his criticism of the Amalgamated Society of Engineers for its conduct in provoking the 1897 lockout:[21]

We all necessarily suffer when a dispute takes place similar to the one just terminated as a large amount of trade is diverted to other countries. That diversion means that less money will come into this country, that there will be less purchasing power among the workers, that they will buy less of other people, and so that other trades will by so much fall off. The round of such effects is well known and understood. The industrial system of a country like this is a most delicate organism, and the most various parts are influenced by each other.

Given the importance of the capital goods industries, and of shipbuilding in particular, at the turning points of the general trade cycle in this period, Knight would have had a basis in more than mere occupational pride for thinking that the outcomes of his union's collective action might have significant wider implications.

It can therefore be suggested that the narrowly focused, dryly economic, and apparently selfish industrial goals set out by Robert Knight in 1892 were in fact merely the practical and short-term targets of a more generous vision of the advance of the working classes. Not only was it expected that in the pursuit of their own immediate interests craft unions would produce benefits for the less well organised labour in their industries, it was also argued that they would produce benefits for the consumers of the products concerned, for workers in related sectors, and, through increased effective demand, for the general prosperity of the national economy. Thus, while unregulated market forces were likely to diminish freedom by producing excesses of prosperity and poverty, brought under some degree of control by the collective organisation of workers, the market could become a more benevolent means of transmitting the effects of sectional advance throughout the working population as a whole.

III

Given this commitment to a market economy, albeit a significantly regulated one, it is worth examining in more detail the nature of Robert Knight's rejection of *laissez-faire* individualism. And it is significant to note at the outset that, whereas his strategy for market regulation was only worked out in full during the revival in trade union strength from

---

[20] USBISS 1876, p. 11.
[21] USBISS 1897, p. ix. It is likely that this reflects the influence of works by J. A. Hobson which had been published in the early 1890s, especially *The Problem of the Unemployed* (London, 1896).

1888, and was at least partly a response to the sudden emergence of socialist views in the labour movement, his forceful rejection of *laissez-faire* individualism was strongest during the preceding long period of depression, and was a direct response to sustained assaults by employers on his members' wages and working conditions. One of the most extensive of Knight's comments on this subject is contained in the Boilermakers' Society's *Annual Report* for 1877, where it also becomes clear that this rejection of *laissez-faire* had deep roots in his Christian beliefs. For Knight, along with many of his colleagues among late nineteenth-century trade union leaders was an active Nonconformist, in his case as the deacon of a Congregationalist chapel.[22]

As Stephen Mayor pointed out some years ago, the nature and full extent of Christianity's influence on the labour movement in this period has been somewhat distorted by an excessive focus on Methodism.[23] For, while Primitive Methodism was indeed concentrated among miners, agricultural labourers, and fishermen, the urban working classes, far from all having become convinced secularists or apathetic non-attenders, were frequently still active adherents of Old Dissent.[24] The Baptists, Congregationalists and Presbyterians had always been committed to rational argument and local democracy, and by the late nineteenth century the latter two denominations were becoming increasingly liberal, both in their theology and in their outlook on social questions.[25] The Congregationalists in particular played a leading role in radical politics in England throughout the second half of the nineteenth century. Among the middle classes they produced important figures in the mid-nineteenth-century campaigns for political and legal reform like Edward Miall, the Chartist sympathiser and Church disestablishment activist, and Samuel Morley, a close friend of organised labour among the manufacturers, both of whom were elected as Radical MPs in the late 1860s. Members of this denomination also played a leading role in the emergence of the more socially oriented radicalism of the late nineteenth century, for it was two of their

[22] *Dictionary of Labour Biography*, vol. 6, pp. 153, 156.
[23] S. Mayor, *The Churches and the Labour Movement* (London, 1967), pp. 353–4, 360–4. For a recent account of Methodism among coal miners which stresses its role in providing continuity in popular politics, see R. Colls, *The Pitmen of the Northern Coalfield. Work, Culture, and Protest, 1790–1850* (Manchester, 1987), especially pp. 201–2, 306–7.
[24] For recent arguments for a greater working-class religious adherence in the nineteenth century than has previously been assumed, see H. McLeod, *Religion and the Working Class in Nineteenth Century Britain* (London, 1984); C. G. Brown, *The Social History of Religion in Scotland since 1730* (London, 1987), pp. 130–68.
[25] A. Peel, *These Hundred Years. A History of the Congregational Union of England and Wales, 1831–1931* (London, 1931), pp. 266–72, 300–1, 328, 332–3; Brown, *Religion in Scotland*, pp. 169–6; K. D. Brown, *A Social History of the Nonconformist Ministry in England and Wales, 1800–1930* (Oxford, 1988), pp. 80–123, 198–221.

ministers, Andrew Mearns and W. C. Preston, who wrote *The Bitter Cry of Outcast London* in 1883, which achieved much of its wider influence through the articles written about it by the journalist W. T. Stead, who was also a Congregationalist.[26] Although generally seen as one of the more middle class of the Nonconformist Churches, the Congregationalists also had a significant following among skilled workers and strong links with the leaders of organised labour.[27] In the mid-nineteenth-century generation of craft union leaders this included George Potter alongside Knight, while the Co-operative movement was largely led by Congregationalist working men: even its most prominent secularist leader G. J. Holyoake came from a Congregationalist family.[28] Interestingly enough, the denomination's influence was just as marked on the younger generation of late-nineteenth-century labour activists, especially among those who joined the Independent Labour Party, with Margaret Bondfield, Fred Jowett, Ben Tillett and Keir Hardie himself retaining active links with Congregationalist churches during their adult political careers.[29] Given the predominance of Presbyterianism throughout Scotland, it would therefore seem likely that the combined Congregationalist-Presbyterian impact on the British labour movement was at least as great as that of Methodism and, as Kenneth Brown suggests in his contribution to this collection (ch. 5) it was probably more assertively radical in its influence.[30]

Further distortions of the influence of Nonconformity on organised labour have arisen as a result of a misunderstanding of the nature of Protestantism's emphasis on the individual.[31] Here it is crucial to distinguish between arguments about the right relationship between man and God and arguments about the right relationship between man and man. It is in the case of the former that Protestantism is assertively

---

[26] Mayor, *Churches*, pp. 46–7, 56, 315; Miall had also sat as an MP between 1852 and 1857.
[27] For local links see S. Mayor, 'Some Congregational relations with the labour movement', *Congregational Historical Society Transactions*, 18 (1956), pp. 23–35, especially pp. 28–9; E. R. Wickham, *Church and People in an Industrial City* [Sheffield] (London, 1957), pp. 135–7; S. Yeo, *Religion and Voluntary Organizations in Crisis* [Reading] (London, 1976), pp. 59, 280–3, 291. In the following individual cases, strict criteria of active adult participation have been used, as suggested in K. D. Brown, 'Nonconformity and the British labour movement: a case study', *Journal of Social History*, 8 (1975), pp. 113–20.
[28] *Dictionary of Labour Biography*, vol. 6 (London, 1982), p. 227 for Potter; Mayor *Churches*, pp. 20, 153–7 for co-operation, where it emerges that, far from having been abandoned after 1850, the idea of producers' co-operation was particularly strong among Congregationalists; see TUC 1884, p. 30 for Knight's support for it.
[29] Mayor, *Churches*, pp. 14, 38, 309–13, 321–2; M. A. Hamilton, *Margaret Bondfield* (London, 1924).
[30] W. Knox (ed.), *Scottish Labour Leaders. 1918–39. A Biographical Dictionary* (Edinburgh, 1984), editor's 'Introduction', pp. 26–33.
[31] A point also touched on in Mayor, *Churches*, pp. 354–5.

individualistic: each individual Christian should have an unmediated relationship with God, and should pursue theological truth through reading the Scriptures, prayer and self-examination. However, it is also assumed that the result of this individual search will be an increasing capacity for compassion and an increasing sense of social responsibility towards one's fellow men and women: Protestants are only able to be so thoroughly liberal because of their confidence in the ultimate collective outcome. Assertions that Nonconformity contributed unambiguously to a popular acceptance of *laissez-faire* economics and individualist views of society therefore need to confront more directly not only the controversies over the meaning of Jesus's comments on the difficulties for the rich in entering the Kingdom of Heaven, but also the centrality of the sentiments evoked by the parable of the Good Samaritan.

Since the fundamental moral ideal of Christianity is caring for others and sharing one's resources with them, it was clearly impossible for Knight to accept the assumptions of economic and social individualism, quite apart from the fact that they were being used to justify attacks on his members' hard-won position. On the contrary, he found in his own Christian beliefs a solid basis for criticism of the employers' behaviour and a justification for industrial action in resistance:[32]

Were the masters to put themselves in the place of their men, and the men in the place of their masters, and endeavour to do as they would like to be done unto, it is highly probable that strikes or lock-outs would cease to be. Such a course would have secured a kindly, mutual consideration, too conspicuous by its absence during the past year. When the question in dispute is one of wages, the first consideration should be (especially among those who claim to be Christians, who believe in the brotherhood of men), whether a man can live on what he earns, or whether his work and his hunger are accelerating his passage to the grave. But such a thought is laughed to scorn by most employers, and science, as developed in political economy, is set by them against all such sentiments of humanity in their dealings with their workmen. This we very much regret, but cannot help it, and must therefore take it into account and provide for it.

It is interesting to note that this statement reflected a long-standing attitude on the part of Old Dissent, in recognising the existence of secular laws of supply and demand but at the same time insisting that Christian behaviour involved adjusting market prices to take account of considerations of humanity and social justice.[33]

---

[32] USBISS 1877, pp. xi–xii.

[33] An important influence on these attitudes was the seventeenth-century Presbyterian writer Richard Baxter, see E. D. Bebb, *Nonconformity and Social and Economic Life, 1660–1800* (London, 1935), pp. 101–10. By the late nineteenth century Nonconformists generally supported trade unions in industrial disputes, see for example, Mayor, *Churches*, pp. 80–151; Peel, *Congregational Union*, pp. 299–300, 332; and Kenneth Brown, ch. 5, in this collection.

In so far as there was a willingness on Knight's part to co-operate with employers it was therefore a discriminating form of co-operation, offered only to those who themselves rejected *laissez-faire* assumptions and were prepared to treat their workers with some measure of fairness and human consideration. They were those who, in Knight's vocabulary, had the moral feelings of gentlemen and since many of them were likely to have been Nonconformists, that would have added another element of common feeling to their relations with the craft unions.[34] The attitudes of the more selfish employers, on the other hand, were closely linked by Knight to the causes of the intense fluctuations of shipbuilding output and employment, for it was this type of person who would be drawn into speculative investment in shipping when prices were high, thus exacerbating over-production in the boom; and it was this type of person who would be prepared to take part in excessive competition for orders in the slump, on the basis of vicious wage cuts for their workers.[35] In this equation of bad behaviour on the part of industrial employers with 'speculation' there is a clear link with Christianity's long-standing suspicions of usury and its tendency to focus criticism on commercial and financial capital in particular. Even in the case of the 'ungentlemanly' industrialist engaged in forcing down wages, the really big profits would be going to the ship owner who was able to buy the product at an absurdly low price, an activity more often than not backed up by the 'fatal facilities for credit offered by our wholly unsound banking system'.[36] Moreover, the other main cause of the intense shipbuilding cycle identified by Knight was equally to be condemned from a Christian point of view, for it was the spending of large sums of money on armaments throughout Europe, and the consequent diversion of resources from peaceful civilian consumption.[37] It was on the basis of this interpretation of the trade cycle that Knight was able to resist a forceful cross-examination from shipbuilding employers at the Royal Commission on the Depression of Trade and Industry in June 1886, and to reject firmly all their arguments that the long slump had been caused by high wages and shorter hours driving contracts for new ships away from British yards.[38] And it was on this same basis

---

[34] USBISS 1873, pp. 5, 8; USBISS 1876, p. 12.

[35] USBISS 1873, p. 5; also USBISS 1878, pp. vi–vii, USBISS 1884, p. viii, USBISS 1886, p. vi.

[36] USBISS 1875, p. 5, also pp. 8–13.

[37] USBISS 1875, p. 5; USBISS 1878, p. ix; USBISS 1886, pp. ix–x. See Peel, *Congregational Union*, pp. 296–8 for the strong support for disarmament among Congregationalists in these years.

[38] Royal Commission on the Depression of Trade and Industry, *Final Report and Minutes of Evidence* (1886 c.4893) (hereafter RC Depression 1886), Q 14,733–979.

that he was then able to mount his own counter-attack to regulate the behaviour of employers in the interests of labour after 1888.

Even before the elaboration of a detailed strategy for the assertive use of self-organisation, Knight had been quite clear that it was only by building up their collective solidarity that workers would have any real defence against unfair pressure from employers in years of depression. To take up the quotation from the 1877 *Annual Report* where it was left off:[39]

This we very much regret but cannot help it, and must therefore take it into account and provide for it. Our experience has taught us that we can never get a fair remuneration for our labour, or enforce our just claims, without the power given by organisation. The grand work for each of us is to use every effort to make our association as complete as possible, as we are only respected in proportion as we are strong. Organise, organise, organise, must be our watchword. Real union in any trade can do more than all reason, eloquence, or justice. We do not plead against these; on the contrary we insist that reason and justice should never be absent from the dealings of men; but we nevertheless affirm that these, without power to enforce them, are of little or no use in the disputes of employers and employed.

If Knight sounds here surprisingly like celebrated militants from the annals of labour history, the impression is not a wholly misleading one. For his actual industrial strategy was considerably less collaborative than has often been suggested by historians and, faced with the strains of a long depression, this Liberal in politics was prepared to make some surprising statements on industrial matters. He frequently voiced such standard defences of trade unionism as employers' economic power making them individually as strong as combinations of workers, and the impossibility of workers stockpiling their labour when the price offered fell too low, but by 1887 things had got so bad that Knight was openly arguing for moral and economic coercion to enforce the closed shop.[40] As was generally the case with his positions, he had given some serious thought to its justification: every adult, he argued, is a citizen of a state whether he wants to be or not, he benefits from the rule of law and as a result does not have absolute freedom to chose whether or not to obey the law himself; similarly, every worker in a craft industry experiences the benefits of strong trade unionism and therefore does not have absolute freedom to choose whether or not to join the union himself, if he will not join those who are already members in furthering the common good, they have as much right to deprive him of employment as the state has to deprive criminals of their rights as citizens.[41]

[39] USBISS 1877, p. xii.
[40] For examples of the standard defences of trade unionism see USBISS 1887, pp. xi–xii and USBISS 1898, pp. vi–vii.
[41] USBISS 1887, pp. xii–xiii.

As well as reflecting on the liberal political tradition, Knight drew on his Christian beliefs to justify his strong commitment to collective organisation, and occasionally called on these same principles to criticise his own members. For example, in commenting on those who regarded their membership simply as a form of individual welfare insurance he emphasised the origins of trade unionism in mutual help in times of need:[42]

> Providence has so ordained that we are wonderfully dependent on one another, and one hardly knows which is the worse – the self-conceited man who imagines he can stand alone, or the selfishness of the man who has no desire to help a brother ... By each bearing the other's burthens, helping the other's progress, gladdening the other's heart, cherishing the other's life, we each find our own aim and hope fulfilled in no private advantage, but in the good of a great whole.

Similarly, as trade began to improve he urged his members to participate more fully in branch affairs, to make sure that the rules of the society were followed properly and to keep their brothers on the straight and narrow path.[43] Knight clearly regarded active trade unionism as a practical manifestation of Christian belief, and occasionally used explicitly religious language to promote his arguments for a more active membership, for example during the revival in union strength in the 1890s: 'In the early part of this address we gave you credit for being firm in trades-union faith, but, as the Good Book tells us, faith alone without good works avails us nothing.'[44] Indeed when responding to external threats, like the mounting employers' assault on wages and conditions in the late 1870s, Knight sometimes presented trade unionism as itself a form of natural religion:

> It was hatred of Trade Societies that prompted the masters to act as they did, but their attempt to erase them out was as futile as Mrs Partington's attempt to sweep back the waves of the Atlantic with a mop. The principles of Trade Unions are as strong in human hearts as are the waters of the ocean.[45]

Knight, moreover, was far from blind to the wider social implications of the Christian principle of brotherhood, for in these years he made repeated demands for more equality between capital and labour both in the workplace itself and in the distribution of the product. The former

---

[42] USBISS 1879, p. iv. Both in the language used and in the personification of moral attitudes, there are surely strong overtones in this passage of John Bunyan's *Pilgrim's Progress* (London, 1678).

[43] USBISS 1890, p. xi.

[44] USBISS 1894, p. xi.

[45] USBISS 1877, p. x. It is interesting to note that references to Mrs Partington were common among late-nineteenth-century trade unionists and that, while she was supposedly a real person from the Devon coast, she had been introduced into radical imagery, as well as into general English usage, by Sidney Smith when he ridiculed the House of Lords' opposition to parliamentary reform in October 1831, see *Brewer's Dictionary of Phrase and Fable* (2nd edition) p. 825.

demand is to be found as a basic assumption behind many of his statements and, as in the case of the Christian basis of his trade unionism, it finds its clearest expression in his 1877 *Annual Report*:[46]

Unfortunately, capital plumes its feathers and crows over labour; here lies their mistake, as we have a just claim to equal rights with capital as to the disposal of our services. The day is gone by for workmen to be treated as a mere serf. We hold out the hand of fellowship to capital, and only ask to be treated as equals in the bargain to be made.

This passage throws a striking new light on the commonly quoted statements of Knight and other craft union leaders of the period regarding harmonious relations between capital and labour, for it suggests that behind them lay, not an attitude of willing subservience, but rather an assertion of equal rights and a perception of anything else as a form of slavery. Their ideal may well have been the unity of capital and labour but it was to be a unity on labour's as much as on capital's terms.[47] Moreover, during the next decade Knight was to address himself to the issue of fair shares of the product on more than one occasion, finding much to be shocked at in the existing distribution of the national wealth and also showing a clear understanding of the rejection of the theory of the 'wages fund' by contemporary Radical economists.[48] Thus in 1880 he argued not only that collective bargaining accelerated the operation of market forces but also that, since the real value of labour could not be determined without access to particular company accounts, and it was obvious that labour was not maintaining its relative share of the national wealth, his members were justified in demanding whatever they could get: 'Left to our own judgment we arrive at the conclusion that fair wages means whatever the workman is able to obtain from the employer, and this process is more easily accomplished and more effective when done collectively than when it is attempted individually'.[49]

By looking at Robert Knight's statements during the years of depression and industrial uncertainty between 1874 and 1888 in the light of his Christian beliefs it can be seen that his perspective on labour matters

[46] USBISS 1877, p. xi.
[47] For a similar stress on the fundamentally egalitarian aspirations of trade unionism arising from Nonconformist convictions, see George Howell, *Trade Unionism New and Old* (London, 1891), p. 230, and Evans, *Mabon*, pp. 11, 13, 98; and for the general support for industrial co-partnership in the Nonconformist press, see Mayor, *Churches*, pp. 95–6. In contrast, see K. McClelland, 'Time to work, time to live; some aspects of work and the reformation of class in Britain, 1850–1880', in P. Joyce (ed.), *The Historical Meanings of Work* (Cambridge, 1987), pp 180–209, which also highlights the persistence of moral attitudes among trade unionists, but argues that they contributed to the acceptance of subordination.
[48] USBISS 1885, p. vii; Biagini, 'Trade unions and popular political economy', pp. 819–32.
[49] USBISS 1880, p. ix; Hobsbawm 'Custom, wages and workload', pp. 350–1.

was much richer and more progressive than might be assumed. For, as well as the broader understanding of economic interrelationships already outlined, it is now clear that Knight had deeply held views on social morality, mutuality and equality, and strong feelings of outrage when these principles were violated. However, it is also important to remember that, as a Christian, Knight did not believe that employers were compelled towards certain kinds of behaviour by economic forces, but rather that they still had the choice of whether to behave well or badly, whether to be fair or exploitative towards their workforce. Social injustice from this point of view was not a necessary consequence of the existence of private property, but rather of the moral failings of many of those privileged to be its owners.

IV

Given Robert Knight's strong criticisms of unregulated industries and immoral capitalists, and given his commitment to the collective organisation of labour to bring them under control in the name of efficiency and equality, it is not surprising that in the early 1890s the Webbs should have regarded him as a potential ally in their campaign to convert the Liberal party to socialism.[50] They were of course disappointed, for Knight still saw virtues in the market and in private property which they did not, and he was extremely uneasy about the extension of the powers of central government implied by the socialist goals of state social reform and state ownership of industry. His major statements on this subject are to be found in the course of his opposition to the New Unionism at the Trades Union Congress between 1889 and 1894, where it became clear that his objections were based on serious thought and deeply held political principles which had their roots in the radical tradition.

One of the major formative experiences for Knight, as for most other members of his generation of union leaders, had been the success of the campaigns for the decriminalisation of trade union activity in the late 1860s and early 1870s, discussed in Jonathan Spain's contribution to this collection (ch. 6). As one of the rising young men in trade union circles in the period, Knight had played a central role in the final act of this drama for, as the chairman of the Parliamentary Committee of the TUC in 1875, he had assisted its Secretary George Howell in organising the campaigning and lobbying for the repeal of the Criminal Law Amendment Act, and he had been the first to congratulate the delegates on their unprecedented

---

[50] It is striking, for example, how they held Knight up as a paragon of progressive industrial policies, see S. and B. Webb, *The History of Trade Unionism* (London, 1894), pp. 307, 336 note, 341 note, 408.

successes at the Glasgow Congress that autumn.[51] This speech, like others he and his colleagues had made over the previous months, was strongly infused with the rhetoric of liberty, equality and justice, and was assertively radical in its references to slavery, as well as in its emphasis on the need for struggle and self-reliance:[52]

A man might not have chains on his ankles, but he might be far from enjoying liberty. If there was anything that prevented his proper development as a man – anything in his relations with those that employ him that curbed his opportunities of bettering his condition – that man is not free ... today they could rejoice because we are free. If he were to ask what had purchased their freedom, he felt assured they would, with united voice reply it had been their associations which have gained it – (applause) ... with a thorough determination to gain what they considered their rights, their suit had been forced. He might say also that justice is the distinguishing characteristic of our associations, and, as working men, they claimed equality with other portions of the nation – not the equality that sprang from fortune, but the equality of self-reliance and independent spirit – (applause).

The success of these campaigns for labour law reform played a crucial role in convincing trade unionists that it was possible to obtain equal treatment under the law if they were well enough organised, and it therefore encouraged an interest in further measures of legal reform, as well as helping to put the final nail in the coffin of arguments in favour of revolutionary methods.[53]

The legacy of these campaigns, apart from the crucial victory of 1875 itself, which had given the unions some defence against the onslaughts of the ensuing long depression, had therefore been a reaffirmation of the radical principle that the central requirement for labour's advance was freedom from external restraint, and a corresponding characterisation of any government interference in industry as reactionary in the literal sense of the word.[54] Consequently, Knight was genuinely appalled by the proposal for statutory enforcement of the eight-hour working day put forward by the younger socialist activists of the New Unionism in the early 1890s. For, should they be successful in achieving it, they would have legitimised once again the principle of parliamentary interference in the

---

[51] TUC October 1875, pp. 8, 16, 22, 26; Leventhal, *Respectable Radical*, pp. 183–5.

[52] TUC October 1875, p. 3.

[53] TUC October 1875, p. 3. For Knight's special interest in the simplification of the criminal law and the abolition of imprisonment for small debtors, see TUC 1877, p. 20, TUC 1878, pp. 27–8, TUC 1880, p. 34, TUC 1882, pp. 27–8, TUC 1884, p. 32.

[54] For widespread popular distrust of the legal system and of the extension of the power of the state, both in trade union affairs and in the area of social reform, see H. Pelling, 'The working class and the origins of the welfare state', in *Popular Politics*, pp. 1–18, and 'Trade unions, workers and the law', in *Popular Politics*, pp. 62–81; also P. Thane, 'The working class and state "welfare" in Britain, 1880–1914', *Historical Journal*, 27 (1984), pp. 877–900. For the general tendency of the strong crafts to be more radical than other groups of workers see Pelling, 'Labour aristocracy', pp. 56–61.

conditions and wages of work, which could then just as easily be turned against them by requiring longer hours and lower wages, perhaps backed up by arguments about foreign competition of the type which had been so prominent at the Royal Commission on the Depression only a few years before. Such a thing had not been heard of since the bad old days of absolute monarchy, the effects of which had not been completely removed until the successful campaigns of the early 1870s:[55]

> The decline of absolute power and the growth of freedom has been the result of continual struggles on the part of working men to shake off the fetters that had so long bound them . . . All we want is liberty of action. We want no Parliamentary interference. We want the right to combine, and this we have; and the power that Union gives us will enable us to obtain all we can reasonably expect.

The attitudes of the Old Unionists were, however, not quite as simple as this, for there was one significant area in which they did accept the legitimacy of government intervention in industry, and which provided part of the motivation for their continued interest in parliamentary affairs and that was the issue of safety at work and compensation for accidents.[56] For, as George Howell argued, this was an exceptional area in which workers were unable to look after their interests individually, in which the law had a responsibility for the protection of persons, and in which the state's involvement in establishing a safe framework for industrial activity would not imply any interference in free bargaining between capital and labour.[57] Moreover, it is also important to note that a number of the more radical trade union leaders were already proposing an extensive range of political and social reforms by the mid-1880s.[58] Interestingly enough, Knight himself had been one of the first of the TUC leaders to mention issues other than labour law for, bringing up the rear of the platform at a public meeting held to celebrate the victory of 1875, it was he who had put forward a vision of the future:[59]

[55] USBISS 1889, p. xi; the opening sentence of this passage repeats almost word for word a section of Knight's celebration speech of 1875, see TUC October 1875, p. 3. See also C. Bradlaugh, *Socialism: Its Fallacies and Dangers* (London, 1887), p. 9, reprinted in J. Saville (ed.), *A Selection of the Political Pamphlets of Charles Bradlaugh* (New York, 1970).

[56] For Knight's active involvement in this issue see TUC 1879, p. 18, TUC 1881, p. 15, TUC 1882, pp. 21 and 23, TUC 1883, p. 28, TUC 1884, p. 40, TUC 1887, pp. 24–5, TUC 1888, p. 22, TUC 1896, pp. viii–ix.

[57] See G. Howell, 'Liberty for labour', in T. Mackay (ed.), *A Plea for Liberty. An Argument Against Socialism and Socialistic Legislation* (London, 1891), pp. 109–41, especially pp. 120–2, 124–5; and for the up-hill nature of the struggle as long as the 'doctrine of common employment' remained in place see Pelling 'Trade unions, workers and the law', pp. 66–8.

[58] See Clegg *et al.*, *Trade Unions*, pp. 52–4 for an earlier recognition of this development, in some contrast to B. C. Roberts, *The Trades Union Congress 1868–1921* (London, 1958), pp. 92–132, which largely repeats the socialist criticisms of the 1890s.

[59] TUC October 1875, pp. 16–17.

But they were not now to fold their arms and be content, because there was more for them to do. They required better homes for their poor, not only in their large towns, but in their country villages scattered throughout the length and breadth of the land. Then there was the question of education for working men to interest themselves in. Although they were possessed of an Education Act, it was a dead letter in three parts of the United Kingdom, and they never would have the benefit of that Act until they had School Boards in every locality throughout the length and breadth of the land.

However, in this respect Knight was rather ahead of his time, and such ambitious proposals were to be overshadowed by a decade and more of economic depression, accompanied by a major decline in trade union strength, a preoccupation with organisational survival, and the growth of Conservatism and imperialism in labour circles.[60] Thus although tenants' land rights were to emerge as a controversial issue in the early 1880s, the TUC did not begin to show a consistent interest in non-industrial questions until after the 1884 extension of the parliamentary franchise, the subsequent large increase in labour MPs, and the inclusion of leading figures like Henry Broadhurst and John Burnett in Gladstone's new administration.[61] In 1885 Thomas Threlfall gave the most wide-ranging presidential address to date calling for, among other things, improved public education and more generous poor relief, and in supporting it Knight pointed out that 'the working classes had now been given the power of making laws for their benefit, and removing from the statute book those laws which in the past had prevented the progress of the labouring population. (Applause)'.[62] This development was accompanied by an intensification of union support for increased labour representation in the form of Threlfall's Labour Electoral Association, as well as by an increasingly detailed grasp of policy issues. The following year, for example, Knight put forward a more sophisticated motion on education, calling for free elementary schooling under the control of elected representatives, and justifying it with reference to the precedent of free public libraries as well as to the need for improved industrial training to keep up with other nations.[63] It is therefore interesting to note that, at the 1887 Congress, the proposer and seconder of the formal vote of thanks for the presidential address, calling for land reform, publicly funded housing, reform of the Poor Law, and unity of the skilled and the unskilled in

[60] Roberts, *Trades Union Congress*, pp. 107–8; see also Jon Lawrence, ch. 4, in this collection.
[61] See Roberts, *Trades Union Congress*, pp. 103–12; see also John Shepherd, ch. 9, in this collection.
[62] TUC 1885, p. 20.
[63] TUC 1886, p. 46; for Knight's support for the Labour Electoral Association see TUC 1886, p. 37. The Congregationalists had supported publicly funded secular education since the late 1860s, and were officially to support local democratic control of schools from 1890, see Peel, *Congregational Union*, pp. 183–9, 362–3.

support of a parliamentary labour party, were none other than Robert Knight and Keir Hardie.[64]

However, as far as economic matters were concerned, radicals like Knight were still strong supporters of private property and a market economy, albeit a regulated one, and they were therefore bound to come into conflict eventually with the younger socialist activists, keen to apply their new ideas to industrial questions. Although the arguments between these two groups were to have much of the passion of a conflict between generations, it should not be thought that the Old Unionists were merely refusing to move with the times; on the contrary, their opposition to socialism was based on the central political principle of independence for working people, which extended from opposition to state intervention in industrial relations, to a concern that any measures of economic and social reform should not reduce the sphere of personal liberty.[65] Thus, on the one occasion on which he did accept that central government might pursue more interventionist policies on unemployment, Knight followed this immediately with a call for self-improvement to minimise the extension of the state:[66]

With the State, thus spurred on by the voice of Labour, rests the responsibility of removing some of the causes [of unemployment]; but we believe it possible for the workers themselves to mitigate, to some extent at least, the sufferings and miseries which from it flow. How is this to be done? Our answer is by the study and practice of those principles of thrift and self-help to which we have already alluded. Self-reform is by far the most needful and pressing, as it is also the most practical and useful of the many reforms that engage public attention. Its advantages far outreach any other, it works automatically, the mind supplies the motive power, there being no complex state machinery required to put it into operation, and its effects are immediate.

It is striking that in his public statements, Knight had rarely proposed individual thrift and temperance before the threat of socialism emerged in the 1890s, and that an uncharacteristic loss of control then occasionally did become evident.[67] However, before dismissing this as merely an old man's reversion to the outdated doctrines of his youth in a time of crisis, it is worth remembering the precarious nature of most working-

[64] TUC 1887, p. 21.
[65] USBISS 1894, p. xi; USBISS 1898, p. xiii; for an impassioned attack on the uniformity implicit in state socialism see Howell 'Liberty for labour', pp. 138–40; also Bradlaugh, *Socialism*, p. 12.
[66] USBISS 1894, p. ix.
[67] See especially the long outburst, written in March 1895, in USBISS 1894, pp. viii–xi; and also USBISS 1890, p. xii; USBISS 1892, p. xii–xiii; USBISS 1898, p. xiii.

class household budgets in the period, the vast quantities and poor quality of the alcohol involved, and the public support for temperance shown by prominent members of the younger generation, like Burns, Hardie, Mann and Tillett.[68] For his part, Knight was prepared to concede that freedom did have an economic dimension and that many of the poorest workers did not possess the preliminary conditions for self-improving activity, however, the difference between the generations still remained, for the central means of social advance in Knight's view should be collective self-organisation, and the goal of that advance should still be independence:[69]

We, as a Society [the Boilermakers' Society], have done much to remove all restrictions, so that everyone may have a fair start, and the opportunity to show what he is made of. At present everyone has not this opportunity. How can the docker, whose whole energy of thought is concentrated on the problem whether he shall get a meal today or the sweater who is kept stitching at shoddy coats for sixteen hours a day. But we do look forward to the good time coming when

> Man to man the whole world o'er
> Shall brithers be and a' that-

when the poorest and meanest shall be given the power, if he has the will, to elevate himself – in that time we shall have social justice, but we shall not have equality.

The overtones in this statement of key moments in the history of radicalism are interesting. The verse is, of course from the conclusion of Robert Burns's 'A man's a man for a' that', a classic radical attack on the pretensions of the aristocracy, written as a New Year statement for 1795 in the immediate aftermath of the intensification of repression of British republicans by the passing of the Two Acts.[70] Moreover, it may not be too fanciful to see a reference in the rest of the sentence to the famous statements of the Leveller leader Colonel Thomas Rainborough at the 1647 Putney Debates on the extension of the franchise: 'really I thinke that the poorest hee that is in England hath a life to live as the greatest hee . . .

---

[68] See Mayor, *Churches*, p. 158; Knox, *Labour Leaders*, pp. 22–6.

[69] USBISS 1890, p. xii; see also USBISS June 1873, p. 8, USBISS 1891, p. xiv. George Howell took the same view, and therefore welcomed the organisation of the unskilled while deploring the political aims of the New Unionist leaders, *Trade Unionism*, p. 235. See also Thane, 'State "welfare"' for the widespread preference among organised workers for full employment, higher wages and personal saving rather than dependence on the state, and for the widespread hostility among poorer workers to the inquisitorial aspect of much state social reform.

[70] R. Burns, *Poetical Works*, vol. 3 (Popular edition, William Paterson, Edinburgh, 1885), pp. 161–3, for the poem and an editorial note which makes the historical context explicit.

Therfore I say, that either itt must bee the law of God or the law of man that must prohibite the meanest man in the Kingdome to have this benefitt as well as the greatest.'[71]

The younger generation's challenge to the 'Old Guard' at the TUC came about largely as the result of an unexpected explosion in unskilled unionism in 1889, followed by a temporarily uncontrolled increase in the influx of new delegates to the annual Congress. For while Keir Hardie had been criticising the Parliamentary Committee since 1887, this had been in the form of a largely personal attack on Broadhurst, and strong support was not evident for eight-hours' legislation until 1890, or for the nationalisation of industry until 1893.[72] Whereas the more progressive radicals like Knight and Threlfall had attempted to avoid getting involved in the bitter disputes between Hardie and Broadhurst, they could no longer ignore the socialist challenge after 1889, and significantly enough it was Knight himself who emerged as the outstanding opponent of the New Unionists, partly because he was so persistent in his objections, and also because he was able to take the radical case on from traditional libertarianism to a detailed and penetrating criticism of socialist principles.

As far as the eight-hour day was concerned, there can be no question of Knight's sincerity in supporting it as a goal. He had, after all, been active in the successful industrial campaign for a nine-hour day in the early 1870s, and had staunchly defended this advance against later criticisms, above all at the Royal Commission on the Depression in 1886:[73]

Machinery is made that the workman might not be made a machine of, and he thereby has leisure to live, leisure to love and leisure to taste his freedom ... the working man should also receive the benefit of the introduction of machinery, as he has done by lessening the hours of labour already, and if it was necessary we might still further lessen the hours of labour.

In 1891 he supported the London joiners' strike for an eight-hour day, and in 1893 he welcomed its introduction at the Woolwich Arsenal, remarking to his members, 'what we want is plenty of intelligent work, and ample leisure in which to increase and enjoy that intelligence'.[74] Knight's objection to Keir Hardie's motion at the 1889 Congress, then, really was

---

[71] The likelihood that Knight was consciously referring to Rainborough is increased by the publication, at around the time he would have been writing his Report for 1890, of both the first text of the Putney Debates and the first use of them in a historical account of the period, see respectively C. H. Firth (ed.), *The Clarke Papers*, vol. 1 (Camden Society, London, 1891), pp. 301, 304 for the passages cited, and S. R. Gardiner, *History of the Great Civil War*, vol. 3, *1647–1649* (London, 1891), pp. 225–6.

[72] Roberts, *Trades Union Congress*, pp. 116–27; Clegg *et al.*, *Trade Unions*, pp. 255–62, 291–4.

[73] RC Depression 1886, Q 14, 976–7.

[74] TUC 1891, p. 32; USBISS 1893, pp. vi, xii.

an objection regarding means and not ends, its basis was the traditional libertarian opposition to state interference, and enough present were in agreement to resist the socialist pressure for an eight-hours bill.[75]

However, by the following Congress the socialist presence was larger and, with the current of opinion flowing strongly against the older generation, it was necessary to tackle the eight-hours proposals in more detail. Thus in 1890 and 1891 Knight became the main spokesman at the TUC of the radical opposition to statutory enforcement of hours and conditions of work on the grounds that general national standards would be too rigid and unresponsive to local conditions. What was to happen, for example, in the case of pieceworkers in the steel industry or in shipbuilding who had to work with hot metal, were they to end their shifts exactly at the hour stipulated even if they had spent the first few hours waiting for their furnaces to heat up? What about workers in industries affected by the seasons? Again this included shipbuilding, in which Knight reckoned that the working day probably already averaged eight hours over the whole year, but was longer in the summer and shorter in the winter. What about variations in individual strength and weakness, or indeed in individual needs for money income? Paradoxically, of course, this latter would apply particularly to time workers on low pay who would need to work for longer than eight hours to earn a subsisitence wage.[76] Finally in 1891, to lighten the atmosphere after a particularly fierce set of exchanges Knight half-jokingly, but also half-seriously, added 'when this eight hours Act of Parliament is passed will the following be included in it: – Editors of newspapers, reporters, commercial travellers – they are workpeople – workingmen members of Parliament – they are work-people – (laughter) – male and female servants of all kinds, and general secretaries of labour organisations? (Laughter and cheers)'.[77] Thus for Knight, as for his colleagues among the parliamentary Radicals like Howell and Bradlaugh, only collective organisation by the people on the spot could guarantee enough flexibility in the regulation of the conditions of working life.[78] Moreover, any version of protective legislation would still have the undesirable side effects of encouraging condescension on the

---

[75] TUC 1889, pp. 55, 57. See also C. Bradlaugh, *The Eight Hours' Movement* (London, 1889), pp. 3, 11–6, reprinted in Saville, *Political Pamphlets.*

[76] TUC 1890, p. 49; TUC 1891, p. 42; RC Labour 1893, Q 20,825–9.

[77] TUC 1891, p. 52.

[78] Howell 'Liberty for labour', pp. 128–36; Bradlaugh, *Eight Hours*, pp. 4–6. It should also be noted that the well-known opposition of the Durham miners to the implied lengthening of their seven-hour day was also phrased in terms of the rigidity of any general legislation, see J. Wilson, *A History of the Durham Miners' Association, 1870–1904* (Durham, 1907), pp. 249–50. Similar arguments had been used in the early-nineteenth-century campaigns against the New Poor Law, see B. Harrison and P. Hollis, 'Chartism, Liberalism and the life of Robert Lowery', *English Historical Review*, 82 (1967), pp. 503–35, especially p. 523.

part of the state and apathy on the part of the worker, for 'is it not insulting to the workman to talk of legislation to help him to do what he could do for himself if permitted?'[79]

As far as the more ambitious goals of the socialists were concerned the disagreement went deeper than it had over the eight-hours question, including ends as well as means, for Knight and his radical colleagues were opposed in principle to the abolition of private property. This was partly because of their concern to defend widespread small-scale property ownership, especially during the debates of the early 1880s over land reform.[80] But it was mainly because of the economic, social and political results which they predicted would flow from nationalisation, with Knight's particular contribution being a characteristic focus on the practical details of the methods proposed for achieving the socialist millennium. Thus in the major debate at the Congress of 1893 he supported the motion by Havelock Wilson and Ben Tillett for a political levy to finance labour candidates, but opposed James Macdonald's famous, and successful, socialist amendment by asking an apparently simple question which had penetrating ramifications, and to which the supporters of the socialist proposal had no answer:[81]

Mr Knight (Newcastle) said he did not quite follow the amendment. He thought it was incomplete, as it did not say into whose hands the collective ownership of the income of production, distribution, and exchange could pass. (Hear, hear.) Was it proposed to place it in the hands of the Government, and did they think it would be for the betterment of their condition?

As he elaborated this point, both immediately and over the next few years, it became clear that Knight had two major objections to the nationalisation of British industry. Firstly, that the national political system was imperfectly democratic and socially biased against the interests of labour, a point which he had touched on during the eight-hours controversy, but now developed with telling effect:[82]

He for one was not prepared to hand over means of production and distribution to the Government of the country. Before they could do anything they would have to get a new House of Commons and do away with the House of Lords. (Applause) He would recommend them to set about getting a new House of Commons rather than go for a visionary scheme such as this.

---

[79] USBISS 1889,. p. xi.
[80] TUC 1883, p. 39; C. Bradlaugh, *The Atheistic Platform VII: Some Objections to Socialism* (London, 1884), pp. 102–8, reprinted in Saville, *Political Pamphlets*.
[81] TUC 1893, p. 47.
[82] TUC 1893, p. 47; also USBISS 1889, p. x for similar comments in the context of the eight-hours issue. Just how visionary the socialist proposals really were at this stage is strikingly indicated by the defeat of a motion of Keir Hardie's calling for the establishment of an independent labour party immediately after the passing of Macdonald's socialist amendment, TUC 1893, p. 49.

Reporting back some years later on the outcome of a TUC delegation to the Admiralty, Knight raised a point which had even more disturbing implications for the operation of parliamentary government, and that was the issue of accountability to the legislature, for 'the First Lord appeared as a special pleader for the sweater-contractor. He did now wonder at this, because anyone who knew anything about Government departments know that the [Fair Wages] resolution of the House of Commons was violated in principle every day in every Government department.'[83]

Knight's second major objection to the public ownership of industry related to the nature of its management, a matter which he was one of the few trade union leaders at the time to have had direct experience of, as a result of his fourteen years as an employee in the Royal Dockyard at Devonport in Plymouth. Once the policy of socialism had been adopted at the Congresses of 1893 and 1894, Knight focused his energies on this second objection by mounting a sustained campaign against the Admiralty: insisting on the proper publication of the location of government contracts in private industry so that wages and working conditions could be monitored by the unions, demanding that the Dockyards stop employing semi-skilled labour on craft tasks, and pressing for all government departments to follow the 1891 Fair Wages Resolution of the House of Commons.[84] It is likely that there was a double intention behind this, on the one hand to remind his colleagues continually of the shortcomings of state management, and on the other hand to build up a basis for influencing government should it emerge after all that nationalisation really was inevitable. While Knight himself tended to present these issues as matters of practical trade unionism, the Boilermakers' District Delegate for Cardiff, Frank Fox, was prepared to be more outspoken about the political intentions behind the campaign:[85]

the resolution conveyed but a very vague and indefinite idea of the grossly unfair and utterly untrade-union-like system that obtained in the Government dockyards in regard to the construction of Her Majesty's ships. He confessed that he was a warm supporter of the principle of the nationalisation of land and of industries that might with advantage be managed by the State, but if he thought that the State would manage nationalised property in the same loose, thriftless, and extravagant fashion they now managed, or rather mismanaged, shipbuilding in the dockyards he would immediately cease to be a nationaliser. (Hear, hear)

---

[83] TUC 1897, p. 32.
[84] TUC 1894, p. 45; TUC 1896, p. 60; TUC 1897, pp. 32, 44–5, 51; TUC 1898, pp. 52, 55–6. This also seems to have involved Knight's conversion to contract compliance which he had previously rejected in favour of stronger trade unionism, see TUC 1895, pp. 57–8; TUC 1890, p. 39.
[85] TUC 1896, p. 60.

Robert Knight's opposition to socialism at the Trades Union Congresses of the early 1890s was based, then, on an almost instinctive libertarianism which was widespread among craft unionists and which he developed into a number of serious objections to the extension of state intervention: national legislation was likely to be too rigid in its application to local conditions, the country's political institutions were themselves urgently in need of reform to make them more democratically accountable and more responsive to the interests of labour, and the quality of government economic management was seriously open to question on grounds both of efficiency and fairness. Given the persistence of his objections it is not surprising that he became a major target for criticism and abuse from socialist activists at the time, and from socialist historians in due course. What would be surprising would be if it were not now possible, after a generation of practical experience of centralised welfare and nationalised industry, to see that Knight's opposition was based on considerably more than narrow-minded obstruction and old-fashioned prejudice.

V

Robert Knight was probably more thoughtful and more articulate than many of his colleagues, but that does not mean that he was unique in terms either of the influences on his thinking or of the conclusions he drew from them. At the same time, it cannot be claimed that he was an entirely typical trade unionist of his period, for there was still a strong attachment to the Conservative party among the Lancashire textile trades, and a closer affinity with official Liberalism in many of the regional coalfields. In any case the British labour movement has included a number of different political strands in every phase of its development. What can be said is that Knight was an influential spokesman for an important group of radical liberal craft unionists, whose leading figures also included Alexander Wilkie of the shipwrights and W. J. Davis of the brassworkers, and who became increasingly influential within the TUC after the retirement of Broadhurst from the secretaryship, and the Congress rule revisions of 1895 which excluded most of the leading socialist activists.[86]

Pulling together the various strands of Robert Knight's broader outlook demonstrates the importance of three major influences on his thinking: trade unionism, Nonconformity and libertarianism. Even simply listing them like this already suggests a marked continuity with the

---

[86] *Dictionary of Labour Biography*, vol. 3 (London, 1976), pp. 206–8 for Alexander Wilkie, and vol. 6 (London, 1982), pp. 92–8 for W. J. Davis. For the revision of the TUC rules see Roberts, *Trades Union Congress*, pp. 143–52, and Clegg *et al., Trade Unions*, pp. 255–68.

popular radicalism of earlier periods. Moreover, Knight's arguments on industrial issues can be matched point for point, and often phrase for phrase, with the 'moral economy' of early-nineteenth-century artisans; the arguments he used against nationalisation have strong affinities with the Chartist emphasis on the priority of political reform; and even his attacks on drink and gambling, which might be thought to be typical of a new 'respectability' in the second half of the nineteenth century, were in fact just as typical of early-nineteenth-century radicalism.[87] This should not, after all, be surprising. For despite many historians' emphasis on a sharp divide in working-class history in the middle of the nineteenth century, only two generations had passed since the days of Paine and Cobbett, the Boilermakers' Society could trace its own formal organisation back to Manchester two years after the 1832 Reform Act, and Knight himself was already a teenager in 1848.

Perhaps some might argue that, with the rise of socialism, radical liberalism had at last become out of date by the 1890s, in which case it would still be necessary to 'rescue the poor craft union leader from the enormous condescension of posterity'![88] However, such an argument would be based on an exaggeration of the support for socialism among trade unionists in this period for, although both the eight-hours' bill and nationalisation formally remained TUC policy, it was in fact the line of the older generation which won out in practice in the second half of the 1890s. Thus on the eight-hours' question, following Knight's light-hearted intervention in 1891, Hardie had acknowledged the force of his objections and had carried an amendment to his own motion of the previous year, adding the possibility of opting out in industries in which the majority of trade unionists preferred it.[89] Thereafter, the eight-hours' campaign fragmented, with Congress repeatedly reelecting a notorious opponent of statutory regulation as Secretary of the Parliamentary Committee and government intervention being pursued only by those unions with a long-standing commitment to legislative enactment, while the rest quietly acknowledged the dependence of the bulk of their members on large amounts of overtime.[90] Similarly, while there was no complete reverse for nationalisation, it was diluted in 1896 to cover only land, mines and public

---

[87] E. P. Thompson, *The Making of the English Working Class* (London, 1963), pp. 328–31; I. Prothero, *Artisans and Politics in Early Nineteenth Century London. John Gast and his times* (London, 1979), pp. 225–9, 328–40; G. Stedman Jones, 'Rethinking Chartism', in *Languages of Class*, pp. 90–178, especially pp. 100–7, 168–78; Harrison and Hollis, 'Robert Lowery', pp. 519–28.

[88] An adaptation of Thompson's famous manifesto in *English Working Class*, p. 14.

[89] TUC 1891, pp. 53–4.

[90] Clegg *et al., Trade Unions*, pp. 293–4, Roberts, *Trades Union Congress*, pp. 136–9.

utilities, and even this soon became a ritual gesture which was widely supported without the expectation of any practical consequences. The socialist organisations themselves began to decline in strength from the mid-1890s, and the political focus of the TUC shifted once again to the more traditional radical causes of opposition to a Conservative government, renewed vigilance over changes in trade union law and the pursuit of increased labour representation.[91]

This reconsideration of the content and the impact of Robert Knight's political thinking helps to throw new light on the significance of two better known radicals of the period, who expressed their views more extensively in print: Charles Bradlaugh and George Howell. The first thing to note is the striking overlap in life histories: all three men were born in the same year (1833), Bradlaugh and Howell both recalled an early involvement in Chartism,[92] and went on to collaborate on the campaign for the 1867 Reform Act; while Howell and Knight worked together on the campaign for the repeal of the anti-union Criminal Law Amendment Act in 1875. Moreover, given the significant overlap in basic ideas between all three men which has been noted in the course of analysing Knight's public statements, it would seem that the common characterisation of Bradlaugh and Howell as increasingly out of date and out of touch with developments in the late-nineteenth-century labour movement is misleading: they were, on the contrary, closely in tune with one of the more thoughtful figures within the TUC in the 1890s, whose own influence has in turn been considerably underestimated.

It is also interesting to consider the points made by these labour radicals against state socialism alongside Stefan Collini's illuminating account of the forms of argument used by contemporary intellectual opponents of Collectivism, for there are striking respects in which Knight and his colleagues were both more and less traditional than their middle-class counterparts.[93] The most marked contrast is in the different relationship of the two groups to 'political' and 'economic' forms of argument, for in respect of the former, the labour radicals were more traditional in regarding the infringement of popular liberty and democracy as a sufficient ground for the rejection of government initiatives, especially when

---

[91] Clegg *et al.*, *Trade Unions*, pp. 302–4; Roberts, *Trades Union Congress*, pp. 142, 155–8.

[92] C. Bradlaugh, *Will Socialism Benefit the English People?* p. 25; *The Autobiography of C. Bradlaugh* (London, 1891), pp. 6–8, both reprinted in Saville, *Political Pamphlets*; Leventhal, *George Howell*, pp. 6–8, 212–3.

[93] S. Collini, *Liberalism and Sociology. L. T. Hobhouse and Political Argument in England, 1880–1914* (Cambridge, 1979), especially pp. 22–32. It is also interesting to note that 'scientific' (evolutionary) arguments for liberty were completely absent from Knight's statements, and that he seems to have begun the shift from 'self-reliance' to 'self-development' relatively early (in the 1870s).

combined with an equally traditional emphasis on the inefficiency and corruption to be expected of central government activity. Many of them therefore remained sceptical about the proposals for state social reform put forward by middle class New Liberals. On the other hand, in respect of economic issues labour radicals had for a long time been deeply hostile to *laissez-faire*, and were far more willing than their middle-class counterparts to extend collective self-government into forms of market regulation: labelling them as Individualists will therefore be misleading if it diverts attention from their strong and consistent support for trade unionism, co-operation (both in distribution and in production), and the redistribution of income through taxes on wealth. These areas of convergence and divergence between labour radicalism and different strands of middle-class liberalism were, as Duncan Tanner points out in his contribution to this collection (ch. 12), important elements contributing towards the separate identity which labour's parliamentary representatives were to retain within the context of the broad alliance of Edwardian Progressivism.

There can be no disputing the 'reformist' nature of this tradition of labour radicalism, for its proponents were consciously committed to gradual and constitutional change as a matter of principle, in order to avoid provoking political reaction and the suffering involved in revolution and civil war. But in terms of the particular kind of 'reformism' they stood for, the notion of 'labourism' as outlined by John Saville is unhelpful in almost every respect. In the first place, the slogan of 'A Fair Day's Wage for a Fair Day's Work', with its implicit acceptance of the existing organisation of industry, does not adequately sum up the goals of craft unionism. As has been seen, Knight in fact had the more ambitious goal of regulating the market, and when he talked of his desire for the unity of capital and labour he meant it to be on an equal footing, not with labour subordinate to capital's existing forms of management. As far as social attitudes are concerned, the claim that Nonconformity encouraged individualism is not borne out by Knight's public statements. Christianity appears rather as a consistent moral basis for mutuality and equality, not only in the internal affairs of workers' own organisations but also over the broader question of social justice in the distribution of the national wealth. Equally in the political arena Knight may have been in favour of peaceful reforms but, far from being a proponent of naive 'parliamentarianism', he championed the abolition of the House of Lords, improved accountability of the civil service and increased labour representation.

Thus the larger Marxist claims that the outlook of organised labour in the late nineteenth century was 'economistic', limited, dependent, defensive and 'fractured' are not likely to survive careful scrutiny. In fact

Knight's political attitudes were the result of a clear grasp of radical arguments about government and not of narrow-minded trade unionism; he had a very real sense of the power of the national labour movement, especially following a decade of significant growth in union membership from 1889; and he had a long-standing willingness to resort to extra-parliamentary pressure by the TUC which went back as far as the 1870s. Moreover, Knight had a positive vision of an ideal future in which social justice would be achieved through democracy and genuinely equal opportunities for all. In fact trade unionism in industry and radical liberalism in politics seem to fit together rather well, if anything it is the relationship between sectional militancy and state socialism which is a 'fractured' one.[94]

Recasting the politics of an influential section of the late-nineteenth-century labour leadership in terms of the radical tradition also helps to resolve some remaining tensions in Henry Pelling's valuable account of popular political attitudes in the period. For his description of the trade union leadership itself remained rather ambiguous, tending on the one hand to portray them as an un-intellectual and narrow interest group when stressing that the early Labour party was not a socialist organisation, and on the other hand to present them as a literate and socially progressive leadership when stressing that, in so far as there was a 'labour aristocracy' of craft workers, they were generally politically more advanced than the unskilled. There was also a tension between Pelling's picture of an essentially conservative and apolitical Labour party and the strong overtones of a wider popular radicalism to be seen in his accounts of working-class hostility to the law and to state interference, as well as of the massive popularity of Gladstone and his political programme.

All of these pieces fall more neatly into place once a leading group among late-nineteenth-century trade unionists is seen more clearly as belonging to a long-standing tradition of popular radicalism and, like many middle-class intellectuals of the time, adapting its liberal and democratic goals to the conditions of the late nineteenth and early twentieth centuries, and using it as a progressive basis for the repudiation of state socialism. Such an interpretation is in any case strongly implied in Pelling's separate discussions of organised labour's criticism of the Boer War, its opposition to the Conservatives' 1902 Education Act and Tariff

---

[94] Pelling, 'Trade unions, workers and the law', pp. 80–1; H. Pelling, *A History of British Trade Unionism* 4th edn, (London, 1987), pp. 313–5; E. J. Hobsbawm, 'The forward march of labour halted?' in M. Jacques and F. Mulhern (eds.), *The Forward March of Labour Halted?* (London, 1981), pp. 1–19; A. J. Reid, 'Politics and economics in the formation of the British working class: a response to H. F. Moorhouse', *Social History*, 3 (1978), pp. 347–61.

Reform proposals, and its pursuit of such legal reforms as a more democratic system of jury service as well, of course, as a return to pre-Taff Vale labour law.[95] In electoral terms such a radical programme was likely to have considerable appeal in the post-Gladstonian era, though it was also likely to come up against widespread popular cynicism and apathy, as well as substantial pockets of working-class Conservatism rooted in particular regional and occupational circumstances.[96] In this political context it was clearly socialism which would be the loser all round, except among some sections of the progressive middle classes. The more perceptive and realistic among the working-class socialists, led by Keir Hardie and Ramsay MacDonald, had in fact become aware of this predicament remarkably quickly in the 1890s, and as a result had decided by 1900 to throw in their lot with the trade union radicals, with whom they had in any case a great deal in common.[97] The Labour party which resulted, then, should be seen neither as an entirely new departure in working-class politics nor as the demise of socialism in the deadly embrace of 'labourist' Old Unionism, but rather as a dynamic recomposition of popular radicalism in adaptation to a new political environment.

[95] Pelling, *Popular Politics*, pp. 16–7, 64–5, 76–9, 82–7.
[96] Pelling 'The working class and the origins of the welfare state', pp. 1–18.
[97] H. Pelling, *The Origins of the Labour Party 1880–1900* (London, 1954); K. O. Morgan, *Keir Hardie, Radical and Socialist* (London, 1975); D. Marquand, *Ramsay MacDonald* (London, 1977); D. Howell, *British Workers and the Independent Labour Party 1888–1906* (Manchester, 1983).

11 Labour and local politics: radicalism, democracy and social reform, 1880–1914

Pat Thane

I

This chapter seeks to elaborate on the final comment of Alastair Reid's contribution: 'The Labour party ... should be seen neither as an entirely new departure in working-class politics nor as the demise of socialism in the deadly embrace of 'labourist' Old Unionism, but rather as a dynamic recomposition of popular radicalism in adaptation to a new political environment.' It aims to examine this process of 'recomposition' firstly through a survey of aspects of municipal politics between the 1880s and 1914. The proliferating range of local elections – for town councils as more towns acquired incorporation, county councils from 1889, vestries, boards of poor law guardians, school boards (until 1904), parish, urban district and rural district councils from 1894, London boroughs from 1900 – and their frequency, offered opportunities for political parties to build up and to exercise party machinery. Their cheapness also enabled new groups to enter politics. Local government had powers to transform essential features of everyday life – or death – which were increasing from the 1870s (e.g. in the important area of sanitation)[1] and it offered more immediate prospects of democratic control of policy making and administration than did central government. There was every reason for radical critics of late Victorian society to take participation in local government extremely seriously.[2] It was one of the paths whereby social reform became central to the politics of the quarter century before 1914 and brought a qualitative change to it.[3] Independent labour, in various guises, emerged as a political challenge to official Liberalism and popular Conservatism at an earlier date in local than in national politics. At the

---

[1] S. Szreter, 'The importance of sanitary intervention in Britain's mortality decline c. 1850–1914: a re-interpretation of the role of public health', *Social History of Medicine*, 1, 1 (1988), pp. 1–38.

[2] P. Hollis, *Ladies Elect. Women in English Local Government. 1865–1914* (Oxford, 1987).

[3] P. F. Clarke, *Lancashire and the New Liberalism* (Cambridge, 1971); H. V. Emy, *Liberals, Radicals and Social Politics, 1892–1914* (Cambridge, 1973).

local level it offered voters a clear programme of measures designed to bring 'socialism' closer some time before the Independent Labour Party (ILP) developed a national programme[4] and this local experience influenced the thinking of the national leadership. Examining these local activities offers an opportunity to explore the meaning and appeal of that socialism.

Party organisation became more important in local as in national politics in Britain from the 1860s, but local elections varied in the interest which they aroused, were often uncontested and where contests occurred turn outs were often low. From the early 1880s the combination of the entry of independent labour into local elections, the increasing centrality of locally administered social reform to politics and growing debate about the relationship between central and local government in the implementation and financing of reform, stimulated both party and popular interest in local elections. This both led to and was enhanced by the local government reforms of 1894 which reduced the property qualification for members of local authorities and created new lower tier, highly localised parish, urban and rural district councils. The parties fought to win this partially revivified popular electorate (though we should not *exaggerate* levels of enthusiasm for local elections even after 1894). The context, in particular the salience of redistributive social reform, the increased role for government and the changed relationship between state and individual implied by reform demands, offered both a challenge to and an opportunity for political action in the popular radical tradition.

II

Radicals seized the opportunity most dramatically, as John Davis has impressively shown, in London with the formation of the London County Council (LCC) in 1889.[5] Its creation injected party politics into London local government where previously it had been weak. Official Liberalism was particularly feeble. London was, however, notable for its network of radical clubs, direct links with the politics of the earlier nineteenth century. The changed politics of the 1880s gave London radicalism renewed dynamism and spurred Liberals to improve their organisation. This took place under strong radical influence. The Liberals – or

---

[4] J. Keir Hardie and J. Ramsay MacDonald, 'The Independent Labour Party's programme', *The Nineteenth Century* (Jan. 1899), p. 26.
[5] J. Davis, *Reforming London. The London Government Problem, 1855–1900* (Oxford, 1988). J. Davis, 'Radical clubs and London politics, 1870–1900', in D. Feldman and G. Stedman Jones (eds.), *Metropolis. London. Histories and Representations since 1800* (London, 1989).

Progressives as they were known in London – fought the first LCC election on a clearly defined policy of municipal reform.

The progressive reforming character of the early LCC is well known, but historians have had difficulty in assigning it to a clear ideological category. One of John Davis' important contributions is to point out the firmly, classically, but also dynamically radical character of LCC progressivism. He also establishes the degree to which its politics were 'not handed down by salon theorists or intellectual journalists, but pushed up from the constituency parties'.[6] Policy was shaped in the manner most acceptable to the London Liberal activist, with an emphasis upon the radical element in traditional Liberalism. The first London County Council campaign was dominated by social reform issues but equal stress was placed on the assault upon privilege and monopoly, and 'the older values of Nonconformist "puritanism" and temperance were also well entrenched'.[7] The radical Progressives controlled the LCC until the Conservative victory of 1907.

Their 1889 programme grew directly out of the ferment of London social politics in the mid-1880s.[8] This centred upon the issues of housing, sanitation, unemployment, sweated labour and the length of the working day. Fundamental issues of human survival – death and sickness rates, levels of income, the quality of living space – became politicised as never before, and as never before were backed by a real hope and a determination that change was possible, above all through democratic action at the local level. Housebuilding, purified water supplies, work creation, a commitment to insist upon the insertion of a 'fair wages and conditions' clause in all contracts entered into by the new council, employment of labour directly by the council whenever possible, and improved conditions and pay for the growing army of municipal employees were the central components of the programme. The gasworkers' strike of 1889 gave still greater saliency to some of these issues, just as changes in local politics must have contributed to the strength and successes of the strike, a high proportion of gasworkers being municipal employees.

Also important was an assault on vested interests on behalf of the community: on ground landlords, the Corporation of the City of London and the public utility monopolists. For a classic radical such as John Williams Benn 'who stood for equality of opportunity and for the freedom of the individual ... public ownership of public monopolies was an indestructible part of his creed and he held that the major task of the Council was to deliver London from the stranglehold of private corpor-

[6] Davis, *London*, p. 119.
[7] *Ibid.*
[8] G. Stedman Jones, *Outcast London* (Oxford, 1971).

ations upon the public sphere'.[9] For LCC radicals public ownership was preferable to private especially when, indeed on condition that, ownership was to be taken into the hands of a democratically elected body sensitive to the necessity for public accountability. In this as in other respects radicalism went through a process of change from the 1880s. Above all it became more collectivist, developing a new conception of the role of the state in a society in which the potential for effective, socially progressive and non-coercive state action, and for its democratic control, appeared to have grown since the 1840s. To some at least the state was less potentially threatening than it had appeared to critics in previous times. The LCC pressed for control of water and tramways and supported the taxation of land values as a means of extracting from Privilege the means to finance social improvement without recourse to the rates. Such essentials as a pure water supply, it seemed obvious to them, could reliably be supplied only by a publicly accountable authority, in view of the manifest failure of private control; but public control was acceptable always on the condition of adequate democratic safeguards. Local government should be accountable to the electorate, not to an elected oligarchy.

Where possible, in their use of income they sought to be actively redistributive, concentrating expenditure from the London-wide rate and other income upon poorer districts. But they stressed always that such redistribution would benefit the *whole* community in indirect as well as direct ways, rather than benefiting one class at the expense of another. However, their sphere of activity was limited. They were prevented by law from achieving many of their ambitions because a great deal of social responsibility lay with the second tier authorities, which until 1900 in London were the vestries. The LCC Progressives therefore campaigned for democratisation of the lower tier of London government in order to extend the radical programme throughout London. They proposed 'democratic district councils' open to women and working men who would be in close contact with a relatively small community; and democratisation of the finances of lower tier authorities through rating equalisation. A serious problem of local government was the regressive character of local authority finance.[10] Rate equalisation was therefore a major radical demand throughout the period and of London Labour parties after 1918.[11]

It is easier to expound a theory of democratic government than to practise it. It is not clear that LCC radicalism in all respects long survived

[9] Davis, *London*, p. 122.
[10] Davis, *London*, p. 168ff.
[11] See Eugenio Biagini in ch. 7, this collection.

the early years of the council. It was longer lived at the lower tier of London government.

III

This lower tier was indeed reviving even before 1889. The 'economist' radicalism of the shopocracy was replaced by a new generation of social reforming radicals, middle as well as working class. As vestries became more politicised election turn outs and turnover of members increased. The outcome before the abolition of the vestries was impressive. The number of sanitary inspectors increased rapidly. The LCC sanctioned loans totalling £317,000 for the provision of parks and open spaces by the vestries during the 1890s and £1.8 million for paving works. In the ten years following 1886 eighteen baths and washhouses were opened and thirty-five parishes adopted the Public Libraries Act where only two had done so before. St Pancras, Hampstead and a handful of other authorities undertook municipal electric lighting; Camberwell vestry opened a school of art and supported a technical college. Shoreditch opened Municipal Technical Schools, carried through an imaginative housing project and built a library and town hall. In working-class areas vestries pursued active labour policies, especially in the wake of the gas and dock strikes, greatly increasing the use of direct rather than contract labour, providing improved conditions of work and pay for previously sweated sectors of labour. They provided work or relief for the unemployed, often under strong pressure from those who were unemployed, especially in the period of severe unemployment in the mid-1890s.[12] When Moderate (i.e. Conservative) replaced Progressive control of particular vestries they frequently carried on established municipal practices and indeed even initiated reforming policies, which suggests that the popularity of such measures outweighed their expense.[13]

More dynamic vestry action appears to have improved the quality of their appointed officials and also the degree of popular participation in local government. This included an apparently greater willingness of people to complain about bad conditions, when there was some realistic possibility that they might be changed. But such activities were costly and the Moderates increasingly organised around resistance to rising rates.[14]

---

[12] Davis, *London*, p. 162; Szreter, 'Social intervention', pp. 19–32.

[13] Davis, *London*, pp. 159–63.

[14] Davis, *London*, p. 166ff. A. Offer, *Property and Politics 1870–1914* (Cambridge, 1981); K. Young, *Local Politics and the Rise of Party. The London Municipal Society and the Conservative Intervention in Local Elections, 1894–1963* (Leicester, 1975), p. 88ff.

Nor did all vestries take up reform; Bethnal Green, for example, with its stable artisan community, remained a retrenching Liberal shopocracy.[15]

The London Government Act (1899) abolished the vestries and replaced them with 28 larger Borough Councils; 1,362 councillors replaced 4,170 vestrymen. From 1900 Progressivism in London weakened, though not fatally, against a resurgent Conservatism organised mainly around the rates issue. Progressives controlled 10 out of 28 boroughs in 1903, only 2 in 1906, though they remained a powerful minority even where they lost control, and they retained important pockets of strength. In the first postwar elections, in 1919, Labour, generally offering programmes indistinguishable from those of pre-war Progressives, won outright majorities in 13 of the 28 Metropolitan Borough Councils and was the largest party in two others. Despite serious setbacks in 1922 Labour thereafter gradually recovered its sudden postwar strength. It was slower to make significant gains on the LCC.[16]

Notable among the boroughs where strong pre-war Progressivism shaded into postwar Labour strength was Battersea. There was an early radical takeover of Liberalism, in this largely working-class district; Battersea radical Liberals were willing and able to work with local trade unionists and socialists and they gained much from the peculiar dominance of Battersea by the powerful figure of John Burns.[17] This radical success was built upon discontent about bad housing, the sickness and death associated with it, and the heavy unemployment of the mid-1880s, which affected all grades of worker. Battersea Liberalism came to express local support for an independent progressive politics. This propelled more orthodox Liberals out of the party. Burns was elected to the first LCC as a 'social democrat' (he refused to stand as a 'radical' or 'labour' candidate) largely on the strength of his activism on unemployment and other labour issues.

Battersea radical Liberalism attracted small businessmen and intellectuals as well as working people. Through the 1890s and up to 1906 an alliance of Liberals, radicals, independent labour activists and local trades unionists worked together in a Progressive Alliance, co-ordinated through the Battersea Trades and Labour Council, their unity assisted by Burns' drift from the social democracy of the Social Democratic Federation (SDF) to the Liberals, and his hostility to the preference of the ILP for working independently of the Liberals. As he shifted, his policy concerns

---

[15] P. Thompson, *Socialists, Liberals and Labour. The Struggle for London, 1885–1914* (London, 1967), p. 183.

[16] Young, *Local Politics*, pp. 223–5.

[17] K. D. Brown, *John Burns* (London, 1977).

became increasingly centred upon advocacy of municipal socialism, social welfare and localism – local control of local responses to local needs.

The Battersea Trades and Labour Council gave priority to placing their supporters on locally elected bodies, which they did with some success, the Liberal Association providing the election machinery. The outcome was one of the most actively reforming vestries in the country in the mid-1890s. It employed direct labour, on a 48-hour week at trade union rates, provided municipal housing, electric lighting, libraries and baths. The direct labour force built libraries, baths, the public laundry, swimming baths, the sterilised milk depot, the electric light station and, by 1903, four housing estates. Of the latter Burns was proud that they were 'not ... tainted with an off-licence or degraded by a beer-shop'.[18] The vestry was also noted for its advanced treatment of the unemployed, under strong pressure from below.[19] From the early 1890s it had not only established a labour bureau, but the vestry surveyor set aside necessary public works for the winter when the need for employment was greatest. It was the only London vestry to do this, although some Lancashire councils did so. There was good reason for Battersea Progressives to hold popular support. With some vicissitudes they held together until the wartime split in the Liberal party. The Progressives were replaced by a firm Labour party majority after the war which operated in accordance with principles which were a recognisable continuation of the pre-war Progressivist programme.[20]

A similar convergence of radicalism, trade unionism and minority socialism around a radical social reform programme similar to that of the early LCC and Battersea emerged in the outlying boroughs of West Ham and Woolwich. That in both these cases the majority described themselves as 'Labour' can be attributed to the greater prominence of the local trades council and ILP (and in West Ham the SDF) in relation to local Liberalism in the radical alliances which emerged.

In 1898 a cross-class 'Labour' coalition took control of West Ham, the first Labour controlled council in the country, promoting policies similar to those of Battersea; but it kept power for only a year. Labour was poorly organised and a high proportion of working people in the borough were not on the electoral register. However it remained a strong minority group until the war, after which it gained control.[21]

In Woolwich from 1898 the local LRC and Liberal and radical clubs

[18] C. Wrigley, 'Liberals and the desire for working-class representatives in Battersea, 1886–1922', in K. D. Brown (ed.) *Essays in Anti-Labour History* (London, 1974), p. 140.
[19] K. D. Brown, *Labour and Unemployment, 1900–1914* (Newton Abbot, 1971).
[20] Wrigley, 'Battersea', p. 151.
[21] Thompson, *Struggle for London*, p. 133.

joined an alliance in which the trades council and the Royal Arsenal Co-operative were prominent. It took control from 1903 to 1906, remained a strong opposition until the war and regained control in 1919. As in Woolwich official Liberalism was weakly organised; also Nonconformity and cross-class Conservatism were strong. The Labour council followed the type of programme broadly supported by 'advanced' reformers, whether they called themselves Liberal, Labour, radical or Progressive; all of these terms had a flexible and, though not infinitely, variable range of meanings at this time. Such programmes included: a direct labour force, trade union rates of pay and conditions, improved sanitary administration, house-building etc. They also developed an elaborate means of ensuring the accountability of councillors to the party and a model party organisation. They introduced evening council meetings to encourage working people to stand as councillors,

tightened up the labour clauses in contracts, negotiated tramway extensions with the LCC, eliminated the contractors in dust collection, introduced a 30s minimum wage for council employees, engaged more sanitary inspectors, set up a works department, built the Plumstead Baths and Library, started a brickmaking plant and an electricity scheme and provided a large amount of winter work for the unemployed . . . the house scheme begun under the previous council was continued and work was begun on a library and baths in Eltham.[22]

A similar pattern emerged closer to central London, in Bow and Bromley, especially in the Poor Law politics of Poplar. In the 1890s the ILP, SDF and progressive Liberals, organised around the trades council, agreed on a broad approach to the urgent problems of poverty and unemployment: demands for equalisation of the rate burden between rich and poor boroughs, direct employment of labour at fair wages by the local authority, provision of temporarily useful work for the unemployed and humane treatment of such deserving pauper groups as old people, widows, children and the infirm.

An important underlying principle on which they were also agreed was that local authorities, including boards of guardians, were potential instruments of democratic control of policy making and administration which it was important to preserve or extend. When Harry Quelch of the SDF in 1910 opposed the proposals of the minority report of the Royal Commission on the Poor Laws for the abolition of boards of guardians on the grounds that this would be anti-democratic, he voiced sentiments widely held across the radical-socialist spectrum. He argued 'The Guardians were the most democratically elected body in the kingdom, and if they had not been so good as they should have been, it was the fault of the

22 Thompson, *Struggle for London*, pp. 253–64.

people, and their business was to elect proper Guardians.'[23] He also argued that the sub-committees of county councils which were proposed to replace them would be more remote and less directly accountable. On similar principles radical and labour organisations everywhere opposed the abolition of separately elected school boards in 1902 and the transfer of their powers to sub-committees of municipal and county councils, which were much larger administrative units and also (until the women protested vigorously) excluded women, as the school boards did not.[24] The belief in democratic accountability combined with popular participation had an important place in Labour and radical politics in the 1890s and 1900s.

The progressive alliance remained intact and in control of the Poplar Guardians until 1903. Bow and Bromley also had a 'very advanced radical', a member of the Rainbow Circle, J. A. Murray Macdonald, as Liberal MP from 1892 to 1895. He was especially active in parliament on issues concerning unemployment, and was a member of the London School Board, 1897–1902.[25] Sharply rising unemployment and pressure from the unemployed then led the independent labour members of the Board in alliance with the radical Liberals to advocate, and, so far as they were able, to implement, the principles of the labour movement's national commitment to the 'right to work or full maintenance'. This meant in practice: fair pay rather than poor law rates for the undeservedly unemployed, who were when possible put to work in the labour colony or the workhouse; and rates of relief adequate for respectable survival for those who could not be provided with work. All such relief was to be conditional upon strict controls against malingering. Lengthy dependence upon conditional welfare was, as George Lansbury, leader of the Labour group on Poplar Guardians put it, 'demoralising', leaving its victims unable either to help themselves or to support mutual aid organisations such as those of the labour movement.[26] The right to relief must be reciprocated by acknowledging the obligation to the community to take work when it was available. In its turn the community should be obliged to ensure that suitable work or training was indeed available. It had the right to punish those who refused such work though it was assumed that malingerers would be few. This framework of rights and obligations,

[23] J. A. Gillespie, 'Economic and political change in the East End of London during the 1920s' (University of Cambridge Ph.D. 1984), p. 372.
[24] Hollis, *Ladies Elect* pp. 128–9.
[25] Emy, *Social Politics*, p. 49; M. Freeden (ed.), *Minutes of the Rainbow Circle, 1894–1924* (London, 1989), p. 363 and *passim*.
[26] P. Ryan, 'Poplarism, 1894–1930', in P. Thane (ed.), *Origins of British Social Policy* (London, 1978), pp. 59–66.

humanely applied, was assumed to be capable of guaranteeing in difficult economic circumstances the dignity of labour and the sense of independence which flowed from it. Establishing human equality in this sense lay at the heart of the value system which bound together the progressive alliances which were so widely emerging out of the range of liberal, labour and socialist politics.

Poplar's approach to the treatment of the unemployed, however, alienated orthodox Liberals who objected to the concept of the 'right' to work on grounds both of principle and of cost. From 1903 they allied with Conservatives and kept the progressives out of power until after the war. Labour was then elected with almost identical policies to those of the pre-war progressives. Even before 1914, these policies in all their aspects appeared popular with poorer voters. Even critics of the progressives acknowledged that their success owed much to the fact that the guardians lived among the unemployed, understood the needs and problems of the heterogeneous poor neighbourhood and sought to devise policies acceptable to and suited to its inhabitants.[27]

This survey of the strength of radical democratic reforming politics in London between the 1880s and 1914 sheds light on the apparent weakness of Labour in London before 1914. Far from being a product or a symptom of an apolitical, inward looking defensiveness on the part of London workers[28] it was rather that they had other places to look than independent socialist groups for a genuinely progressive, dynamic, reforming democratic politics. This was more radical than socialist in its inspiration and had social reform as much as employment issues at its core; the two were indeed complementary. As Davis has put it, 'the transition from a work-centred form of politics' of the type of the older artisan radicalism 'to one based on neighbourhood and community was part of the evolution of London labour politics'.[29] Where it was active, whether under a 'Labour' or 'Progressive' banner local politics regained their vitality. Support for this progressive politics, given the composition of the registered electorate, cannot have been exclusively working-class, but rather included substantial middle-class, and increasingly female, support.

This strength of pre-war radicalism makes less mysterious the Labour party's postwar strength in London politics. It should also be noted that in parliamentary elections Liberals, mainly radicals, made substantial gains

[27] Ryan, 'Poplarism', pp. 68–9.
[28] G. Stedman Jones, 'Working-class culture and working-class politics in London, 1870–1900: notes on the remaking of a working class', in *Languages of Class* (Cambridge, 1983), pp. 236–8. See also Thompson, *Struggle for London, passim.*
[29] Davis, 'Radical clubs', p. 114.

in working-class districts of London in 1892, which they held on to. Even in 1910 the Conservative resurgence was least in London and in Lancashire.[30] This suggests that Labour's postwar success cannot be explained purely in terms of the growth of the working-class franchise, important though this was after 1918 (though it was more limited at local than at parliamentary level), of improved Labour organisation, or of political responses to changes in the London economy. Rather, following the split in the Liberal party, Labour took over leadership of the radical alliance for which before the war it had competed with the Liberals; and it fought and won on policies little different from those of the alliance before the war.[31] These policies stressed social and economic reform and, above all, democratic accountability. The attraction to voters lay in what the progressive groupings, whatever their labels, stood for and did.

IV

The story elsewhere in English local government where information is available, was similar: Liberals, Labour and on occasion Conservatives competed for a popular vote attracted by radical democratic collectivism. In the West Riding of Yorkshire, in contrast to London, official Liberalism was strong and secure and saw no need in the 1890s, and in some parts of the region for much longer, to abandon retrenchment for social reform, or to make gestures to labour or radical sentiment. Its leaders opposed the eight-hour day, old age pensions, free or subsidised school meals, indeed almost all of the standard progressive reform proposals of the quarter century preceding 1914. Where it was necessary and possible they preferred to encourage voluntary effort.

There had long been tension between radical and moderate Liberalism in the West Riding. This finally ruptured in the mid-1890s as radical Liberals allied with independent labour, alienated by official Liberalism's refusal of compromise, even to the extent of adopting working-class candidates.[32] Here also, campaigning for local government elections played a large part in ILP strategy. The first ILP councillor was elected in Bradford in 1891, by 1900 there were 19 ILP councillors in the West Riding. The total number of Labour representatives on West Riding local authorities rose from 53 in 1900, to 89 in 1906 and 202 in 1914 despite the abolition of school boards in 1904.[33]

[30] Emy, *Social Politics*, pp. 50, 236.
[31] Gillespie, 'East End', pp. 364–70.
[32] K. Laybourn and J. Reynolds, *Liberalism and the Rise of Labour, 1890–1918* (London, 1984), p. 30.
[33] *Ibid.*, pp. 65, 109, 149.

Again, trades councils were at the centre of independent labour organisation. First the strike wave of 1889–90, then the unemployment of the mid-1890s made the trades councils politically more pugnacious. Their consequent development of social reform and municipalisation programmes as means of creating work, improving work conditions and of alleviating hardship due to unemployment and under-employment and low pay, widened the appeal of the political alliances of which they formed the core. They made limited gains from the mid-1890s, more permanent ones from 1903, when the return of high unemployment as elsewhere provided an opportunity for their permanent substantial presence in local government. In consequence Leeds, for example, in 1903 had 1 Labour city councillor, 18 Conservatives and 29 Liberals, in 1913 14 Labour, 25 Conservatives and 12 Liberals (these numbers exclude aldermen).[34] In 1910 the Liberal programme still advocated retrenchment, whilst that of Labour advocated municipal provision of coal and milk, a 48-hour week for municipal employees and 1/2d tram fares. Municipalisation was another issue which divided radical from orthodox Liberals. Labour's municipal success in Leeds was based upon an advanced programme of social reform to which democratic principles were central.[35]

Similar patterns can be seen in Bradford and elsewhere in Yorkshire, with unemployment again proving the issue which exposed the limits of the reforming instincts of orthodox Liberalism and the source of independent Labour success.[36] Liberal intransigence enabled Labour to take over West Riding progressivism. Radicals saw little to gain from remaining within Liberalism. In the 1906 general election Jowett, with an impressive reputation in Bradford local government behind him, was the only Labour candidate in the country to win, in Bradford West, against Liberal opposition.[37] His programme emphasised school feeding and other measures to combat poverty and unemployment. His Liberal opponent had more in common with the Conservative candidate in advocating free trade, Home Rule, religious teaching in schools, licensing reform and Chinese labour.[38] He came bottom of the poll. Following this shock Bradford Liberalism showed signs of movement towards progressive

[34] G. L. Bernstein, 'Liberalism and the Progressive Alliance in the constituencies, 1900–1914: three case studies', *Historical Journal*, 26, 3 (1983), pp. 617–40; E. P. Hennock, *Fit and Proper Persons: Ideal and Reality in Nineteenth Century Urban Government* (London, 1973), p. 359.

[35] Bernstein, 'Three case studies', pp. 625–9.

[36] Laybourne and Reynolds, *Rise of Labour, passim*. D. Clark, *Colne Valley: Radicalism to Socialism* (London, 1981).

[37] F. Brockway, *Socialism Over Sixty Years: The Life of Jowett of Bradford* (London, 1946).

[38] *Ibid.*, p. 132.

reforms in particular in respect of the provision of school meals and municipal housing.

But such signs were slight by 1914, as elsewhere in West Yorkshire. In contrast, the indications of growing, if hardly yet overwhelming, popular support for advanced democratic reforming politics with a discernible debt to radicalism were strong. In West Yorkshire the intransigence of orthodox Liberalism handed the benefit to independent Labour.

V

Leicester experienced a third blend of the complex relationships linking radicalism, Liberalism and independent Labour. It was a Liberal dominated town where the tensions between official and radical Liberalism had long been evident and both were influential. 'During the 1860s and 70s Leicester politics had generally returned to the old opposition of People and Privilege.'[39] The campaign against vaccination, which was at its most active in Leicester in the 1870s and 1880s, was the issue on which this polarity was most starkly revealed.[40]

The Liberal leadership in the town kept its distance from the trade unions. From the early 1890s a political labour movement began to gather around the trades council. The ILP branch developed a progressive municipal programme but won little support before 1895, even on the unemployment issue. In part this was because radical Liberals remained in the Liberal party and worked hard to keep working people within the Liberal fold, emphasising the traditional alliance between Liberalism and radical and working-class movements. When, in 1893, they established a fund to provide a memorial to Thomas Cooper the Chartist, the Liberal candidate told a crowded meeting that he 'expected the ILPers back in the fold just like the Chartists'.[41] Meanwhile the Leicester ILP claimed legitimate descent from such 'radical icons' as Cooper and Peter Alfred Taylor, one of the Town's previous Radical MPs, a supporter of John Stuart Mill and Mazzini.[42] When James Ramsey MacDonald became candidate for one of Leicester's two parliamentary seats in 1900, he set about attempting to woo the radical vote without alienating official Liberalism; carefully creating the idea of a party which was independent, but not cut off from or antagonistic to Liberalism.

[39] B. Lancaster, *Radicalism, Cooperation and Socialism. Leicester Working Class Politics, 1860–1906* (Leicester, 1987), p. 80.
[40] *Ibid.*, p. 82.
[41] *Ibid.*, p. 131.
[42] D. Howell, *British Workers and the Independent Labour Party 1888–1906* (Manchester, 1983).

Unemployment, however, eventually played the largest role in causing voters to shift their allegiance to Labour. Between 1902 and 1904 it was at especially high levels in the dominant Leicester boot and shoe-making industry due largely to technological change. Organisation of the unemployed, culminating in a march to London in 1905, appears to have been the main agency transforming Labour's position. By 1906 the local Liberal organisation was seriously weakened as its radical wing slipped away. A new generation of Labour activists emerged out of the unemployment agitation and the ward parties rather than from the trades council,[43] often lacking the Liberal loyalties of the older generation.

Labour and Liberal now became more clearly differentiated. In the more equal battle which followed, both Labour and the Liberals refined their language and programmes in response to one another and to their sense of the wishes of the electorate for which they competed. As Labour became an unmistakable local force, orthodox Liberals began to define Liberalism as a positive moderate alternative to socialism – which they described as a danger which would 'deprive the individual of the power of initiative and destroy his right to develop as he thinks best the talents and powers with which he has been endowed'.[44] Labour, meanwhile, increasingly abandoned the language of class for that of community and gave less prominence to their commitment of the 1890s to 'the nationalisation of the whole of the means of production, distribution and exchange'; they sought to outbid the electoral programmes of the Liberals but never by very much, asserting Labour's independence, but in such a way as to avoid alienating Liberal radicals.[45]

Again, the 'right to work or full maintenance' was the crucial test of the party divide, as it was also in the House of Commons (along with the 'fair wage clause' issue).[46] Both favoured labour colonies – MacDonald of two sorts 'one penal for rogues and vagabonds and one educational for honest men'[47] – but Labour supported fair rates of pay; as elsewhere Labour insisted upon 'relief without pauperisation', to maintain the human dignity of those whose poverty was not their own fault.

In 1906 Labour had 10 members on the city council; in 1913–14, Liberals 18, Conservatives 16.[48] Labour's success continued despite the decline   of serious unemployment as a local problem after 1906. Labour candidates

[43] Lancaster, *Leicester*, p. 175.
[44] *Ibid.*, p. 636.
[45] Howell, *Independent Labour Party*, pp. 240–1.
[46] Emy, *Social Politics*, pp. 54, 59, 156–7.
[47] Lancaster, *Leicester*, p. 166.
[48] Bernstein, 'Three case studies', p. 636.

now gave prominence to such issues as housing and school meals, indeed to a progressive reform package. Though the Liberals opposed Labour and lost ground to them, they did not shift into alliance with the Conservatives, despite Conservative attempts to seduce them. By 1914 they accepted a viable three party system, radical Liberal support having largely shifted to Labour.

VI

Other local evidence supports this picture of growing popular support for a radical reforming local government programme.[49] Before 1914 local circumstances dictated whether Liberals, or in some places Conservatives, gained from this growth or whether it fuelled the rise of independent Labour. Such a rise was clear from local election results. Labour had increased success in local elections in the years leading up to 1914, at the expense of both Liberals and Conservatives, e.g. estimates indicate that in 1906, 91 candidates were successful in municipal elections in provincial England and Wales, in 1912, 101, in 1913, 171.[50] It remained of course by far the weakest of the three parties.

The variety of relationships between Liberals and Labour was considerable: from the antagonism of Bradford, to the more tolerant rivalry of Leicester, to the dominance of different varieties of Liberalism in Battersea and Birmingham, and of Labour in Woolwich, Manchester and Salford. In Preston, Liberals in the 1890s, desperate to break local Conservative control, formed a Progressive party which advocated advanced reform. But its appeal and effectiveness were limited by its fears of alienating ratepayers and, partly for this reason, it failed to win trade union support. Its chief effect was to undermine support for Conservatism by stressing the need for such reforms as public washhouses and council house building, which paved the way for Labour to become the dominant force in Preston politics by 1929.[51]

---

[49] J. Lawrence, 'Party politics and the people: continuity and change in the political history of Wolverhampton, 1815–1914' (University of Cambridge Ph.D. thesis, 1989); Hennock, *Fit and Proper*; A. Briggs, *A History of Birmingham*, vol. 2, *1865–1938* (Oxford, 1952), p. 172; J. Hill 'Manchester and Salford politics and the early development of the ILP', *International Review of Social History*, 36 (1981); Bernstein, 'Three case studies'; J. Melling, *Rent Strikes. Peoples' Struggle for Housing in West Scotland, 1890–1916* (Edinburgh, 1983).

[50] M. G. Sheppard and J. L. Halstead, 'Labour's municipal election performance in provincial England and Wales, 1901–13', *Bulletin of the Society for the Study of Labour History*, 39 (Autumn 1979), pp. 39–62.

[51] M. Savage, *The Dynamics of Working-Class Politics. The Labour Movement in Preston 1880–1940* (Cambridge, 1987), pp. 149ff.

Very many voters must have remained open-minded about the choice of Liberal or Labour or simply uncertain as to the difference. What made an individual a radical Liberal, a 'Lib.–Lab.' within the Liberal party or independent Labour remains elusive but it appears often to have been as contingent upon local political alignments, or alignments on specific political issues, notably unemployment, as upon serious ideological differences.[52] The appeal of radical Liberalism was summed up by a leading Norwich socialist and ex-LCC councillor Fred Henderson in 1903:

The simple fact was that Liberalism in England today stood for collectivism to an extent that even its own leaders had not yet realized. And it was reasonable and natural that it should be so; *for the fundamental principle of Liberalism was the right of the people to manage their own affairs, instead of having them managed for them by a privileged class, and socialism was only the application of that principle to industry as well as to the political organization of the country.*[53] (my emphasis)

By 1906, after longer experience of inflexible Norwich Liberalism, he was less convinced that Liberalism rather than Labour was the vehicle to carry forward these principles.

There was one other important feature of the democratic politics of the period: women became more actively involved in Liberal, radical and increasingly, Labour politics. The Women's Liberal Federation grew rapidly from the mid-1880s, initially attracting women across classes. It was strongly independent within the party, increasingly suffragist, and encouraged women to be active especially on social issues, and to stand as local government candidates.[54] The large Women's Co-operative Guild and the Women's Labour League from its foundation in 1906 played a similar role for largely working-class memberships. As the suffrage movement intensified active members of the Women's Liberal Federation were alienated from Liberalism by the leadership's opposition to the suffrage. Some transferred and worked to build the Labour party, whose democratic record was somewhat better. Women were also drawn into Labour politics through campaigns on social issues, notably housing.[55] Women played a significant part in building and sustaining local Labour parties. An important change in the radicalism on the period was that women's suffrage and more generally women's rights became firmly

[52] Emy, *Social Politics*, pp. xi–xii, 136ff, 184ff, 238ff.
[53] Bernstein, 'Three case studies', p. 622.
[54] L. Walker, 'Party political women: a comparative study of Liberal women and the Primrose League, 1890–1914', in J. Rendall (ed.), *Equal or Different. Women's Politics, 1800–1914.* (Oxford, 1987).
[55] Melling, *Rent Strikes, passim.*

established on the radical agenda.[56] By 1914 'democracy' could no longer be discussed in isolation from the question of women's suffrage, and democracy was central to progressive politics.

Successful radical reform programmes had in common not only specific practical reforms but important ideals and principles, though of course proponents differed about details and emphases. The common core focused on acceptance of the need for publicly funded and directed action to bring about a society in which the worst social evils were eliminated, and in which rewards and opportunities were fairly distributed; this might include where necessary public ownership of property and certainly an assault upon privilege and monopoly. Such action, though sanctioned and given a legal framework and direction by the central state, should be so far as possible decentralised in its administration and control, responsive to local need and democratically accountable, incorporating mechanisms for active popular participation in policy making and administration. Robert Knight's objection to increasing the power of the profoundly undemocratic nineteenth-century state over the economy or anything else was widely shared, as Reid describes;[57] democratisation and decentralisation had first place in the progressive politics of the late nineteenth century, as it had in Chartism, as a necessary first step to economic and social change.

It was a politics of a community of active participating citizens whose objective was to secure independence and a civilised life for all, in part by providing work for all. The community involved was generally wider than the working class, though Labour and radicals varied in the extent to which they saw themselves as class spokesmen. Differences of emphasis on this point merit further investigation. Increasingly women were seen explicitly as part of that community. But for most the aim was a society which benefited all classes and both sexes, though in differing ways and to differing degrees. Few denied that working people should gain most in power and in material terms because they currently lacked most; but the better off would also gain from enhanced stability and national prosperity provided that they made a positive contribution to society. 'Parasites', whether idle *rentiers* or malingering workers deserved to lose. In this sense

[56] S. Holton, *Feminism and Democracy. Women's Suffrage and Reform Politics in Britain, 1900–1918* (Cambridge, 1986); J. Liddington, *The Life and Times of a Respectable Rebel. Selina Cooper, 1864–1946* (London, 1984). Walker 'Party political women'; J. Hannam 'In the comradeship of the sexes lies the hope of progress and social regeneration: women in the West Riding ILP c.1890–1914', in Rendell, *Equal or Different*; P. Thane 'The British Labour party and feminism, 1906–1945', in H. L. Smith (ed.), *British Feminism in the Twentieth Century* (London, 1990); C. Collette, *For Labour and for Women. The Women's Labour League, 1906–1918* (Manchester. 1989); J. Gaffin and D. Thoms, *Caring and Sharing. The Centenary History of the Co-operative Women's Guild* (Manchester, 1983), pp. 43–6; F. Leventhal, *Arthur Henderson* (Manchester, 1989), pp. 43–6; J. Liddington and J. Norris, *One Hand Tied Behind Us* (London, 1978), pp. 231–51; B. Harrison, 'Class and gender in modern British labour history', *Past and Present*, 124, (1989), pp. 153–8.
[57] See Alastair Reid, ch. 10, this collection.

it remained essentially a 'popular' politics. An intrusive, 'bureaucratic' central state was as bitterly opposed as by the early radicals, but post-1880s radicals were optimistic that the scope of state action could simultaneously be extended and controlled by democratic institutions.

These principles were essential constituents of an ideology best, if inelegantly, characterised as a dynamic collectivistic democratic radicalism. As always in politics there were gaps separating ideal, practicability and practice, but the support it obtained derived from its increasingly successful application to the most severe social and industrial problems of late Victorian and Edwardian society. To an important degree Labour built its early strength upon practical everyday engagement with mundane but, literally, vital issues of sanitation and water supplies, seeking to improve health and survival chances, housing, education and poor relief as well as employment questions. But before 1914 it was still not clear whether Labour or the Liberals or some realignment of the two would be the long-term beneficiaries of the appeal of reforming politics.

It was the events of the war which brought both Arthur Henderson and Ramsay MacDonald among Labour party leaders to conclude that Labour rather than Liberalism must take the lead in carrying on the radical democratic tradition and redefining it to meet changed needs.[58] MacDonald as the one political leader who risked his career to uphold the radical anti-war tradition could make the claim with particular conviction. They saw the post-1917 Labour party as a radical democratic reforming alliance cutting across class and gender.[59] Labour's success in winning postwar local elections on programmes substantially similar to those of the pre-war progressive alliances confirmed these beliefs.

If Henderson, with such allies as Herbert Morrison, put the 'dynamic recomposition of popular radicalism' consciously into practical effect in building the postwar Labour party, it was MacDonald who developed it both as a theory and as a programme. The congruence of his ideas and proposals, as expressed in his writing from the 1890s to 1914 with those expressed in local Labour and progressive politics is striking, and his ideas were clearly influenced by what he saw as 'the most fruitful period ... in local government ... we have ever experienced'.[60]

VII

The care, depth and self-awareness with which MacDonald conducted this 'recomposition', on both theoretical and programmatic levels have been

[58] Leventhal, *Arthur Henderson*, pp. 72–3.
[59] *Ibid.*, pp. 73.
[60] J. R. MacDonald, *Socialism and Society* (London, 1907), p. 161.

underestimated.[61] An early statement was *The New Charter: a programme of working class politics*, whose title, no doubt consciously, signalled the connection to the past. This originated in his programme as parliamentary candidate in Dover in 1892 and was published as a series of articles in the *Daily Express*. MacDonald, the journalist, was the principle presenter to non-believers, in books, pamphlets and journalism, of what the Labour party stood for between the 1890s and 1914. The pamphlet summed up MacDonald's politics as they were throughout that time. 'The Labour party is no class champion. In politics it is frankly democratic, in economics it is co-operative . . . It was not brought into being to revenge the wage-earner and mercilessly smash the capitalist . . . Capitalist and labourer alike feel that some new order must evolve if England is to exist.' First in his programme was 'Political reform': adult suffrage, payment of MPs, shorter parliaments, abolition of the House of Lords and decentralisation. 'There is too much expected of parliament. Localities should manage their own affairs and unions of localities should be formed when necessary to look after common interests. Our county councils are excellent beginnings in this direction.' Next in importance was 'The question of the Land Monopoly . . . the root of our social difficulties', to be solved by taxation of rents and ground values, the proceeds to go to county and town councils who should also own land where possible. There followed poor law reform: popular participation in administration should be increased by removing the property qualification for membership of boards of guardians, and relief should be paid, where possible in return only for useful and adequately remunerated work. He anticipated that this would encourage and maintain, in both claimants and ratepayers, a sense of citizenship which he believed that the present system served only to incapacitate. He also advocated old age pensions, a state court of arbitration, greater legal powers for municipalities, in particular to employ labour directly, and statutory enactment of the eight-hour day, though 'operating only as the various trades resolve to take advantage of it'.[62]

---

[61] R. Barker, 'Socialism and progressivism in the political thought of Ramsay MacDonald', in A. J. A. Morris (ed.), *Edwardian Radicalism 1900–1914* (London, 1974), pp. 114–30 is a perceptive essay which notes but underestimates the radical influence on MacDonald's thinking and quite wrongly asserts that he made no concrete reform proposals (p. 127). D. Marquand, *Ramsay MacDonald* (London, 1977) recognises MacDonald's seriousness as a political thinker but underestimates the centrality of his commitment to democratic political reform whilst mistakenly criticising him for failing to propose mechanisms for socialisation of the economy, p. 92. S. Macintyre, *A Proletarian Science. Marxism in Britain 1917–1933* (Cambridge, 1980), more sweepingly and wrongly describes as characteristic of all 'Labour socialism' a lack of concern with the practical mechanics of achieving socialism, pp. 47–65.

[62] J. R. MacDonald, *The New Charter: A Programme of Working Class Politics* (Dover Labour Electoral Association, 1892).

The debt to radicalism in the formation of a distinctively 'British socialism' was made quite explicit in the article published under the joint names of MacDonald and Hardie in 1899 (though probably written by MacDonald)[63] 'The Independent Labour Party's Programme'. They argued that political reform, with the purpose of extending democratic participation, must take priority, not just as an end in itself, but as the necessary precondition for social and economic change. An Independent Labour Party was the best vehicle for such change, for:

The mass of the Liberal Party will no doubt continue progressive, but their organisation is not now the sole custodian of the progressive cause ... The Independent Labour Party is in the true line of the progressive apostolic succession. It alone is able to interpret the spirit of the time ...
... the task of the practical democratic reformer is now to show how the work of democratic liberty begun so well by the early Radicals but dropped by their modern representatives is to be completed: how the golden bridge of palliatives between political and social democracy is to be built: and how the foundations of social democracy are to be laid.

Though it is reasonable to assume that MacDonald had tactical reasons for stressing the ILP's debt to a political tradition with a strong appeal to working-class voters, consciousness of it so suffuses his writing that there is good reason to believe that the debt was real. The first step in the socialist programme was to be 'The perfecting of the means of expressing the popular will and of making that will supreme in the nation ... The Independent Labour Party declares for democracy in the political and socialism in the industrial world.'

MacDonald's conception of the relationship between state and society and of the nature of the socialist state was most fully developed in his complementary *Socialism and Society* (1907) and *Socialism and Government* (1909). The first set out MacDonald's holistic, organic conception of modern society. This he described, as throughout his writing of this period, as undergoing an organic evolution from liberalism to socialism as the framework best suited to the simultaneous increase in the complexity and scale, and the increasing interdependence of individuals and of economic units, in the modern world. Such change necessitated greater public ownership and central direction in order to maximise both the individual and the collective good, but on democratic, participatory lines, retaining important roles for private property and initiative, for religion, the family and voluntary organisation; the latter being responses to the most frequent contemporary criticisms of socialism.[64]

---

[63] Marquand, *MacDonald*, p. 62.
[64] S. Collini, *Liberalism and Sociology* (Cambridge, 1979), p. 35.

He insisted that society did not change by means of sharp discontinuities and conflict, rather the new grew out of the old. Marx and Engels had misread recent British history:

The England of 1844 did not break out into revolt; Chartism did not develop into socialism ... The class war created trade unionism; the working classes became citizens; law, morality, the force of combination, lifted to some extent the pall of darkness which hung over the land. The Marxian today still wonders why England fell from grace. Neither Marx nor Engels saw deep enough to discover the possibilities of peaceful advance which lay hidden beneath the surface ...[65]

MacDonald believed that social division and indeed conflict existed but in more complex ways than in Marxian analysis. There were not just two 'great economic classes'. Marx had failed to recognise 'the conflicting interests of the receivers of rent and of profits', and between producers and consumers. He had overlooked among the proletariat 'many differences and oppositions which have been growing for some time rather than diminishing'. The growth of Co-operatives and Building Societies were making workers into employers and owners, 'the psychological basis of class is being undermined'. He added:

Of course (it could be said that) they are making a mistake from the point of view of their own interests and that if they were properly enlightened they would see that they belong to an exploited class, one and indivisible. That may be true, but a mode of action which is ineffective until men are 'fully enlightened' is a chimera.[66]

Moreover MacDonald saw no inevitability in the political responses to social and economic conditions. Deprivation, he believed, might as readily make people greedy and sycophantic as conscious of collective interests or revolutionary.

On the basis of this analysis of society, he concluded that:

The voting strength of this movement will come from the ranks of labour – the organised intelligent workers – the men who have had municipal and trade union experience –the men of self-respect who know the capacity of the people ... they are to be the constructive agents of the next stage in our industrial evolution. But they are not to stand alone. Socialism is no class movement. Socialism is a movement of opinion, not an organisation of status. It is not the rule of the working class; it is the organisation of the community. Therefore to my mind, one of the most significant facts of the times is the conversion of the intellectual middle class to socialism.[67]

[65] *Ibid.*, pp. 107–8.
[66] *Ibid.*, p. 112.
[67] J. R. MacDonald, *Socialism* (London, 1907), pp. 122–23.

How the socialist state was to be achieved and what its character was to be were more fully discussed in *Socialism and Government*. Attacking those socialists, anarchists and syndicalists who rejected political reform as a 'red herring' MacDonald asserted: 'The economic truths of socialism ... must remain the vainest of vain dreamings unless we preserve among the people the political frame of mind which can appreciate democratic liberty and worth. When "A man's a man for a' that" is recited without making the blood tingle, the *man* has ceased to be.' Robert Burns' poem was a classic statement of the essential dignity, equality and independence of all men, and for MacDonald 'a people who greet the praises of political freedom with a yawn are already offering their wrists for the shackles of servitude'.[68]

Contrary to assertions that 'Late Victorian labour leaders had no concrete conception of politics or the state'[69] MacDonald insisted that 'Socialism must have a conception of a governmental machine otherwise it will be misled by superficial appearances.'[70] He certainly explicitly rejected the Marxist conception of the state as an irredeemable expression of class control, as well as the notion that any complex society could function without a state apparatus. Rather he argued that existing state institutions should and could be radically democratised. He offered a fully worked out theory of the relationship between state and community and a blueprint for the democratic reform of the existing state.

The first step to democratisation was adult suffrage. He defended women's suffrage at length ('the socialist state cannot be masculine'), proposed abolition of the House of Lords and the replacement of what he regarded as its only vital function by a small revising chamber of law lords. He thought republicanism a 'more defensible system of government' than monarchy.[71] The central problems were the relationship between MPs and voters and ensuring that a representative assembly was kept in touch with and accountable to public opinion. He insisted that democracy meant much more than the act of voting. A democratic state was one 'where the democracy does the thinking as well as the electing',[72] in which there was maximum popular interest in politics and criticism of its outcomes. He discussed at length and rejected the various forms of proportional representation as unsuited to effective democracy, above all because they broke the possibility of the direct link between MP and constituency which he thought essential to an effective system of

[68] J. R. MacDonald, *Socialism and Government* (London, 1909), pp. xxiv–xxvi.
[69] Stedman Jones, 'Working-class culture', p. 238.
[70] MacDonald, *Socialism and Government*, p. vii.
[71] J. R. MacDonald, *The Socialist Movement* (London, 1911), p. 150.
[72] MacDonald, *Socialism and Government*, vol. 2, pp. 131–2.

democratic accountability. He believed that proportional representation reduced rather than increased the influence of the voter upon the most important choice of all – the choice of government, which could emerge as a compromise which no one had chosen. It should be said that on this as on other detailed proposals for the democratisation of the state there were strong disagreements within the Labour party to which MacDonald was consciously making a polemical contribution.[73]

His solution to the undoubted shortcomings of the existing system also included frequent adjustment of constituency boundaries to ensure that the House of Commons indeed represented the nation; and shorter (three to four year) parliaments. Like the radicals of an earlier period discussed by Miles Taylor (ch. 2) and Jon Lawrence (ch. 4) in this collection,[74] MacDonald wanted a lively party system which sought genuinely to express popular feeling, as distinct from the 'partisanship' which he disliked in the existing system. Similarly he was keen to introduce the maximum decentralisation of policy making and administration, to avoid the dangers of excessive centralisation, bureaucratic distance from popular accountability and the overloading of parliament with business. This would include 'Home Rule all Round', for Ireland, Scotland and Wales. This had been a radical Liberal demand in 1896.[75]

Equally important was strong local government. This was to be the starting point of the socialist programme and indeed MacDonald thought that the first steps had already been taken, and that socialism was already evolving, proceeding from the municipalisation of 'water to trains and from light to milk ...' Next they would move on to issues which could only be tackled on the national level, social measures such as factory legislation, school feeding, old age pensions.[76] Then 'we shall begin the process of nationalising capital with services like the railways, or with exploitation of natural resources like mines; and we shall begin the process of industrial reconstruction by agrarian policies which will bring the towns into contact with the country, repopulate the deserted villages and re-till the waste fields'.[77] MacDonald avoided 'shopping lists' of what should and should not be nationalised, arguing that this would depend upon the circumstances of the time. Moreover, in economic as in political life decentralisation was essential:

The great factory industries will be controlled by associations of consumers ... the socialist state will mainly concern itself with co-ordinating production and

[73] See Duncan Tanner, ch. 12, this collection.
[74] See Miles Taylor, ch. 2, and Jon Lawrence, ch. 4, this collection.
[75] Emy, *Social Politics*, p. 65.
[76] MacDonald, *The Socialist Movement*, p. 152.
[77] MacDonald, *Socialism and Society*, p. 180.

consumption so as to prevent gluts, useless labour, unearned income, industrial loss, surplus value ... Yet greater liberty will be given to localities to regulate their own affairs to acquire property for that purpose, to promulgate byelaws and more particularly to organise themselves as markets after the manner of co-operative societies.[78]

MacDonald recognised however, that expensive services such as education required growing central government subsidies; that technological change made national rather than municipal production of such essentials as electricity cheaper and more efficient; and that improved transport meant that people lived and worked in different communities. Thus a variety of pressures were shifting the boundaries of central and local government and tending towards the increasing centralisation of control. He recognised that this increased the urgency of devising methods of decentralisation suited to modern conditions and ensuring democratic accountability, and also the difficulty of making it into a reality. Perhaps the greatest failure of MacDonald and others in labour and progressive politics once they were closer to power after the First World War, was that they appear not to have pursued and found effective solutions to these central problems of twentieth-century society.

For MacDonald the practical mechanisms for the organisation of the state and the economy could not be dissociated from their role in 'advancing human character'.[79] Social reform measures had an especially important role. They should be provided in such a way as to reinforce personal independence rather than dependence upon 'state charity' which 'is not socialism but may become the greatest menace that the Socialist Movement [has been] threatened with'.[80] He was firm in his definition of acceptable social reform:

The idea that a lax administration of the poor law is socialistic, that putting an unemployed man on a farm for six weeks at the public expense is socialistic, that feeding schoolchildren is the beginning of the socialistic state is absurd. We can deal with our unemployed, our sweated workers, our derelicts, only by attacking the causes of unemployment, of sweating, of human deterioration and though at a crisis our humanitarianism will compel us to resort to palliatives and give temporary relief, our action at such times should not be a willing and proud thing but one which is hesitating and temporary.[81]

Such principles fitted with the belief, which also united radicals, supporters of independent labour and socialists, in the centrality of

---

[78] MacDonald, *Socialism and Government*, p. 119–22.
[79] J. R. MacDonald, 'The Labour party and its policy', *The Independent Review*, 8 (March 1906), pp. 267–9. I am grateful to Mr John Stewart for this reference.
[80] J. Ramsay MacDonald papers, Labour Party Headquarters: LP/MAC/08/1 item 263ii. I am grateful to Mr Stewart for this reference also.
[81] MacDonald, *Socialism*, pp. 119–20.

fulfilling work to human experience and identity – that in an ideal world people would look forward to work with as much enthusiasm as to leisure. Hence the emphasis of progressive unemployment policies on the need to provide not only relief to the unemployed but also work, to pay for it at a fair rate and to discipline the 'shirker'. Such comments as that of Harry Quelch that 'an able-bodied pauper appears to us to be an anachronism in a rational civilised society',[82] and the expressions of despair or criticism of the slum-dweller which are frequently to be found in speeches and writings across a progressive spectrum, are too readily interpreted as expressions of contempt or ignorance by the secure working class or the middle class for the underclass, as symptomatic of the association of the labour movement only with the elite of the working class. Sometimes this is justified, but, carefully read, they very rarely appear to blame the individual for his or her condition, but rather blame the structures which brought it about and they express a desire to create alternative structures which could give constructive help without undermining human dignity. Criticism of the malingerer could be an attack on the poor; it also expressed affirmation of the dignity of labour and rejection of the conditions which withdrew that dignity from human beings.

MacDonald claimed: 'The political demands of socialism cannot be understood better than by a study of the concept of the 'Right to work', which 'was put forward more frequently than any single demand in the socialist programme'.[83] This encapsulated the framework of rights and obligations which he believed essential for a socialist society.

For MacDonald social reform was not just an end in itself, nor simply a matter of sympathising with or caring for society's victims, it was an essential part of a wider restructuring of the moral basis of the relationship between state and society. Policies democratically arrived at and then democratically administered, preferably at local level, financed through rates and taxes of equitable incidence should be directed firstly, towards maximising opportunities for permanent, fairly paid and fulfilling employment. Where this was impossible or inappropriate individuals had a right to expect publicly funded support at a level sufficient, and so administered, as to uphold human dignity. Only the state, and not individual employers could make this 'right' effective. But inseparable from this *right* was the *obligation* to co-operate fully in the 'ethical democracy', to behave in a dignified and responsible manner, to work wherever suitable work was available, to be active and responsible citizens of the state at all levels. The 'socialist state' was one 'which did not remove responsibility from people

[82] Ryan, 'Poplarism', p. 60.
[83] MacDonald, *Socialist Movement*, pp. 163–7.

because it insisted on their participation ... the State does not concern itself primarily with man as a possessor of rights, but with man as the doer of duties'.[84] He spoke a language recently appropriated by Conservatism in the 1970s, which Labour has been struggling to regain in the 1980s.

VIII

Such sentiments had long radical roots. Furthermore, MacDonald's political ideas and the language in which they were expressed – for example, the pervasive organicist analogy – had clear affinities with the ideas discussed, and to varying degrees shared, by members of the Rainbow Circle of which MacDonald was an active member. He read them papers discussing some of the ideas described above. From 1894 to 1924 the Circle drew together some of the most influential thinkers and activists of advanced liberalism and moderate socialism. They 'saw themselves as the true inheritors of the mantle of philosophic radicalism',[85] which they sought to recast in a collectivist mode. Ideally, in the minds of many of them, their purpose was to provide the intellectual foundations for a political programme to be promoted by a new progressive party, an alliance of liberals and socialists of the type that had emerged in parts of London.[86]

Central to Labour's own conception of the socialist state, as expressed both by MacDonald's writings and in the words and practice of Labour activists in a variety of settings, were quintessentially radical notions of rights, justice, 'fairness', independence, dignity and individual freedom. They carried on the reworking of these concepts that had gone on throughout the preceding century. The insistence upon the need for a reciprocal, participatory relationship between state and citizen embodied a shift from the old radical theory of rights. For rights were no longer simply natural, but were to be earned through active participation in state and society, including through work.[87] Labour moved beyond the older radicalism in accepting a stronger role for the state, but still insisted on democratic checks upon its activities. As for earlier radicals, democracy was the inescapable route to change, but it required new institutional forms in twentieth-century conditions. The character of these institutions was at the heart of the political debate among Labour thinkers. They sought, for example, effective ways to put into practice the theory long held in the labour movement of the need for market regulation by

[84] MacDonald, *Socialism and Government*, p. 11.
[85] Freeden, *Rainbow Circle*, p. 1.
[86] *Ibid.*, p. 10.
[87] *Ibid.*, p. 17.

collective trade union action, for it had long been recognised what inequalities of power and resources resulted from the operations of uncontrolled capitalism. An essential element in the stronger role which Labour now required of the democratic state in the twentieth century was the democratic control of key sectors of the economy. The wholly unmerited 'privilege' of the parasitic *rentier* or of any undeserving holder of power was still to be attacked, but 'British socialism' began to incorporate into the older analyses its own theories of the nature of advanced industrial society and the inequalities which resulted.

12 Ideological debate in Edwardian labour politics: radicalism, Revisionism and socialism

Duncan Tanner

I

Ideological debate within Edwardian labour and socialist politics is not a subject which has attracted a great deal of historical attention. Edwardian labour ideology has been dismissed by some as a defensive and simplistic creed because not socialist,[1] (a factor which has hampered the study of social democracy in general).[2] Others see the Labour party as the product of a muted sense of class consciousness, not of a Marxism which was unattractive given the social and economic realities of Edwardian Britain. For this second group Labour ideology was an irrelevance. Social and economic factors, and the ethos and aims of the trade unions which represented these forces, dominated Labour's outlook and its policy.[3]

While historians have always noted the existence of Labour intellectuals, particularly the Fabians, other intellectual currents have not until recently been studied in depth (and Fabianism has been miscast or dismissed as politically unimportant).[4] None the less, historians have now started to show that there were alternatives to a sectional, trade union created, 'Labourism', and that Labour intellectuals (the Webbs, R. H. Tawney, G. D. H. Cole) could develop sophisticated, in part competing,

---

[1] See, e.g., J. Saville, 'The ideology of labourism', in R. Benewick *et al.*, *Knowledge and Belief in Politics* (London, 1973). The author wishes to thank the University of Kent for additional research/travel funds.

[2] L. Kolakowski, *Main Currents of Marxism* (Oxford, 1978), pp. 114–15, 243–54; G. Lichtheim, *Marxism: An Historical and Critical Survey* (London, 1961), ch. 6.

[3] R. I. McKibbin, *The Evolution of the Labour Party 1910–24* (Oxford, 1974), and his articles, 'Labour and politics in the Great War', *Bulletin of the Society for the Study of Labour History*, 34 (1977), pp. 3–7, 'Why was there no Marxism in Britain?', *English Historical Review*, 99 (1984). This is also the logic behind much of Henry Pelling's work on the Labour party. For 'Labourism' as a cultural force, albeit with less emphasis on the role of the unions, G. Stedman Jones, 'Working-class culture and working-class politics in London: notes on the remaking of a working class', reprinted in his *Languages of Class* (Cambridge, 1983).

[4] A. M. McBriar, *Fabian Socialism and English Politics 1884–1918* (Cambridge, 1962). For the reinterpretation of Fabianism, I. Brittain, *Fabianism and Culture* (Cambridge, 1978), L. Radice, *Beatrice and Sidney Webb* (London, 1984).

ideological and political arguments.[5] Historians have also noted that many Labour activists were rooted in a radical, ethical critique of the existing order which developed in the 1890s, largely from within the radical Nonconformist tradition.[6] Yet this 'ethical socialism' is still frequently dismissed as derivative and ideologically unsophisticated (like Fabianism), while the ideas of the more well-known Labour thinkers are dismissed as politically insignificant.[7] Neither has the relationship between Labour's various ideological components, and the practical political aims and strategies of party leaders, received more than cursory attention. This is partially because the leading politicians are viewed as ideologically naive.[8] But it is also because even in otherwise excellent accounts, 'practical' policies and tactics are seen as having nothing to do with ideology.[9]

This is odd because the questions which dominated socialist debate even in Europe after Marx's death were essentially questions concerning the role of socialist parties in a changing political and social climate. It was obvious by the 1890s that the transition to socialism was more problematic than some Marxists had suggested. Economic changes were not such that the revolution was imminent. Socialists would have to compete for popular support in the electoral market-place. Politicians would have now to answer questions about the kind of society which they and their supporters wished to create, and about how they would create real changes in society and in the economy. The short-term aims and means of socialist parties (rather than abstract philosophical questions), and the ways in which these short-term aims would contribute to the achievement of socialism, were the essence of socialist debate in Europe, while questions concerning the likely structure of the state under the left were a

---

[5] J. Winter, *Socialism and the Challenge of War* (London, 1974), A. W. Wright, *G.D.H. Cole and Socialist Democracy* (Oxford, 1979) and his *R.H. Tawney* (Manchester, 1987), and *British Socialism* (London, 1987). On the intellectual basis of the ILP, D. Howell, *British Workers and the Independent Labour Party 1888–1906* (Manchester, 1983), pp. 52–62.

[6] S. Pierson, *Marxism and the Origins of British Socialism* (Ithaca, 1973) and his *British Socialists. The Journey from Fantasy to Politics* (London, 1979), S. Yeo, 'A new life: the religion of socialism in Britain', *History Workshop*, 4 (1977), D. Clark, *Colne Valley. From Radicalism to Socialism* (London, 1980), K. O. Morgan, *Keir Hardie* (London, 1975), ch. 10.

[7] Pierson, *British Socialists*, chs. 5–6, G. Foote, *The Labour Party's Political Thought: A History* (London, 1985), ch. 3.

[8] This is the case even in quite sophisticated treatments: see, e.g. R. Barker, 'Socialism and Progressivism in the political thought of Ramsay MacDonald', in A. J. A. Morris (ed.), *Edwardian Radicalism 1900–1914* (London, 1974), and D. Marquand, *Ramsay Mac-Donald* (London, 1977), pp. 87–93.

[9] R. I. McKibbin, 'James Ramsay MacDonald and the problem of the independence of the Labour party, 1910–14', *Journal of Modern History*, 42 (1970), C. Howard, 'MacDonald, Henderson, and the outbreak of war, 1914', *Historical Journal*, 20 (1977).

not unrelated feature of the discussions.[10] The Revisionist ideas which emerged in Europe should thus be seen as part of the political history of socialist parties, not as a question of political philosophy to be viewed apart from politics.

Labour politicians in Britain had to face a particularly fierce form of the general socialist ideological/political problem. Economic deterioration and political oppression had not materialised as much as they had in Europe. Support for the existing parties was even more strongly rooted.[11] Yet socialist organisations, and socialists, emerged from within this situation. Many British socialists saw the opportunity of merging an indigenous popular radical tradition (which formed their own initial background) with newer socialist ideas, giving them an altered form and substance. They were not unique in this respect. In Europe some Revisionists and moderate socialists (leaders and activists) drew on non-socialist ethical and radical traditions.[12] One historian of German socialism has gone further, stressing the political importance of the *least* socialist of German Social Democrats. The German popular radical tradition, he argues, was a more significant influence on the party's approach in certain areas than the newer socialist ideas of Marx or even Bernstein.[13] In Britain, however, studies of the interaction between moderate ideas and reforming policies, and between old ideas and new intellectual influences, have been confined very largely to the study of key Liberal figures.[14] The

---

[10] The most sophisticated analysis emanating from Europe was probably by Hilferding and Bauer. Hilferding's economic analysis did not lead him towards more socialist economic policies that MacDonald, while Bauer's ideas on nationalism and socialism had their equivalent in Britain. See H. James, *The German Slump* (Oxford, 1986), D. Howell, *A Lost Left* (Manchester, 1987).

[11] The British New Liberals had recognised that European Liberal parties had allowed socialists to seize the reforming initiative (J. A. Hobson, *The Crisis of Liberalism* [London, 1909], pp. xii–xiii). Socialists saw the revitalisation of Liberal radicalism in Britain as a major cause of British socialism's comparatively limited success (Bernstein's view, cited in R. Fletcher, 'Bernstein in Britain: Revisionism and foreign affairs', *International History Review*, 1 (1979), p. 365, W. John to J. R. M., 29 Jan. 1913, JRM MS PRO 30/69/1157).

[12] Kolakowski, *Marxism*, pp. 245–54, F. Andreucci, 'The diffusion of Marxism in Italy during the late nineteenth century', in R. Samuel and G. Stedman Jones (eds.), *Culture, Ideology and Politics* (London 1983), R. Fletcher, *Revisionism and Empire* (London 1984), pp. 24–41, and his 'Revisionism and Wilhelmine Imperialism', *Journal of Contemporary History*, 23 (1988). Study of the reading material of European socialists does not indicate a much greater familiarity with socialist theory (see extensive lists of references cited in R. J. Evans (ed.), *The German Working Class* (London, 1982), p. 23 and C. Levy (ed.), *Socialism and the Intelligentsia* (London, 1987), p. 34 n. 31).

[13] See references to Fletcher, above, note 12.

[14] P. F. Clarke, *Liberals and Social Democrats* (Cambridge, 1978), and his *The Keynesian Revolution in the Making, 1924–36* (Oxford, 1988). There are some suggestive thoughts in L. Barrow, 'Determinism and environmentalism in socialist thought', and R. Samuel and G. Stedman Jones, 'The Labour party and social democracy', in Samuel and Stedman Jones (eds.), *Culture, Ideology and Politics*.

extent to which ideas – old, new or otherwise – influenced British socialist practice has not been considered.

The following is a tentative step towards such an analysis.[15] I attempt first to indicate the sophistication and coherence of ideas put forward by various Labour politicians, and to show that these were not in essence markedly dissimilar from debates within European socialism. Secondly, I note the challenge presented to a popular radical tradition by new circumstances and new ideas (particularly, but not exclusively, socialism). It is suggested that the popular radical tradition was not written in tablets of stone, and that its salience had to be updated by renewal from within or from without. Thirdly, the bifurcation of the radical and socialist traditions in Britain is noted (with divisions in the latter seen as parallel to those within European socialism). The way in which different mixtures of the 'old' and 'new' radical ideologies could sustain different forms of reforming Labour politics, particularly when combined with differing economic outlooks and ideas, is then discussed. The analysis is concerned largely with the views of James Ramsay MacDonald on the one hand, and the rather different views of Fred Jowett and George Lansbury on the other. However, in the final section it is suggested that these differing types of politics might have been attractive to particular (and different) sections of the party. Whilst the identified approaches were not entirely dissimilar, and party activists were increasingly steeped in a common intellectual culture which might make them sympathetic to either, the differences between the two stances were of both contemporary, and possibly more long-term, significance.

II

Ramsay MacDonald, the leading strategic thinker in Labour politics before 1914, has often been seen (by contemporaries and historians) as in reality a liberal. Yet MacDonald had a considerable, if often neglected, interest in moderate socialist (i.e. Revisionist) ideas. In 1911, he stated his hope that the *Socialist Review*, the journal he founded to increase intellectual debate within the labour movement, would develop 'a strong school of Revisionist Socialism in Britain'. In books and articles he discussed and criticised Engels' conception of socialism, and praised Jaurès and Bernstein (the major European moderate socialist intellec-

---

[15] A full examination would of course involve a closer look at the genesis and nature of ideologies, and a much fuller analysis of policy details, in which other groups – such as the Fabians and the unions – would no doubt loom larger than they do in the following pages. See the contributions to this collection by Alastair Reid (ch. 10) and Pat Thane (ch. 11) for discussions of trade unions and local politics.

tuals).[16] He befriended Bernstein during Bernstein's long residence in Britain, and encouraged the publication of his opinions in the *Socialist Review* and the *Labour Leader*.[17] He also wrote an introduction to Jaurès' *Studies in Socialism* when it was published in Britain, arguing that 'it is of the utmost moment that British Socialists should study Continental Socialist methods'. He referred in particular to the ethical aims, and policies of co-operation with other parties – tendencies which dominated continental practice.[18] Through MacDonald's influence, and the writing of other socialists, the details and merits of Revisionism became a major topic of debate in national and local British socialist journals and newspapers.[19]

There were several points at which MacDonald's views and those of some major Revisionists coincided. First, MacDonald rejected the scientific 'iron law' of extending immiseration (like Bernstein) as historically inaccurate. Capitalist economic development was *not* producing greater poverty in Western Europe; neither was there a compression of the class structure, and an ever-expanding proletariat, as Marx had anticipated. Secondly, he cast doubt on the idea of class struggle as a force for real social change. For Bernstein, the class war was becoming less apparent. For Bernstein, Jaurès *and* MacDonald, change would only be *desirable* (even if it were inevitable) if people were ethically committed to a new social order. Without ethical commitment there could be no real change. 'Any victory won as the result of siding with any one party in the struggle', MacDonald wrote, 'only perpetuates what it desires to eliminate.'[20]

Thirdly, MacDonald argued that the depressive impact of social conditions was such that the working class was hardly fit material at the moment to forge the socialist state. The poor, MacDonald noted, would readily 'sell their souls for a mess of potage'.[21] However, if this suggested that changes in attitudes would only come when the economy produced

---

[16] J. R. M. to Francis Johnson, 29 June 1911, Francis Johnson MS, FJ 1911/181 (Harvester microfilm) and see similarly, W. C. Anderson to J. R. M., 3 Aug. 1910, JRM MS, PRO 30/69/1154. For attacks on Engels, e.g. J.R.M., *Socialism and Government* (1909), ch. 6.

[17] *Labour Leader* (*LL*), 5 Apr. 1907, and 'Revisionism and Social Democracy', *Socialist Review* (*SR*), Mar. 1910.

[18] J. Jaurès, *Studies in Socialism* (Socialist Library, 2nd edn, London 1908), p. xiv. I am grateful to Emlyn Sherrington of UCNW Bangor for bringing this book to my attention. See also MacDonald's article on Jaurès, *Contemporary Review*, Sept. 1914.

[19] R. Gibb, 'Socialism in Germany', *Daily Citizen*, 11 May 1914, 'French Municipal Socialism a word for the critics', *LL*, 24 Jan. 1908, *Railway Review*, 28 June 1912. See also references at n. 70 below.

[20] J. R. M., *The Socialist Movement* (London, 1911), p. 148. For a similar line, P. Snowden, *Socialism and Syndicalism* (London, 1913), p. 78. The general points are from P. Gay, *The Dilemma of Democratic Socialism* (London, 1952), pp. 170, 219, 225–6.

[21] Cited in Marquand, *Ramsay MacDonald*, p. 90.

prosperity, most Revisionists could supply an alternative. Their fourth point was that because ethics were to be the basis of change, so change could be supported by all social groups. Ethically motivated men of ideas, the new professional middle class, could thus support socialist aims and help bring about material and moral change. They could also play a more important positive role. As a group above the pettiness and intellectual stultification induced by poverty, these intellectuals, and their ideas, could become a vital force in initiating progress.

Fifthly, and like Bernstein, MacDonald argued that alliances with groups led or inspired by such people were ideologically justified, if this led to attacks on adverse conditions. Through alliances, socialists could force the pace of local and national legislative change to improve the material condition of the people: 'it's social progress', Bernstein wrote, 'as well as ... agitation which leads to the achievement of (real) change'. MacDonald's argument that legislative intervention moved the country gradually closer to socialism, and his emphasis on achieving positions of practical influence, accords well with this view.[22] Only by tackling the conditions of working-class life, Revisionists argued (to differing extents) could socialism make any headway.

Many Revisionists did not think that social change was imminent, or that it would be achieved easily. New ideas, MacDonald argued, would not readily be accepted. Socialists should recognise the power of 'inherited habits, modes of thought, axioms of conduct, traditions both of thought and activity'. Change would therefore be gradual. Socialists had to tread carefully to see that roots in past tradition were not ruptured. MacDonald's affinity with a popular radical tradition was thus both personally and politically important.[23]

The New Liberalism also had a significant impact on MacDonald's ideological and strategic thinking. Contact with New Liberals in the 1890s helped convince him that if 'ethical socialism', and its accompanying attacks on the Liberal party, could be superseded by a more policy-minded and co-operative Labour ideology, then 'Progressives' (i.e. New Liberal and Labour members) could put pressure on the more conservative members of the Liberal party.[24] Changes in policy would follow. Perhaps most significantly, in accepting the 'futility of direct assaults upon

---

[22] Cited in W. L. Guttsman, *The German Social Democratic Party 1875–1933* (London, 1981), p. 293.

[23] J. R. M., *Socialism: Critical and Constructive* (London, 1921), p. 2.

[24] Clarke, *Liberals and Social Democrats*, pp. 56–61. New Liberals and Fabians also had an effect on Bernstein (Fletcher, 'Bernstein in Britain', and his 'British radicalism and German Revisionism: the case of Eduard Bernstein', *International Review of Social History* [1982], p. 152; E. Pease, *The History of the Fabian Society* [New York, 1916], p. 239).

deep-rooted habits', MacDonald drew lessons not unassociated with popular radical (or Revisionist) attitudes, but which he took to lengths more usually associated with a section of the Liberal party. MacDonald accepted that change would be gradual and based on existing attitudes: but he also emphasised as much, if not more, than the New Liberals, that *reason* – not working-class communitarian humanity or class solidarity – would have the dominant part to play in creating new attitudes.[25] As he reflected later, 'The protection of practical reason which instinctive action needs ... threatens to stifle the instinct, and yet without it the instinct is blown and swayed by every gust of passion'.[26] MacDonald respected those who saw the simple virtues of working-class life as morally ideal (witness his interest in Thoreau and Tolstoy and his depiction of the 'good-natured', honest trade unionist, with his instinctive unease about titles, pomp and social superiority); but he was equally influenced, he noted, by Tolstoy's critics.[27] By 1914 he generally came down on the side of reason and practical politics, not this intuitive egalitarianism: 'opinion and conviction are ultimately the only foundations for permanent social change', he wrote. In blacker moments, he revealed his doubts about whether the working class would ever be capable of the motivations which he deemed essential: 'I do not believe I have ever understood the working of the ordinary mind', he wrote, 'It is not interested in an impartial truth. It works only on nerves and impulses.' MacDonald's faith in *reason* – which in policy discussions increasingly became deference to conventional experts – was to have some importance in the future, although its consequences were not fully evident before 1914.[28]

Other aspects of MacDonald's thought and approach reflected his roots in a popular radical tradition. As Pat Thane argues in her contribution to this collection, MacDonald, in full conformity with this radical tradition, hoped to create a social system in which welfare reforms were just part of a society which allowed people independence, self-respect and dignity. The state was not there to be a source of income. State 'charity', he argued, was not socialism but was potentially the greatest menace that the socialist movement had ever been threatened with.[29] He amplified the point later. Capitalism, he wrote, created a system in which individual expression and

[25] For New Liberal ambiguities on the working class as a force for change, P. F. Clarke, 'The social democratic theory of the class struggle', in J. Winter (ed.), *The Working Class in Modern British History* (Cambridge, 1983), pp. 12–13.

[26] J.R.M., *Wanderings and Excursions* (London, 1925), p. 299.

[27] J.R.M., *At Home and Abroad* (London, 1935), pp. 11–12; J.R.M. to G. Murray, 6 Oct. 1914, Gilbert Murray MS 153 fol. 10 (Bodleian Library, Oxford).

[28] J.R.M. introduction to Jaurès, *Studies in Socialism*, p. xvii; J.R.M. diary, 1 Oct. 1914, JRM MS PRO 30/69/1753.

[29] Thane, above p. 267.

a *personal* commitment to certain moral and social values (including co-operative beliefs and a concern for others) were being attacked. State intervention had created a dependence on state institutions to teach or supply morally desirable attitudes.[30] This was precisely what MacDonald was concerned with before 1914. The state should act, he had argued, not to *replace* individual responsibility and commitment, but to *reinforce* it. It should have an important, but not dominant, role: it should supply the economic climate, and should encourage – through concrete, structural changes – a climate in which individuals could work to create a more dignified independence: 'Unless good emotion in society', MacDonald wrote, 'finds expression through a system of social relations [it] will sink to mere sentimentality.'[31]

MacDonald was also concerned that dependence, and the erosion of the individual's self-motivated desire to act in a dignified and egalitarian manner, might be accompanied by an escalation of the pursuit of individual gain. If institutions reinforced good citizenship they were to be encouraged; if they did not, they should be condemned. Thus, on trade unions: 'If the new Labour movement was simply an attempt of trade unionists to use their political power for purely sectional purposes ... it would be a menace to all the qualities that mark public life with distinction and honour'. Trade unions should identify 'with something higher and wider than trade union industrial demands. It must set these demands into a system of national well-being; the wage earner must become the citizen: the union must become the guardian of economic justice.'[32]

MacDonald's ideas were reinforced by his economic outlook. Although precise details of MacDonald's views in this area in particular require further investigation, it would seem that, like most nineteenth-century radicals, he blamed Britain's economic problems on the existence, and values, of the idle rich, calling for a union of the industrious classes to oppose them.[33] He advocated the improvement of conciliation machinery, although he had no desire to prejudice the non-corporate position of the trade unions by so doing. He also supported improved technical education, as union leaders had done for many years. His views contained little of a socialist critique of a capitalist economy. He did, however, see a significant role for the state (as did most socialists) in economic development. Writing on the *Zollverein*, he argued that large economic trusts were 'the line of British advance', adding that, 'in this country the introduction

[30] J.R.M., *Parliament and Democracy* (London, 1920), pp. 68–72.
[31] J.R.M., *Socialism After the War* (London, 1917), p. 2.
[32] J.R.M., 'The new Labour movement', *New Liberal Review* (Sept. 1903), p. 161.
[33] For the centrality of this attitude in early nineteenth-century radicalism see G. Stedman Jones, 'Rethinking Chartism', in *Languages of Class*, pp. 90–178.

of the Trust should be marked by public ownership'. State control of land in particular was 'the economic bedrock on which all other reform is based'.[34] A democratised state had a role to play in stimulating productive enterprise, and in encouraging and controlling development through state regulation. It was also to watch over the large scale enterprises which could control markets and eliminate wasteful competition.

MacDonald's electoral plans reflected his Revisionist/popular radical views. Alliance with a radical Liberal party was desirable because many moderate trade unionists wanted such an arrangement. It was acceptable because a section of the Liberal party embraced similar political, economic and social ideas to MacDonald. A loose alliance would allow Labour to influence legislation while giving it the opportunity to build support by consistent campaigning, especially at municipal level.[35] Such an alliance was also consistent with Revisionist practice and ideas. MacDonald none the less hoped to gradually expand Labour's support. Whatever his broad agreement with Liberal radicals, he did not believe that they were a majority of the Liberal party, nor so entrenched that they were certain to influence policy.[36]

III

The theoretical arguments of the European Revisionists (and the practice of those European social democrats who had departed from a 'socialist' approach) did not escape criticism on the continent. The initial opposition of Kautsky and other Marxist socialists to Revisionism is well known, as is the later opposition of Rosa Luxembourg, Georges Sorel and the syndicalists to the declining virulence of this hostility on the left. The opposition of democratic socialists like Jaurès to Revisionism is less well known but of some significance. Jaurès was more optimistic than Bernstein or MacDonald about the working class as an instrument of change. His religious and philosophical beliefs convinced him that human nature contained the capacity for mutual sympathy and hence the ability to support a better system of social relations. The working class, as the most oppressed group, was logically the mouthpiece of moral justice. It was also already forging socialism within capitalism through its own co-operative

---

[34] J.R.M. 'The electorate and the tariff temptation', *New Liberal Review* (Nov. 1903), pp. 441–7, Marquand, *MacDonald*, p. 87. For land reform, C. Llewelyn Davies to D. Lloyd George, 4 Aug. 1912, Lloyd George MS, LG C/9/3/10.

[35] For this, D. M. Tanner, *Political Change and the Labour Party 1900–18* (Cambridge, 1990), ch. 1.

[36] J.R.M. to L.C. Money, 30 Apr. 1907, LP GC 14/240 (Labour party archives).

organisations and institutions. Change would come by building on these ideas and these instances of communal solidarity. Like other Revisionists, Jaurès was less willing than either Bernstein or MacDonald to forge long-standing electoral agreements with middle-class non-socialist radicals.[37] The middle and working classes were, he argued, very different. They could only travel so far together.

British socialists also criticised MacDonald's approach and his ideological perspective, in ways similar to the various European anti-Revisionists: we should not assume that more militant forms of socialism than that of MacDonald – or Jaurès – were unknown in Britain. Marx's ideas had been studied, largely in education classes, but sometimes in simplified pamphlets, by many of the late Victorian and Edwardian socialists who disagreed with MacDonald. Kautsky's attack on Bernstein in the 1890s was reflected in Britain through men like Theodore Rothstein. Attitudes also hardened over time. Founders of the Independent Labour Party (ILP), such as Russell Smart and Joseph Burgess, initially attacked only aspects of MacDonald's approach, but gradually came to reject his whole analysis and adopt a more militant socialist outlook.[38] Other more well-known critics of MacDonald acknowledged the influence of Marx on their thinking, including George Lansbury, Fred Jowett, James O'Grady, Will Thorne and John MacLean.[39]

In fact, from around 1909 British socialist debate revolved around the conflict between 'Revisionism' and 'Revolutionism'. As one activist put it, 'reform or revolution, revisionism or revolutionism', became the major question of the day.[40] The point was made explicitly in the 'Green Manifesto', *Let Us Reform the Labour Party*, the most direct of the pre-war assaults on MacDonald's approach.[41] The authors of the manifesto also went on to emphasise this apparent polarity at every possible

[37] Kolakowski, *Marxism*, ch. 5.
[38] In Glasgow, socialists studied Marx through classes run by W. Reid and W. Nairn, or by reading A. P. Hazell's penny pamphlet, *A Summary of Marx's Capital* (H. MacShane and J. Smith (eds.), *Harry MacShane: No Mean Fighter* (London, 1978), p. 29). Others amongst the Labour rank and file also studied Marx in this manner: W. Stephen Sanders, *Early Socialist Days* (London, 1927), pp. 28–30, J. Toole, *Fighting Through Life* (London, 1935), p. 80, J. Clunnie, *Literature and Labour* (Dunfermline, 1967), pp. 190–1. For Rothstein, see Pierson, *British Socialists*, pp. 82–4.
[39] W. T. Stead, 'The Labour party and the books that helped to make it', *Review of Reviews* (1906), G. Lansbury, 'How I became a Socialist', *LL*, 17 May 1912, N. Milton (ed.), *John MacLean. In the Rapids of Revolution* (London, 1978), pp. 10–11, 27–45.
[40] Clunnie, *Literature and Labour*, p. 156. See also J. Paton, *Proletarian Pilgrimage* (London, 1935), pp. 208–10.
[41] L. Hall et al., *Let Us Reform the Labour Party* (London, 1910), esp. p. 7. The following from D. Morris, 'Labour or Socialism? Opposition and dissent within the ILP, with special reference to Lancashire', Manchester Ph.D. thesis 1982, p. 210. See also e.g., *Forward*, 28 Jan. 1911, *SR*, Aug. 1913.

opportunity. As C. P. Douthwaite, one of the Green Manifesto authors, put it, party leaders should be made to understand 'that Revisionism is one of the seven deadly sins'.

Support for the Green Manifesto group extended beyond the deterministic Marxist camp. Most of those who had read Marx, and many who had not, cited William Morris as a particular influence on their outlook, an indication that their socialism was of the more humanistic kind. In reality many opponents of MacDonald were what Peter Clarke has called *moral* revolutionaries; optimistic believers in the capacity of the working class to effect change, if necessary through class struggle, but not through the imposition of values or political structures.[42] The British left critics of a strategy of compromise were not generally hardened sympathisers with a deterministic Marxism, but they were not without socialist credentials.

The 'moral revolutionist' diagnosis of the failures of Revisionism was shared by many party activists. Liberal collectivism – sustained and encouraged by MacDonald – was not producing socialism. As Lancelot Eden, in an article entitled 'Philip Snowden's Revisionism', put it, many socialists were 'becoming uneasy with regard to the continuous extension of national ownership in the absence of democratic control'.[43] Joseph Burgess argued that 'municipalisation and nationalisation in present conditions actually strengthens Capitalism'. 'It is necessary', another wrote, 'that we should examine very carefully the industries we now possess with a view to finding out [how] to limit the power of those now controlling them.'[44] State control, Jowett argued, simply meant an unaccountable bureaucracy. Belloc and Chesterton's idea of a 'Servile State' – a state catering *for* people, not involving them in any way – was adopted by the left both in Britain and perhaps also in parts of Europe.[45] Social reforms, it was generally argued, were not enough. Unless people's attitudes were changed, Keir Hardie wrote, the Servile State would stifle true change; 'there is no success', Fred Henderson added, 'that will stand the wear and tear of life, other than the success of converting public opinion to Socialism'.[46]

The solutions to the problem diagnosed by many socialists (including Lansbury/Jowett and those associated with the Green Manifesto) were

---

[42] Clarke, *Liberals and Social Democrats*, pp. 5, 29.
[43] *SR*, Aug. 1913.
[44] *Bradford Pioneer*, 10 Apr. 1913, *Sheffield Guardian*, 23 May 1913.
[45] F. W. Jowett, *What is the Use of Parliament?* (London, 1909), p. 28. Belloc and Chesterton were not entirely happy about this: *Daily Herald* (*DH*) debate, 14 Mar. 1913, H. Belloc to F. Henderson, 5 Mar. 1910, 16 Feb. 1912, Henderson MS 43/1 and 2 (Norfolk County Record Office). For Europe, C. Levy, 'Conclusion: historiography and the New Class', in Levy (ed.), *Socialism and the Intelligentsia*, p. 280.
[46] *Scotsman*, 5 Jan. 1914, *Clarion*, 12 July 1912.

initially very similar, even if there were some tactical/temperamental differences, particularly between Jowett and Victor Grayson.[47] They suggested that Labour – under MacDonald's influence – was currently too concerned with Liberal policy, and that socialist aims should be given more prominence. Like European socialists they called for a return to basic principles, and an avoidance of pragmatism. Moreover, if Liberal legislation was not creating an acceptable kind of social system, then electoral alliance with the Liberals was unnecessary and undesirable. Like many European socialists they argued for an independent working-class party, and against alliance with bourgeois radicals. Labour should attack the Liberals at every opportunity – in parliament, in by-elections and in general elections – advertising socialism's distinct attraction in the process.[48] To this end, there were parliamentary demonstrations, by MPs like Victor Grayson, Keir Hardie and George Lansbury, and calls, by these and others, for an end to Labour's electoral alliance with the Liberals.[49]

The leading left-wing critics of MacDonald, like many European anti-Revisionists, were optimistic about working-class capabilities. Russell Smart saw the working class as inherently capable of effecting change, and specifically referred to William Morris' views in justifying his optimism.[50] It was simply a matter of motivation. 'It is not Statesmen we want in Parliament', he wrote in 1907, 'but agitators who will use Parliament as a platform.'[51] This confidence in the working-class capacity for change was increased by industrial unrest after 1910. Strikes, Keir Hardie noted, were an opportunity to mobilise opinion because they 'stimulated the moral fibre of those participating', displaying and keeping alive the 'spirit of rebellion' which would 'awaken society and revolutionise it along Socialist lines'. If the Parliamentary Labour Party would give a lead, the *Herald* noted, 'there will be such an uprising as will astonish the country'.[52]

Here again British and European socialism did not move on fundamentally different lines. In Europe, new critiques of the attitudes and approach of socialist parties had become more widespread after 1910, as Sorel and Luxembourg amongst others voiced their opposition to the increasingly moderate practice of socialist parties. The full details of these critiques did not feature prominently in the British socialist press. None the less, work by the irrationalists, Bergson, Sorel and Nietsche, and by the famous anarchist, Kropotkin, were common elements in the intellectual biogra-

[47] Jowett had been unhappy about Grayson's temperamental outbursts, and about his lack of constructive thought.
[48] Tanner, *Political Change*, pp. 51–4.
[49] *Ibid.*, pp. 72–5.
[50] *Huddersfield Worker*, 3, 24 Feb. 1912.
[51] *LL*, 17 May 1907. See also ILP *Conference Report* 1908, pp. 34–7, 1909, pp. 35–6.
[52] *DH*, 15 Apr., 3 July 1912.

phies of British socialist militants.[53] Their views were influential not as formal ideology, but because – to British eyes – they seemed to be based on faith in the working class and its ethical, or non-rational, motivations. British critics of Revisionism absorbed ideas concerning individual psychology, popular morality and the importance of historical myth. In this respect European ideas were paralleled in the ideas of British critics of MacDonald. MacDonald's emphasis on the importance of rational conviction in political mobilisation, critics argued, had been overstated, for the working class was by instinct and by fact of oppression capable of supporting and recognising the value of total social reconstruction. As J. M. McLachlan put it, 'Students of human nature ... scarcely need to be reminded that men are stirred to action by their emotions, not by cognition or reason. Cognition of itself can never produce action. It is only emotion which can stir men to action – with or without cognition.' Instinct, and especially working-class instinct, could be a vital agent of change.[54]

If state bureaucracy was stifling true socialism, party bureaucracy had the same effect, as it kept left critics from assuming positions of leadership and responsibility. Leonard Hall, McLachlan, and Russell Smart proposed a series of internal reforms of the ILP's institutional structure which would undermine what they saw as a leadership clique. Lansbury and others attacked the idea that ILP MPs should be required to follow the Labour line in parliament.[55] Jowett's suggestion that MPs should vote on the merits of particular proposals, rather than as the whips dictated, was both an attempt to weaken the power of the political caucus, and an attempt to allow Labour to advertise distinct, non-Liberal, views on every aspect of legislative interest. Lansbury's decision to resign from parliament in 1912, and fight a by-election, was a protest not just over women's suffrage, as is generally argued, but over the PLP's subservience to the Liberals in parliament and in the country, and the party leadership's suppression of this fact.[56] While these attacks paralleled the European

[53] E. Muir, *An Autobiography* (London 1954), pp. 8–14; R. M. Fox, *Smokey Crusade* (London 1937), p. 54; Paton, *Proletarian Pilgrimage*, pp. 209, 212; Toole, *Fighting Through Life*, p. 81; H. Snell, *Men, Movements and Myself* (London, 1938), pp. 77, 114; Clunnie, *Literature and Labour*, pp. 190–1. The psychology of mass action, often with particular reference to Sorel, was a common subject. See, e.g., J. R. M., *Syndicalism* (London, 1912), ch. 3, P. Snowden, 'The psychology of the strike', *Sheffield Guardian*, 29 Aug. 1913; L. Haden Guest, 'The problem of our democracy', *DH*, 3 Dec. 1912. However, contrast Bruce Glasier's view that Nietsche's work was 'the political philosophy of the baboon' (J. Bruce Glasier diary, 1 July 1910, Liverpool University Library).

[54] *LL*, 29 May 1908.

[55] *LL*, 22 May 1908. Smart's proposals were defeated at the ILP Conference in 1909. See also J. Bruce Glasier diary, 26 June 1912.

[56] G. Lansbury to M. Coates-Hanson, 31 Oct. 1912, Lansbury MS LL 6 fos. 77–9 (BLPES) and Tanner, *Political Change*, pp. 72, 179.

socialist critiques of party bureaucrats, a general hostility to leadership 'juntas' and 'caucuses', and the vigorous affirmation of local branch autonomy, had also been a strong feature of radical politics in Britain throughout the nineteenth century.[57]

The anti-Revisionist camp in Britain soon divided into its differing ideological elements. The division between moderate and militant critics of MacDonald's stance – between a particular species of moral reformer and moral revolutionaries – occurred because of the moral revolutionaries' lack of a constructive policy.[58] Smart had argued in 1908 that the whole of Labour's attention should be focused on the need to tackle poverty. The Right to Work campaigns which sprang up across the country in 1908 were largely the work of Victor Grayson, Smart, Joseph Burgess, and the Green Manifesto authors and their allies. Yet the campaigns revealed that they had few practical proposals for tackling the immediate economic problems of working-class life. Joseph Burgess amongst others even rejected Hobson's radical underconsumptionist ideas.[59] Hobson's suggestion that the current economic system, suitably altered, could produce material improvements for the bulk of the population, Burgess argued, was simply capitalist camouflage. Fred Henderson developed this argument in a series of articles in the socialist press:

A Labour party which is preaching the virtues of the minimum wage ... or any social reform within the existing order instead of Socialism and the expropriation of the master class, cannot fight the New Liberals ... because to do so would be to include its own clap-trap in a common condemnation with Liberalism.[60]

Most of those who held this view gradually embraced more revolutionary ideas. They left the ILP to form the British Socialist Party (BSP) or to join other fringe left organisations, such as the Socialist Labour Party (SLP).[61] The ideas of men like Lansbury and Jowett, moral revolutionaries by origin, but with an awareness of the need for immediate social reform – men closer to the ideas of Jaurès than to Kautsky – therefore dominated the opposition to MacDonald within the ILP after 1910.

Neither Jowett nor Lansbury have had a good press. Lansbury was more than a 'bleeding heart'. His broad aim, like that of William Morris, was to 'make workers want, and want badly, better conditions' – to encourage workers to demand reforms which bourgeois parties could not

---

[57] D. Morris, 'The origins of the British Socialist Party', *North West Labour History Society*, Bulletin 8 (1982–3). See also the contribution by Jon Lawrence to the present collection.

[58] For varieties of moral reformers, Tanner, *Political Change*, pp. 30–40.

[59] J. Burgess, *A Potential Poet?* (Ilford, 1927), pp. 201, 205.

[60] *Clarion*, 19 July 1912.

[61] Morris, 'BSP', passim. See also J. M. McLachlan, *Which Way? Assimilation versus Independence* (London, 1911).

implement.[62] He attacked the Poor Law, for example, as inimicable to human dignity, and contributory national insurance as a means of making the poor finance their own social benefits.[63] In this, however, Lansbury and Jowett, like MacDonald, drew on a popular radical tradition. When advocating intervention by the state, or by the local authority, to redress grievances they attempted to maintain human dignity in the process (portraying benefits as a moral right, and not as charity, and therefore seeing intervention as a positive policy). However, they were less concerned than MacDonald with the dangers of intervention, and more concerned that intervention should be used to attack the poverty which they thought prevented real individual improvement. As socialists with an acute awareness of immediate problems, and a desire to move towards a much better social system, they wanted to demonstrate the practical importance of socialism by showing that only socialists recognised the need, and had the commitment, to transform the material realities of working-class life. As municipal politicians, Jowett and Lansbury tried to do this through interventionist municipal policies. Before 1914, in Lansbury's case, this meant providing work wherever possible, after 1918 it meant generous social provision (despite the opposition of MacDonald and others to what they called a policy of public doles).[64] Lansbury also rejected the accusation that his policies were economically unrealistic. It was possible, and only possible, he argued (departing from MacDonald's view) to help the poor by taking money from the rich. He and Jowett were thus insistent that the money for social reforms *had* to be found, and that it should come from national taxation of the rich, not from the rates or from the contributions of the working class itself.[65]

MacDonald was a bitter opponent of this approach. For MacDonald, socialism was a guiding ideal, in which the ultimate aims were greater individual dignity, individuality and liberty of thought and expression. The state, he thought, could easily restrict improvements through its

---

[62] G. Lansbury to B. Webb, 28 Oct. 1913, Passfield MS 11 4f fol. 166 (BLPES).

[63] P. Thane, 'The working class and state "welfare" in Britain, 1880–1914', *Historical Journal*, 28 (1984), p. 898.

[64] P. A. Ryan, 'Poplarism 1894–1930', in P. Thane (ed.), *The Origins of British Social Policy* (London 1978); J. Reynolds and K. Laybourn, 'The emergence of the Independent Labour Party in Bradford', *International Review of Social History*, 20 (1975). For other related examples, J. W. Marriott, 'London over the border: a study of West Ham during rapid growth', Cambridge Ph.D. thesis 1984; T. Woodhouse, 'The working class', in D. Fraser (ed.), *A History of Modern Leeds* (Manchester, 1980). The postwar political conflicts over Poplarism are best discussed in J. S. Rowett, 'The Labour party in local government: theory and practice in the inter-war years', Oxford D.Phil. thesis 1979, esp. pp. 142–4; J. A. Gillespie, 'Economic and political change in the East End of London during the 1920s', University of Cambridge Ph.D. thesis 1984, ch. 8.

[65] *DH*, 20 May 1912, A. Fenner Brockway, *Socialism Over Sixty Years. The Life of Jowett of Bradford* (London, 1946), ch. 4.

intervention. Intervention should be limited and the state should be democratised to ensure that necessary intervention was both controlled and rendered compatible with individual liberty. Democratisation would ensure that governments did not engage in class legislation which was favourable to the aristocracy; indirect encouragement of change would allow real and genuine changes in working-class self-esteem to become apparent.

MacDonald's views in this respect are much more extensive and sophisticated than has previously been recognised.[66] But Jowett and Lansbury also represented a sophisticated but different combination of 'old' and 'new' ideological currents. They went even further in their attempt to control what they hoped would be a more interventionist state. As far as political structures were concerned, Lansbury and Jowett supported the introduction of the referendum to ensure continuous accountability. The left generally supported proportional representation.[67] Lansbury and Jowett also had more to say than did MacDonald about the dangers of an uncontrolled domination of the state mainly because they saw the state as a potentially coercive force. They were more concerned than MacDonald, for example, with the potentially undemocratic impact of state bureaucracy. These left critics argued that intervention and democratisation should go hand in hand. Jowett, for example, called for parliamentary control of the legislature through the introduction of the committee system which operated in local government. This would break down party power *and* make executive control of monopolies a reality.[68] Others stressed the need for industrial democracy. There was also some support amongst Jowett's sympathisers at least for extensive municipalisation, as an alternative to more nationalisation, and as a means of securing greater public control.[69] None the less, the difficulty of tackling economic injustice at the local level ultimately led to Jowett calling for state (not local authority) intervention. It was difficult to finance a decentralised, municipal, approach.[70]

IV

The attack on MacDonald's approach was defeated. MacDonald's ideas on the correct policy for the Parliamentary Labour Party (PLP) were

---

[66] See Thane, above pp. 261–70.
[67] Jowett, *What is the Use of Parliament?*, *DH*, 20 Dec. 1912, and e.g. support for P.R. from Burgess, *Bradford Pioneer*, 18 Aug. 1913, from the ASE, ASE, *Monthly Journal*, Feb. 1914.
[68] Jowett, *What is the Use of Parliament?*
[69] Winter, *Socialism and War*, pp. 107–13; *Huddersfield Worker*, 15 July 1911 (leader).
[70] *LL*, 11 Nov. 1910.

repeatedly endorsed. Bruce Glasier described Victor Grayson's parliamentary protests as 'the footlight heroics of a blatent windbag'. More seriously, and not unusually, E. P. Wake denounced criticism of MacDonald's strategy by reference to the actions of European socialist parties: 'the impossibilism of that British section finds no counterpart in the present methods of our German comrades. Liebknecht quickly renounced the impossibilist idea of using the Reichstag as a platform of protest from which to give dramatic displays to satisfy the hunger for sensation of frothy revolutionaries.'[71] MacDonald's by-election strategy was also endorsed by the PLP and by individual trade unions, ultimately – and despite considerable opposition – at a special session of the Labour party conference in 1914.[72]

MacDonald's policy of a tacit electoral alliance with the Liberals also commanded considerable support within the moderate wing of the party. Liberal policy incorporated aspects of a popular radical tradition which Labour moderates did not wish to see sacrificed through electoral conflict. The Liberals' hostility to the idle rich – and their support for popular control of parliament with the assault on the Lords in 1910 – were far more attractive than Jowett's argument that the constitution was a secondary issue. A. E. Fletcher, in the Engineers' *Journal* in 1909, argued that 'All other considerations are now overshadowed by the question of whether the people or the peers are to control the people's destiny.' The Secretary of the Boilermakers' Society, declining to pursue candidatures in seats where Liberal success might thus be jeopardised, noted, 'There is a strong feeling amongst our members for a closing up of the Progressive ranks, to end for ever the veto of the Lords on measures passed by overwhelming majorities of the people's representatives.'[73] The point was made with equal force in 1914, when it appeared that the army in Ireland was attempting to dictate policy to the elected British government.[74]

If popular control of government was important, here was another good reason not to oppose the Liberals. New Liberals were *more* concerned than MacDonald, and as concerned as Lansbury, Jowett and

[71] *Manchester Weekly Citizen*, 27 Jan. 1912, and Glasier's observations, J. Bruce Glasier to E. Bruce Glasier, 30 Oct. 1908, JBG 08/12. This approach was also used in rejecting Jowett's constitutional schemes (J. Arnott, 'The Parliamentary Committee system in France', *SR*, June 1913; W. C. Anderson debate with McLachlan, *LL*, 5 Aug. 1910, cited in Morris thesis, p. 210).

[72] Tanner, *Political Change*, pp. 74–6, 320–5.

[73] Amalgamated Society of Engineers *Monthly Journal*, Dec. 1909, United Society of Boilermakers, *Monthly Report*, Dec. 1909.

[74] *Railway Review*, 3 Apr. 1914, *Typographical Circular*, Mar. 1914; Amalgamated Society of Carpenters and Joiners, *Monthly Journal*, Aug. 1914. See MacDonald's similar views, Marquand, *Ramsay MacDonald*, pp. 160–1.

European socialists, to ensure that the legislature was accountable to the people. To this end, Hobson supported the referendum, like Jowett and Lansbury, and with other New Liberals welcomed Jowett's schemes for the scrutiny of government policy by parliamentary committees.[75] The government, under New Liberal pressure, had in fact already formed committees to oversee some areas of public expenditure, and agreed to a Royal Commission to investigate the 'secretive' working of the civil service. There was also an unofficial Liberal committee to watch over foreign policy.[76]

The popular radical hostility to welfare, as opposed to wages, to 'charity' as opposed to 'independence', is equally apparent in the support which many skilled unions gave to reforms which MacDonald and the Liberals supported, and which Lansbury and Jowett opposed. The Liberal policy of having a *contributory* national insurance scheme, for example, was an extension of the popular radicals' collective individualism, especially if kept under union control. The insurance legislation, Hill of the Boilermakers came to argue, was 'the greatest measure of social reform ever placed on the Statute book'. For one railwayman writer, it was 'the largest measure of social reform ever enacted ... many members [would] have cause to thank God for it'.[77] Moreover, even for more socialist reformers, the Liberals were forcing through collectivist policies which provided a platform on which Labour could build.

Other aspects of the Liberals' partial intervention in the economy were also supported. Many Labour leaders were suspicious of attempts to substantially improve wage rates in the sweated trades through minimum wage legislation. MacDonald and others argued that extensive state legislation would dampen enthusiasm for union activity as a means of securing real improvements. They also argued that if wage rates were set too high, they would simply put people out of work.[78] Minimum wages and the nationalisation of certain industries would come, MacDonald argued, but this was not a priority. Minimum wages for government employees (e.g. in the dockyards) should also be introduced, because the government should set a standard – but living standards for these workers would be raised 'in the same way as we raise the standard of life all round'.[79] The government workers had

[75] *Nation*, 3 June 1911, and later views, noted in *Bradford Pioneer*, 10 July 1914.

[76] R. A. Jones, 'Peace, retrenchment and reform: the British Radicals before 1914', *Parliament, Estates, and Representation* 4 (1984) pp. 75–8.

[77] Boilermakers' *Annual Report* 1911, *Locomotive Journal*, Jan. 1912.

[78] MacDonald's views noted in Bruce Glasier's diary, 6 Sept. 1912, Fabian Conference report, *Fabian News*, Jan. 1913.

[79] *Leicester Pioneer*, 16, 25 Nov. 1911. One of MacDonald's sometime allies, George Barnes, similarly opposed subsidised state housing because it would promote low rents, and hence

little reason to think that Labour legislation would supply prosperity, rather than a safety net. This limited state intervention attracted support. Miners in the north-east, for example, opposed the legal implementation of an eight-hour day in 1908–10, and a national minimum wage in 1911–12, in part because they did not trust the state, but also because an eight-hour day and nationalisation were not deemed to be economically credible. A national minimum wage, dependent on political, not economic, factors was unrealistic. 'Wages follow prices', J. J. Lawson ruefully commented, 'that is Durham philosophy'. Policies consistent with MacDonald's social philosophy and economic outlook were popular: breaks from that tradition (as with Labour's support for an eight-hours bill in the north-east) caused major local revolts against party policy.[80]

V

The elements of MacDonald's ideology discussed above no doubt meshed together in a more complex manner than a brief analysis can reveal. There is certainly far more work to be done on MacDonald's policies, outlook and ideas, and even more on those of his supporters. However, it is clear from this preliminary account that MacDonald's Revisionism was not a dramatic break from his previous views: it was an extension of them, modified by new intellectual and political factors. There is evidence to suggest that some of MacDonald's supporters at least shared a similar analysis and intellectual inspiration.[81] Moreover, and although the point cannot be developed here, it would appear that MacDonald's version of a moderate social democracy appealed to people from a particular strand within the radical tradition, even if aspects of their views were different or expressed in a less sophisticated manner. Nonconformity, a radical family tradition, and personal experience of cultural or economic deprivation, feature prominently as formative influences on many moderate Labour activists.[82] Local studies also stress the importance of existing radical currents by noting the role of Nonconformity as a motivating force

---

low wages, when higher wages were in fact the answer (cited in Brockway, *Socialism Over Sixty Years*, p. 51).

[80] J. J. Lawson, *A Minimum Wage for Miners* (London, 1911), p. 6; Tanner, *Political Change*, pp. 76–8, 209–11. Some railwaymen were hostile to the eight-hours bill introduced by Labour's W. Hudson (*Locomotive Journal*, Feb. 1911).

[81] See, e.g., W. C. Anderson's article on Jaurès, *LL*, 11 Nov. 1910.

[82] See the series 'How I became a Socialist', *LL*, e.g. 24 May, 7, 20 June, 1912, and autobiographies such as J. Griffiths, *Pages from Memory* (London, 1969), pp. 18–19, W. J. Edwards, *From the Valley I Came* (London, 1956), p. 103.

amongst early ILP activists.[83] Yet continuities with the past, and cultural parallels between Liberals and some early Labour supporters, should not suggest that the only differences between Liberals and Labour were of social origin (even if the differences were not politically effective before 1914).[84] If the views of Robert Knight and Ramsay MacDonald are anything to go by, the views of trade unionists and moderate Labour sympathisers with an ILP past were more sophisticated, and more part of a popular radical tradition, than many have suggested. For some – even amongst MacDonald's supporters – socialism played a part in shaping their opinions; for others, clearly it did not. The extent to which the views of 'MacDonaldites' from 'union' or 'ILP' backgrounds differed, and the relationship between their views and those of the Liberals, would repay further analysis.[85] It is clear, however, that a popular radical tradition, amended and expounded by MacDonald, was the guiding principle of a section of the party, and an important part of what the party represented.

The political orientation of Lansbury and Jowett was equally a merger of old radical outlooks and new influences. Their synthesis differed quite dramatically from MacDonald's. The difference between the views of those like Lansbury and Jowett, and the views of those who sympathised with MacDonald, can often be traced to three factors. First, men like Lansbury, or even Attlee and Tawney, were far more willing to accept working-class behaviour, or to identify the latent morality of working-class instinct. As devoutly religious men, they recognised the importance of the irrational: Christianity, and especially their Christianity, was built on faith. Their form of religion also made them both optimistic about the possibility of compassion and brotherhood, and aware, and tolerant, of the fact that this could coexist with sin. Their belief in the positive side of human nature could, and did, withstand their experience of slum life in the East End of London and their experience of the First World War. Attlee, Lansbury and Tawney were of course Anglicans, while some sympathisers with MacDonald's critics (like Jack Jones) were Roman Catholics. It *may*

---

[83] Clark, *Colne Valley*; T. Brennan, E. W. Cooney and H. Pollins, *Social Change in South-West Wales* (London, 1954), p. 20; S. Awberry, *Labour's Early Struggles in Swansea* (Swansea, 1949), pp. 54–5; R. Moore, *Pit-men, Preachers and Politics* (Cambridge, 1974), ch. 7.

[84] As in D. Martin, 'Ideology and composition', in K. D. Brown (ed.), *The First Labour Party, 1906–1914* (London 1985), ch. 1.

[85] Individual points of difference noted in Tanner, *Political change*, pp. 36–7, 361–2, 365–72. A conventional economic training could tie some moderate socialists to traditional policies. For this training and outlook, C. Cross, *Philip Snowden* (London, 1966), ch. 6; T. N. Graham, *Willie Graham* (London, 1948), pp. 50, 76, 93, 103, 144; Snell, *Men, Movements and Myself*, pp. 103–4. For Knight's views, see Alastair Reid, ch. 10 in this collection.

be the case that Nonconformist ideas in individual redemption were more compatible with MacDonald's conception and outlook.[86]

A second, and sometimes related, difference was anti-intellectualism. Jowett, for example, suggested that the working class leaned naturally towards socialist values, while the middle-class was far more inclined to be selfish and aquisitive. Lansbury consistently declared his faith in the poor, and disparaged the role which intellectuals might play in creating change: 'I think the only intellectual in our party has not been good for it', he told Tawney (Tawney was sufficiently modest not to take this as a personal criticism). Lansbury's admiration for Lenin was based not on Lenin's Marxism, but on the fact that, to Lansbury, Lenin was an intellectual serving the working class, not setting himself above it. He displayed no pomp, no pride and no affectation despite his position.[87] The common notion in Labour writing and preaching of 'service' – to a class which one respected, and from whom one might oneself learn much – contrasted markedly with the notions of moral improvement evident in the ILP's ethical socialism, and with MacDonald's expressed doubts about the working class and the trade unions. It also contrasts with the emphasis of MacDonald and the New Liberals on the vital role of middle-class rational intellect. If this faith in the working class was sometimes the product of an active middle-class conscience, it was also the case that notions of loyal service to a working-class community of equals, and a hostility to those intellectuals who criticised its values, were common amongst working-class activists (Nonconformists, Anglicans or neither). That working-class values, and working-class common sense knowledge, were not deemed of equal importance to middle-class 'expert' knowledge could cause opposition to MacDonald's views. This was especially true if this emphasis on policies which were deemed 'rational' by the official experts meant avoiding approaches which were thought to contain the potential for making improvements in living conditions.[88]

The third factor to consider is economics. Lansbury's insistence that

[86] G. Lansbury, *My Life* (London, 1928), p. 8: 'Socialism has for years meant for me the first fullest expression of everything religious'; Winter, *Socialism and War*, pp. 154–6; J. Jones, *My Lively Life* (London, 1928), esp. pp. 25–6 opposing 'temperence fanatics', and p. 105, noticing the primary significance of 'beer, work and football'.

[87] F. W. Jowett, *What Made Me a Socialist* (London, 1925); J. M. Winter and D. M. Joslin (eds.), *Tawney's Commonplace Book* (Cambridge, 1972), p. 4; Lansbury, *My Life*, pp. 245–7, 288. See also Lansbury's *What I Saw in Russia* (London, 1920).

[88] T. D. Benson, *Socialism and Service* (London, 1906); J. J. Lawson, *Peter Lee* (London, 1949), p. 141; F. Blackburn, *George Tomlinson* (London 1954), pp. 21–2. Cf. S. Collini, 'The role of character in Victorian political thought', *Transactions of the Royal Historical Society*, 35 (1985), p. 30. See also J. Smith, 'Labour tradition in Glasgow and Liverpool', *History Workshop*, 17 (1984), pp. 32–3, L. Barrow, *Independent Spirits. Spiritualism and English Plebians 1850–1910* (London 1986), e.g. p. 272. The poorest could also, however, be amongst the economically *most* conservative.

poverty could be tackled if Labour possessed the political will, was matched by a broader sympathy amongst his supporters for ideas which rationalised this view. Hobson's underconsumptionist ideas, for example, were rejected even by his political friends in the Liberal party, but spread rapidly through the Labour left.[89] In general, MacDonald's critics on the left were more concerned to attack poverty as an obstacle to changes in working-class self-esteem, while MacDonald was more concerned that the remedy might be worse than the disease.

Some of the ideas associated with critics of MacDonald had a much broader appeal. The Right to Work campaigns, the attacks on Mac-Donald's election strategy, and Jowett's voting on merits proposals, all attracted wide support at party conferences. The value of Labour's political independence, an aspect of the popular radical tradition which Jowett and Lansbury emphasised, was a further idea which attracted broad support. Calls for more activism may also have claimed adherents amongst moderates. MacDonald's movement towards a dry rationalistic approach antagonised erstwhile supporters like Bruce Glasier.[90] None the less, the militant, class-conscious ideas of Jowett and Lansbury did not dominate Labour politics. Support for *elements* of the analysis was not the same as support for the whole package.

An approach *similar* to that of MacDonald's critics, however, *was* popular with a substantial section of the party. A reluctance to criticise working-class life, an emphasis on local communal solidarity, especially in municipal politics, a concern to protect local living standards by munici-pal intervention, and hostility to the moralistic preaching of the state (and of some Liberal and Labour activists), were part of a radical past which had been half-incorporated into a popular *Conservative* tradition by the 1890s. It was Labour's ability to tap this tradition which helped create the MacDonald–Gladstone pact of 1903. Party members from within this tradition (often former Tories) were particularly common in Lancashire and London.[91] As some, especially of the more constitutional, elements of the left's approach became less pronounced, so the differences between this approach and that of Jowett and Lansbury became less evident, and the scale of sympathy increased.[92]

[89] Attack by L. C. Money, *Daily News*, 1 June 1909, doubts of Hobhouse noted in Clarke, *Liberals and Social Democrats*, p. 126. For Labour's greater interest, F. Keeling's review of Hobson's *The Industrial Spirit*, *SR*, Aug. 1909, replies to W. T. Stead by O'Grady, Wardle, comments by Toole, *Fighting Through Life*, p. 81.

[90] Tanner, *Political Change*, pp. 73, 142, 174–7, 187, 258, 264, 300, 337.

[91] For the Tory origins of 40 per cent of Labour activists in Blackburn, G. N. Trodd, 'Political change and the working class in Blackburn and Burnley 1880–1914', Lancaster Ph.D. thesis 1978, p. 334.

[92] For the shifts between these approaches in London before 1914, Tanner, *Political Change*, pp. 176–8.

Labour represented not one, but at least two major political outlooks. These contained some common principles, but drew on different aspects of past traditions, and different aspects of new ideas and approaches. This gave the party the capacity for identifying and expressing a variety of problems, and putting forward a number of solutions. It meant that there was support for change through the collective individualism associated with MacDonald, and support for the more interventionist measures represented by Jowett and Lansbury. They were likely to appeal to different social groups.

It may be that *both* aspects of Labour's appeal had an electorally *positive* role in the politics of the 1920s.[93] At the same time, the existence of differing ideological outlooks (and differing immediate interests) in the Labour party was also a potentially destructive factor in policy discussions. A growing tradition of suspicion and conflict between party leaders and officials on the one hand, and members of the rank and file on the other, made the position worse. Between 1929 and 1931 Labour had to tackle an economic crisis which existing policies could not 'solve'. Ideas – whether from the left or the right – had to be adapted. It is possible that MacDonald's brand of reformism was not easily adapted to these conditions. It is even more likely that tensions between the two main ideological groups prevented geniune co-operation, and hindered a renewal of Labour ideology which might have limited the political and economic damage caused by the slump.

[93] For the existence of different successful Labour approaches in the 1920s, M. Savage, *The Dynamics of Working-Class Politics* (Cambridge, 1987), ch. 2 and pp. 195–8, I. McLean, *The Legend of Red Clydeside* (Edinburgh, 1983), ch. 13, S. Macintyre *Little Moscows* (London, 1980), pp. 157–63, 192, Gillespie (thesis), ch. 8.

Index